# GOD'S
# GENERALS

*Why They Succeeded*
*and Why Some Failed*

# GOD'S GENERALS

## *Why They Succeeded and Why Some Failed*

ROBERTS LIARDON

WHITAKER
HOUSE

All Scripture quotations are from the King James Version of the Holy Bible.
Excerpts from *Sister Aimee: The Life of Aimee Semple McPherson*, © 1993 by Daniel Mark Epstein, reprinted by permission of Harcourt, Inc.
Excerpts from *Smith Wigglesworth: Apostle of Faith* by Stanley Howard Frodsham, used by permission of Gospel Publishing House.
All possible efforts were made by ALBURY PUBLISHING and WHITAKER HOUSE to secure permission and to insure proper credit was given for every entry within this book.

---

### GOD'S GENERALS:
*Why They Succeeded and Why Some Failed*
hardcover reprint edition

---

Roberts Liardon Ministries
P.O. Box 2989
Sarasota, Florida 34230
www.robertsliardon.org

ISBN-13: 978-0-88368-944-8 • ISBN-10: 0-88368-944-8
Printed in the United States of America
© 1996 by Roberts Liardon

Whitaker House
1030 Hunt Valley Circle
New Kensington, PA 15068
www.whitakerhouse.com

**Library of Congress Cataloging-in-Publication Data**

Liardon, Roberts.
  God's generals : why they succeeded and why some failed / Roberts Liardon.— Reprint ed.
    p.  cm.
Originally published: Tulsa, OK : Albury Pub., ©1996.
Includes bibliographical references.
  ISBN 0-88368-944-8 (hardcover : alk. paper) 1. Evangelists—Biography. 2. Healers—Biography. 3. Pentecostals—Biography. 4. Evangelists—United States—Biography. 5. Healers—United States—Biography. 6. Pentecostals—United States—Biography. I. Title.
  BV3780.L47 2003
  270.8'092'2—dc22
                          2003015625

12  13  14  **UI**  19

# Endorsements

The strength and power of the body of Christ today did not come by accident. True, it is a work of the Holy Spirit, but the Holy Spirit anoints faithful and humble servants to bring about His purposes. In this book, Roberts Liardon has done a masterful job of opening new windows of insight upon the lives of some of the greatest heroes of the faith. *God's Generals* will encourage you and strengthen you to succeed in whatever purpose God has for you in His kingdom.

Dr. C. Peter Wagner
Author and Professor of Church Growth, Fuller Theological Seminary
Pasadena, California

A project which combines the stories of great twentieth century Pentecostal preachers into one book has been much needed, and I am sure this publication will be greatly appreciated. I am glad my mother, Aimee Semple McPherson, has been included among God's other Generals, for she served wholeheartedly as a pioneer in the front line trenches for the greatest of all Generals, her Lord Jesus Christ. I appreciate the tribute this book has given her.

Rolf K. McPherson
President, International Church of the Foursquare Gospel
Los Angeles, California

Until Roberts Liardon came along, very few people here had heard of John Alexander Dowie, Maria Woodworth-Etter, Jack Coe, and the likes. His teachings have impacted the young churches of Asia in a very profound way. The lessons we can learn from the great revivalists of the twentieth century – what attributed to their successes and failures – are absolutely vital to propel an emerging generation to greater spiritual heights as we enter a brand new millennium.

Hee Kong
Pastor, City Harvest Church; President, City Harvest Bible Training Centre
Singapore

I've known Roberts Liardon since he was a teenager. I met him when he was searching for information about my father, Jack Coe Sr., who is one of the twelve Generals studied in this book. I was impressed with Roberts' diligence then, and am happy to see the fruit that has been born from his life and ministry today. I recommend this book for not only its historical value, but for the insight into what it takes to carry the very power of God.

Jack Coe Jr.
International Evangelist; President, Christian Fellowship
Dallas, Texas

Roberts Liardon is one of America's leading experts on the dynamic healing ministries of the nineteenth and twentieth centuries. Having spent almost two decades researching and studying the most significant spiritual leaders whose lives have been characterized by signs, wonders, and miracles, Liardon presents a powerful and inspirational panorama of their ministries. This is the first comprehensive volume to bring together a thorough survey of these giants of the faith. It is church history at its best.

Paul G. Chappell, Ph.D.
Dean of Graduate School of Theology, Oral Roberts University
Tulsa, Oklahoma

God's pioneers are controversial figures. They often get things wrong, perhaps, because few if any have been this way before. Roberts Liardon has done an excellent job in providing well researched material on God's Generals, the pioneers of Pentecostal and Charismatic history. Through reading this book your faith will be inspired, and you shall learn a few lessons along the way.

Gerald Coates
Pioneer International

We need to rediscover our Pentecostal heritage. As we seek to tap into the pure stream of Pentecost that stretches from the pages of the New Testament to the revivals of this century — we will see God take us to our full potential in Him. Roberts Liardon has recognized the importance of honoring those who have gone before us, learning from their mistakes, and drawing inspiration from their testimonies. I know from hearing Pastor Roberts' presentation on the material in this book, that the years he has spent studying the lives of these great men and women of God have resulted in a resource that will encourage, exhort, and teach many in this generation. I give it my highest recommendation knowing that it will change lives and re-introduce to us an element of Pentecostal living with which many are unfamiliar.

Colin Dye B. D.
Pastor, Kensington Temple
London, England

# Dedication

I want to dedicate this book to the people who have stood with me and fought to see God's vision for the ministry come to pass:

To my staff, you are the backbone of Roberts Liardon Ministries. Your hard work and dedication have become an incredible force in the earth that I appreciate so deeply. I know God is grateful to you as well.

To the Embassy Christian Center family, you are a faithful family, selfless and full of unconditional love. Thank you for your loyalty and steadfast labor of love.

To the Operation 500 missionaries worldwide, you are why the rest of us keep going. We want to see His Kingdom come, and we watch that unfold everyday through your tireless work in the field. Thank you for that.

My friends, we must keep reaching to lay hold of what God has for us.

# Contents

# Foreword

I want to commend my dear friend and fellow minister, Roberts Liardon, for this contribution to making known the history of the great moving of God through the ministry of His true Generals. This book will show you their strengths and their weaknesses.

It is clear that this is not the work of a man, but of the Holy Spirit of the living God. It will show you that it is not what we are, or what we possess in ourselves that God is depending on, but what He can make of us!

As you read this most inspiring book, you will be stirred to remember that the God of Elijah is your God – just as He was the God of His other past Generals. So take your Bible now and read Hebrews 11:1-12:2 before you embark on this historic journey, and you will see that "all truth is parallel."

God has always had His Generals – "For many are called, but few are chosen" (Matthew 22:14). God would not have us to forget this as we see many new Generals emerging on the battlefields today. So always let us look to "Jesus the author and finisher of our faith" (Hebrews 12:2).

This literary work is destined to be a spiritual classic. It will show you that even the smallest, seemingly insignificant person can be used by God. Roberts' commentary is powerful and practical, and will leave you with great hope to succeed.

God's Generals were diamonds in the rough – mostly unsophisticated, uneducated by man's standards – yet vessels God recognized who possessed the unique characteristics that He could use if they would surrender their call.

Will you?

Dr. Morris Cerullo, President
Morris Cerullo World Evangelism
San Diego, California

# Preface

Roberts has always had a hunger to understand the calls of great men and women of God. As his mother, I saw his spiritual hunger develop in two ways. First, as a very young boy, Roberts' interest grew because my mother told him so many stories about great ministers and their camp meetings, of which she had been a part. Her descriptions were lively and vivid, and with almost every story, she would have a lesson to preach.

Second, when Roberts was twelve years old, the Lord appeared to him and instructed him to study the lives of the great men and women of God. The Lord told Roberts that this intensive study would be an important part of his training for the ministry.

Immediately after that visitation from the Lord, Roberts began to study. In our house there was already an atmosphere conducive to study. I spent many years pursuing my education while the children were growing up, and I myself had a well-developed library. The combination of my mother's influence and my diligence to study seemed to impart into Roberts what he needed for that hour. I remember many nights when each of us would sit around the table, pouring over and highlighting books.

Roberts began to dig into every book he could find that had to do with a move of God. If he came upon a name in the book, he would research everything he could about that person. If in his research he discovered that the person had died, he searched until he found the closest living relative or friend. God's favor on Roberts' life was so evident. He would always be granted interviews with these people and inevitably was able to develop personal relationships with them. These people seemed to give Roberts whatever he asked for, whether it was artifacts, pictures, or books.

There never seemed to be any fear or inhibitions about Roberts' pursuits. I remember one particular incident when he was in junior high school. I had come home from work to find that somehow, Roberts had made contact with someone overseas who was eager to help him do research on the revivalists and reformers like Evan Roberts and John Wesley. The more he studied, the more the doors would open to him. He was obeying God, so the doors had to open. When other people who were pursuing the same end as Roberts would hear of the success that he had in obtaining materials they would ask, "How did you get these things?" He would answer simply, "I just asked."

I was a student and staff member at Oral Roberts University during the years Roberts was researching the lives of the Generals. Roberts spent a great deal of time there studying the research materials at the Holy Spirit Research Center. In fact, he worked there for two summers, volunteering as they needed him. When the ORU staff discovered all the memorabilia that Roberts himself had obtained, they were very surprised. They offered to buy it. He actually considered the offer, but I put my foot down. Today, those materials are in the Reformers and Revivalists Library at his Bible college.

Roberts' desire to know and understand the lives of these men and women was as pure as it was diligent. I distinctly remember that when Roberts first stepped into the pulpit at age sixteen, his research was complete. He had fulfilled his assignment for that hour. He had no formal training, no connections, and no expertise. He just obeyed God. He was faithful to what was put before him, and that faithfulness matured into an international call. To me that is such a testimony of someone who not only understood the season of his life, but also completed it.

Roberts will probably always continue to research the lives of God's Generals. It is still part of his call. Now, the ministry has a research department responsible for continuing on with the research where Roberts left off when he stepped into his call to help prepare the nations for the return of the Lord.

Carol M. Liardon, B.S., M.L.S.
Executive Vice President, Roberts Liardon Ministries
Irvine, California

# Acknowledgments

I want to personally thank two people:

My Editor, Denyse Cummings, and my Research Director, Laurel McDonald. As a team, we waded through endless research, interviews, writings, and edits, to put this book together and make it work. You two have helped me to fulfill a vital part of my call in the earth. Thank you, my friends.

# Introduction

When I was almost twelve years old, the Lord appeared to me in a vision. In this vision, He told me to study the lives of the great preachers, to learn of their successes, and of their failures. From that day on, I gave a large portion of my life to the study of church history.

When prominent people in the secular world die, people begin to look at their natural accomplishments. But when leaders in the body of Christ die, I believe Jesus would have us look at not only what was accomplished in the natural world through their lives, but at what they also accomplished within the body of Christ. The purpose of their remembrance is not to praise or criticize the leaders, but to see him or her as an example for our own lives.

The "Generals" that are written of in this book were human. Their stories represent a collaboration of the way life is. I have not made anyone out to be superhuman or bionic. I have told of their tears, their laughter, their successes, and their failures. They were all persecuted, lied to, betrayed, slandered, as well as honored, adored, and supported.

But most importantly, I have attempted to reveal the secrets of the power in their individual calls to the ministry – how they operated, what they believed, and what motivated them to CHANGE each of their generations for God.

The failures that took place in the lives of these great men and women will attempt to take place again. But their successes also challenge us, and are waiting to be grasped again. There is nothing new under the sun. If there is something new to you, it is because you are new under the sun.

It takes more than a desire to fulfill the will of God. It takes spiritual strength. As you read these chapters, allow the Spirit of God to take you on a journey that points out the areas in your life which need to be focused or subdued. Then, determine that your life and ministry will be a spiritual success in this generation that will bless the nations of the earth to the glory of God.

Roberts Liardon

# CHAPTER ONE

# John Alexander Dowie

## *"The Healing Apostle"*

# "THE HEALING APOSTLE"

"'Will he dare pray for rain?...If he does and no rain comes, then he's not Elijah. If he doesn't, then he's afraid to — and that's almost worse.'

"At last the preacher dropped on his knees behind the pulpit. Never before had an audience followed his prayers with more strained attention. '...God, our Father, we have seen the distress of this land...look upon it now in Thy mercy and send rain....'

"Suddenly the General Overseer stopped...then said, 'Get to your homes quickly, for there is sound of abundance of rain.' But he was too late. Just as the multitude turned to go, rain descended in torrents."[1]

Few in our generation today know of the fascinating and dramatic ministry of John Alexander Dowie. Undoubtedly, this man succeeded in shaking the world at the turn of the century. He brought to the forefront of society, the visible Church of the living God — primarily in the area of divine healing and repentance. Whether one agreed with Dr. Dowie or not, the fact remains that his incredible story is one of unflinching faith and powerful vision. John Alexander Dowie's recorded converts numbered in untold millions. Although the end of his ministry is a tragic one, rarely has there been a mission containing more strength and vitality. His apostolic ministry was world-changing. From coast to coast it single-handedly challenged and triumphed over the great apostasy and lethargy of his time, demonstrating soundly that Jesus Christ is the same yesterday, today, and forever.

> *Against hypocritical, opposing clergy, fierce and slanderous tabloids, murderous mobs, and relentless city officials, Dr. Dowie wore his apostolic calling as a crown from God, and his persecution as a badge of honor.*

Against hypocritical, opposing clergy, fierce and slanderous tabloids, murderous mobs, and relentless city officials, Dr. Dowie wore his apostolic calling as a crown from God, and his persecution as a badge of honor.

## MORE THAN ORDINARY

John Alexander Dowie was born May 25, 1847, in Edinburgh, Scotland. His Christian parents, Mr. and Mrs. John Murray Dowie, named him what they hoped he would grow up to be: "John," meaning "by the grace of God;" and "Alexander," "a helper of men."

Born in poverty, one would have to see through the eyes of faith to ever believe what was to come in the future for this small child. Although his school attendance was irregular due to frequent illness, young Dowie portrayed brilliance and enthusiasm. His parents trained and helped him because they had hope for his call. Young Dowie was an active part of their prayer meetings and Bible studies. They never left him out of the ministry, and loved him dearly. This parental security produced a key element in his early foundation.

At the mere age of six, young Dowie read the Bible through from cover to cover. Deeply convicted by what he had read, he developed an intense hatred for the use of alcoholic beverages. A Temperance Movement was on the rise in Scotland at the time, and without even realizing the hand of God upon him, he campaigned against alcohol abuse and signed a petition to never partake of it.

Dowie continued to read the Bible and accompany his father as much as possible on "preaching journeys." On one such journey, he came upon a humble street preacher by the name of Henry Wright. As young Dowie listened to the details of the Gospel, he gave his heart to Jesus Christ.

*...God continually spoke to him. His heart was constantly tugged toward full-time ministry. He realized there were many truths in the Bible that had been neglected by the clergy of that day.*

At the tender age of seven, Dowie received his call to the ministry. But he didn't yet know how to answer.

At the age of thirteen, John and his parents left Scotland for a six-month journey to Australia. Once situated in this new country, John began to earn his living by working for his uncle in the shoe business. He soon left his uncle and began working at various other places, always in menial positions. And even then, his peers noticed that he was a "more than ordinary" young businessman. Dowie soon became the assistant to a firm's partner in a business that grossed more than $2 million a year.

Through these years of "climbing the occupational ladder," God continually spoke to him. His heart was constantly tugged toward full-time ministry. He realized there were many truths in the Bible that had been neglected by the clergy of that day. One such teaching – divine healing – had been realized at his own expense. Dowie had been a sickly child. And he suffered from "chronic dyspepsia," a severe indigestion problem that plagued him in his teen years. But, after reading the will of God concerning healing, Dowie petitioned the Lord and was "completely delivered of the affliction."[2] And this divine manifestation was only a token of the revelation that was to come in his life.

Finally, at the age of twenty-one, Dowie made an absolute decision to answer the call of God. He would take the money he had saved from his occupation and begin studying under a private tutor to prepare for the ministry. Fifteen months later, he left Australia to enroll in Edinburgh University, to study in the Free Church School. Majoring in theology and political science, he was not regarded as a model student because of his disagreements with the professors and their doctrine. He challenged their lethargic interpretations brilliantly. John Dowie had an incredible hunger and thirst for the Word of God. He read constantly, and had a photographic memory. This established him far beyond his superiors in substance and accuracy.

While in Edinburgh, Dowie became the "honorary chaplain" of the Edinburgh Infirmary. It was there that he had the unique opportunity to sit under the famous surgeons of his day, comparing their diagnoses with the Word of God. But as patients lay helplessly under chloroform, Dowie heard these surgeons lecture on their medical inadequacies. It was then that he realized these surgeons could not heal, and that they could only resort to removing the diseased organs, hoping for a cure. He watched many surgeries end with deadly results. As he heard from the lips of these medical professors the confession that they were only guessing in the dark, and witnessed their experiments, Dowie developed a strong antipathy to surgery and medicine.[3]

Many today still accuse Dowie of condemning the medical field. But I want to point out that in his time, the medical practice was very primitive. And he was one of the privileged few who saw behind the scenes. He witnessed how the physicians of his day offered great hope to patients, but confessed in private that they knew nothing. He saw poor victims paying untold amounts of money in the hope for a cure, while receiving the worst of results. He despised falsehood, so, he searched for an answer. And when he began to publicly come against their deceiving methods, his accusations proved true.

While studying at Edinburgh University, Dowie received a cablegram from his father in Australia. In response, he made a hasty return home to free himself from any inheritance in the family business because of his love for the ministry.

Because he dropped everything and returned home so quickly, he was under a tremendous financial strain. But, he resolved that this setback would not hinder him and vowed that he would fulfill the mission of his life. He would be an ambassador for God in full-time ministry.

Soon Dowie accepted an invitation to pastor the Congregational Church in Alma, Australia. His duties were divided among several churches. And as was to be expected, his bold preaching sent uneasy rifts throughout the church. Persecution quickly arose against him and resentment was openly voiced because of his penetrating method of ministry. Dowie was a visionary, but despite his repeated endeavors, he was unable to arouse the people from their lethargy. Although he needed the church financially, he chose to resign the pastorate because he felt it a waste of time to continue with them.

John Alexander Dowie was a reformer and a revivalist. This kind of calling *has to see results* because of the passion for God that burns so strongly within them. He loved people, but his commitment to the truth caused him to focus only on groups that would respond.

Soon after his resignation, he was asked to pastor the Congregational Church in Manly Beach. He was warmly received. But, once again, he was distraught over their lack of repentance and sensitivity to the Word of God. Still, Dowie remained with this pastorate. His congregation was small and it gave him the time to pursue his studies and gain direction.

*He knew he was a man on a mission, but he had no idea of where or how his mission would be accomplished.*

As time passed, Dowie continued to have a tossing restlessness in his spirit. He knew he was a man on a mission, but he had no idea of where or how his mission would be accomplished.

He began to long for larger congregations, and an opportunity soon opened to pastor a larger group in Newton, a suburb of Sydney. So in 1875, Dowie moved again. Unknown to him at the time, this move would take him into the revelation that would launch his ministry into worldwide acclaim.

## "OH, COME AT ONCE! MARY IS DYING...."

While pastoring in Newton, a death-wreaking plague swept through the region, particularly in the outskirts of Sydney. People were dying at such a high rate that the population was totally paralyzed with fear and dread. Within a few short weeks at his new appointment, Dowie had presided over forty funerals. Sickness and death seemed to be waiting at every corner. The tragedy of it all struck the heart of Dowie to such an extreme, that he sought for immediate answers. And he knew those answers were available in God's Word. Listen to the sense of tragedy the young pastor wrote in his own words:

"I sat in my study in the parsonage of the Congregational Church, at Newton, a suburb of Sydney, Australia. My heart was very heavy, for I had been visiting the sick and dying beds of more than thirty in my flock, and I had cast the dust to its kindred dust into more than forty graves within a few weeks. Where, oh where, was He Who used to heal His suffering children? No prayer for healing seemed to reach His ear, and yet I knew His hand had not been shortened.... It seemed sometimes as if I could almost hear the triumphant mockery of fiends ringing in my ear whilst I spoke to the bereaved ones the words of Christian hope and consolation. Disease, the foul offspring of its father, Satan, and its mother, Sin, was defiling and destroying ...and there was no deliverer.

"And there I sat with sorrow-bowed head for my afflicted people, until the bitter tears came to relieve my burning heart. Then I prayed for some message.... Then the words of the Holy Ghost inspired in Acts 10:38, stood before me all radiant with light, revealing Satan as the Defiler, and Christ as the Healer. My tears were wiped away, my heart was strong, I saw the way of healing...I said, 'God help me now to preach the Word to all the dying around, and tell them how 'tis Satan still defiles, and Jesus still delivers, for He is just the same today.'

"A loud ring and several loud raps at the outer door...two panting messengers who said, 'Oh, come at once, Mary is dying; come and pray.' ...I rushed from my house and ran hatless down the street, and entered the room of the dying maiden. There she lay, groaning, grinding her teeth in the agony of the conflict with the destroyer...I looked at her and then my anger burned....

"In a strange way it came to pass...the sword I needed was still in my hands...and never will I lay it down. The

**doctor, a good Christian man, was quietly walking up and down the room.... Presently, he stood at my side and said, 'Sir, are not God's ways mysterious?' 'God's way!...No sir, that is the devil's work and it is time we called on Him Who came to "destroy the work of the devil."'[4]**

Offended by the words of Dowie, the doctor left the room. Dowie turned to Mary's mother and asked why she had sent for him. Learning that she wanted the prayer of faith, Dowie bowed by the girl's bed and cried out to God. Instantly the girl lay still. The mother asked if her daughter was dead, but Dowie replied, **"No...she will live. The fever is gone."[5]**

Soon, the young girl was sitting up in bed and eating. She apologized for sleeping so long and exclaimed how well she felt. And as the small group thanked the Lord, Dowie went into the room of her brother and sister, prayed for them, and they were instantly healed.[6]

From that moment on, the plague was stayed as far as Dowie's congregation was concerned. Not another member of his flock died of the epidemic. And as a result of this revelation, the great healing ministry of John Alexander Dowie was launched.

*From right to left: John, Gladstone, Jeanie, and Esther Dowie*

## WEDDING BELLS

Soon after his remarkable revelation of divine healing, Dowie began to think about a possible mate. When he did, he found he was in love with his first cousin, Jeanie, and that he could not be happy without her. After many controversial discussions with family members, it was agreed that the two should marry. So at the age of twenty-nine, on May 26, 1876, John Dowie married Jeanie and the two began their incredible mission together.

Their first son, Gladstone, was born in 1877. But Dowie had misjudged certain persons in financial matters and found himself in great financial hardship. So Jeanie and Gladstone were sent to live with her parents until the situation could be worked out. Needless to say, such a decision caused an even greater turmoil, due to the in-laws' mistrust of their son-in-law. However, even through these shaky hardships, Dowie remained a man of divine vision. In the midst of the chaos, he held fast to the work before them and wrote this to his beloved wife: **"...I can see that future far more clearly than I can solve the mysteries of the immediate present."**[7]

Every ministry has a future. But we must believe in that future or we will never take the first step. Like Dowie, we must determine to hold fast to the Word of God and fight for what is ours in the earth. Setbacks are always present, but we determine if the problem is to remain permanent. Even though we are called, we still have to war against spiritual evils that are sent to destroy our vision and to discourage us. God's angels can help, but the war for our destiny is a personal responsibility that we must win.

## NO MORE RELIGION!

During this trying time, Dowie made an unprecedented decision to leave the denomination he was a part of. He couldn't understand or operate with the cold, lethargic state of their leadership. And he burned with a passion to proclaim the message of divine healing throughout the city. His congregations had grown to over twice the size of the others. But his success spoke to deaf ears, and he was constantly fighting through the politics and "letter of the law" theology that threatened to dampen his faith.

Because of the hostility presented by denominational leaders, he found himself constantly on the defensive. In a letter to his wife proclaiming his decision to begin an independent ministry, Dowie wrote that the political system of his denominational church:

> **"...killed initiative and individual energy, made men denominational tools, or worse, caused them to become worldly-minded, and left them high and dry and useless for the most part – good ships, but badly steered and terribly overladen with worldliness and apathy."**[8]

Dowie had come to realize that revival was possible if the church could be awakened. He considered the vast opportunities that lay ahead of him. He studied the lethargic side of the church, then he studied the unchurched. He made the decision that reaching the vast number of the unchurched would result in a greater fervor for Jesus Christ. And he decided to stop his laborings among the cynical. So he determined that his mission would reach the uncared for and perishing masses of the city with the revelation that Christ was the same yesterday, today, and forever.

In 1878, Dowie broke free from his denomination and secured the Royal Theatre in Sydney to begin an independent ministry. Hundreds flooded the theatre to hear his powerful messages. But, once again, a lack of funds halted his work. Though the crowds were large, many had no financial income. The only answer Dowie could see was to sell his home and furnishings, put the money into the work, and move to a smaller residence. After Dowie did this, the work flourished. In a message describing his decision, he said:

> *...he determined that his mission would reach the uncared for and perishing masses of the city with the revelation that Christ was the same yesterday, today, and forever.*

**"My beautiful furniture and pictures were gone, but there came in place of them men and women that were brought to the feet of Jesus by the sale of my earthly goods."**[9]

In Dowie's passion, he had no thought for the strong opposition that arose against him. He vehemently denounced the evils of the day and formed a group to distribute literature city-wide. Violent persecution, mostly from local pastors, arose from these pamphlets. Still Dowie was merciless in dealing with the lethargic clergy. He didn't mince his words, responding that he **"did not recognize their right to request any information of his actions, nor did he have any respect for their judgment."** He answered one minister:

> **"I consider your judgment to be as feeble and incapable as your ministry.... I wish I knew who distributed these 'obnoxious tracts' among your flock; I would certainly commend his choice of a field...."**[10]

Part of Dowie's call was to deal with moral evils. A strong stance on morals usually goes with a strong healing ministry. (Sin causes much of the sickness and disease.) But Dowie paralyzed his critics with such astute sharpness, that it led them to consort and plan in private to destroy him. And so the stage was set for the seemingly invincible John Alexander Dowie.

## MISREADING THE CALL

Dowie was an apostle who didn't have the complete understanding of that office. The anointing he carried pierced the religious theocracies of his day, but there were few who understood him, including himself. As a result, he misunderstood several administrations that came with the passion of his office. One passion was in the area of politics.

Dowie's leadership was gaining a strong national influence. So seeing his potential and knowing his stand, the Temperance Society asked him to run for Parliament. At first, he opposed the idea. But he later changed his mind, thinking he could possibly influence more in the political arena and decided to enter the race.

But Dowie suffered a sound defeat in the elections. The local newspapers that had been so damaged by his ministry, waged an all-out attack against him. The politicians and alcoholic beverage industry paid untold amounts of money to see him slandered and defeated. After the election, Dowie had wounded his church, and disgraced his ministry.

Dowie was moved by such strong spiritual yearnings that he sought to fulfill them in the natural. I can only speculate why he made this move. It could have been because the church world wasn't grasping the truth fast enough to satisfy him. Whatever his reason, he misread the timing and plan of God for his ministry.

We need to understand that God has a central point from which every aspect of our lives operate, whether individually or corporately. That area is called "timing." From the operation of that one word, lives can move forward with God or be hindered. Nations can advance spiritually, or regress. Life in the spirit realm has a timing to it just as life in the natural. Therefore, it is vitally important for us to follow the leading of our spirit. We must learn that it's not always right to move into action because it seems like the thing to do. This kind of obedience only comes from seasons of prayer and intercession.

Politicians and the political arena have never changed the world, church-wise or government-wise. Only a people whose hearts are changed by the Gospel can transform civil laws and regulations. Politics are meant for compromise to please people as a whole. The apostolic office presents the Word of the Lord, then it is up to the people to conform to and follow it. The apostolic and political don't mix. Dowie with his calling, should have never resorted to a political lifestyle.

While campaigning for office, Dowie also neglected his commandment to preach divine healing. He simply steered away from his calling to pursue a personal goal, thinking he could reach a greater mass of people. And as a result, the rest of his time in Australia was spent in darkness and futility.

## PEOPLE CAME FROM EVERYWHERE

Dowie finally repented and in 1880 returned to the message of divine healing, with great physical and spiritual blessings coming to him as a result. The gifts of the Spirit began to manifest in his life and revelation abounded like never before. Because of his spiritual obedience, thousands were healed under his ministry. Persecution abounded, even to the point that his enemies in organized crime once schemed to plant a bomb under his desk. The bomb was set to explode during the late hours Dowie kept, but he heard a voice that said "Arise, go!" The third time he heard it, he grabbed his coat and went home to finish his work. Within minutes after arriving safely home, the bomb exploded under his desk, several blocks away.

> *The gifts of the Spirit began to manifest in his life and revelation abounded like never before. Because of his spiritual obedience, thousands were healed under his ministry.*

In 1888, Dowie sensed the unction to come to America, then possibly on to England. His unction became reality in June of that year as he passed under the Golden Gate Bridge in San Francisco. Newspapers carried the story that Dowie was heading for America, and that people were coming from all parts of California to be healed. From morning until evening, halls would overflow with people waiting for an audience with Dowie, and he would pray for only one person.

The reformer had a unique way of praying for the sick. He fervently believed no one could come for healing unless they were born again and had repented of any lifestyle contrary to the Gospel. He was usually indignant if he sensed worldliness on someone who came for healing. As a result, he prayed for very few people early in his ministry – but the ones he did pray for were instantly healed.

## FORSAKING THE DIVINE

Soon Dowie began healing crusades up and down the coast of California. It was during this time that he met Maria Woodworth-Etter, the great woman healing evangelist. But there arose a conflict between them, and Dowie denounced her method of ministry. I believe this was a tragic mistake on his part.

In our lives, we have many relationships, casual and sometimes intimate. But the most significant ones to the kingdom of God are "divine relationships." In every call, whether secular or ministerial, God sends divine relationships to help strengthen your walk with Him. We may have many casual relationships, but divine relationships are very few. They can usually be counted on one hand.

I believe Dowie and his family missed a tremendous opportunity to have a divine relationship with Maria Woodworth-Etter. But for some reason, possibly a "manly-ministerial" pride, Dowie crucified Etter every chance he got. Once he attended her meeting, took the stage, and proclaimed her to be of God. But he forsook that leading of the Spirit, and later renounced her.

Etter's method of ministry made Dowie uneasy, because he didn't understand it. But he never took the time to speak with her privately about it, heart to heart. His ministry "preference," or favorite style of ministry, caused him to cut Maria off. Etter also had a revelation of divine healing, but she was more experienced in cooperating with the Spirit. And she had the spiritual strength to speak into Dowie's life. She could have instructed him on how to live out of his spirit while resting his body at the same time. Dowie had a problem in this area. He sometimes worked forty-three hours straight in his passion. Through Maria, he could have befriended others of like faith and call, furthering his own ministry. But he didn't.

As a result, Dowie experienced only casual relationships with certain followers, rather than the kind of divine relationship he could have had with other fellow leaders.

I think it's interesting to note that Dowie interviewed the great impostor of his day, Jacob Schweinfurth, who claimed to be Jesus Christ.[11] He also challenged the famous atheist, Robert Ingersoll, to a confrontation.[12] But he never gave Sister Etter the courtesy of a conversation.

Don't miss your divine relationships in life. There will always be fellow laborers, but divine relationships are few and far between.

## FINALLY, A HOME

Persecution from envious ministers began to rise feverishly against Dowie. But by this time, he had become a veteran in the art of facing opposition. Persecution brought out his brilliance and strength and he never gave those bringing it thought *unless* they were in the immediate way of his mission.

Dowie toured the regions of America and eventually chose to settle in Evanston, Illinois, outside of Chicago. The Chicago newspapers bitterly attacked him, calling him a false prophet and impostor. They boldly declared that he was not wanted in Chicago. But none of their attacks caused Dowie to flinch. He remained where he had chosen, and ministered wherever he felt led to go.

Once while speaking at a divine healing convention in Chicago, he was summoned to pray for a lady dying from a fibroid tumor. At the time, Chicago was the second largest city in America. There were strong, evil spiritual influences ruling Chicago, and Dowie was very interested in establishing his headquarters there. So he took this woman's request for healing as a test as to whether or not he should begin a work in the city. The woman's tumor was reportedly the size of a coconut that had grown into various parts of her body. When Dowie prayed for her, she was instantly healed. In fact, the healing was so remarkable that several Chicago newspapers ran the story. Now he was convinced, and Dowie made his worldwide headquarters within the city. His enemies didn't like it, but Dowie didn't care.

The World's Fair was to open within a matter of months, so Dowie built a small wooden "hut" outside its gates. From the top of the hut named, "Zion Tabernacle," hung a flag with the words, "Christ is All." Services went on day and night. Though the beginning was small, the crowds grew steadily, and soon people had to stand outside in the snow to get a glimpse of the miraculous healings taking place inside.

> *...Dowie built a small wooden "hut" outside its gates. From the top of it hung a flag..., "Christ is All."*

As was true in Australia, Dowie had opened the doors to the city of Chicago by way of divine healing. Never before or since has one man so captured a city. Still, Dowie experienced the fight of his life in those early years. He demonstrated God's Word in power, and by so doing, the medical profession and the religious churches suffered financially. So the newspapers frantically formed a list of allies, including ministers, to pull out all the stops to paralyze his ministry. But none could tarnish his work. To their dismay, the constant articles and unrelenting slander only caused his work to increase.

## ANOTHER HOME — JAIL!

By now, hundreds of people flooded the city of Chicago to attend Dowie's services. As a result, lodging was difficult to come by, so Dowie opened several large rooming houses called "Healing Homes." Here, the sick who had come for healing could find shelter and rest between the services held at Zion Tabernacle. Once there, they were able to receive constant ministry from the Word until their faith mounted to the place of complete manifestation. But the newspapers, mainly the *Chicago Dispatch*, were merciless, calling the homes "Lunatic Asylums" and continued to print every lie imaginable.[13]

Because of these healing homes, Dowie's enemies thought they had found a vulnerable spot. So early in 1895, they arrested him on the charge of "practicing medicine without a license." Obviously untrue, Dowie would have been the last person to allow medicine into his homes. He hired a brilliant attorney, but he only kept Dowie advised of the legal matters. So Dowie chose to represent himself in court because no one else could articulate his call as accurately as himself.

Dowie's superior intellect was not enough to overrule the evil jurisdiction of the court. Despite his profound arguments, the court fined him. But they never dreamed he would take the case to a higher court, costing much more money than the fines they had issued. When he did, the higher court denounced the evil of the lower court, and reversed the decision.

The city hoped Dowie would get discouraged if they continued to arrest and fine him. So before the year was over, he had been arrested one hundred times. Although severely persecuted, he was never discouraged. Persecution brought out great resiliency in his character. He actually thrived on his persecutor's affliction and interrogation.

Evil will always try to persecute the power of God. But Dowie was supernaturally secure and anchored in his godly authority. The supernatural never bows to the natural.

## LEAVES OF HEALING

Having foiled the legal system, his enemies then plotted to take away his mailing privileges. By 1894, Dowie's newsletter, *Leaves of Healing*, had a weekly worldwide circulation. It was filled with teachings and healing testimonies. Needless to say, the newsletter was very dear to his heart. Dowie fondly spoke of it as the "Little White Dove."

True to his form, Dowie never minced words in his writings. He fervently denounced sin and exposed evil industries. And those who were the most hurt by the publication saw it as another opportunity to end his ministry. *Leaves of Healing* also warned its readers of lethargic and controlling denominations.

People loved Dowie's dramatics and straightforward talk. Many wanted to say the same thing themselves, so they looked to him as their voice. Even those who despised him read the newsletter to see what he had to say. As a result, circulation increased rapidly. Much of his support and ministry was attributed to this publication.

The Postmaster General of Chicago was a devout Catholic. So to take his mailing privileges, Dowie's enemies gave one of his sermons that renounced the infallibility of the Pope to this man. The Postmaster was instantly offended and revoked his second-class mailing privileges, forcing Dowie to pay fourteen times the usual cost!

But Dowie could not be outdone. He paid the increase and solicited his readers to write Washington, D.C., to tell of this injustice. His supporters came out in full force, and he was granted an immediate audience with the Postmaster General in Washington. Once Dowie shared his story and showed the malicious lies printed in the Chicago newspaper, both the editor and the paper were denounced by the U.S. government. In fact, by 1896, this particular editor, one of Dowie's greatest persecutors, was put in prison on a separate charge and was made a public spectacle, forever ruined.

While in Washington, Dowie was also granted an audience with President William McKinley. He assured the president of his prayers while in office and the president warmly thanked him. While leaving the White House, Dowie commented to his staff that he feared for McKinley's life. He later asked his followers to pray for the safety of the president because he was not properly guarded.[14] But in spite of Dowie's prophetic warnings, President McKinley was shot in Buffalo, New York, on September 6, 1901. He died eight days later, being the third U.S. president to be killed by an assassin.

## "ZION HAS COME"

By the end of 1896, Dowie had gained great influence over the city of Chicago. His enemies were either dead, in prison, or silent. The local police, who had once arrested him a hundred times, were now his friends and protected him at a moment's notice. The political officials, including the mayor, had all been voted in by Dowie's people. Divine healing was preached on every street corner. Dowie had sectioned off the districts of the city, and sent teams called "The Seventies" proclaiming the Gospel into each area.

*Soon, there was scarcely a person in Chicago who had not heard the Gospel message.*

Soon, there was scarcely a person in Chicago who had not heard the Gospel message. Now Dowie was praying for thousands every week to receive divine healing. Sadie Cody, niece of Buffalo Bill Cody, was miraculously healed, having first read a copy of *Leaves of Healing*. Among other notable healings were Amanda Hicks, cousin of Abraham Lincoln; Dr. Lillian Yeomans; Rev. F. A. Graves; John G. Lake's wife; and the wife of a U.S. congressman.

Through his apostolic mantle, John Alexander Dowie literally ruled the city of Chicago for Jesus Christ. He leased the largest auditorium in Chicago for six months, and moved the great Zion Tabernacle into the building, filling its six thousand seats at every service.

Now Dowie was finally able to pursue the dream he had long held in his heart – to organize a church on apostolic principles. It had been his lifelong desire to bring back the teachings and foundation of the early church found in the book of Acts. So, in January, he held his first conference and laid the groundwork. The work was named "Christian Catholic Work," with the name "Catholic" meaning "universal," and was by no means connected to the Roman Catholic Church.

He would never allow this church to be known as a "new thing." He looked at it as a "restoration" of the principles that had been lost to the body of Christ. His theology was good in that he warned if something was "new," then it was "false." Within a few years, Dowie's Christian Catholic Church had multiplied into tens of thousands.

I believe without a doubt, that all of the five-fold ministries listed in Ephesians 4 are alive and well today (see verses 11-13). The apostolic office was not done away with when the original twelve died. Nor did God allow His plan for the Church to die when the apostles' flesh did. His new covenant principles were to continue until His return. They aren't bound by men's ideas or theology, nor do His promises end when men get nervous. There have been many more than the original twelve apostles, and men today are still called to that office.

Ephesians 2:20 says the foundations of the Church are built upon the apostles and prophets, with Jesus Himself being the chief cornerstone. Great authority comes with the office of an apostle, and I believe God sovereignly chooses and equips those He wants to stand there. But there has always been a lack of knowledge concerning the administration of that office. I believe Dowie was sovereignly called and equipped as an apostle. And I don't believe his ministry failed because he accepted the apostolic office. But I do believe that because of his lack of knowledge and understanding, that he misread the spiritual operations of his office. And I believe that this in itself was the main spiritual deficiency that caused him to misuse his authority.

During the time in which Dowie's church was being instituted, some very interesting events transpired. This period has been called, "The Golden Years" of Zion.[15] The next three years were quiet, prosperous, and influential. It was then that Dowie made his secret plans for his special city.

*Dowie and wife, Jeanie, seated in front of trophy wall at Christian Catholic Church*

*Dowie preaching in Australia*

*Last photo of Dowie before his death*

Knowing that such an effort would produce curiosity, Dowie diverted the attention of the multitudes by declaring a "Holy War," and announced a coming message entitled "Doctors, Drugs, and Devils." Advertising the message for weeks, the title caused no small stir. Then while his enemies were distracted by it all, Dowie secretly hired proprietors to survey land forty miles north of Chicago to build a city. After they found sixty-six hundred acres on Lake Michigan, Dowie dressed himself up as a tramp so as not to be recognized, then toured the site. And before his enemies could discover what was happening, the land had been purchased, and decisive plans were made for building the city of Zion, Illinois.

Dowie unveiled the architectural plans for Zion at the New Year's Eve Watch Night service on January 1, 1900. His business ability was praised by his people and the secular world, for starting the Zion Land Investment Association. Subdivisions were allotted, and home-building began. The land was not to be sold, instead it was to be leased for a period of some eleven hundred years. The terms of the lease strictly forbade the possession or use of tobacco, liquor, and swine's flesh anywhere within the limits of the city.[16] And in two years' time, houses had been erected and the city was taking shape.

## THE ELIJAH COMPLEX

Though his "moral utopia" seemed to abound, those closest to Dowie noticed a change. Trouble was brewing in Zion. There was no longer any time for divine healing to be preached because all of Dowie's efforts were focused on running the city. He deemed himself as Zion's General Overseer. The rule of the city was to be absolutely in his hands. And problem after problem arose to cleverly divert him from his original ministry command.

*Eventually Dowie had so sadly diverted from God's plan for his life that he embraced the suggestion and proclaimed it as truth. He believed he was Elijah.*

It was during this season that some ministers came to Dowie and proclaimed him to be the Elijah foretold in the Bible. At first, Dowie soundly denounced them. But their words kept "ringing in his ears." Then after awhile Dowie himself said a voice seemed to say, "Elijah must come, and who but you is doing the work of Elijah?"[17]

Eventually Dowie had so sadly diverted from God's plan for his life that he embraced the suggestion and proclaimed it as truth. He believed he was Elijah. He even went on to believe that by establishing other cities like Zion outside of every major city in America, that he could eventually have the money to build outside of Jerusalem. His plan was to buy out the Turks, the Muslims, and the Jews to take over Jerusalem for Jesus so He could establish His city during the millennial reign. Dowie was thoroughly deluded. Soon his preaching had deteriorated into the mere denouncing of his enemies. He also gave "lectures" on political views while he exhorted his hearers to invest more heavily into the work of the city.[18] He took counsel from no one, except in minor matters. And he removed all restraints that could have kept him in check or hindered his plans.

## THE MADISON SQUARE KNOCKOUT

What was once a persecution battle against the Word of God had now become a personal war to maintain Dowie's own level of influence. It was godly persecution that activated the mantle of his apostolic office, but now he was fighting to maintain his own personal influence and success. And it destroyed him.

A vividly sad example of Dowie's vanity in this area happened at what was deemed, the "New York Visitation." The bishop of the Methodist church and the editor of its denominational newspaper, Dr. Buckley, asked for an interview with Dowie. So Dowie granted them audience and thought that he had fully persuaded them to believe his acclamations. But he hadn't. According to Buckley's newspaper article, Dowie was "in the moonlit border land of insanity where large movements of limited duration have sometimes originated." Buckley also added, "If he believes it or not, he is but another impostor."[19] Enraged, Dowie rented the Madison Square Garden, and though financially strained, arranged for eight trains to take thousands of his followers to New York City. Once there, he planned to make an open show of the two men to demonstrate the power he still held. What was once inspired by God's divine direction, was now reduced to

*John Alexander Dowie, General Overseer of Zion in his high priest robe.*

Dowie's own self-appointment. It was totally in the flesh. He reacted out of a hurt and emotional wound and now he was determined to display his vengeance.

The event failed miserably. Though thousands went with Dowie, thousands more came who had another plan. They filled the Garden, but as Dowie took the platform to speak, they began to exit by the droves. The scene confused Dowie terribly and kept him from speaking as he had originally planned. As a whole, the city of New York was virtually unaware that anything had transpired at this meeting. It was as if God silenced the newspapers and had mercy on His servant.

## THE FATEFUL END

By now, the city of Zion was broken financially. So Dowie sought to escape by taking an expensive trip around the world where he found himself unwelcome in many cities. It was on this trip that his train pulled into Pomona, California. There had been a severe drought in the land, and no rain had fallen for eight months. So the reporters chided Dowie, reminding him that Elijah prayed for rain during drought in Israel and rain came. And that if he was Elijah, surely he would do the same for California. Dowie did indeed pray for rain at the end of his service, and before the crowd was dismissed, rain was falling in torrents.

Upon leaving California, Dowie planned a venture into Mexico to establish "Zion Plantation." He was hoping this new venture could pay for the debts of the old. But his followers, now broken financially and disillusioned, had left him in heart. They couldn't help but notice how poor they had become – while Dowie lived in extremes, hosted lavish parties, and left for a world tour.

Some say Dowie built his own city because he was tired of the persecution. But in my personal opinion, that doesn't seem true. Although greatly anointed and sent by God, it seemed that Dowie had a weakness for power and success. He said of himself:

> **"In becoming an apostle, it is not a question of rising high, it is a question of becoming low enough.... I do not think that I have reached a deep enough depth of true humility...of true abasement and self-effacement, for the high office of an apostle...."[20]**

Jesus never commanded us to build communes. Jesus commanded us to "Go!" not "Huddle." The book of Acts "commune" didn't work for long either

(Acts 2:44-47; 5:1-10). Persecution hit the group, and they were scattered to the uttermost regions of the earth. (Acts 8:1.) Why? So the Great Commission in Matthew 28:19-20 could be fulfilled. We are to be lights in the world and penetrate Satan's darkness. Huddling together won't accomplish that feat.

The greatest test of a leader is not in the area of persecution, though many fall there. I think one of the greatest snares comes in the form of power and success. We must never think we've "made it" and begin to dictate our personal power as a result of God-given success. Success brings a multitude of avenues and ventures. If we get caught up in the vast selections that come from success and *fail to develop our spiritual tenacity*, we can fall victim to the "whirlwind." We can't find peace with our past by using the power of the present. With each new height, we must build a new tenacity. That's why some churches grow to a certain level, then become comfortable, or fall. The leadership become too busy with the "avenues" and lose the time and energy to develop both themselves *and* their members for higher levels in God.

Whenever we obey God, success should come. So never be afraid of success! But to properly administrate success, we must hold ourselves in the strength of the Spirit, listening for His direction – *not our own*. It is only through the strength of the Spirit and a hunger for God, that we are able to continue in what God has spoken, pioneering into the next level.

> *We must never think we've "made it" and begin to dictate our personal power as a result of God-given success. Success brings a multitude of avenues and ventures. If we get caught up in the vast selections that come from success and fail to develop our spiritual tenacity, we can fall victim to the "whirlwind."*

Dowie soon proclaimed himself as the First Apostle of a renewed, end-time Church, denounced his last name, and signed his documents as "John Alexander, First Apostle."[21] But not long after his "self appointment," Dowie suffered a stroke on the platform from which he delivered his last sermon. Then while he was out of the country to recover, the city of Zion held an organized meeting to vote Dowie out.

Dowie fought this decision to the last ounce of his strength but never succeeded in regaining his position. He was allowed to live his last days inside of Shiloh House, his home for many years, and slipped into eternity on March 9, 1907. His death was documented with these words by Judge V. V. Barnes:

"...the last night John Alexander spent on earth, he was again in spirit upon this platform talking to the assembled multitudes of his people. He preached during that night and thought he was preaching the principles of the Gospel to the assembled thousands. As he taught the same old truths...he lapsed again into slumber, awaking from time to time and continuing the dispensation of the old gospel message. The last song he ever sang as the morning light began to appear was, 'I Am a Soldier of the Cross.' Then they listened for his last sentence, and he said, 'The millennium has come; I will be back for a thousand years.' These were the last words that he spoke; the last sentence he uttered."[22]

How could such a great life end in such sadness? Are there any answers? Again, I believe the answer lies in a basic misunderstanding of spiritual principles.

Dowie was spiritually assigned by God to the city of Chicago – and he conquered it. While living within that city, and carrying out his divine appointment, principalities and powers couldn't touch him. But Dowie seemed to move out of Chicago through his own desire for power and gave the devil freedom to destroy his life. When he left the city of his calling, the enemy killed his worldwide influence through deception, killed a member of his family, destroyed his marriage, and destroyed Dowie himself with "every form of disease" fastening to his body.[23]

We must remain with the original, anointed plan of God for our lives and allow Him to open the avenues to administrate it. Maybe Dowie should have built *churches* and *Bible schools* instead of a *city*. That avenue would have sent thousands into the ministry from his godly influence.

Dowie did go on in peace to be with the Lord. Those who were with him at the end said he had returned to his faith of the early years. Many even testified that he had become a gentle, loving man who acted as if a tremendous burden had been lifted. And the city of Zion, Illinois, remains today, but the leadership is divided among many brethren, "...as no single person could completely fill Dr. Dowie's shoes."[24]

## A GREAT OBJECT LESSON

Gordon Lindsay, John Alexander Dowie's official biographer and founder of Christ for the Nations in Dallas, Texas, described Dowie's ministry as "the greatest object lesson in the history of the church."[25] Pertaining to ministry, his life was filled with vivid, instructional detail. The lessons we can learn are never meant to degrade or criticize this great man of God. His personal problems should be held separate from the call of God.

John Alexander Dowie went down in history as an impostor, yet he was a genius called of God. Even in the midst of his error, he prophesied the coming of radio and television to our generation. He had his failures, but from his influence came many great men of God. His ministry produced John G. Lake, the great apostle to South Africa; F. F. Bosworth, and his brother B. B. Bosworth, whose healing campaigns touched untold millions; Gordon Lindsay, whose life and ministry resulted in the great interdenominational college, Christ for the Nations, in Dallas, Texas; Raymond T. Richey, healing crusader; and Charles Parham, "The Father of Pentecost," whose Bible school in Topeka, Kansas, ushered in another move of the Holy Spirit. Many more had large radio ministries and powerful mission works.

> *John Alexander Dowie went down in history as an impostor, yet he was a genius called of God.*

Without a doubt, John Alexander Dowie succeeded in making the Bible alive to untold millions. He was an instrument used of God to restore the keys of divine healing and the revelation of repentance to a lukewarm, lethargic generation. If there is a moral to the message of the failure in his life, that message is this: Never sway from what God has commanded you to do in the earth. No matter what your age, your generation has not passed until you exit the earth and enter heaven. So if God has commanded you to fulfill a commission, make *it* your utmost priority as long as you live.

## CHAPTER ONE, JOHN ALEXANDER DOWIE
References

1 Gordon Lindsay, *John Alexander Dowie: A Life Story of Trials, Tragedies and Triumphs* (Dallas, TX: Christ for the Nations, 1986), 228-229.

2 Ibid., 15.

3 Ibid.

4 Ibid., 22-24.

5 Ibid., 25.

6 Ibid.

7 Ibid., 43.

8 Ibid., 44-45.

9 Ibid., 46.

10 Ibid., 49.

11 Ibid., 95.

12 Ibid., 151.

13 Ibid., 107-109.

14 Ibid., 133-135.

15 Ibid., 161.

16 Ibid., 173.

17 Ibid., 188.

18 Ibid., 199.

19 Ibid., 221.

20 Ibid., 155-156.

21 Ibid., 235.

22 Ibid., 260-261.

23 Ibid., 251.

24 *This We Believe*, Handbook of the Christian Catholic Church, 7.

25 Lindsay, *John Alexander Dowie, A Life Story*, Introduction.

# CHAPTER TWO

# Maria Woodworth-Etter

## *"Demonstrator of the Spirit"*

# "DEMONSTRATOR OF THE SPIRIT"

**"T**he Lord has given me a special mission to bring about a spirit of unity and love.... God is raising up people in every land who are reaching out after more of God and saying, 'Come and help us. We want the spirit of love. We want the signs and wonders.'"[1]

There hasn't been a greater demonstrator of God's Spirit since the book of Acts in Pentecostal history than Maria Woodworth-Etter. She was an incredible woman of vision and spiritual strength who stood in the face of fierce opposition, lifted her tiny hand, and allowed the Holy Spirit to spread His fire. Sister Etter lived in the realm of the spirit as a powerful vessel of God's divine leading and His supernatural manifestations. She was a faithful friend of heaven, choosing to lose her earthly reputation to gain a spiritual one.

Maria (pronounced "Ma-ri-ah," not "Ma-ree-ah") was born in 1844 on a Lisbon, Ohio, farm. She was born again at the beginning of the Third Great Awakening at the age of thirteen. The preacher who led her to the Lord prayed that her life "might be a shining light."[2] But little did he realize that this little girl he had just prayed for would become the grandmother of the Pentecostal Movement that would spread throughout the world.

Maria immediately heard the call of God and dedicated her life to the Lord. Of her calling she would later write, "**I heard the voice of Jesus calling me to go out in the highways and hedges and gather in the lost sheep.**"[3] But one thing stopped her – she was a woman – and at that time, women were not allowed to preach. In the mid-nineteenth century, women couldn't even vote in a national election, so to be a woman preacher

> *"I heard the voice of Jesus calling me to go out in the highways and hedges and gather in the lost sheep."*

was definitely frowned upon. And to be a *single* woman in the ministry was out of the question. Therefore, Maria pondered the things the Lord told her, and decided she would have to marry a missionary to fulfill her call. So she planned to continue her education, then enter a formal college to make herself ready.

But tragedy struck her close-knit family. Her father was killed while working in the fields of their farm and she immediately returned home to help support her family. Now her hopes of a formal education were shattered, so she settled into what she thought was a normal Christian lifestyle.

## "ANGELS CAME INTO MY ROOM...."

During the Civil War, Maria met P. H. Woodworth, who had returned home from the conflict after being discharged with a head injury. She had a whirlwind courtship with the former soldier and soon married him. They took up farming, but nothing ever came of their labors. It seemed as if everything was failing.

Over the years, Maria became the mother of six children. So she tried to settle into a normal family home life while the Lord continued to call her. But Maria, exasperated in her role as a wife and mother, couldn't answer the call. She was married to a man with no desire for ministry, she had six children to raise, and she was sickly herself. Then real tragedy struck their home. The Woodworths lost five of their six children to disease. Maria was able to pull herself together after this horrible episode, but her husband never recovered from the loss. She did her best to help him while raising their only surviving daughter. Through all these situations she never grew bitter against God, nor did she harden her heart as a result of the loss.

> *Angels came into her room. They took her to the West, over prairies, lakes, forests, and rivers where she saw a long, wide field of waving golden grain. As the view unfolded she began to preach and saw the grains begin to fall like sheaves.*

But Maria needed answers for the nagging heartache that oppressed her because of the calamity that struck her family. Refusing to give up, she began to search the Word of God. And as she read, she saw how women were repeatedly used by God throughout the Bible. She read Joel's prophecy predicting that the Spirit of God would be poured out upon men AND women. But Maria would look to heaven and say, **"Lord, I can't preach. I don't know what to say and I don't have any education."** Still, she continued to read and find truth in the Word of God while she struggled with her call. She would later write, **"The more I investigated, the more I found to condemn me."**[4]

Then Maria had a great vision. Angels came into her room. They took her to the West, over prairies, lakes, forests, and rivers where she saw a long, wide field of waving golden grain. As the view unfolded she began to preach and saw the grains begin to fall like sheaves. Then Jesus told her that, "just as the grain fell, so people would fall" as she preached.[5] Finally Maria realized that she would never be happy until she yielded to the call. In response to this great vision from God, she humbly answered **"yes"** to His call upon her life and asked Him to anoint her with great power.

## "W-O-M-A-N" DOES NOT SPELL "W-E-A-K"

Many women reading this book are called of God to preach. You have had visions and unctions from God's Spirit to go and set people free. God has spoken to you in the area of divine healing, deliverance, and freedom of the Spirit. So never allow a religious spirit to silence what the Lord has spoken to you. Religion likes to suppress women and their ministries, especially young ones. You need to learn to obey God without question. If Maria had answered from her youth, possibly her children wouldn't have died. I'm not saying that God killed her children. But I am saying that when we directly disobey God, our actions open the door to the works of the devil. His work is to destroy. God's work is to bring life. So learn to obey God with boldness. Boldness brings the power of God and will leave your accusers speechless in your presence. Also find some strong women with solid ministries from whom you can learn. And allow these words of Sister Etter to stir you in your heart:

> **"My dear sister in Christ, as you hear these words may the Spirit of Christ come upon you, and make you willing to do the work the Lord has assigned to you. It is high time for women to let their lights shine; to bring out their talents that have been hidden away rusting; and use them for the glory of God, and do with their might what their hands find to do, trusting God for strength, Who has said, 'I will never leave you.' Let us not plead weakness; God will use the weak things of the world to confound the wise. We are sons and daughters of the Most High God. Should we not honor our high calling and do all we can to save those who sit in the valley and shadow of death? Did He not send Moses, Aaron — *Miriam* to be your leaders? Barak dared not meet the enemy unless Deborah led the van. The Lord raised up men, women, and children of His own choosing — Hannah, Hulda, Anna, Phoebe, Narcissus, Tryphena, Persis, Julia, the Marys and the sisters who co-labored with**

Paul. **Is it less becoming for women to labor in Christ's kingdom and vineyard now than it was then?"**[6]

Seek the Spirit of God for yourself. If you are called, you will have to answer for it. Obey God without question. He will handle the details.

## THEY WEPT THROUGHOUT THE HOUSE

Maria first launched her ministry into her own community. She had no idea of what she would say, but God told her to go and that He would put the words in her mouth.[7] And God fulfilled His Word. As Maria stood before her first crowd, most of them relatives, she opened her mouth, and the crowd began to weep and fall to the floor. Some got up and ran out in tears. After this Maria was highly sought throughout her community. Several churches asked her to come and revive their congregations. Soon she expanded her ministry westward and had held nine revivals, preached two hundred sermons, and started two churches with Sunday school memberships of over a hundred people. God honored Maria and made up for her lost years in a short amount of time.

One particular meeting was held in a town called Devils Den. No minister had ever been successful there, and people came to mock her. They were looking to see the female evangelist who would soon run out of town shattered and defeated. But they received the surprise of their lives! Sister Etter might have been a woman, but she was not one to be taken lightly. She knew the key to spiritual warfare, and the fervency of prayer that unlocked heaven.

For three days Maria preached and sang. No one moved. Finally, on the fourth day, she exercised her spiritual authority through intercession and tore down the demonic principality that ruled over Devils Den. She prayed that God would show a great display of His power to break the people's stiff formality. That night, people throughout the meeting cried and repented to God. It was the greatest manifestation of the presence of God the town had ever witnessed.

## THE DEMOLITION DERBY FORCE

We are not called to give up. We are called to obey God at whatever cost and to let success answer our critics. If it seems you have hit a hard place in your life or ministry, don't whine and complain. Don't offer your reasons for it. Pray! Explanations and excuses rob us of strength and power. Don't shake your head and run. Use the authority that has been given you through Jesus and overthrow the demonic powers that blind the people. Through prayer, take authority and make a clear path for the Spirit of God to minister to the hearts of the people. Sister Etter groomed her spirit through prayer producing invincible strength. She was known as a revivalist who could break towns open.

## THEY CAME SCREAMING FOR MERCY

Sister Etter pioneered the way for the Pentecostal manifestations that are so common in the movement today. It was not until she preached at a church in western Ohio that had lost God's power, that the meaning of her vision about the sheaves of wheat became clear.[8] It was at this church where the people fell into "trances." This was the one spiritual manifestation that marked her ministry highly, but brought fierce persecution.

Up to this point, this manifestation had not been known in the Church the way it is known today. In her own account she wrote:

**"Fifteen came to the altar screaming for mercy. Men and women fell and lay like dead. I had never seen anything like this. I felt it was the work of God, but did not know how to explain it, or what to say."[9]**

After laying on the floor for some time, these people sprang to their feet with shining faces while shouting the praises of God. Sister Etter said that she had never seen such bright conversions. The ministers and elder saints wept and praised the Lord for His "Pentecost Power." And from that meeting on, Sister Etter's ministry would be marked by this particular manifestation that always followed her preaching with hundreds coming to Christ.

*Sister Etter pioneered the way for the Pentecostal manifestations that are so common in the movement today.*

## "TRANCE" TALK

The trances became the talk of the day. Hundreds flocked to taste of this outpouring, while others went to observe or ridicule. At one meeting, fifteen doctors came from different cities to investigate the trances. One of the doctors was a world-class leader in his field. Sister Etter wrote of it this way:

**"He did not want to admit the power was of God. He would have been glad if they could prove it was something else. He came to investigate...but was called to another part of the house. He went, expecting to find something new. To his surprise he found his son at the altar and wanted his father to pray for him. He could not pray. God showed him what he was, and what he was doing. He began to pray for**

*On the road*

**himself. While praying he fell into a trance, and saw the horrors of hell. He was falling in. After a terrible struggle God saved him. He went to work to win souls for Christ."**[10]

Sister Etter also wrote of a party that several young women attended at which they thought they would have fun and act out a trance. But they were immediately gripped by the power of God, and their mocking turned into loud cries to God for mercy.[11]

Once an elderly man who had traveled the world was visiting an area where Maria was ministering. He was a religious man, so he decided to attend one of her meetings out of curiosity. As he witnessed the meeting, he made some joking remark to his friends concerning the display of power. Filled with pride, the man boldly headed for the platform to investigate. But before he reached the pulpit, he was "struck to the floor by the power of God" and laid there for over two hours. While in this state, God showed him a vision of heaven and hell. Realizing he had to choose, he immediately chose God and was born again. Then he came to, praising God.

The only thing this man could say once he came out of the trance was that he regretted having spent sixty years lost in religion, never knowing Jesus

Christ personally.[12] Still, newspapers and unbelieving ministers warned others to stay away from the meetings. They said they "would make a person insane." Nevertheless, thousands were saved, many being "struck down, laying as dead men" even on their way home. It is said that many people also fell under the power in their homes, miles away from the meetings.

What are "trances"? They are one of the four ways God manifests in a vision. The first type of vision is an "inner vision." The picture you see in your inner man, or spirit man, will benefit you greatly if you heed it. Secondly, there is the "open vision." This vision comes when your eyes are wide open. It's like watching a movie screen open up in front of you as it displays a scene God wants to show you. Thirdly, is the night vision. This is when God gives a dream to make you aware of a certain thing. The last type of vision is the "trance vision." In this vision, natural abilities are frozen so God can minister whatever is needed. When people came up from a trance vision in Sister Etter's meetings, they told of seeing both heaven and hell.

Sister Etter's style was, to say the least, "different" from the ministers of her day. She never prohibited the audience from participating. Unlike the stoic church order of the late 1800s, Maria believed in shouting, dancing, singing, and preaching. She believed that emotional displays were important, as long as they were in order. And she believed that a lack of physical manifestation was a sign of apostasy.

> *Unlike the stoic church order of the late 1800s, Maria believed in shouting, dancing, singing, and preaching. She believed that emotional displays were important, as long as they were in order. And she believed that a lack of physical manifestation was a sign of apostasy.*

## FRENZY OR FULFILLMENT?

I believe God is upset with some of the churches today because they refuse to allow the people to openly and freely express themselves to Him. If people can't express themselves to God, then God can't move upon them. Some people are afraid of emotions in the church. They have no problem with them at home, or at a sporting event. But for some religious reason, they think the church should be quiet and serene. But let me tell you something, heaven isn't quiet and serene! Some people are in for a rude awakening when they die and go to heaven. They are going to have to learn how to rejoice along with the rest of us – because heaven is full of life and energy! We have a lot to shout about – both here *and* there!

Our churches *must* have a fresh move of God. And like it or not, *a move of God affects the emotions.* "Well, Roberts, I just don't believe God is in all that shouting and dancing." The shouting and dancing isn't God. It is simply an unconstrained response *to His power.* Listen, have you ever put your finger in a light socket and remained still? How much more when you touch God! When God touches you, you will react! If you say, "Well, what about the extremes?" I say, "Why are we so concerned about the ditch when we should be looking at the highway?"

Focus on the true, and the false will fade away. When the power of God comes upon you, you will enjoy it! And when you enjoy something, you show it. So learn the truth of what God loves in His worshippers, then do it.

Now you say, "Well, people will talk about us." I say, "So what?" The truth outlives a lie. What people don't understand, they persecute. They lied about Jesus, but He still lives today. When those people experience the true touch of God, they will change their minds.

"What if we lose money?" Well, is money your god? Let me remind you that monetary currency can't save souls. The Spirit of God is what draws mankind to Jesus. By obeying the Spirit, we lift up Jesus. There are no payoffs or short-cuts. If you are a church leader, you are commanded by God to obey the Holy Spirit and learn His ways. The Bible says it is those who are led by the Spirit that are the sons of God. (Romans 8:14.) So let Him lead!

If you are led by the Spirit, visions will increase in the Church. We must be spiritually mature to deal with any problems or evil spirits. New Age religions have dug so deeply into the wrong spirit realm that they've made the Church afraid to pursue the true manifestations of God's Spirit. The realm of the spirit holds both God and the demonic, and if the Holy Spirit is not your Guide when you enter, you are subject to the demonic. But New Agers don't enter the spirit realm with Jesus Christ. They come of their own will. And this is one place where they are deceived. We are nothing without the blood of Jesus. Some are afraid that if they pursue God supernaturally, they will be accused of being involved with the New Age. If you are following God's Spirit, He will keep you pure.

So open your church to the move of God, and learn from those who have gone on before you. Where the Spirit of God is, there is liberty, and yes, *order.* But I'm not talking about the fearful restraints of control or denominational suppression. People are hungry to see God and to be free. Some will travel across the continent to hear someone who truly knows God and the manifestations of His Spirit.

## "SHE KNOCKS 'EM SILLY"

By the time Sister Etter reached age forty, she was a national phenomena. Various denominations recognized her ability to stir dead churches, bring in the unconverted, and cheer on a deeper spiritual walk with God. Doctors, lawyers, drunkards, and adulterers – people from all walks of life – were gloriously saved and filled with the Holy Spirit in her meetings. Because of one of her meetings in 1885, the police said they had never seen such a change in their city. The city had been so cleaned up that they had nothing to do![13]

One newspaper reporter wrote of Sister Etter:

"She goes at it like a foot pad tackles his prey. By some supernatural power she just knocks 'em silly when they are not looking for it, and while they are down she applies the hydraulic pressure and pumps the grace of God into them by the bucketful."[14]

Eventually the Lord led Maria to begin praying for the sick. At first, she was reluctant, feeling it would take away from her evangelistic call. But God continued to make His will clear, and she agreed. She studied the Word and began preaching His divine will in healing. It didn't take long to see that evangelism and healing went hand in hand as thousands were won to Christ as a result of seeing others healed.

*She studied the Word and began preaching His divine will in healing. It didn't take long to see that evangelism and healing went hand in hand as thousands were won to Christ as a result of seeing others healed.*

Maria preached that the strong manifestations of the Spirit were **"nothing new; they were just something the Church had lost."**[15] And she refused to get caught up in the pet doctrines of the day, desiring only for the Holy Spirit to do His works.

Once in a meeting, a crowd rushed to the platform and cried out, "What shall we do?" Maria finishes the story:

**"They went down by the mighty wind power of the Holy Ghost. He sat upon the children of God till their faces shone like Stephen's when his enemies said he looked like an angel. Many received gifts; some for ministry, some as**

*Church built by Etter in Indiana known as the Etter Tabernacle*

*Sioux City, Iowa*

*Evangelist Mrs. M. B. Woodworth-Etter. In the last years of her ministry Etter always wore white when she ministered.*

*Etter in state*

**evangelists, some of healing, and hundreds of sinners received the gift of eternal life."**[16]

In another meeting, over twenty-five thousand people crowded in to hear Sister Etter. And remember, in those days, there were no public address systems! Maria wrote that before she even finished preaching, the power of God fell on the multitude and took control of about five hundred as they fell to the ground.[17]

## THE WILD, WILD WEST

Of course, Sister Etter's life was marked with great persecution. There were problems around every corner, not to mention the pressures that came from leading such huge masses of people who were experiencing their first manifestations of the Spirit. In addition to all of this, she was a woman in ministry who was married to an unfaithful man.

While ministering in her controversial crusade in Oakland, California, P. H. Woodworth's infidelity was revealed. Sister Etter stayed in separate quarters, choosing to leave him. Finally, after twenty-six stormy years of marriage, in January of 1891, they were divorced. Then, in less than a year and a half, P. H. Woodworth remarried and publicly slandered Maria's character and ministry. He died not long after on June 21, 1892, of typhoid fever.

Despite her stormy relationship with this man, Maria took time from her ministry schedule to travel to his funeral. It is said that she not only attended the funeral, but also took part in the memorial service.

Etter's greatest trials came while on the West Coast. She believed the West could be won to God, just as it occurred in the Midwest. So in 1889, she arrived in Oakland and purchased an eight-thousand seat tent. And soon, the tent was jammed with onlookers coming to see the trances, hear of the visions, and watch all the other manifestations of the Holy Spirit.

But heavy persecution also visited Maria on the West Coast. Hoodlums, or gangs as we call them today, started harassing her meetings. Several times these men hid explosives in the wood stoves – and miraculously – no one was ever injured. Once a windstorm even ripped the canvas of the tent apart during a meeting. Death threats were sent to her weekly, newspapers slandered her relentlessly, and ministers divided against her. Mischievous people would bring the mentally disturbed to her meetings, knowing they would cause a great emotional scene. This was done so many times, that many naive people thought it was Maria's meetings that drove these people to insanity! And because many misunderstood her theology, the citizens called for the authorities daily to shut her meetings down. Nevertheless, Maria refused to leave Oakland until she felt God was finished.

When it seemed the gangs began to get the upper hand in her meetings, the Oakland Police Department deputized "bouncers" to protect the services. But this got out of hand because the bouncers were inexperienced both in character and common sense.

> *When it seemed the gangs began to get the upper hand in her meetings, the Oakland Police Department deputized "bouncers" to protect the services.*

Then there was the wild prophecy that came from Maria saying disaster would hit the coast and destroy it. After she spoke this, the newspapers terrorized Sister Etter and made her out to be a common criminal. They misquoted and hyped up the prophecy to such a degree that it was not accurately known what was actually said. Then as could be expected, other men and women operating in the counterfeits to the gifts of the Spirit jumped on the prophecy bandwagon. Deceived by the enemy, these people prophesied more doom and gloom for the West Coast, causing great controversy.

Sister Etter had a slew of prominent ministers both for and against her. One was John Alexander Dowie. While she was on the West Coast, he joined her critics and publicly blasted her "trance evangelism," calling it a great delusion.[18] No other minister but Etter matched his own ministry in the area of healing and publicity, so he often referred to her when he spoke of the abuses. Only once did Sister Etter even publicly defend herself against Dowie. She did so with these words:

> **"After stating in our meeting before thousands, that he never saw such power of God, and so wonderfully manifested, and after advising all his people to stand by me, he went up and down the coast preaching against me and the meetings, until he broke up all his missions. His only objection was that some were struck down by the power of God in our meetings.**
>
> **"He lectured against me two or three times in San Francisco, and said I was in line with Satan. Many went to hear him...but his talk was such that many people left in disgust**

while he was talking. I told the people that I had been his friend and had treated him like a brother, and that he was not fighting me, but the Lord and His Word. I always told the people that I would leave him in the hands of God and that I would go right on with the Master.

"I told them to watch and see how we would come out, and they would see that he would go down in disgrace, and that I would be living when he was dead."[19]

Sister Etter outlived John Alexander Dowie by seventeen years.

It can be said that Sister Etter did make some mistakes in her Oakland Crusade. And it isn't any wonder with all the attacks that were plotted against her. However, it should be remembered that in 1906, San Francisco did experience the most devastating earthquake in American history, and Sister Etter's prophecy came forth in 1890.

Sister Etter also made several good friends while there, one being Carrie Judd Montgomery. Montgomery had come from the East Coast to conduct meetings in California. The two met and developed a lifelong friendship. Carrie and her husband, George, were instrumental in the Pentecostal Movement and founded the *Home of Peace* in Oakland. The couple remained strong supporters of Sister Etter throughout their ministry.

## "GIFT FROM GOD"

During this phase of Sister Etter's life, there were also some refreshing highlights. Besides the friendships she made, God didn't want her to carry the ministry mantle alone. It took some time, but ten years after her divorce, Maria met a wonderful man from Hot Springs, Arkansas, named Samuel Etter. God sent her the perfect mate. The two were married in 1902. Sister Etter had great respect for this gentleman and often referred to him as her "gift from God." Later she would write of him:

"He stood bravely with me in the hottest battle, and since the day we were married has never shrank. He will defend the Word and all the gifts, and operations of the Holy Ghost, but does not want any fanaticism, or foolishness. It makes no difference what I call on him to do. He will pray, and preach, and sing, and is very good around the altar. The Lord knew what I needed, and it was all

**brought about by the Lord, through His love and care for me and the work."**[20]

Three years after her marriage to Samuel Etter, Maria disappeared from public ministry and remained silent for the next seven years. No reason has ever been given for this long silence. But when she emerged seven years later, she was just as powerful as before, and now had the loving support of a wonderful husband. Samuel Etter faithfully loved and cared for Maria. He managed her meetings inside and out, and took care of all of her writings and book distribution. In fact, Sister Etter's ministry published several books:

1. *Life, Work, and Experience of Maria Beula Woodworth, Evangelist.*
2. *Marvels and Miracles God Wrought in the Ministry of Mrs. M. B. Woodworth-Etter for Forty Years.*
3. *Signs and Wonders God Wrought in the Ministry of Mrs. M. B. Woodworth-Etter for Forty Years.*
4. *Song Books.*
5. *Questions and Answers on Divine Healing.*
6. *Acts of the Holy Ghost (later published as "A Diary of Signs and Wonders").*

Some of Sister Etter's books were reprinted into several editions, and some were translated into foreign languages. Although we have a large selection of Christian books on the market today, Sister Etter's books are still very rare. I have personally been offered thousands of dollars for my private collection, which I have refused. In my opinion, no amount of money could buy what Sister Etter has written.

So, Samuel Etter – the husband, friend, editor, manager, and minister of helps – "gift from God" – found peace in his position as a support in his wife's ministry. His ability showed a rare and notable character as a man. As a result, he was a vital part of her ministry in almost every capacity until his death twelve years later.

## PERSECUTION, PROBLEMS, AND JAIL TRIALS

Maria was the only leading evangelist of the Holiness Movement who embraced the Pentecostal experience of speaking in tongues. Today, we would have called her a "Pentecostal Holiness" preacher. She embraced the Holiness doctrine as well as the Pentecostal doctrine of speaking in tongues. Many ministers didn't understand the manifestations of the Holy Spirit, nor did they understand her doctrine about it. And Maria so rarely defended herself in public, that it was highly noted whenever she did. She would usually tell the people that she was not called to defend herself, but that she was called to lead others to Jesus Christ.

Sister Etter showed an invincible strength to carry on in the face of opposition. When harassed with life-threatening situations, she would refuse to leave a town until she was finished. And she was never afraid of unknown perils because she knew the Lord would fight for her. Many times, rowdy men would find their way into her meetings to disrupt them because of being paid to do so. Others came on their own volition. She once wrote:

> *Maria was the only leading evangelist of the Holiness Movement who embraced the Pentecostal experience of speaking in tongues.*

**"I have been in great dangers; many times not knowing when I would be shot down, either in the pulpit, or going to and from meetings...But I said I would never run, nor compromise. The Lord would always put His mighty power on me, so that He took all fear away, and made me like a giant...If in any way they had tried to shoot, or kill me, He would have struck them dead, and I sometimes told them so."**[21]

One such man came to her meeting determined to break it up. He marched within ten feet of the platform and let out a stream of vulgarity and cursing. Then suddenly, his tongue refused to obey him as a "strange power seemed to grip his vocal chords." Totally protected by the Spirit of God, Maria seemed oblivious to the man's presence! Questioned later about the experience by two major newspapers, the shaken man replied, "Go up yourself and find out."[22]

Maria was arrested four times during her ministry, but three of the citations never made it to court. New England was the only place where she was arrested and actually taken to court. Her trial in Framingham, Massachusetts, was based on charges that she practiced medicine without a license and hypnotized people with trances. It was a grand spectacle for the cause of Christ. Many people testified on her behalf, retelling their personal testimonies that could be likened to stories in the book of Acts. The great author and founder of Bethel Bible School, E. W. Kenyon, was among those who testified. Kenyon would go on to later have a great healing and teaching ministry. He was a prolific author. Many of his books are used in Bible schools throughout the world.

The love Maria had for different cultures also caused racial persecution. She loved the African American and Native American communities just as she loved white people. She preached many times for the black churches, helped their preachers, and supported their revivals. She also went to an Indian reservation, staying for weeks at her own expense. All social classes were welcome in her home – rich and poor alike. Sister Etter loved them all.

## "NOTHING SHORT OF A CIRCUS"

There is no one volume book that can describe all the acts in the ministry of Maria Woodworth-Etter. She was a humble, spiritual powerhouse who looked "just like your grandmother, but exercised tremendous spiritual authority over sin, disease, and demons."[23] Sister Etter couldn't answer all the invitations she received to minister. And the ones she did accept created a national stir that has never been silenced.

One such meeting was planned by the then young pastor, F. F. Bosworth in Dallas, Texas. His writings of the spectacular meeting that lasted from July through December, shook the world. As a result, Dallas became a hub of the Pentecostal revival.

One night three very dignified ministers walked into the meeting. Since there was no place left to sit, the platform preachers gave up their seats for the men. Reluctantly, the "dignified" took their seats. The service got well underway, with the power of God as strong as usual. Then suddenly, one of the starchy preachers tumbled off his chair and fell into the sawdust, motionless. The other two tried to ignore their friend on the ground. But in just a few minutes, the second minister joined his friend, falling helplessly into the sawdust. Then the third fell off the platform and laid motionless with them. The three laid under the power of God for more than three hours. Then finally, one by one, each got up, brushed himself off, and walked in a daze to the exit![24]

Thousands came to Dallas, some from over two thousand miles away, bringing the sick and afflicted for healing. One man had three broken ribs from a fall. He could hardly stand because of the pain. Sister Etter laid her hands on him and offered the prayer of faith, and instantly, the bones that were turned inward came into place. At first, he flinched when she touched him, but he ended up pounding his ribs realizing the pain and swelling were gone. Another man was brought in on a cot, suffering from tuberculosis. His condition was hopeless, being also plagued with a fistula, an open sore that had left a deep hole in his body. But when Maria prayed, the power of God hit the man. He jumped off his cot and ran up and down in front of the crowd. Then he rode home sitting up with the others and gained four pounds a day from that day on.

Cancer had eaten the entire side of one man's face and neck. The cancer was so painful, he had to be taken from the first meeting. But when Sister Etter laid hands on him and prayed, the power of God hit him. The pain, stiffness, and burning left immediately. He was suddenly able to turn his neck from side to side, then he got up on the altar and preached to the people.

> *The pain, stiffness, and burning left immediately. He was suddenly able to turn his neck from side to side, then he got up on the altar and preached to the people.*

One night, three people that had been deaf and dumb, all strangers to one another, stood at the altar, weeping, hugging and shouting because God had opened their ears and given them their speech. Many others looked on and wept, making their way to the altar to know God and be saved. One of the three formerly deaf and dumb went on to testify:

> "When Sister Etter put her finger in my mouth at the root of my tongue and then in my ears, commanding a 'deaf and dumb' spirit to come out, God instantly opened my ears and gave me my voice."[25]

One woman had a double affliction of cancer and tuberculosis. She was like a living skeleton. All the best physicians of Dallas had given up on her. She was brought in on a cot, and many thought she would die before Sister Etter got to her. When prayed for, she was instantly healed and jumped up from the cot shouting! Then she came to the rest of the meetings every night and sat with the others. Though she was still very thin, all who knew the woman said that she was gaining weight and improving daily.

The great healing evangelist and pastor, F. F. Bosworth, wrote of the Dallas meetings:

> "Night after night, as soon as the invitation was given, all the available space around the fifty-foot altar would be filled with so many suffering with diseases and afflictions and others seeking salvation and the baptism in the Holy Ghost, that it was difficult to get in and out among the seekers."[26]

At every meeting she held there was a demonstration of the power of the Spirit as never seen in our generation. One reporter from Indiana wrote, "Vehicles of all sorts began pouring into the city at an early hour...nothing short of a circus or a political rally ever before brought in so large a crowd."[27] Another wrote that it was the first time that his Iowa community could remember a religious gathering that had "driven out a good show." He wrote that members booked at the opera house went over to the camp meeting to see what had taken their crowds."[28]

## THE SPLITTING ISSUE

A well-established Christian businessman from Los Angeles, Mr. R. J. Scott, visited Dallas during these meetings. He and his wife had been baptized in the Holy Spirit at the Azusa Street revival. But by this time, most of the Azusa revivalists had scattered. Scott was searching for a way to bring a unified, supernatural work back into Los Angeles. He had heard of the miraculous healings and had come to see if they were true and if Maria's doctrine matched his own. Elated by what he experienced, he determined to ask Maria to come to Los Angeles and hold what he thought would be a "dream camp meeting." He felt she had the power that Los Angeles needed. So Sister Etter agreed to come.

As could be imagined, thousands poured into the Los Angeles area for the camp meeting. The meetings ran all day and most of the night, and thousands came from all sections of North America. Tents were erected and people stayed on the grounds. In fact, there were so many tents, that tentative "streets" were established with names such as "Praise Avenue," "Hallelujah Lane," and "Glory Avenue." This made the location of someone's tent much easier to find!

Although the results of the meeting were phenomenal, this 1913 Los Angeles Worldwide Camp Meeting (Azusa/Arroyo Seco Meeting) was also known to birth the issue that split the early Pentecostal Movement. It produced the debate surrounding the "Jesus Only," "Oneness," or "New Issue" doctrine. The teaching originated from John G. Scheppe, a man who had spent a night in prayer during the meetings. Scheppe believed he had seen something new about using the name of Jesus and ran through the camp sharing it with others. As a result, people on the West Coast began to baptize in "Jesus' Name" only, and were told if they were baptized in the Trinity they would have to be re-baptized. The teaching split the Pentecostal Movement. R. J. Scott's "dream camp meeting" was designed to promote unity within the body of Christ. Instead, it produced one of the greatest divisions known in this generation.[29]

Soon the Pentecostal Movement broke into a number of other groups that emphasized a variety of doctrines. Sister Etter did her best to stay clear of these issues. She believed the most important issue was to warn sinners that Jesus was coming soon through the preaching of His Word with signs and wonders. She said it best in a sermon entitled, *Neglect Not the Gift That Is Within Thee.* In this message she said:

> *Years later she called the "Oneness" position "the biggest delusion the devil ever invented."*

"His ambassadors must stop all the contention, all hair-splitting theories must be dropped; this hobby and that hobby with continual harping on finished work or sanctification that antagonizes the saints must be put away. Paul says preaching has to be with demonstration of the Spirit and of power.... Let the Word go forth in demonstration and power so people can see what God has for them."[30]

Sister Etter soon developed a policy of preaching in meetings at which no "hair-splitting" doctrines were spoken of. Years later she called the "Oneness" position **"the biggest delusion the devil ever invented."**[31]

## "ELECTRIFIED US ALL"

Understandably, Sister Etter had mixed emotions regarding the Los Angeles meeting. She was advertised as the main speaker, and thousands drove from all parts of America to be in her meetings. But because of the political controversy, the male ministers took control, and Sister Etter was forced to minister only in the mornings. The men took over the afternoons and evenings to primarily expound on the new "Oneness" doctrine. She was pressured to cut her meetings short so the afternoon speaker could begin. And in spite of it all, hundreds were miraculously healed. It was reported that when her scheduled time would come to a close, Sister Etter would just raise her hands toward heaven as she was leaving the tent, and at that moment, many were healed. A young boy remembered, "She raised her small hands and the power of the Holy Spirit electrified us all."[32]

Invalids walked from their sick beds, the deaf heard, the blind saw, arthritis was instantly healed, tumors destroyed, dropsy eliminated. In short, every manner of sickness and disease that dared to show itself at Sister Etter's meetings, bowed its knee to Jesus Christ and was disintegrated by the fire of the Spirit. And all of this in spite of the doctrinal divisions.

Elizabeth Waters remembered these meetings like this:

"I remember like yesterday, my girlfriend and I rolled my mother in a wheelchair about six or seven long blocks.... Two big men carried the wheelchair in front of the round pulpit as it was already lined up with wheelchairs. It was so hot, my mother begged to be taken home, but I insisted on staying. Praise the Lord, she was pointed out to be put up on the pulpit, where that beautiful little lady I won't ever forget, spoke to my mother. I saw her reply by shaking her head and then she [Sister Etter] hit her on the chest (it looked hard to me). It was like a bolt of lightning struck her, she leaped to her feet and flew around, jumping for joy. All the people yelled and screamed, I doubt if they had ever seen anything like it before. Many more miracles were seen. We almost had to tie my mother in the chair coming home. She wanted to walk, but she was weak as she had been bedfast for two years. When we got

*Etter and ministry associates in Indiana, 1924*

home, my grandmother and more neighbors were waiting for us. My mother stepped out of the wheelchair and walked up the stairs. They all yelled and cried. From that day on my mother was completely healed, healthy, fat, and loved the Lord."[33]

Because of her Dallas and Los Angeles meetings, Sister Etter would remain a leading evangelist for the rest of her life. And though she loved the itinerant lifestyle, God had yet another plan for her. He wasn't finished writing the pages of history.

## TABERNACLE TALES

After forty-five years of ministry and preaching thousands of sermons from coast to coast, God spoke to Maria about building a tabernacle in west Indianapolis. Many had asked her to build a permanent location where they could come at any time to receive from her ministry. All parts of America had offered their region, but she chose Indiana because of its central location. True to the style of Sister Etter, the Tabernacle was a model for the Pentecostal churches of today. She built the church next door to her home, and ministered there for the last six years of her life.

At the time, there were few large churches. So in 1918, when Sister Etter raised the five-hundred seat building, it was no small task. Throughout her ministry, Maria never put pressure on the people to give financially. But in building this Tabernacle, she sent out letters for financial help. The money came in and the building went up. It was dedicated on May 19, 1918, and to date, only one other woman has ever surpassed her "church-building" ability. That woman was the female evangelist who emulated much of Etter's style, Aimee Semple McPherson.

*"People would move toward the altar and fall on the floor before they got there."*

Sister Etter used the Tabernacle as her home base. She had a special insight for choosing associates who would contribute to the revival. As a result, the church remains today – though in a different location – affiliated with the Assemblies of God. People flocked from around America to be in her church, and many remained as faithful members. One man remembered that "people would move toward the altar and fall on the floor before they got there." He said he never saw pre-suggestions or people ever being pushed over – "It was God. Nothing phony about Sister Etter."[34]

One incredible Tabernacle story involved a Romanian family. Their daughter suffered from tuberculosis and two Pentecostal women had come to their house to pray for her. Discovering that their daughter had been healed after the prayer, the family searched for a Pentecostal church and found the Tabernacle. During their first service, a lady who had been miraculously healed from cancer, stood and delivered a message in tongues for twenty-eight minutes. Some wondered why Sister Etter allowed her to continue so freely in the Spirit for such a length of time. But their questions were answered the next Sunday when it was learned that this woman was speaking Romanian, a language she had never heard nor learned.

This little Romanian family heard a message from God in their own language as they sat listening, completely overwhelmed. The father was the only one who could speak English. It has been said that Maria and the Tabernacle members "learned to expect such experiences as much as some congregations expect to sing the doxology at the end of their services."[35]

Another Tabernacle tale involved the healing of a young boy. He had tuberculosis and developed a tumor the size of a fist. When his mother took him to Maria she said, **"We'll just cut it out with the Sword of the Spirit."** With that, Sister Etter took her Bible and "whacked" him on the neck, and the boy was healed.[36]

## GREAT MEETS GREAT

One of my favorite Tabernacle stories is the one that tells about the meeting of Maria Woodworth-Etter and Aimee Semple McPherson. At that time, Aimee was still a traveling evangelist. She truly loved Sister Etter, and eagerly desired to meet with Maria and sit in one of her meetings. In my personal opinion, I believe Aimee devoured all she could read about Sister Etter, and strengthened her own calling from the courage Maria showed.

There had been an influenza ban on the city of Indianapolis until Aimee's "Gospel Car" pulled in. The ban was finally lifted the night she arrived, and Aimee attributed it to an act of God. She writes from her diary, dated October 31, 1918:

> "For years I have been longing to meet Sister Etter, and have been talking more about it in recent months. I have longed to hear her preach and be in her meetings.... Tomorrow Mrs. Etter's tabernacle will be open and I will have the desire of my heart. Glory!"

Following their meeting Aimee wrote:

"We rejoiced and praised the Lord together. The power of God fell...showering His blessings upon us."[37]

Sister McPherson left Indianapolis the next day, no doubt rejoicing on the way to her own divine destination – California. We can only imagine the memories she cherished from meeting with Maria.

While there is no public statement from Sister Etter on what she thought of Aimee, her traveling companion Bertha Schneider, did make a comment. On one occasion, Sister Etter and Aimee were in the same city. It was their night off, so Sister Etter's group attended one of Aimee's services. But Maria chose not to go. The reason Mrs. Schneider gave for this was, "Sister Etter expressed concern over the direction Aimee's ministry was going – theatrical performances and other popular attractions."[38] I personally feel with Sister Etter being from the Holiness background, that her concern was genuine, not critical.

Many great speakers of the day visited the Tabernacle. Though it was never recorded that Sister Etter met the legendary British evangelist, Smith Wigglesworth, many feel he was a disciple of her ministry. It is believed that Wigglesworth picked up several of his mottos from Sister Etter.[39] And Wigglesworth did conduct a series of meetings in the Tabernacle after her death in 1925.

To some of you, these stories may be intimidating. Understand that God is restoring the supernatural to the Church today. Some of you reading this book are afraid of it. God has told some of you to pray for the sick in your churches, and you haven't done it. Maybe you don't know much about God's will for healing. Maybe you feel confused. It is God's will for man to be free. He came to destroy the works of the devil, not to tolerate or live through them. The Church today must learn to deal with the destroyer and bring life to the people.

Too many of us remain inside the confines of a "comfortable" doctrine or a "pick and choose" theology. God wants the whole counsel of His Word to be preached and demonstrated to the people. That's why Jesus gave us His blood. Begin to read the book of Acts and you will learn of the demonstrators of His Spirit and the opposition they aroused. Like the apostles, Sister Etter remained true to the whole counsel of God all the days of her life – despite the pressure and persecution – and we must do the same. She is one who has passed the torch, and we must be faithful to carry it.

## THE TRAILBLAZER

The summer of 1924 was difficult for Maria. At the age of eighty, with failing health from gastritis and dropsy, she received heart-breaking news. Her only daughter, Lizzie, age sixty, was killed in a streetcar accident. Now all of

Maria's immediate family had gone to be with the Lord. And though her health was frail, she was still able to summon enough strength to stand in the pulpit to conduct the funeral. When she did, she exhorted the people to have faith in God and look to the heavens – not into the grave.[40]

During that year, there were times when Sister Etter was so weak she could not walk. But it didn't stop her from preaching. If she couldn't walk, she appointed someone to carry her in and place her behind the pulpit. Eventually, the Tabernacle presented a large wooden chair as a gift to Maria. Then when she seemed too weak to walk, a few strong men would carry the wooden chair from the church to her house, place her in it, and carry her back. The minute her feet hit the platform, the Spirit of God would quicken her and she would walk up and down the platform, preaching and ministering in the supernatural power of God. Hundreds witnessed how weak she seemed, then how incredibly strong she became. At the end of the service, the men would put her back in the chair and carry her home.

> *Sister Etter's faith caused her to continue, when many others would have given up.*

Sister Etter's faith caused her to continue, when many others would have given up. Remember, by now Sister Etter had reached her eighties. There were no airplanes and very few luxuries in her time. There was no air conditioning or modern conveniences. She had traveled across the nation in buggies and trains, many times sleeping in a tent when money was scarce, or no room was provided. But it didn't matter to Etter.

Three weeks before she died, the Lord revealed to Maria that, "It was only a matter of days before she would leave" to go to her reward. During this time, a lady brought her flowers to which Sister Etter replied, **"I will soon be where the flowers will bloom forever."**[41] A number of times she would even preach sermons to those who visited her at home.

Of her death, an associate, August Feich, wrote:

> "A few days before she passed away, she called me to her side and took my hand and said, 'Brother Feich, do you realize that I am going the way of all flesh?' The answer came, 'I do, mother,' to which she replied, 'You have been very faithful in your ministry with me for these many years. Now I trust that God's blessing may continue to rest upon you; soon you will have me no more to help you.'"

Maria Woodworth-Etter's end came without a struggle as she sank away slowly into a deep sleep:

> "Her eyesight was good for a person of her age. Her mental powers were keen to the very end. There was not a single moment during all her sickness but what she could freely converse with you on any topic that came up. The saints around her came in freely at all times to see her and have council with her. Some came as they were led by the Spirit to pray for her; others again to be prayed for by her. She laid hands on the sick and prayed for those who were in need. This she did 'til the very end. She did this while at the same time she knew that her own strength was rapidly slipping away. She has repeatedly said during her ministry that *she would sooner wear out for Jesus than rust out.*"[42]

Before Sister Etter went home to be with the Lord at age eighty, she had buried all six of her children and two husbands; preached thousands of sermons from coast to coast; remained the victor over hoodlums and vicious ministers; blazed the trail for women in ministry; and unflinchingly displayed the power of the Holy Spirit with mighty signs and wonders following.

She wasn't well educated. She didn't care about seminary classes and didn't take the time to explain how God worked. She preached a very simple Gospel, offered herself completely to Him, and believed for signs and wonders. Maria's one passion was for the Gospel to come alive and for people to be led by the Spirit. She preached many times with tears streaming down her face, begging those who heard to come to Christ. Her meetings and teachings paved the way for the founding of many Pentecostal denominations, including the Assemblies of God, Foursquare, and other similar denominations.

## ETTER'S FAMILY TODAY

Etter's immediate heritage was not heard from again until 1977. Her great-great-great grandson, Tom Slevin, had an interest in researching his family tree. Surprisingly to him, he discovered that an immediate relative of his was a "little pioneer-preacher" named Maria Woodworth-Etter, otherwise known as Grandma Etter. She had been a famous evangelist and founder of a church not far from his home. He inquired of her to his mother, Mary; but she could tell him little, as much information had been lost. Mr. Slevin refused to give up. He researched the Etter books and sermons, reading them continuously.

Soon, his own life was influenced by this woman's sermons, some preached over 80 years ago.

Slevin said, "When I first read her books, I thought they might have been blown out of proportion with all the tremendous miracles. So I went to other towns and researched through the microfilms. I read the old newspapers and discovered a wonderful thing. I found the stories in her books were absolutely true and it was the newspapers that had left a lot of miracles out!"

Slevin and his mother became so curious about the life of Etter, that they went to hear an evangelist who had sat under Sister Etter's ministry as a young boy. This evangelist, Roscoe Russell, had been the boy who, when "whacked" in the neck with a Bible by Sister Etter, was miraculously healed. When Slevin's mother went forth for prayer, the evangelist said to her, "The same God that answered the prayers of your grandmother is here today. He will answer your prayers just the same." Afterwards, Slevin's mother was baptized in the church affiliated with Etter's ministry.

Slevin likes to compare his grandmother Etter's ministry to that of Smith Wigglesworth's. He feels their relationship with God was very similiar, especially in the areas of faith. Though he has many favorite stories, Slevin pointed out that John G. Lake met Etter in 1913. After that meeting, it is said that Lake told his people to, "Pray like Mother Etter."

From his research, Slevin gained an insight into the character of his grandmother. "The thing that impressed me the most," he remembered, "was how completely her life was sold out to God. She was unlike so many today. She went wherever God told her to go; whether they had 20 people or a thousand people. Her time belonged to God. She was never "too busy" to do what He said. Everyone was important to her, because they were important to God. That is why she knew God so well. That is why she could 'punch someone in the stomach' or 'whack them on the neck'. She knew God and she knew He would heal them."[43] It is no doubt that through the Slevin family, the spiritual heritage of Sister Etter will continue.

## A PERSONAL VIEW

In my own personal observations, the ministry that Sister Etter carried has passed down and is still in the earth today. Every ministry should have signs and wonders following it. If not, the ministers are just playing with the ministry. If your ministry is following the commands of Jesus, then signs and wonders will follow you.

Styles of ministry and methods of ministry will vary from person to person. No one person will operate in the same way, because we are all individuals and there are different generations to reach.

But when a ministry operates in the same magnitude as one that has gone on before it, I sometimes refer to that operation as the "mantle" that has been passed down. A mantle is a spiritual term that can be described in the natural, like a coat or a shawl. When we "wear" the mantle, we operate similar to the ministry we received it from.

> *If your ministry is following the commands of Jesus, then signs and wonders will follow you.*

From this personal point of view, it seems that Aimee Semple McPherson carried on where Etter left off, through great signs, wonders, and exploits. I believe she received Maria's mantle. From McPherson, a similar mantle seemed to pass on to Kathryn Kuhlman. Kuhlman was also known for the great magnitude of miracles in her ministry and for her hunger for fellowship with the Holy Spirit. Today, in the 1990s, it seems to me that a similar healing mantle has passed from Kuhlman to Benny Hinn, though Hinn doesn't like for that to be said of him. Hinn feels he has his own mantle from God, not someone else's. He is the great pastor and healing evangelist from Orlando, Florida.

## DON'T RUST OUT

Maria Woodworth-Etter reached untold thousands from around America with the liberating message of Jesus Christ. These words were written of her:

> "Glory to God and the Lord Jesus for calling her, enduing her with power, keeping her, and making her a 'Mother in Israel' to us. The same love that watched over her is ours today. Amen."[44]

Mighty signs and wonders are in the earth again. So cultivate the godly treasures within you by experience and the Word, then bring them to the surface by prayer and obedience. Believe God for signs and wonders to come through you. Determine to be used in this hour and press on to the fullness that God has for you. Don't allow setbacks to frustrate or hinder you. Call for the Spirit of might and finish your course in complete victory. Adopt these words of Sister Etter:

**"It's better to wear out for Jesus Christ than to rust out."**

Then don't stop until you are finished. The world is searching for the answer within you.

## CHAPTER TWO, MARIA WOODWORTH-ETTER
References

1 Wayne E. Warner, "Neglect Not the Gift That Is in Thee," Etter Sermon from *The Woman Evangelist* (Metuchen, NJ and London: The Scarecrow Press, Inc., 1986), 307, Appendix C.

2 Ibid., 6.

3 Ibid., 7.

4 Ibid., 8.

5 Ibid., 10.

6 Maria Woodworth-Etter, "A Sermon for Women," *A Diary of Signs & Wonders* (Tulsa, OK: Harrison House, Reprinted from 1916 ed.), 215-216, 30-31.

7 Warner, *The Woman Evangelist,* 14.

8 Ibid., 21.

9 Ibid., 22.

10 Woodworth-Etter, *A Diary of Signs and Wonders* (Tulsa, OK: Harrison House, reprinted from 1916 ed.), 67-68.

11 Warner, *The Woman Evangelist*, 41.

12 Woodworth-Etter, *A Diary of Signs*, 111.

13 Warner, *The Woman Evangelist*, 42.

14 Ibid.

15 Ibid., 148.

16 Ibid., 146.

17 Ibid.

18 Ibid., 81, Footnote 18, John Alexander Dowie, "Trance Evangelism," *Leaves of Healing* (March 8, 1895), 382. Reprinted from *Leaves of Healing* (old issue), 98.

19 Maria Woodworth-Etter, *Life & Testimony of Mrs. M. B. Woodworth-Etter,* 12.

20 Woodworth-Etter, *A Diary of Signs*, 151.

21 Ibid., 184.

22 Warner, *The Woman Evangelist*, 41.

23 Ibid., 213.

24 Ibid., 167.

25 Woodworth-Etter, *A Diary of Signs*, 166.

[26] Ibid., 173.

[27] Warner, *The Woman Evangelist,* 201.

[28] Ibid., 202-203.

[29] Ibid., 172.

[30] Article from *The Latter Rain Evangel* (August, 1913).

[31] Warner, *The Woman Evangelist,* 188, Footnote 42 taken from Maria Woodworth-Etter's *Spirit-Filled Sermons.*

[32] Ibid., 169 from A. C. Valdez's *Fire on Azusa Street.*

[33] Personal letter from Elizabeth Waters to Thomas Slevin, great-great-great grandson of Sister Etter.

[34] Warner, *The Woman Evangelist,* 268, Footnote 21.

[35] Ibid., 256-257, 267, Footnote 13.

[36] Ibid., 256.

[37] Aimee Semple McPherson, *This is That,* (Los Angeles, CA: Echo Park Evangelistic Assoc., Inc., 1923), 149-150.

[38] Warner, *The Woman Evangelist,* 294, Footnote 11.

[39] Ibid., 287.

[40] Ibid., 290.

[41] Woodworth-Etter, *Life & Testimony of Mrs. M. B. Woodworth-Etter,* 123.

[42] Ibid., 124.

[43] Personal interview with Tom Slevin, great-great-great grandson of Sister Etter.

[44] Woodworth-Etter, *Life & Testimony of Mrs. M. B. Woodworth-Etter,* 138.

CHAPTER THREE

# Evan Roberts

*"Welsh Revivalist"*

# "WELSH REVIVALIST"

I n my opinion, the story of the young revivalist from Wales, Evan Roberts, is the saddest study I have conducted on the Generals. This young boy-preacher from the coal mines of southern Wales had an unmistakable dispensation of worldwide revival allotted to him. But because of inexperience, limited revelation, and demonic control, his incredible ministry was cut short long before its time. Before we explore his life, let it be clearly understood that the truths presented here are not intended as criticism. The lessons I will bring to light are constructively inserted so that our generation can learn to guard their hearts, carry the anointing, and prevail successfully in the heat of revival fire.

## COAL-COVERED TRUTH

Evan John Roberts was born June 8, 1878, into the staunch Calvinist-Methodist home of Henry and Hannah Roberts. I believe a "revivalist spirit" was built immediately within him. Evan's parents had a strong influence in cultivating that spirit and nature within him. His nature was one of excellency and sensitivity. The family was known for their love of God's Word and hard work. Each family member, no matter how young, had his own well-worn Bible.

I want to make a point here: Parents, allow your children to be involved with the move of God. I can't stress how vitally important it is to teach and train your children in the things of God. They need to know how to pray, how to study the Word of God, and how to sit under the anointing. Teach them to worship God with you, and show them how to do it. Revival fires die because parents stick their children in the nursery instead of setting them in the move of God. The nursery is a blessing for taking care of infants and toddlers. But there comes a time when they are able to understand proper behavior and can be included in the revival service.

> *His nature was one of excellency and sensitivity.*

How can revival continue without passing it on? Many past revivals and some revivalists didn't take their next generation into account. As a result, God had to search for another generation to rekindle the fire that should have never gone out. Revivals don't have to end. Revivals are meant to continue. The fire of God must be passed on with each new generation. Children are pliable and sensitive, wanting to learn. They are like little sponges eager to draw in everything you share with them. So be their teachers. If you have children, that godly responsibility of passing the fire of God onto them rests in your hands. And it is evident the family of Evan Roberts took that responsibility seriously.

Evan's strong character was the result of his family's training. While still very young, Evan's father was injured in a mining accident. So his father took Evan out of school to help him in the coal mines. Evan never complained.

Soon, Evan had developed the family's habit of memorizing Scripture. He was never seen without his Bible. It has been said that he would even hide his Bible in the clefts of the mine while he worked. One day, a huge fire burned through everything in its path – except young Evan's Bible. Only the pages were scorched, so he continued to carry it every day and memorize Scriptures from it. Each morning, Evan stood at the opening of the mine to give a particular Scripture to each of the passing workers for their workday meditation. Then when young Evan saw them in the evening, he would ask, "What truth did you find in that text?" As these hard-working men passed by the coal-covered boy, they had no idea how God would use him to change their nation.

## "WHAT WOULD JESUS DO?"

Evan was dramatically different from the rest of the boys his age. He never took part in sports, amusements, or coarse joking. He worked in the mines every day, then came home and walked a mile to his church, Moriah Chapel. At thirteen years of age, Evan experienced his first encounter with God. It was then that Evan vowed to commit himself even further to the work of the Lord. One simple yet profound phrase spoken from the pulpit of Moriah Chapel changed Evan's life. The phrase, "What would Jesus do?" became his obsession. He repeatedly asked himself, **"What have I done for Jesus?"** as he further dedicated himself to the work of the Lord.

*While others of his age group became interested in dating, Evan was more likely to be inside the church discussing Scripture with other men.*

Evan was so intense in giving his life to God that he read everything he could pertaining to Him. He used his earnings to purchase instruments that he later learned to play. In fact, he was able to succeed at most everything he put his hand to because he put his whole heart into it. He excelled in any business apprenticeship offered to him, and he excelled in personal character. He was also a prolific writer, having several of his poems and essays published in local newspapers.

While others of his age group became interested in dating, Evan was more likely to be inside the church discussing Scripture with other men. Soon, the elders of the church gave him the responsibility of starting a weekly debate group for young men like himself. But these happy times ended abruptly when the mine Evan worked in suffered an explosion. The single men were the first to be relieved of their duties. So in 1898, Evan began work in Mountain Ash, a town north of where he lived. He left home not realizing the spiritual preparation he had gained.

## "I AM BURNING, WAITING FOR A SIGN"

At that time few people understood the power of prayer. Most attended church as a moral commitment, instead of a spiritual one. But not Evan. Because of his unique desire for the Lord, Evan gave himself to fervent prayer and intercession. So much so, that by the time he was twenty years old, he was known by some as a "mystical lunatic." Stories about him circulated widely. There were whispers about seeing him standing "trance-like" beside the road while uttering deep sighs as his lips moved without the sound of words.[1] It was also said that he meditated in the Word so long that he often missed the evening meal. Sometimes he would stay up half the night discussing and praying with a friend about revival.

Several concerned ministers approached Evan regarding his unusual behavior. He simply answered them, **"But the Spirit moved me."** During this time, friends also introduced him to an American specialist, Dr. Hughes. The doctor told Evan's friends he was suffering from "religious mania." One Christian man said of Evan:

> "We usually had a reading and prayer together before we put out the lamp. Then I could hear Evan calling and groaning in the Spirit. I couldn't understand what was his message to God again, and some holy fear kept me from asking."[2]

Though people didn't understand Evan's methods, the spiritual power he portrayed was unmistakable. On one occasion, he traveled to Builith Wells for a prayer meeting at which he was called on to pray. The people's hearts were melted within them at the power exhibited in Evan's prayer. After the service, the minister approached Evan and advised him to consider full-time ministry.

Evan considered it and answered the call. Through his church, he was required to preach twice at all twelve affiliate churches, and his sermons were met with great approval. He confided to a friend that his heavenly secret was,

"Ask and it shall be given unto you. Practice entire, definite faith in God's promise of the Spirit."[3]

During this period, Evan wrote to a friend and said, "**I have prayed that the Lord will baptize you and me with the Holy Spirit.**"[4] Soon afterward, he got so caught up in the Lord, that his bed shook. Then after that, he was awakened every night at 1:00 A.M. to be "**taken up into divine fellowship.**" He would pray for four hours, fall back to sleep at 5:00 A.M. for another four hours, then pray from 9:00 A.M. until 12 noon.

In December of 1903, Evan knew in his heart that God had planned a great revival for the Welsh community. While preaching at Moriah he said, "**I have reached out my hand and touched the flame. I am burning and waiting for a sign.**"[5]

Let me make a point here. Revival must be in your heart before it comes into the earth. Each revival has nothing to do with the last one, but it has everything to do with the individual who brings it.

During this time, every denomination in Wales was praying for revival. Moriah Chapel had a strong Calvinistic doctrine, so Evan was well-trained in the doctrine of "man, sin, and salvation." The young ministry students were

*Moriah Chapel*

required to listen to great men of their denomination and pattern their preaching styles after them. But Evan was an exception. Though he had been accepted into the Bible college, he couldn't complete his studies because of his burning desire to preach and pray.

## "BEND US! BEND US!"

For Evan Roberts, 1904 was a year of great struggle. He was torn between doing what everyone expected and following what he felt the Spirit of God wanted him to do.

His closest friend, Sidney Evans, attended a prayer meeting and came back very excited. He told Evan of how he had fully surrendered his life to the work of the Lord. But Evan reacted strangely. Fearing he wouldn't be able to receive the fullness of the Spirit of God, he went into a deep depression – a pattern he became known for throughout his ministry. He was so consumed with this thought that no one could soothe him.

Then in September, Evan's friends persuaded him to go with them to hear the rugged evangelist, Seth Joshua. Unknown to Evan, Rev. Joshua had prayed for years that God would raise up another "Elisha" from an ordinary person and "mantle him with power."[9] And Joshua got exactly what he prayed for. When mighty revival came through the leadership of Evan Roberts, the great, dignified preachers of England and Wales were forced to sit at the feet of crude, hard-working miners to see the wonderful works of God.

*When mighty revival came through the leadership of Evan Roberts, the great, dignified preachers of England and Wales were forced to sit at the feet of crude, hardworking miners to see the wonderful works of God.*

Evan remained silent throughout Joshua's service. But when the minister began to pray, "Bend us! Bend us!" Evan's soul stirred within him. After the meeting, the group went to Joshua's house for breakfast, but Evan refused to eat. He was extremely tense and solemn. He was afraid the Holy Spirit would come to him and that he wouldn't accept Him. So once again, Evan put himself in a state of depression.

In my opinion, this showed young Evan's misunderstanding of the ways of the Holy Spirit. This intense, unnatural pressure he put upon himself only led to error later down the road. The Holy Spirit will never force Himself upon anyone. He will never offer you something you can't receive or ask you to perform anything you can't do. The Holy Spirit isn't out to torture your soul, drive you, or pressure you into isolation. He has come to empower you for His service. He came to impart boldness, sensitivity, and strength. All we have to say is, "Come, Holy Spirit." If our lives need adjustment, He will reveal those areas along with His plan to mature them. The kingdom of heaven is righteousness, peace, and joy. Anything else will throw you off balance.

Evan left the company of his friends and went back to the chapel where Rev. Joshua held his meeting. While there, he began to respond to Joshua's earlier prayer by crying out to the Lord, "**Bend me! Bend me!**" In this prayer of total submission, he received a revelation of the love of God. Evan surrendered to the will of God that day and allowed His compassion to fill him. One of Evan's friends described him during this period as a "particle of radium whose fire in their midst was consuming."[6]

Though many times it seemed Evan Roberts was unnaturally driven toward the things of God, it can also be said that he carried a great love for the Holy Spirit and His move in the earth.

## AN ARM OUTSTRETCHED FROM THE MOON

Evan wasn't one normally given to visions. He had his first vision in October of 1904.

While strolling in a garden with Sidney Evans, Evan noticed that Sidney was in a daze, staring at the moon. So Evan looked into the sky and inquired, "**What are you looking at? What do you see?**" Then suddenly, Evan saw it too. He saw an arm seemed to be outstretched from the moon, reaching down into Wales.

Evan had been fervently praying for one hundred thousand souls to be added to the kingdom of God, and he received this rare vision as a direct answer to his prayers.

He later told Sidney Evans: "I have wonderful news for you. I had a vision of all Wales being lifted up to heaven. We are going to see the mightiest revival that Wales has ever known—and the Holy Spirit is coming just now. We must get ready."[7] Now he was even more determined to launch his ministry. He was ready to give all his time and money to the work before him. His statement, "**We can do nothing without the Holy Spirit,**"[8] set the precedence for the rest of his ministry. Sometimes it was effective while at other times it was extreme.

Fervent for the Holy Spirit, Evan seemed to take up a personal defense for Him at times. Once while sitting in a service, he jumped to his feet, disrupted the sermon, and accused those in the congregation of not being sincere and earnest. His friends were concerned while others labeled him as a lunatic. As quickly as Evan turned extreme, he would often become level-headed and instruct those around him how to obtain peace with God.

## THE LOST KEYS

Evan finally obtained approval to begin a small series of meetings. What began on October 31 as a small church meeting quickly grew into a major revival and lasted for two weeks!

The group began with a few consecrated believers who listened intently to Evan's message. Instead of standing behind the pulpit, the young revivalist walked up and down the aisles, preaching and asking questions of those sitting in the pews. This was unheard of in his day. The goal of those first meetings was to dedicate and train intercessors for the coming revival. Evan succeeded in his goal. He believed that revival would come through knowledge of the Holy Spirit and that one must "co-work" with the Spirit in order to operate in power. Even the children were trained to pray morning and night for God to "send the Spirit to Moriah for Jesus Christ's sake!"

*Instead of standing behind the pulpit, the young revivalist walked up and down the aisles, preaching and asking questions to those sitting in the pews.*

Soon, the services grew to a fervor, and Evan sent word to the Bible college to request more workers. Strong moves of intercession flooded the room during each service, and many times the services would go past midnight. Once, Evan prayed all night with a congregation and didn't return home until the next morning. This small group of intercessors led by the young evangelist transformed the entire community. Some meetings lasted until 4:00 A.M. with crowds gathering outside for 6:00 A.M. prayer. In two years, all of Wales would know the name of Evan Roberts.

During this whirlwind of revival, Evan refused to be recognized as its leader. He denounced anyone who sought him as such and even refused to be photographed. It is said that he once even hid behind the pulpit when a

*February, 1905*

newspaper photographer came into a meeting with a camera. As a result, the only photographs we have of Evan are family possessions.

One eye witness of the revival said that what drew people to Evan "perhaps more than any other thing, was the unfeigned humility in all his actions."[9] His services were marked with laughing, crying, dancing, joy, and brokenness. Soon, the newspapers began covering them, and the revival became a national story.

Political meetings were cancelled. Soccer matches had neither players on the field nor fans in the stands. Theatres closed down due to low attendance. Gambling and alcohol business lost their trade. And doctrinal barriers came tumbling down as Christians from all denominations worshipped together in the Spirit's move.[10] Some of the reporters themselves were converted at the meetings. As the revival spread with great fervor throughout Wales. Soon bars and movie houses closed. Former prostitutes started holding Bible studies. People began to pay their longstanding debts. And those who once selfishly wasted their money on alcohol suddenly became a great joy and support to their families.

The Wales revival meetings had no choirs or special ceremonies. There were no offerings, no hymnbooks, no committees, no song leaders, and no paid advertising. Leaders from denominations who were hungry for God attended the meetings. It is said that in one city, all the ministers exchanged pulpits for a day in an effort to break down denominational walls and establish unity. Even the women were welcome to participate. Up until that time, the women of Wales had been banned from any public role in church life, but now could be seen praying and praising openly. Eventually Evan even encouraged national and racial barriers to be broken.

The Wales revival was founded on these four points: (1) Confess all known sin. (2) Search out all secret and doubtful things. (3) Confess the Lord Jesus openly. (4) Pledge your word that you will fully obey the Spirit.

Evan Roberts had discovered the keys to revival. And if those keys were important then, they are certainly important now. I believe "repentance" is a word that is somewhat tarnished today. It has lost much of its meaning due to social issues and wrong attitudes. Some people are so carried away with God's law of grace and mercy that they overlook the rest of His laws. Grace and mercy don't give us license to live however we want to. We don't live under cheap grace and mercy. The righteousness we enjoy as believers was purchased by the blood of Jesus – a price too great for words. If we don't obey, we won't receive. Repentance brought us into the kingdom of God, and repentance will keep us moving with His cloud.

Also, we must love God more than we love anything else. When I was a young boy, I felt impressed to quit playing basketball. There's nothing wrong with basketball. But at the time, I knew what God had called me to do, and it seemed I loved basketball more than I loved to pray. So I quit playing basketball. God had set the plan for my life. I agreed to it, and prayer became my life-giving force. It's fine to enjoy life. Just make sure you don't love life more than God.

## "GOD HAS MADE ME STRONG AND MANLY"

Roberts' revival meetings were unlike any Wales had ever seen. One such service began with two girls standing in the pulpit. One pleaded and prayed for the people to surrender to the Holy Spirit. Then the other gave her testimony in song before bursting into tears. They called this, "warming the atmosphere." If the congregation wondered why Evan Roberts didn't take the platform after the two girls finished, they only needed to look at him. He was on his knees, weeping and pleading with God. Many said it was not the eloquence of Evan Roberts that broke men – it was his tears. In his book, *Azusa Street*, Frank Bartleman quotes an eyewitness as saying, "Roberts in the intensity of his agony would fall in the pulpit, while many in the crowd fainted."

It was common in Evan's meetings for members in the congregation to suddenly fall on their knees and pray aloud. Waves of joy and sorrow would flood the congregation. Women fell to their knees and men laid in the aisles weeping, laughing, and praying. All the while, there was no Bible reading or instrument playing. A few were inspired to stand and sing hymns. It was even said the congregation was so caught up in God that they would forget to go home for Sunday dinner. This was unheard of in southern Wales in those days. As the day progressed, the evening service would become a continual prayer meeting. Evan could be seen walking up and down the aisles swinging his arms, clapping his hands, and jumping up and down.

> *If Evan didn't sense the unction to preach, he remained quiet.*

Though his success had become the talk of the nation, many still didn't know what to think of Evan Roberts. They were used to the fiery eyes of the old-time preachers, and Evan never raised his voice. Sometimes he was called the "silent preacher." If Evan didn't sense the unction to preach, he remained quiet. On one occasion, Evan sat on the front row for three or four hours, then rose up to preach for only fifteen minutes.

Also in that day, most people were accustomed to the preachers with stern, dignified faces. But Evan was the opposite. His face constantly beamed. Once when a minister read from a list of thirty-three converts, Evan threw his arms around him and exclaimed, **"Is this not glorious?"**

As a result of the revival, local stores couldn't keep Bibles in stock. The Welsh coal mining industry also took on a new look. Their workhorses had previously been trained to respond to instructions that included profanity. But with the coal mining crew now born again, they found that their horses had to be re-trained because the animals didn't know how to follow a normal command without a curse word in it.

Of course, there was the usual concern. People were murmuring because there seemed to be no order in the services. And Evan was operating around the clock without rest. When asked about it once, he replied:

**"Tired? Not once. God has made me strong and manly. I can face thousands. My body is full of electricity day and night and I have no sleep before I am back in meetings again."**[11]

It is a documented fact that Evan Roberts slept and ate very little during the first two months of this great revival. In fact, he only slept two or three hours a night.

## HEAR THIS: REST

In order to continually walk in the Spirit, we must obey the universal laws instituted by God. One of those laws is to take care of your physical body. While it is true that the Spirit is greater than the flesh, if we don't take care of that flesh while on earth, the body will break down, or even die. If the body dies, the spirit must depart. God established a universal law that says our bodies need proper rest and nourishment. God Himself rested on the seventh day after the work of creation, establishing the principle for us.

When I am in the anointing, it affects every part of me. My body feels energized, and my mind is submitted to the will of God. Why? Because the anointing brings life. However, the physical demands of my body continue, anointing or not. My blood still needs oxygen and nutrients, and my mind still needs rest. We are not in our glorified bodies yet. So mature revivalists *must* learn to care for their physical bodies. You *can* live out of your spirit, operate in the anointing, and get the rest you need. If you don't, disaster is pending. The Holy Spirit will never drive you – He leads you. You can't follow God and hear Him accurately if your body is exhausted and driven. *Pressure and need abound when revival hits* because mankind is made aware of his spiritual condition. A revivalist must know how to *lead* and *rest* in order to remain a vital instrument of God. I believe *one* of the main reasons Evan Roberts' ministry was cut short was because he didn't learn this principle.

Evan was soon showing many signs of emotional strain. But despite the overload, he continued to go from town to town and pleaded with residents to think of the lost. Whenever friends would encourage him to rest, he reacted strongly against them. Though his body was rapidly wearing down, the power of God continued to feed the hunger of the people. One newspaper reported that while some were shouting with conviction, others were literally shaking.

## DEMONSTRATING THE DIVINE

It was a supernatural experience to be in an Evan Roberts meeting. He carried the ability to usher in the presence of the Holy Spirit as almost a tangible force. He made the common church-goer aware of the spirit world, especially in the area of purity and holiness toward God. Since he rarely preached, Evan allowed three female singers – Annie Davies, Maggie Davies, and S. A. Jones – to travel with him. Many times, they sang an inspired message from God to the congregation. Evan would rebuke anyone who tried to hush the singing. He believed the Holy Spirit should be given the primary role and that no one had the right to interrupt Him. He felt that so doing invited the wrong kind of authority and control.

To Evan, the Holy Spirit wasn't some unseen force, but a Divine Person who must be praised and adored in His own right and totally obeyed. It even came to the point that when one or two people in the congregation wouldn't participate, Evan would stand up and say, **"The Spirit can't be with us now."**[12] Then, many times he would leave the service.

Residents from local towns and surrounding communities would often pour into the buildings for Evan's meetings. In a town with a population of three thousand people, over one thousand would attend the meetings. If they didn't arrive early enough to get a seat, the people remained outside just to catch a glimpse. Amazed, newspaper reporters noted that communities had never seen so many visitors as when Evan Roberts came to town.

*Amazed, newspaper reporters noted that communities had never seen so many visitors as when Evan Roberts came to town.*

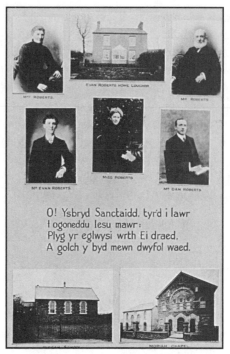

O! Ysbryd Sanctaidd. tyr'd i lawr
I ogoneddu Iesu mawr:
Plyg yr eglwysi wrth Ei draed,
A golch y byd mewn dwyfol waed.

*Mrs. Roberts, Evan Roberts Home Loughor, Mr. Roberts,*
*Mr. Evan Roberts, Miss Roberts, and Mr. Dan Roberts*

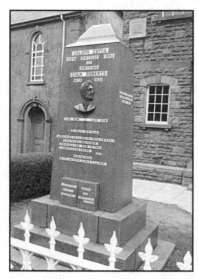

*Roberts Monument*

*Welsh Revivalist*

*Roberts and his singing ladies*

*Roberts reading the Word*

*Evan Roberts in back seat of car with friends*

*On fire for God*

Soon, word of this revival spread to other nations. The people of South Africa, Russia, India, Ireland, Norway, Canada, and Holland rushed to Wales. One group of Americans came just to say, "I was there when the miracles happened." Many came to carry a portion of this revival back to their own nations. It is said that during this time, the California evangelist and journalist, Frank Bartleman, wrote to Evan and asked how to bring revival to America. Evan corresponded several times with Bartleman, each time listing principles for revival while encouraging him to pursue it, and assuring him of the prayers from Wales. Bartleman would later become instrumental in recording the events of the Azusa Street Revival that originated in Southern California in 1906. There is no doubt that the revival in Wales started a worldwide hunger for God.

## CONFUSION AND COLLAPSE

In 1905, Evan Roberts' mind became confused. A Congregational minister's published criticisms of the young revivalist unsettled him greatly, but he pushed on.[13] He often said that he wanted to enter into the **"sufferings of the Master."** Sometimes, he would start a service in gentleness and joy, then suddenly jump up, wave his arms, and sharply rebuke those who weren't pure in heart. Then he would threaten to leave the service. He commented to his friend, Sidney Evans, that he was afraid of speaking words that weren't of God. He heard many voices, and sometimes he wasn't sure which was God's and which was his. He was also constantly examining himself for any unconfessed sin. His number one fear was that people would exalt him instead of God.

Revival attendees in the town of Neath were confused and disappointed by Evan's sudden decision to remain in seclusion for seven days in the home of his host. He received no visitors and spoke to no one during that time.[14]

As the revival continued and specific needs became apparent, Evan began to operate in the gifts of the Spirit. Out of ignorance, the people labeled Evan telepathic, since they didn't understand how he could be so spiritually accurate. But instead of stopping to teach the people concerning the gifts of the Spirit, Evan simply continued to operate in them.

At times, Evan would be preaching, then suddenly would stop. He would look up into the balcony and exclaim that someone there needed salvation. Within seconds, a person would fall to his knees and cry out in repentance to God. This happened often in his services.

Sometimes Evan would name a specific sin that was present and call for immediate repentance. Other times, he would know of a person outside the building agonizing before God. Evan would abruptly leave the building, head out into the street, and find that person on his knees crying to God.

The voices Evan was hearing began to trouble him greatly. But instead of receiving counsel from mature leaders, he chose to continue following the signs and to ignore the uneasiness within. It was at this time that Evan Roberts suffered his first emotional collapse. He was forced to remain in the home of a friend and cancel his meetings.

## "OBSTACLES ARRIVING...AND DEPARTING"

When the people heard of his cancellation, they were outraged and offended. Though still severely fatigued, Evan was swayed by their pressure and rescheduled the meeting.

But as to be expected, at the meeting he was hazy in mind and rebuked the crowd sharply. He even began to point out "**obstacles arriving**" and "**obstacles departing.**" The people became more concerned with the conflict he was pointing out than with their hunger for God. After this, complaints and criticism abounded against Evan from every corner of Wales. They labeled him a "hypnotist," "exhibitionist," and "occultist." In retaliation, Evan began to condemn entire congregations for the cold hearts of one or two who would show up at his meetings. He once even condemned a man's "soul" forbidding anyone to pray for him.

Accusation and criticism spread like wildfire. Every day produced new, bitter charges in the newspapers and letters. And each new meeting was filled with challenging agnostics who called him a "bearer of false fire" or "profaner." Friends tried to justify his actions, saying he was a young, inexperienced minister and subject to making "a young man's mistake."

Soon, Evan Roberts suffered another physical and emotional breakdown. Much to his critics' delight, Evan canceled all his meetings. He was branded as unbalanced, and revival converts began to wonder if they had been deceived by Satan. In response to the outburst, a psychologist who examined Evan published this remark: "Our organisms can't support such pitiless tensions and violent repeated shocks, shaking the nerves and exhausting the brain and body."[15] With this, Evan went into silence for a season.

## GREAT GLORY, GREAT STRAIN

Not to be outdone by critics, the supporting public flooded Evan's secretary with requests for him to minister. After a short season of rest, he agreed to accept the invitations, and he published an itinerary of the meetings in the newspapers.

On the day of his first meeting, the streets were packed. Hundreds arrived early to get a seat. As it was about to begin, his secretary took the platform and read a note from Evan: **"Tell the people I shall not come to the service. The Spirit prevents my coming and I can't speak."**[16] There were great cries of disappointment and anger. Even Evan's friends couldn't support this "leading of the Spirit." The best they could say of him was that he was under great strain.

Evan locked himself away to spend time in the Word and prayer. Then after another short season of rest, he returned to public ministry. This time the results looked like the days of the early revival. Evan saw himself as "the Lord's special messenger who would arouse the churches for their task of saving the nation."

Again sharp criticism arose. Evan, no longer known for his gentleness, openly rebuked public leaders and announced of one particular church he was ministering in that it was not "founded upon the Rock." One devastating blow came at a men's meeting in this same church when Evan filled in for the absent pastor, facing hundreds of disturbed men. When he arrived, he wouldn't step up to the platform, choosing instead to sit silent in his chair for two hours. As criticism was openly voiced by the ministers there, Evan got up and left the chapel. When the pastor returned, he vowed the meetings would continue in peace and begged the ministers to conduct themselves peacefully. When Evan took the platform that night, he smiled and exhorted them to study the true Shepherd in Ezekiel 34.

> *...now he saw himself as "the Lord's special messenger who would arouse the churches for their task of saving the nation."*

Because of his failing condition, Evan's emotional wounds became more difficult to heal. He became greatly disturbed at small things. He took it personally when he heard of converts "barking after the devil," or "following healers and prophetesses." As a result, he remained depressed most of the time.

The critical point of Evan Roberts' downfall came when he returned to northern Wales in the summer of 1906. He was asked to participate in a Keswick-type Easter convention for ministers and church leaders. It was there that Evan spoke on what he called his "new burden," which was the identification with Christ through suffering. Soon afterwards, he became tremendously overstrained and broke down again.

## ENTER JEZEBEL

At the Keswick meeting, Mrs. Jessie Penn-Lewis introduced herself to Evan. Mrs. Penn-Lewis was a socially influential and wealthy woman from England.

*Mr. and Mrs. Penn-Lewis*

She was also a minister, but her ministry had been scorned by the Welsh due to serious doctrinal conflicts. They rejected her "suffering" teachings and abolished her ministry in their nation.

When Mrs. Penn-Lewis heard Evan's message on the cross, she aligned herself with him to gain his acceptance. And she confided to friends that she felt Evan "had too been shattered and would need some type of getaway." Then she convinced Evan of her position while pointing out his excellent teaching and the abuses he was suffering because of it. In his weakened condition, Evan succumbed to her influence. Less than a month after being constantly paired with Penn-Lewis, Evan suffered his fourth and most serious nervous breakdown.

Newly discovered letters show that Penn-Lewis had ulterior motives with Evan Roberts. She used his name repeatedly while exonerating her own methods and beliefs. She also told the ministers of Wales that she was so hurt by their opinion of her and her doctrine that she wouldn't return to their nation. And she added that it was best for Evan to stay away from Wales because he, like her, was "too shattered to do anything."

After this announcement by Penn-Lewis, Roberts was transported quickly and quietly by train from his beloved homeland and place of his call. Penn-Lewis and her husband retired Evan to their estate in England called, Woodlands. Then they built their new home around Evan Roberts' needs. They built him a bedroom, a prayer room, and his own private stairway. It was here that the great evangelist was confined to bed.

> *From this point on, Evan determined from Mrs. Penn-Lewis' counsel that he would no longer trust any moving of the supernatural.*

## FIRST KINGS 21?

While at Woodlands, Penn-Lewis visited Evan daily. Evan listened respectfully as she told him of the mistakes and wrong judgments she felt he made while in the ministry. But Evan wasn't able to discern that everything the woman said was based entirely on her opinions.

When one local minister was forbidden a personal interview with Roberts while gathering information for a book, he was angered by Penn-Lewis' complete control over the revivalist's affairs. Convinced Penn-Lewis had destroyed Evans' effectiveness, he wrote that she and those working with her had done "much towards marring his usefulness."[17] This minister's letters were intercepted by Penn-Lewis and never seen by Evan. Other correspondence went completely unanswered, and rumors circulated wildly concerning Roberts' disappearance from the field.[18]

As Penn-Lewis counseled Evan in his seclusion, she questioned him about the supernatural gifts that operated through him. She determined that Evan's depression was caused from this spiritual operation. Denouncing these gifts given to Evan, Penn-Lewis lectured that unless he was totally crucified to self, he was deceived. Filled with condemnation, Evan finally agreed that all the supernatural operations he had experienced couldn't have been of God. Besides confounding the multitudes, Evan concluded that he too, had been deceived by the supernatural operations.

From this point on, Evan determined from Mrs. Penn-Lewis' counsel that he would no longer trust any moving of the supernatural. And he concluded that in order for the Holy Spirit to move through any believer, he or she would have to have a far greater wisdom and experience than that which he possessed. The depressed revivalist's condition was extremely frail and was further frustrated by the repeated prodding and drilling of Penn-Lewis.

I wonder if Evan ever considered the thousands that turned to God and became born again because of those gifts. Could he remember the multitudes that came from other nations to receive from his ministry and carry it to their countries? No doubt he heard of their glowing reports in their own nations.

I wonder if he thought of the multitudes, hungry for a touch, who stood in the streets because he had been so transparent for the Holy Spirit to use. Did he ever once consider that his lack of rest – not a lack of consecration – caused his confusion? Did he think the mistakes he made from exhaustion summed the total fruit of his ministry?

If Evan Roberts ever did consider these things, the thought never turned to action. Thus, the spiritual equipment that came as a result of his call was severely damaged for any future manifestation.

## PULPIT MINISTRY? NEVER AGAIN

Faced with much criticism for her actions with Evan, Mrs. Penn-Lewis wrote to a respected revivalist. In the letter she stated how Evan Roberts needed to be "safe-guarded" and that he was maturing at a "great rate, seeing how he had been misled." She later wrote the same minister, this time stating how Evan had grown spiritually and that she could see how the two of them were being "specially trained for a special work."

In my opinion, it seems that Mrs. Penn-Lewis was using the strength and call of Evan Roberts to promote herself. From past record, she didn't have the strength, character, or call to make it on her own. Therefore, I believe she needed something that would prove her spiritual validity. And that "something" was Evan Roberts. If she could gain his partnership, then she could share his platform.

Though Evan remained isolated at the home of Penn-Lewis, a minister and a friend were allowed to visit him. As they counseled and prayed with him, they greatly influenced his recovery. Their love helped to encourage Evan spiritually, but it was still another year before the emotionally shattered revivalist was able to physically stand or walk.

After a year, medical advisors told Evan to never undertake pulpit ministry again. He would be able to do informal counseling, but he was advised to never preach again. Obviously, for more reasons than health, Penn-Lewis agreed.

Unaware of his physical condition, the Welsh revival converts were very hurt. They felt deserted by their leader. A year or so after Evan's move to Woodlands, concerned friends made accusations that Penn-Lewis was guilty of misleading Evan and that she had been far too secretive concerning their relationship. Evan answered their criticism by saying that he remained at her estate of his own free will. He also said Penn-Lewis was "one sent by God" and that her work could only be understood by "the faithful ones of God whose eyes are opened of God."[19] But sadly, with eyes wide open, it was Evan who refused to see.

> *Don't ever cut your family off. Whether or not you see "eye to eye" with them is irrelevant.*

## SEVERING THE BLOOD TIE

Shortly thereafter, Evan began to refuse visits from his closest relatives. When his mother became seriously ill, the news wasn't passed on to him because of his nervous condition. It seems the decision was made by Penn-Lewis. But once when Evan's father came to see him, it was not Penn-Lewis, but Evan himself who refused to speak with him. The reason given for not seeing his father was that **"he had been set apart for a highly spiritual task and had thus been obliged to forget ties of blood."**[20]

There is an important point I want to make here. *Don't ever cut your family off.* Whether or not you see "eye to eye" with them is irrelevant. Many of you are where you are today because of the prayers of your family. The old saying, "Blood is thicker than water," is true. When all of hell turns against you, you can usually count on your family to love and care for you, especially if you were raised in a Christian home. By cutting off your blood ties, you cut off part of your own heritage. For some reason, it seems revivalists can be misled in this area, especially if they feel their family isn't spiritual enough for them. John Alexander Dowie went through the same thing. He even forsook his last name for a season. You can never become so spiritual that you forsake the Word of God that commands: "Honour thy father and mother; which is the first commandment with promise; That it may be well with thee, and thou mayest live long on the earth" (Ephesians 6:2,3).

According to the Word, if you dishonor your family, you will not be at peace and your life could be shortened. If you feel too spiritual for your family, then love them to your level. Never forsake them.

## WAR ON THE RANKS

During these isolated years, Penn-Lewis relied on the anointing of Evan Roberts and wrote a number of books. The first one, *War on the Saints*, was published in 1913. Mrs. Penn-Lewis stated the book was birthed from six years of prayer and testing of the truth. It is believed the two authored the book together, but she received the credit. And rightfully so. Intended to be a complete answer manual to spiritual problems, it was instead, a compiled work of spiritual confusion.

Within a year after the book was published, Roberts denounced it. He told friends it had been a **"failed weapon which had confused and divided the Lord's people."**

Though his opinion eventually changed, during the years of writing *War on the Saints*, Evan seemed mesmerized by Penn-Lewis, saying, **"I know of none equal to her in understanding of spiritual things, she is a veteran in heavenly things."**[21] At this stage of Evan's recovery, Penn-Lewis convinced him that his sufferings were a divine plan of God to equip him to do battle against satanic powers and to train others for battle. As a result, she persuaded him to translate into Welsh *her* revelations on warfare and to compose booklets of it into English.

It is amazing to see how a national revivalist, once so strong and invincible from the power of the Holy Spirit, could now become so harnessed, subdued, and deceived. The biblical stories of Elijah and Jezebel, or of Samson and Delilah, continue to repeat themselves throughout history.

## SERMONS IN THE SHADOWS

The newly-formed team of Roberts and Penn-Lewis also published a magazine entitled, *The Overcomer.* This was a Penn-Lewis idea in which Evan wrote an essay and she wrote the remainder of the issue. From my personal view, the magazine was just another tool of Penn-Lewis' continued need to bring validity and popularity to her work. It attacked early Pentecostal groups and listed their practices as satanic. But with a mailing list of approximately five thousand people, the magazine circulated throughout Britain, Europe, North America, South Africa, Korea, and China.

*"I would like to reach a state of prayer where my life would be nought but one prayer from morn to night."*

Penn-Lewis fell ill in late 1913. In her absence, Evan wrote most of the magazine. Then several months after her health returned, she announced she was closing the magazine. She decided to hold what she called, "Christian Workers' Conferences" where she would preach. During these conferences, Evan was to stay in the prayer room, and at times, he would be allowed to counsel groups of people. This was justified by the fact that his medical advisors had told him to never again stand behind the pulpit. So Evan submitted and used his gifts in counseling. One person who sat under his group counsel said, "What strikes me most is Evan Roberts' accuracy of insight, for he is rarely at fault in his diagnosis and his spiritual discernment."

How could one, who once seemed so invincible from the might of the Holy Spirit, and who balked at anyone who suggested otherwise, now be contained to only counseling sessions?

Penn-Lewis' conferences eventually became less popular over the years. When they did subside, Evan found his outlet through The School of Prayer. The school came out of "The Prayer Watch" that was instituted during the Swansea Convention of 1908. In The School of Prayer, Evan taught how to intercede for families, ministers, and churches. And he wrote essays on various aspects and degrees of prayer. Several ministers commented that everything they knew about prayer came from Evan's teachings.

Evan came alive when he spoke of prayer. The school sparked a new flame inside him. Eventually he detached himself from The Prayer Watch and turned privately toward his own prayer life.

For awhile, several met with him in his prayer room within the Penn-Lewis home. Then he pulled himself away from the group and chose to intercede privately before the Lord. Evan once commented to a friend, "I would like to reach a state of prayer where my life would be nought but one prayer from morn to night."

Evan seemed thrilled to be called to a life of intercession. His prayer ministry focused on Christian leaders and believers around the world. When a group of French Salvation Army officers asked him about aggressive warfare, he answered:

> **"In Luke it does not say, 'preach and faint not,' but 'pray and faint not.' It is not difficult to preach. But while you pray, you are alone in some solitary place, fighting in a prayer-battle against the powers of darkness. And you will know the secret of victory."[22]**

I believe this statement supported Evan's choice to leave public ministry. In fact, he became so detached from humanity that he could no longer relate to people. Penn-Lewis wrote this of his behavior:

> "Those who are around him can't get into conversation with him — even if present in the same house."[23]

Evan Roberts remained inside the walls of the Penn-Lewis home for eight years.

The life of Evan Roberts was complex. I find it interesting that even though Penn-Lewis used Evan's ministry influence for her own ulterior motives, Evan obviously allowed it. In the beginning, he probably had little choice because of his invalid-like condition. However, the young revivalist remained in her household for *eight years*. And this leaves me with a multitude of questions. Was the Penn-Lewis home a comfort zone for him? Did he lose all confidence in his public image? Why didn't he go home? Did his emotional breakdowns cause him to feel secure with someone else in control? The only thing we can conclude for sure is that Evan Roberts made a choice to leave the public forefront. And the Penn-Lewis home is where he wanted to be.

## "SHALL WE HAVE REVIVAL AGAIN?"

It is not exactly clear how or why Penn-Lewis and Evan Roberts separated. First, it was noticed in 1920 that he was no longer contributing to any of her writings. When asked about his absence, she responded, "It is remarkable that

Mr. Roberts has never been able to take part in the work again, but his work has been carried on by others."[24]

Then sometime between 1919 and 1921, Evan moved to Brighton, in Sussex. He had purchased a typewriter and began to write several booklets. But they were unorganized and much of the Scripture was out of context. The booklets were never a success.

> *"Something like electricity went through us. One felt that if he had gone on there would have been another revival then and there."*

Evan had written to several friends in his homeland to tell them how he had never forgotten their love and support. England and Wales were bitterly divided at this time. Returning to his homeland wouldn't be easy without the support and the permission from the citizens of Wales. Besides the fact that Evan had left, the converts of the Welsh Revival were shocked and outraged at what they had read in *War on the Saints*. It seemed to them their leader was now contradicting everything he once stood for. The Welsh didn't know what to think of the young revivalist now. They thought they had known his heart, but they couldn't explain his actions.

Evan wrote to his denomination and congratulated a minister who received a new position in it. The minister was elated to receive the letter and asked if he could publish it to break Evan's ten-year silence. Evan consented, and was invited to return to Wales at his convenience. Evan did just that.

In 1926, Evan's father fell ill. When Evan returned home for a visit, the family was receptive. All the members were happy to see him and assured him that all was forgiven. And while he was there, some members of a particular chapel asked him to hold a service. Obviously forgetting the medical advisor's warning, Evan took the pulpit. While the congregation was surprised at his middle-aged appearance, they recognized the power of the Holy Spirit that still rung through Evan's voice. The people became so excited that it was murmured throughout northern Wales, "Shall we have revival again?"

Mrs. Penn-Lewis died of lung disease in 1927. Evan had been longing for his homeland of Wales for some time. After her death in 1927, Evan returned home permanently. It is interesting to note that though he began to *visit* Wales, he never *moved* there from England until Penn-Lewis died.

## "THE ROOM FLOODED WITH LIGHT"

Evan's father died in 1928, and at the funeral service, Evan did something unusual. As his father was being somberly eulogized, he suddenly interrupted the ritual and said, **"This is not a death but a resurrection. Let us bear witness to this truth."** Of that day, one person remarked, "Something like electricity went through us. One felt that if he had gone on there would have been another revival then and there."

Indeed, there was a short revival. The deacons of Moriah asked Evan to take part in a special service. When he decided to speak, the exciting news traveled throughout Wales. Visitors poured into northern Wales, and locals rushed to the chapel after work. Two hours before the service began, the chapel was full. Outside in the streets, another large crowd had assembled. Young people were eager to hear the man their parents spoke of. Evan calmly addressed the crowd. Then he went outside to address the overflow of people.

During this brief period, he visited various chapels and warned against the choking materialism that had crept into the church. Once, two parents brought their child to Evan in his prayer room. As he prayed for the child, "the room was flooded with light and with a sense of the Spirit of God." The parents began to praise and worship God at the top of their voice. Soon, nearby workers heard them and left their jobs to join the group. Shoppers in the same district also heard the celebration and ran to take part. In a matter of time, there was such a large crowd gathered that wagons couldn't get through the streets. According to an eyewitness, Evan prayed for healings and deliverances and operated in the gift of prophecy. But he is said to have openly rebuked someone who tried to speak in tongues. Nevertheless, some thought Evan Roberts had become Pentecostal. Healings, conversions, and answered prayers were the most talked about results of this small revival. A year later, Evan Roberts totally disappeared from public life.

## A SHADOW OF SUCCESS

By 1931, Evan was almost a forgotten man. He stayed in a room provided by Mrs. Oswald Williams. She wanted nothing from Evan but to ensure his peace of mind. He spent the last years of his life writing poetry and letters to ministers. He kept a daily journal and enjoyed watching sports and theater. In May, 1949, Evan had to stay in bed all day for the first time. One word was written in the September, 1950, portion of his journal. It was the word, **"ill."**

Evan Roberts was buried on January 29, 1951, at the age of seventy-two. He was buried in the family plot behind Moriah Chapel in northern Wales. Some years later, a memorial column was raised in front of Moriah commemorating his efforts to stir revival.

The funeral service itself turned into a memorial. Hundreds who loved Evan Roberts but had lost sight of him through the years, attended and sang his favorite hymns.

Of the many tributes to him, the memorial in *The Western Mail* eulogized him best. It read:

> *If a move of God fades away, it is partly because the people never continued in what they received. So we are in error if we solely blame the leader.*

"He was a man who had experienced strange things. In his youth, he had seemed to hold the nation in the palms of his hands. He endured strains and underwent great changes of opinion and outlook but his religious convictions remained firm to the end."

Indeed, Evan Roberts was a great revivalist who held the keys of spiritual awakening. He pioneered a tremendous move of the Spirit of God in Wales. However, forty years later, not a trace of this revival could be found in his homeland. It would remain as only a memory in the hearts of those who experienced it.

But, why just "a memory"?

Because one man can't carry the weight of revival alone. He can *lead* a move of God, but the people also have their part to play. If a move of God fades away, it is partly because the people never continued in what they received. So we are in error if we solely blame the leader.

There are a multitude of unanswered questions circling Evan Roberts' life. Some believe Evan was ordained by God for a two-year public ministry, then was called to spend the rest of his life in worldwide prayer and intercession. If this were totally true, I believe he would have died a happy man. But dark and depressing poetry was found written in his journals. In his sixties, he wondered if there was any purpose left in his life. His reaction was a mixture of "personal loss, loneliness, and failure." It seemed he continually searched for the part he was to play.

I believe Evan Roberts carried the spiritual truths that would shake the world, but those truths were only in his heart. It seemed he could never find the keys to emotional strength. Evan wanted his personality to fade into the shadows and he said repeatedly, **"I do not want to be seen."** Yet, in my opinion, the weakness of his emotional disposition caused him to be seen more than if he had taken his place in the authoritative leadership that comes in the move of God.

To carry the weight that comes with leading a revival – especially for a nation – all three parts of the human being – spirit, soul, and body – must be made strong. So as we can see from his life, there is more to revival than spiritual revelation. Spiritual hunger and revelation are always where it *begins*. But we are more than spiritual beings. The human body and emotions must be strong through the Word of God in order to maintain revival in the earth.

Your work for God doesn't have to fail or be cut short. Strengthen your body, season your soul, and yield your spirit to the plan of God. You *can* have revival in your nation and run with it successfully!

## CHAPTER THREE, EVAN ROBERTS
### References

[1] Brynmor Pierce Jones, *An Instrument of Revival: The Complete Life of Evan Roberts 1878-1951* (South Plainfield, NJ: Bridge Publishing, 1995), 10.

[2] Ibid., 10-12, 19.

[3] Ibid., 14.

[4] Ibid.

[5] Ibid., 15.

[6] Charles Clarke, *Pioneers of Revival* (Plainfield, NJ: Logos International, 1971), 26.

[7] James Alexander Stewart, *Invasion of Wales by the Spirit Through Evan Roberts* (Asheville, NC: Revival Literature, 1963), 28.

[8] Jones, *An Instrument of Revival,* 26.

[9] David Matthews, *I Saw the Welsh Revival* (Kimmel, IN: Pioneer Books), 75.

[10] Stewart, *Invasion of Wales by the Spirit Through Evan Roberts,* 64, 65.

[11] Jones, *An Instrument of Revival,* 41.

[12] Ibid., 58-59.

[13] Charles Clarke, *Pioneers of Revival,* 29.

[14] David Matthews, *I Saw the Welsh Revival,* 76.

[15] Ibid., 92-98.

[16] Ibid., 109.

[17] Eifion Evans, *The Welsh Revival of 1904* (Bridgend, Mid Glam, Wales: Evangelical Press of Wales, 1969), 174.

[18] David Matthews, *I Saw the Welsh Revival,* 115-116.

[19] Jones, *An Instrument of Revival,* 168.

[20] Ibid., 170.

[21] Ibid., 169-170.

[22] Ibid., 192.

[23] Ibid., 198.

[24] Ibid., 204.

# Charles F. Parham

## *"The Father of Pentecost"*

# "THE FATHER OF PENTECOST"

"At Christ's Second Coming the Church will be found with the same power that the Apostles and the early Church possessed. The power of Pentecost is manifest in us. The Christian religion must be demonstrated. The world wants to be shown. Then let God's power be manifest through us."[1]

Charles Fox Parham gave his life to restore the revolutionary truths of healing and the baptism of the Holy Spirit to the Church. *(Note: whenever the "Baptism of the Holy Spirit" is referred to in this chapter, it is inferred that the experience is always accompanied with the "evidence of speaking in tongues.")* The first forty years of the twentieth century were powerfully visited by this man's Pentecostal message that changed the lives of thousands around the world.

The miracles that occurred in Charles Parham's ministry are too numerous to record. Multiplied thousands found salvation, healing, deliverance, and the baptism of the Holy Spirit. When he proclaimed to the world in 1901 that, **"Speaking in tongues was the evidence of the baptism of the Holy Spirit,"** the Pentecostal truths of the early church were wonderfully restored. But the evangelist paid a price for it. The relentless backlash of persecution and slander Parham endured throughout his life would have destroyed others of lesser character. But for Parham, it only served to strengthen his hardened determination and purposeful faith.

> *When he proclaimed to the world in 1901 that, "Speaking in tongues was the evidence of the baptism of the Holy Spirit," the Pentecostal truths of the early church were wonderfully restored.*

## PREACH 'TIL THE COWS COME HOME

Charles F. Parham was born on June 4, 1873. After his birth in Muscatine, Iowa, his parents, William and Ann Maria Parham, moved south to Cheney, Kansas. They truly lived as and considered themselves American pioneers.

Aside from the rugged pioneer life, early childhood was not easy for young Parham. At six months of age, he was stricken with a fever that left him bedridden. For the first five years of his life, he was plagued with dramatic spasms, and his forehead swelled making his head abnormally large. Then, at the tender age of seven, his mother died.

Though Parham had four other brothers, he felt an overwhelming sense of grief and loneliness when his beloved mother died. His memories left him melancholy and despondent, as he thought of his mother's loving attention during his illness. As his mother said her last good-byes before dying, she looked at young Parham and said, "Charlie, be good." There, in the presence of God and his dying mother, he vowed to meet her in heaven.[2] Those simple words made a deep impression on him. It has been said that they were influential in his later decision to give his life to God. Parham's father would later remarry a young woman, Harriett Miller, who was greatly loved and needed by the entire family.

When Parham was nine he contracted inflammatory rheumatism. The condition left his body tied in knots. When the affliction finally lifted, his skin was completely transparent. The boy then developed a tapeworm which required such strong medications that the lining of his stomach was eaten away and destroyed. His many trials progressed as the medications stunted his growth for three years.[3]

It was also at the tender age of nine that Parham was called to the ministry. Because he and his brothers had been taken to Sunday school during their first years of life, Parham enjoyed an early awareness of God. Even before he was converted, the boy's constant thoughts were, **"Woe is me, if I preach not the Gospel."**[4]

So he began to prepare himself for God's calling by pursuing literature. Though Kansas was not yet modernized, and libraries weren't readily available, he managed to collect a few history books along with his Bible. And he found other ways to prepare himself for the ministry by doing his chores and helping his brothers. While working with the family livestock, Parham was often known to give the cattle rousing sermons on various subjects ranging from heaven to hell.

## "LIGHTNING" THAT PENETRATED

Parham never regretted that he had to do so much studying on his own. It actually worked to his advantage. There were so few churches and preachers on the prairie, and with no one to teach him otherwise, Parham studied God's

Word and took it literally. There were no inferences of man-made theology in his doctrine, and there were no traditions to break through. From an early age, up to the age of thirteen, Parham had only heard the sermons of two preachers. It was during one of these meetings that Parham was converted.

Parham believed that deep repentance must take place within a convert's heart, yet he felt void of such an emotional experience. So when he sought to be saved at the meeting, on the walk home, he began to question his conversion. He was so weighed down with a heavy heart that he was unable to pray. He found himself humming the song, *"I Am Coming to the Cross,"* and upon reaching the third verse, Parham immediately became assured of his conversion. Of the experience he later said, **"There flashed from the heavens a light above the brightness of the sun, like a stroke of lightning it penetrated, thrilling every fiber of my being."**[5] From that moment forward, Parham was never swayed from the "Anchor" of his salvation.

## "WILL YOU PREACH?"

After his dramatic conversion, Parham served as a Sunday school teacher and worker. He held his first public meeting at the age of fifteen, with marked results. He preached for a short time, then entered Southwestern Kansas College at the age of sixteen.

When he entered college, Parham had every intention of entering the ministry, but he began to notice the disrespect and general disgust that the secular world held toward ministers. And he began to hear about the conditions of poverty that accompanied ministry. Discouraged by these stories, he looked upon other professions with great interest. Soon, Parham denied his calling and began to backslide.

> *When he entered college, Parham had every intention of entering the ministry, but he began to notice the disrespect and general disgust that the secular world held toward ministers.*

In remembering his traumatic childhood illnesses, Parham reasoned that the medical field would be a good pursuit. So he began studying to be a physician. But he was constantly tormented in remembering his promise to become a missionary, and soon contracted rheumatic fever.

After suffering for months from the flames of the fever, a physician visited his bedside and pronounced Parham near death. But those bedridden months had prompted Parham to remember the words that had once rung in his ears, "Will you preach? WILL YOU PREACH?" Again he hungered to answer his call, but he didn't want to live in the impoverished conditions that seemed unavoidable for ministers of his day. So he cried out to God: **"If You will let me go somewhere, someplace, where I wouldn't have to take collections or beg for a living, I will preach."**

Parham was so sedated with morphine in his condition that he was unable to think of more words to pray. So he began reciting The Lord's Prayer. When he came to words "...thy will be done in earth as it is in heaven," his mind cleared and he envisioned God's majesty. He caught a slight glimpse of how God's will was manifested through every ounce of creation and realized that it was God's will to heal. So he cried out to God, praying, **"If Thy will is done in me, I shall be whole."** As he said this prayer, every joint in his body loosened and every organ was healed. Only his ankles remained weak. But his lungs were clear and his body recovered.

Following his recovery, Parham was quickly asked to hold an evangelistic meeting. So he renewed his promise to God, and vowed to quit college to enter the ministry if God would heal his ankles. Crawling under a tree, Parham began to pray and God immediately sent a "mighty electric current" through his ankles making them whole.[6]

## A "BUMPKIN" WITH POWER

Parham held his first evangelistic meeting at the age of eighteen, in the Pleasant Valley School House, near Tonganoxie, Kansas. He was a stranger to the country community when he asked permission to hold a revival at their school. So when they gave their approval, Parham went up on a hillside, stretched his hand out over the valley and prayed that the entire community be taken for God.[7]

The first night of the meeting, the attendance was good, but most of the people weren't used to active participation. He received few responses at first, but before the evening was over, there were many conversions.

The Thistlewaites attended this meeting and wrote of it to their daughter. Their daughter, Sarah, had grown up in the community and was in Kansas City attending school. When she returned home, the meeting had closed, but the community had arranged for Parham to come back the next Sunday.

At the meeting, the refined Sarah Thistlewaite was surprised by what she saw. Parham looked much different from the wealthy, cultured preachers she had been used to in Kansas City. And when he took the pulpit, he didn't have his sermon written out like the preachers she had seen. In fact, Parham never wrote down what he was going to say. He relied on the Holy Spirit to give him inspiration. Then as Sarah listened to the young evangelist preach, she realized her lack of devotion to the faith. She knew she was following Jesus from "far off," and made the decision to consecrate her life totally to the Lord. She also began to cultivate her friendship with Charles Parham and soon, what began as a simple interest, turned into a union of purpose and destiny.

## DENOMINATIONS? NO MORE!

When Parham was nineteen years old he was asked to pastor the Methodist church in Eudora, Kansas. This he did faithfully, while also pastoring in Linwood on Sunday afternoons. Sarah and her family attended his services regularly.

The congregation grew steadily and a new building was built to hold the people. The denomination's leadership saw a great future for Parham, and they would have given him most any pastorate or assignment if he would have submitted to their authority. But all was not well between Parham and the Methodist denomination. Parham had vowed to follow the leading of the Holy Spirit, despite what other men asked him to do. In advising new converts, he would exhort them to find any church home, even if it wasn't the Methodist church. He explained that joining a denomination was not a prerequisite for heaven, and that denominations spent more time preaching on their particular church and its leaders than they did on Jesus Christ and His covenant. This caused many conflicts within his denominational ranks. Speaking of these conflicts, Parham said:

*Many slanderous accusations had been leveled against him, and he was concerned that the rising persecution would forever ruin his work. Then one day while deep in prayer, he heard these words, "I made Myself of no reputation."*

**"Finding the confines of a pastorate, and feeling the narrowness of sectarian churchism, I was often in conflict with the higher authorities, which eventually resulted in open rupture; and I left denominationalism forever, though suffering bitter persecution at the hands of the church.... Oh, the narrowness of many who call themselves the Lord's own!"[8]**

Parham's parents were greatly disappointed in their son, since they were strong supporters of the church. So when Parham resigned, he sought rest in the home of friends, who welcomed him as their own son.

Parham began to pray for direction. Many slanderous accusations had been leveled against him, and he was concerned that the rising persecution would forever ruin his work. Then one day while deep in prayer, he heard these words, "I made Myself of no reputation." Immediately, Parham was strengthened and encouraged. As the Spirit of God continued to give him Scripture, he set his course. He would enter the evangelistic field, unassociated with any form of denomination. He would hold his meetings in schools, halls, churches, tabernacles – wherever he could – and believe for the Holy Spirit to manifest Himself in a mighty way.

While holding a meeting in western Kansas, Parham wrote to Sarah Thistlewaite and proposed marriage. He warned Sarah that his life was totally dedicated to the Lord and that his future was unclear, but if she could trust God with him, they should marry. Charles and Sarah were married six months later, on December 31, 1896, in her grandfather's home.

## HEAL YOURSELF!

As the young couple started traveling, they were received with great approval. September of 1897 saw the birth of their first son, Claude. But the joy of the event was short-lived when Charles fell ill with heart disease. No amount of medicine seemed to work as he grew weaker. Then, without warning, tiny Claude was stricken with a high fever. The Parham's walked the floor praying for the baby, but to no avail. The physician couldn't diagnose Claude's fever, and therefore, had no cure.

Parham was called to pray for another man who was ill, so in his own weakened state, he left for the man's home. While praying for the man, the Scripture, "Physician, heal thyself," exploded inside of Parham and while he was praying, the power of God had touched Parham. He was healed instantly.

Parham eagerly rushed home after the visit, grabbed Sarah, and told her of his experience, then prayed for his baby. He then threw away all of his medicines, vowing to never again trust anything but the Word of God. The fever left Claude's body, and he grew to be a healthy child.

I want to say something here. Parham's healing ministry was always controversial to those who misunderstood it. He lived in a time when physicians, as a whole, stood contrary to the Gospel. It was Parham's *personal faith* that inspired him to throw away his medicine. He believed that to trust totally in medicine was to deny the blood of Jesus and the price Christ paid on the cross. When true revelation comes, it is invincible. It will always produce the success it illustrates. Parham's deep revelation was transferred to his family and medicine was forbidden in his home. But he left the final decision regarding their use of medication to anyone else. There will always be those who follow the inspiration of another, without any revelation themselves. Because of this we have seen entire sections of the body of Christ refuse to use medication and call those who do "sinners." Parham never taught this so it would be a mistake to blame him, as so many have, for the errors some believers have made about divine healing.

## THE "LIVE OR DIE" VOW

Not long after Parham and his son were healed, he received some heart-breaking news. Within the time frame of a week, two of his closest friends had died. Consumed with grief, Parham hurried to their graves. It was a day that marked the rest of his ministry:

**"As I knelt between the graves of my two loved friends, who might have lived if I had but told them of the power of Christ to heal, I made a vow that 'Live or Die' I would preach this Gospel of healing."[9]**

Parham moved his family to Ottawa, Kansas, where he held his first divine healing meeting. During the meeting, he boldly proclaimed the truths of God's Word. A woman with dropsy, given three days to live, was instantly healed. Another young invalid lady, blind and ill with the consumption, felt a tearing sensation through her chest and was completely healed. God also instantly restored her eyesight, and she spent the rest of her life sewing for a living.

*The truths of divine healing were rare in the Church during these years.*

The truths of divine healing were rare in the Church during these years. Dowie and Etter had great success, but these truths were virtually unknown in the Prairie. Though results couldn't be denied, many claimed the power that manifested through Parham was of the devil. The accusations drove Parham to shut himself in a room to establish himself in the truth. As he prayed and searched the Scriptures, Parham found that everywhere he looked in the Bible, healing was present. He realized that healing, just as salvation, came through the atoning work of Jesus' blood, and from that point on, persecution and slander never slighted him. Then a revolutionary idea had come to him: he would provide a refuge home for those seeking healing. Parham was filled with joy!

## A FAITH HOME "ALL THE WAY"

A daughter was born to the Parhams in November of 1898 on Thanksgiving Day. They named her Esther Marie. Not long after, Parham opened his divine healing home in Topeka, Kansas, which he and Sarah named "Bethel." The purpose was to provide a home-like atmosphere for those who trusted God for healing. The ground floor had a chapel, a reading room, and a printing office. The top floor had fourteen rooms with large windows. The Parhams kept the windows filled with fresh flowers, making the atmosphere of the home peaceful and beautiful. Chapel services were held daily, where the Word of God was powerfully taught. And prayer was offered individually, several times throughout the day and night.

Bethel also offered special classes for ministers and evangelists which prepared and trained them for the ministry. This place of refuge also found Christian homes for orphans, and jobs for the unemployed.

One guest at Bethel wrote:

"Who can think of a sweeter name than 'Bethel'? Surely it is the House of God. Everything moves in love and harmony. On entering the rooms one is impressed with the divine influence shed abroad here.... It is a Faith Home all the way through."[10]

Parham's newsletter, *The Apostolic Faith*, published bi-weekly, had a subscription price at first. But Parham quickly changed this by asking readers to study Isaiah 55:1, then give to the paper as they felt led. The newsletter published wonderful testimonies of healing and many of the sermons that were taught at Bethel.

Parham always believed that God would provide the financial support for Bethel. Once, after a hard day of ministry, he realized the rent was due the next morning and he didn't have the money to meet it. Tired and weary, he looked to the sky and told the Lord that he must have rest and that he knew God wouldn't fail him. The next morning, a man showed up at Bethel, saying, "I was suddenly awakened with the thought of you and your work; no sleep came to me until I promised to bring you this." It was the exact sum for the rent.

Another time, Parham only had a partial sum to pay on a bill that was due. So he set out to the bank to pay what he had and while on the way, he passed an acquaintance who handed Parham some money. When Parham got to the bank, he found the money was the exact amount he needed to pay the bill in full.[11] And there are many other incredible stories of financial provision surrounding Parham's ministry.

The Parham family was blessed with another son in March of 1900. They named him, Charles, after his father. Now his family seemed to be outgrowing the Bethel Home, so a parsonage was built. Along with his growing family, Parham's spiritual hunger was growing so he felt he should leave Bethel and visit different ministries. Leaving two Holiness ministers in charge, Parham set out to visit the ministries of several different godly men in Chicago, New York, and Maine. He returned home, refreshed and renewed with an even deeper hunger:

**"I returned home fully convinced that while many had obtained real experience in sanctification and the anointing that abideth, there still remained a great outpouring of power for the Christians who were to close this age."[12]**

These words contained the seeds of the truths Parham would later unveil.

## SURROUNDED BY A HALO

Because of his tremendous success at Bethel, many began to urge Parham to open a Bible school. So again, Parham shut himself away to fast and pray. Then in October of 1900, he obtained a beautiful structure in Topeka, Kansas, for the purpose of beginning a Bible school, and called it, "Stone's Folly."

The building was patterned after an English castle. But the builder ran out of money before the structure could be completed in style. The staircase that joined the first and second floor was carved with finished woodwork of cedar, cherrywood, maple, and pine. The third floor was finished in common wood and paint.

*The outside of Stone's Folly was laid in red brick and white stone, with a winding stairway leading to an observatory. Another doorway led from there to a small room known as the Prayer Tower. Students took turns to pray three hours each day in this special tower.*

The outside of Stone's Folly was laid in red brick and white stone, with a winding stairway leading to an observatory. Another doorway led from there to a small room known as the Prayer Tower. Students took turns to pray three hours each day in this special tower.

When Stone's Folly was dedicated, a man looked out from the Prayer Tower and saw a vision above Stone's Folly of a "vast lake of fresh water about to overflow, containing enough to satisfy every thirsty need."[13] It would prove to be a sign of things to come.

Parham's Bible school was open to every Christian minister and believer, who was willing to "forsake all." They were to arrive willing to study the Word deeply and believe God for all their personal needs. The student's faith was their only tuition; everyone was to believe that God would supply their needs.

Examinations were given that December on the subjects of repentance, conversion, consecration, sanctification, healing, and the future coming of the Lord. When the book of Acts was included for the study of these subjects, Parham gave his students a historical assignment. They were to diligently study the Bible's evidence of the baptism in the Holy Spirit and report on their findings in three days. After assigning this homework, Parham left his students for a meeting in Kansas City. Then he returned to Stone's Folly for the annual Watch Night Service.

*Stone's Folly, Topeka, Kansas*

On the morning that the assignments were due, Parham listened to the reports of forty students, and was astonished by what he heard. While different manifestations of the Spirit occurred during the outpouring of Pentecost in Acts, every student had arrived at the same general conclusion: *Every recipient baptized by the Holy Spirit spoke in other tongues!*

Now there was a great excitement and new interest at Stone's Folly surrounding the book of Acts. Anticipation filled the atmosphere as seventy-five people crowded around one another at the school for the evening Watch Night Service.

During the service, a spiritual freshness seemed to blanket the meeting. Then a student, Agnes Ozman, approached Parham and asked him to lay his hands on her so she would receive the baptism of the Holy Spirit. Ozman believed she was called to the mission field and wanted to be equipped with spiritual power. At first Parham hesitated, telling her that he himself didn't speak in other tongues. But she persisted, and Parham humbly laid his hands upon her head. Parham would later write of the incident, explaining it like this:

**"I had scarcely repeated three dozen sentences when a glory fell upon her, a halo seemed to surround her head and face, and she began speaking in the Chinese language, and was unable to speak English for three days."**[14]

Ozman later testified that she had already received a few of these same words while in the Prayer Tower. But after Parham laid hands on her, she completely overflowed with the supernatural power of God.

## THE TONGUES OF FIRE

After witnessing this incredible outpouring of the Holy Spirit, the students moved their beds from the upper dormitory and turned it into a prayer room. For two nights and three days, the school waited upon the Lord.

*They were sitting, kneeling, and standing with hands raised, and they were all speaking in other tongues. Some were trembling under the power of God.*

In January of 1901, Parham preached at a church in Topeka, telling the people of the wonderful experiences that were happening at Stone's Folly. And he told them that he believed he would soon speak in other tongues. That night after returning home from the meeting, he was met by one of the students who led him into the Prayer Room. When he stepped inside, he was amazed at the sight of twelve denominational ministers. They were sitting, kneeling, and standing with hands raised, and they were all speaking in other tongues. Some were trembling under the power of God. An elderly lady approached Parham, to relate how moments before he had entered the room, "tongues of fire" sat upon their heads.

Overcome by what he saw, Parham fell to his knees behind a table praising God. Then he asked God for the same blessing, and when he did, Parham distinctly heard God's calling to stand up in the world. He was to reveal the truth of this mighty outpouring everywhere he would go. The enlightened minister was also made aware of the severe persecutions that would accompany his stand. But he counted the cost and decided to obey; just as he had obeyed in proclaiming divine healing. It was then that Charles Parham himself was filled with the Holy Spirit, and spoke in other tongues.

**"Right then and there came a slight twist in my throat, a glory fell over me and I began to worship God in a Swedish tongue, which later changed to other languages and continued...."** [15]

Soon the news of what God was doing had Stone's Folly beseiged by newspaper reporters, language professors, and government interpreters. They sat in on the services to tell the whole world of this incredible phenomenon. They had come to the consensus that Stone's Folly's students were speaking in the languages of the world. And their newspapers screamed with the headlines "Pentecost! Pentecost!" Newsboys shouted, "Read about the Pentecost!"

On January 21, 1901, Parham preached the first sermon dedicated to the sole experience of the baptism of the Holy Spirit with the evidence of speaking in other tongues.

## DOORWAY TO THE SUPERNATURAL

Some say today that "tongues have passed away." But my friend, when miracles pass away, when signs and wonders pass away, when the manifestations of the Holy Spirit pass away, tongues will pass away too. Then we will have no need for other tongues. But as long as we are on planet earth, these things shall remain. The book of Acts continues to be lived out in the life of the Church today. The only thing that has passed away is the sacrificing of lambs, because

Jesus fulfilled the sacrifice system of shedding of blood and removed the veil separating God and man.

Praying in other tongues will birth the will of God in your spirit. You will no longer depend on your intellect or the direction of others. You will "know" for yourself what the will of the Father is for your life. Sometimes we are limited in our prayer life by our national language, and don't always know how to pray for a situation. The Word tells us that "praying in the spirit," or in tongues, enables us to pray the perfect will of God into every situation because praying in tongues moves us into the realm of the Spirit. You can go to heaven without the baptism of the Holy Spirit, but it is not God's highest desire for you.

There are several different operations of tongues spoken of in the Bible. First, tongues can manifest in a supernatural language that other nationalities can understand (see Acts 2:8-11). Secondly, the gift of tongues can be spoken out by one person in a public setting and then followed with the interpretation of that language, which brings edification to the people gathered there (see 1 Corinthians 14:27-28). And there is the prayerful language of tongues, that will edify and build your faith. Finally, praying in the spirit will bring boldness, strength, direction, and guidance into a believer's life. Praying in tongues is also one of the most powerful forms of spiritual intercession (see 1 Corinthians 14:4; Jude 20; Romans 8:26-27; Ephesians 6:18).

If you haven't experienced the baptism of the Holy Spirit with the evidence of other tongues, then earnestly seek God for this. Speaking in other tongues is not just "for some." It is for *everyone*, just like salvation. When you choose to enter into this measure of God's fullness, your life will never be the same.

> *"I am healed of my infidelity; I have heard in my own tongue the 23rd Psalm that I learned at my mother's knee."*

## SPIRITUAL FATHERHOOD

At this stage of Parham's life, there had never been such "refined glory" and peace in his household. Parham went throughout the country, preaching the truths of the baptism of the Holy Spirit in wonderful demonstration. Once in a service, he began to speak in other tongues, then when he had finished, a man in the congregation stood up and said, "I am healed of my infidelity; I have heard in my own tongue the 23rd Psalm that I learned at my mother's knee."[16] This was only one of the countless testimonies regarding the gift of other tongues that came out of Parham's ministry. Soon, hundreds upon hundreds began to receive this manifestation. But along with this mighty outpouring came a slanderous persecution of those who despised it.

Then, tragedy struck the Parham household again. Their youngest child, Charles, died on March 16, 1901. The family was grief-stricken. Their sorrow was compounded even further when those who stood against the Parhams persecuted them for contributing to the death of their son. Then many who loved the family, but didn't believe in divine healing, added to the sadness by encouraging the Parhams to forsake their belief in this area. But through it all, the Parhams showed tremendous character by choosing to keep their hearts tender toward the Lord and win this test of faith. As a result Parham would continue in an even greater fervency in the preaching of Christ's *miraculous* Gospel – around the world.

In the fall of 1901, the Bible school in Topeka was unexpectedly sold out from under Parham, for the purposes of secular use. Parham warned the new buyers if they used the school for secular reasons, the building would be destroyed. But they ignored his prophetic warning, and by the end of December news had reached Parham that the building had been totally destroyed by a fire.

After Stone's Folly sold, the Parhams moved into a rented home in Kansas City. It was then that Parham began to hold meetings around the country. Hundreds of people, from every denomination, received the baptism of the Holy Spirit and divine healing. As is true with every pioneering revivalist, Parham was either greatly loved or hated by the public, but his colorful personality and warm heart were recognized by all. One Kansas newspaper wrote: "Whatever may be said about him, he has attracted more attention to religion than any other religious worker in years."[17]

In 1901 Parham published his first book, *A Voice Crying in the Wilderness*. The book was filled with sermons on salvation, healing, and sanctification. Many ministers throughout the world studied and taught from it.

Another son, Philip Arlington, was born to the Parhams in June of 1902. By now Charles had become a father of the Pentecostal outpouring, and was continually watching over his spiritual children to help them grow in the truth. Parham had his first experience with fanaticism in 1903. He preached at a church where wild and fleshly manifestations took place. The experience would add a new dimension to his teaching. Though he never allowed himself to be called the leader in this Pentecostal Movement, Parham felt personally responsible in seeing that the baptism of the Holy Spirit was manifested according to the Word. So he endeavored to learn the personality of the Holy Spirit, and spoke strongly against anything contrary to what he had learned.

Perhaps it was this personal passion that caused him to speak out against the manifestations at Azusa in later years.

## "HE PREACHES IN BIG CHUNKS"

In the fall of 1903, the Parhams moved to Galena, Kansas, and erected a large tent. The tent could hold two thousand people, but it was still too small to accommodate the crowds. So a building was located as winter set in. But even then, the doors had to be left open during services so those outside could participate. Huge numbers poured into Galena from surrounding towns when strong manifestations of the Spirit occurred, and hundreds were miraculously healed and saved.

*"Many...came to scoff but remained to pray."*

In those days, cards were handed to people who came for healing. The common procedure was to write numbers on the cards and hand the cards to those who were seeking prayer. Then during the service, the numbers were randomly called out and prayer was offered for those holding the card number called. So with this practice everyone was given an equal chance. But Parham shunned the practice and chose to pray for all who came, despite the length of time that it took.

Two newspapers, the *Joplin Herald* and the *Cincinnati Inquirer*, declared Parham's Galena meetings to be the greatest demonstration of power and miracles since the time of the Apostles, writing, "Many...came to scoff but remained to pray."[18]

On March 16, 1904, Wilfred Charles was born to the Parhams. One month later, Charles moved the family to Baxter Springs, Kansas, then continued to hold tremendous meetings around the state.

Parham always warned the crowds to never call him "healer," reminding them that he no more had the power to heal than he had the power to save. One observer said, "Brother Parham surely preached God's Holy Word straight from the shoulder; in chunks big, pure, and hard enough to knock the scales from our eyes."[19]

The revivalist's meetings were always very interesting. Parham was known to have a great love for the Holy Land, and always implemented its beliefs in his teachings. So besides the many miracles, he would often display a great array of garments from the Holy Land that he had collected over a period of time. The newspapers always highlighted this aspect of his ministry favorably.

*Stone's Folly Students, 1905*

*Crusade Team, Houston, Texas, 1905*

In 1905, Parham traveled to Orchard, Texas. He did so in response to certain believers who had attended his Kansas meetings and had fervently prayed for him to come to their part of the country. When ministering in Orchard, there was such a great outpouring of the Spirit, that Parham was inspired to begin holding his "Rally Days." These were a series of meetings that were strategically planned and held throughout America. Many workers volunteered to assist in the outreach once Parham returned to Kansas.

## EVERYTHING'S BIG IN TEXAS!

The first Rally Day was planned for Houston, Texas. Parham and twenty-five workers held this meeting in a place called Bryn Hall, where they were advertised as non-denominational and invited anyone who wanted to experience more of the power of God. The newspapers loved the novelty of Parham's Holy Land array, and favorably wrote of all the miracles that happened.

After these meetings, Parham and his group held large parades, marching down the streets of Houston in their Holy Land garments. The parades helped to spark the interest of many who attended the evening services. When the Rally Days were over, Parham's group returned to Kansas, rejoicing in the Lord.

Due to high public demand, the team returned to Houston once more, but this time, heavy persecution came their way. Several of Parham's workers were poisoned during one meeting making them very ill, with severe pain. But Parham prayed for each of them immediately, and they recovered completely.

*Parham's schools were never meant to be theological seminaries.*

Parham's own life was threatened several times, but he always escaped. Once, after taking a drink of water on the platform, Parham was doubled over with tremendous pain. But he began to pray and the pain left instantly. Later when the water from his glass was examined chemically, it was found to contain enough poison to kill a dozen men.[20]

Undaunted by the persecution, Parham announced the opening of a new Bible school in Houston, then moved his headquarters there in the winter of 1905. The school was supported like the one in Topeka, through freewill offerings. There was no tuition and each student had to believe for their own means. It was said that a military style of order was practiced at the school and that each person understood how to work in harmony.[21]

Parham's schools were never meant to be theological seminaries. They were training centers where the truths of God were taught in the most practical manner – with prayer as a key ingredient. Many ministers left his schools to serve God throughout the world.

It was in Houston that Parham met William J. Seymour. Up to this time, the Jim Crow Laws forbid blacks and whites from attending school together. And Parham's meetings were segregated, but it was because blacks didn't ask to attend the schools, that is until Seymour. Seymour's humility and hunger for the Word so moved Parham that he decided to ignore the racist rules of the day. Seymour was given a place in the school where he experienced revolutionary truths on the baptism of the Holy Spirit. William Seymour would later become the leader of the Azusa Street Mission in Los Angeles, California.

After Parham's historical Houston school came to a close, he moved his family back to Kansas, and on June 1, 1906, Robert (their last child) was born.

Parham continued to hold meetings throughout the country and was in great demand. It was at this time that he received letters from Seymour, asking him to come to the Mission in Los Angeles at Azusa Street. It was said that Seymour wrote "urgent letters appealing for help, as spiritualistic manifestations, hypnotic forces and fleshly contortions...had broken loose in the meeting. He wanted Mr. Parham to come quickly and help him discern between that which was real and that which was false."[22] In spite of the plea, Parham felt led by God to hold a rally in Zion City, Illinois, instead.

## WALKING ON THE WATER AT ZION

When Parham arrived in Zion, he found the community in great distress. Dowie had been discredited in his ministry there, and others were in the process of taking control of the city. There was a strong oppression hanging over the town, because people from all nations and all walks of life had invested their future in the hands of Dowie. Discouraged and broken, these people had lost hope. Parham saw this as a wonderful opportunity to bring the baptism of the Holy Spirit to Zion. He could think of no greater blessing or joy, than to introduce the fullness of the Spirit to these people.

When Parham arrived in Zion, he met with great opposition, and was unable to secure a building for the meetings. So all doors of opportunity seemed to close. Finally, at the invitation of a hotel manager, he was able to set up a meeting in a private room. The next night, two rooms and the hallway were crowded and attendance grew steadily from there.

Soon Parham began cottage meetings in the best homes of the city. One of these homes belonged to the great healing evangelist and author, F. F.

Bosworth. Bosworth's home was literally turned into a meeting house during Parham's stay. Every night, Parham led five different meetings in five different homes, all beginning at 7:00 P.M. When his workers would arrive, he would go preaching from meeting to meeting, driving rapidly to make sure he reached each one. As a result, hundreds of ministers and evangelists went out from Zion filled with the power of the Spirit to preach God's Word with signs.

Though Zion was a Christian community, it seemed the persecution against Parham was the greatest ever there. Secular newspapers had a media blitz, citing the "Prophet Parham" as taking the ground of the "Prophet Dowie."[23] Dowie himself went on public record to criticize Parham's message and actions. The new Overseer of Zion, Wilbur Voliva, was eager to see Parham leave the city. Voliva wrote Parham to ask how long he intended staying in Zion. Parham replied, **"As long as the Lord wants me here."**[24]

In October of 1906, Parham felt released from Zion and hurried to Los Angeles to answer Seymour's call.

## SHAKE, RATTLE, AND ROLL: THE L. A. STORY

It was told to Parham that Seymour had gone to Los Angeles with a humble spirit. Those from Texas who moved to Los Angeles with Seymour were impressed with his ability. It was clear that God was doing a wonderful work in Seymour's life. But it was also clear that Satan was trying to "tear it to pieces."[25] Because Seymour had been a student at Parham's school, Parham felt responsible for what was happening.

*Parham was exiled from the meetings, and the door to the mission was padlocked so he couldn't return.*

Parham's experiences at Azusa added to his understanding of fanaticism. According to Parham, there were many genuine experiences of receiving the true baptism, but there were also many false manifestations. Parham held two or three services at Azusa, but was unable to convince Seymour to change his ways. The door to the mission was padlocked so Parham couldn't return. But instead of leaving Los Angeles, Parham rented a large building and held great services that ministered deliverance from evil spirits to the crowds who had previously attended the meetings.

Parham regarded the Seymour conflict as an example of spiritual pride. He wrote about it in his newsletter and noted that fanaticism always produces an unteachable spirit in those given over to it. He explained that those under the influence of these false spirits:

**"...feel exalted, thinking they have a greater experience than anyone else, not needing instruction or advice...placing them out of reach from those who can help."**

He ended his newsletter "deposition" by saying:

**"...although many forms of fanaticism have crept in, I believe every true child of God will come out of this mist and shadow stronger and better equipped against all extremes that are liable to present themselves at any time in meetings of this kind."[26]**

## "PART HAM"

Parham returned to Zion from Los Angeles in December of 1906. Unable to obtain a building, he pitched a large tent in a vacant lot. Parham's tent meetings were well attended by some two thousand people. On New Year's Eve, he preached for two hours on the baptism in the Holy Spirit, and produced such an intense excitement that several men approached Parham with the idea of beginning a "movement" and a large church.

But Parham was against the idea. He told the men that he was not there for personal gain and that his idea of coming to Zion was to bring the peace of God to replace its oppression. Parham believed America had enough churches and said that what Zion needed was more spirituality in the churches they already had. Parham felt that if his message had value, then the people would support it without an organization. He was concerned that groups who gathered around the truth of the "baptism of the Holy Spirit" would eventually develop a worldly, secular objective.

After confronting these issues, Parham officially resigned as the "projector" of the Apostolic Faith Movement. Many controversies over leadership had already developed in other states that adopted the movement. He wrote in his newsletter:

**"Now that they [apostolic faith tenets] are generally accepted, I simply take my place among my brethren to push this Gospel of the kingdom as a witness to all nations."[27]**

Parham's position created many new enemies at Zion and when his meetings closed, he traveled alone to Canada and New England to preach.

His family remained in Zion and were greatly persecuted. Each day at school brought new persecutions to the Parham children. Pork was forbidden in the city, and therefore, children began to call the Parhams, "Part Ham," so the children came home from school very often in tears. The Parham family believed they were persecuted mainly because they wouldn't organize a movement. Later, Charles would write:

**"If I differ at all from Zion with respect to any of these truths, it is only as individuals in Zion differ among themselves."**[28]

Then one day, Mrs. Parham received a disturbing letter from a Zion citizen that threatened her husband in a scandalous manner. She denounced the letter as a lie, but conditions and persecutions grew so bad that she decided to take her children back to Kansas.

## FLAMES FROM HELL: THE SCANDAL

It is here that we come to the greatest controversy in the life of Charles Parham. Clearly, Parham had many enemies in prominent Christian organizations. But his main antagonist was Wilbur Voliva, the General Overseer of Zion. After Parham's public resignation as "projector" of the Apostolic Faith Movement, various rumors were circulated throughout Pentecostal circles that Parham had been arrested for sexual immorality. The *Waukegan Daily Sun* suggested that Parham's sudden departure from Zion had been prompted by "mysterious men, said to be detectives, ready to arrest him on some equally mysterious charge." The paper later admitted that its report was based on rumor and that the Zion police department knew nothing of the incident.[29] But much damage had been done.

> *Parham had many enemies in prominent Christian organizations.*

In the summer of 1907, Parham was preaching in a former Zion mission located in San Antonio when a story reported in the *San Antonio Light* made national news. Its headline read: "Evangelist Is Arrested. C. F. Parham, Who Has Been Prominent in Meeting Here, Taken Into Custody."[30] The story said Parham had been charged with sodomy, a felony under Texas law. And that he had been arrested with his supposed companion, J. J. Jourdan who, along with him was allegedly released after making a payment of one thousand dollars.

Parham immediately fought back with rage. He secured a lawyer, C. A. Davis, and announced that he had been "elaborately framed" by his old nemesis, Wilbur Voliva. Parham was certain that Voliva was furious over a Zion city church that Parham had preached in. It had once belonged to Zion, but left the Zion association and joined the Apostolic Faith Movement.

Parham pledged to clear his name and indignantly refused to leave town. But Mrs. Parham, having previously read the rumors in a letter in Zion, left Kansas for San Antonio. The case never made it to court and Parham's name disappeared from the headlines of secular newspapers as quickly as it appeared. No formal indictment was ever filed, and to date there is no record of the incident at the Bexar County Courthouse.[31]

But the religious newspapers weren't as kind to Parham as the secular. Their press seemed to locate even more details about "his affairs." Two newspapers that took liberty with the story were the *Burning Bush*, and the *Zion Herald* (the official newspaper of Wilbur Voliva's church in Zion). These newspapers were said to have quoted the *San Antonio Light*, along with an eyewitness account of Parham's alleged improprieties, including a written confession. But when researched, it was found the articles "quoted" in the *Herald* and *Bush* *never appeared* in the San Antonio paper. It was also learned that the scandal was only publicized in certain areas – every source of which could be traced to the *Zion Herald*. If the rumor went nationwide, it traveled by the grapevine.[32]

Without a doubt, it seemed that Voliva was making the best of the scandal, "leaving no stone unturned." Though no one could actually pinpoint Voliva as the instigator of the accusations, he had been known to spread rumors frequently about immorality against his chief rivals. In addition to Parham, Voliva had launched many verbal attacks on his associates in Zion, calling them "adulterers," and "immoral." Parham's associates attempted legal action with the U. S. postal authorities for "unlawful defamation," but they refused to act on the matter.[33]

Mrs. Parham felt their enemies must have had great faith in Parham's beliefs because, if this kind of onslaught had befallen a secular person, court action would have surely followed. But Parham never discussed the incident in public. He left the matter to the discretion of his followers, believing that those who were faithful would never believe the charges.[34] On his fortieth birthday Parham wrote:

**"I think the greatest sorrow of my life is the thought that my enemies, in seeking my destruction, have ruined and destroyed so many precious souls."[35]**

But sorrow and destruction make no difference to those who oppose the ministry of God. When Parham returned to preach in Zion nine years later, the Voliva followers fabricated posters and fliers that showed a signed confession of guilt in the crime of sodomy.[36]

## LIVING IN THE LONG-AWAITED DREAM

During the years that followed the scandal, Parham continued to evangelize throughout the nation. Many said his sermons were critical of Pentecostal Christians, others said he was never able to recover from Voliva's accusations. In 1913, he was met by a mob in Wichita who were armed with clubs and pitchforks. But a friend rescued Parham by secreting him away by a different route, and the meeting continued as scheduled. Hundreds were said to have repented in Wichita, and many were healed.

Though wounded by those he thought were his friends, Parham never backed away from the cities to which God had led him. He even returned to Los Angeles and held a tremendous meeting, in which thousands were converted, baptized in the Holy Spirit, healed and delivered. In the winter of 1924, Parham held meetings in Oregon and Washington. It was at one of these that Gordon Lindsay found salvation. Lindsay went on to do a great work for God, establishing the international Bible college, Christ For The Nations, located in Dallas, Texas.

*"I am living on the edge of the Glory Land these days and it's all so real on the other side of the curtain that I feel mightily tempted to cross over."*

Finally, in 1927, the lifetime dream of Charles F. Parham came true. Funds were collected by friends and Parham was able to visit Jerusalem. The trip was a great joy to Parham. He was thrilled as he walked through Galilee, Samaria, and Nazareth. It was here that Parham encountered his favorite passage of Scripture, Psalm 23. In Palestine the reality of the Shepherd and His sheep came alive to Parham, bringing great peace and comfort. When he returned to New York Harbor in April of 1928, he carried with him the slides of the land he loved. From then on, Parham's meetings consisted of the showing these slides that he called "The 23rd Psalm."

## "PEACE, PEACE LIKE A RIVER"

By August of 1928, Parham had grown tired and worn. He told friends that his work was nearly over. To one he wrote:

**"I am living on the edge of the Glory Land these days and it's all so real on the other side of the curtain that I feel mightily tempted to cross over."**[37]

After spending Christmas of 1929 with his family, Parham was scheduled to preach and show his Holy Land slides in Temple, Texas. His family was concerned with his departure because his health had deteriorated, but Parham was determined to go. Several days later, the family received word that Parham had collapsed during a meeting while showing his Holy Land slides. It is said that while on the floor, Parham regained consciousness and only spoke of wanting to continue the slideshow.

The Parham family set out for Temple to assess his condition. Once they arrived, a decision was made to cancel the meetings and bring Charles home to Kansas by train. Parham, so weak from a heart condition that he could barely speak, waited for his son Wilfred to return from ministry in California. While waiting for him, Parham refused all medication, saying that to do so "would fail his belief." He asked only for prayer.

His youngest son, Robert, quit his job with a department store to come home to fast and pray in the house where his father lay. After several days, he came to Parham's bedside to tell him he had also "surrendered his life to the call of ministry." Thrilled in the knowledge that two of his sons would carry on the work of the Gospel, Parham gained enough strength to say:

*Though several men sought to destroy him, they couldn't touch the pillar of strength that was built within his spirit.*

**"I can't boast of any good works I have done when I meet my Master face to face, but I can say, I have been faithful to the message He gave me, and lived a pure, clean life."**

Sarah said she would never forget her beloved's face, knowing "with a joy and a look of peaceful satisfaction that his prayer for many years was answered."[38]

His last day on earth, Charles Fox Parham was heard quoting, **"Peace, peace, like a river. That is what I have been thinking all day."** During the night, he sang part of the song, "Power in the Blood," then asked his family to finish the song for him. When they had finished, he asked them to, **"Sing it again."**[39]

The next day, on January 29, 1929, at fifty-six years of age, Charles F. Parham went to be with the Lord.

His funeral was attended by over twenty-five hundred people, who visited his grave in the newly fallen snow. A choir of fifty occupied the stage, along with a number of ministers from different parts of the nation. Offerings poured in from all over the country, enabling the family to purchase a granite pulpit for a grave memorial. On the memorial was carved "John 15:13," the last passage of Scripture that Parham had read as he had held his final meeting on this earth: "Greater love hath no man than this, that a man lay down his life for his friends."

## THE TRULY FAITHFUL

*I challenge you today to take account of your life, to count the cost, and to analyze where you stand in the area of faithfulness.*

Before Charles Parham died, his ministry contributed to over two million conversions, both directly and indirectly. His crowds often exceeded seven thousand people. And though some spoke in tongues long before Topeka, Kansas, it was Parham who pioneered the truth of tongues as the evidence of the baptism of the Holy Spirit.

His life exemplifies the harsh reality of the persecution and conflict that accompany God's revivalists. Though several men sought to destroy him, they couldn't touch the pillar of strength that was built within his spirit. He was never moved from his calling because of the slander waged against him. And when he left earth, he did so because he *willed* it. Although some will not accept Parham's ministry because of his support for the Ku Klux Klan,[40] most remember Parham for his sacrificial love, and primarily, for his faithfulness. The utmost cry of God is that we be found faithful to His plan. And for Charles Fox Parham, he could live no other plan than what God had prescribed. Faithfulness will always endure the conflict that comes to challenge it.

God has called us to an area of service. Whether we stand before the masses or before the few in our families, we, like Charles Parham, must prove our faithfulness too. But in our fast-paced, "feel good" generation, faithfulness seems to have been compromised. Still, no matter what generation we speak of, God's Word remains the same. First Corinthians 4:2 states that faithfulness is a *requirement* for believers.

*Believing* the Word of God and *trusting* God to fulfill His promises to you, in spite of life's conflicts, produce faithfulness. How wonderful it will be to hear the Lord say, "Well done, my good and *faithful* servant!" instead of Him saying only, "Well...?"

I challenge you today to take account of your life, to count the cost, and to analyze where you stand in the area of faithfulness. I challenge you to know what you believe in, and what you are against, then to stand true to those convictions. Demonstrate the "cutting edge" of truth to the nations of the earth and never allow yourself to be counted among the persecutors, the despisers or the envious. Whatever your call in life may be, always stand true on God's side. Be faithful.

## CHAPTER FOUR, CHARLES F. PARHAM
### References

1 Mrs. Charles Parham, *The Life of Charles F. Parham*, (Birmingham, AL: Commercial Printing Company, 1930), 59, 74.

2 Ibid., 1.

3 Ibid., 2.

4 Ibid.

5 Ibid., 5.

6 Ibid., 6-9.

7 Ibid., 11.

8 Ibid., 23.

9 Ibid., 33.

10 Ibid., 42.

11 Ibid., 46-47.

12 Ibid., 48.

13 Ibid., 57.

14 Ibid., 52-53.

15 Ibid., 54.

16 Ibid., 62.

17 Ibid., 76.

18 Ibid., 95-97.

19 Ibid., 100.

20 Ibid., 134.

21 Ibid., 136.

22 Ibid., 155-156.

23 Ibid., 158-159.

24 Ibid., 159.

25 Ibid., 161-162.

26 Ibid., 163-164, 168.

27 Ibid., 176.

28 Ibid., 182.

29 James R. Goff Jr., *Fields White Unto Harvest*, (Fayetteville and London: The University of Arkansas Press, 1988), 136, 223, Footnote 32.

30 Ibid., 136.

31 Ibid., 136-137, 224, Footnote 39.

[32] Ibid., 138-139, 224-225, Footnote 41.

[33] Ibid., 225-226, Footnote 44 & 45.

[34] Ibid., 141.

[35] Parham, *The Life of Charles F. Parham*, 201.

[36] Ibid., 260-261 and Goff, middle section, photos of posters.

[37] Parham, *The Life of Charles F. Parham*, 406.

[38] Ibid., 200, 410.

[39] Ibid., 413.

[40] Goff, *Fields White Unto Harvest*, 157.

# CHAPTER FIVE

# William J. Seymour

## *"The Catalyst of Pentecost"*

# "THE CATALYST OF PENTECOST"

**"A**s she looked at me through her gold-handled lorgnette, she said, 'Reverend, I believe in the baptism of the Holy Ghost and fire...but I don't appreciate the noise, the shouting.'

"'Sister, you are just like I am, I responded. There are many manifestations that I see among God's people that I don't appreciate myself, but, do you know, when the Spirit of the Lord comes upon me, I enjoy it.'

"Her small mouth pursed in mild disagreement, but I continued:

"'...Now, my little sister, if you want to go into the prayer room and pray to be baptized in the Holy Spirit, please go ahead. And when it happens, don't shout unless you feel like it. Just be yourself.'

"She nodded vigorously, 'Oh, indeed I will.'

"...I was busy in an office about seventy-five feet away and soon forgot that she was there. Suddenly,...I heard a penetrating outcry.

"Quickly I jerked open the door to look through the church and there came the little lady out of the prayer room as if she had been shot from a cannon. She began jumping, dancing, and shouting in the Lord. It was something to see this reserved, refined lady with the gold-handled lorgnette, dancing and swaying...crying out and singing intermittently in tongues and in English.

"I went out to meet her and smiling on the inside, commented, 'Sister, what you are doing doesn't appeal to me.'

"She made an undignified jump into the air and shouted, 'Maybe not, but it sure appeals to me!'"[1]

Serving as the "catalyst" of the "Pentecostal Movement" in the twentieth century, William J. Seymour turned a tiny Los Angeles horse stable on Azusa

Street into an international center of revival. Because the baptism of the Holy Spirit with the evidence of speaking in tongues was a major part of the meetings held there, Seymour became the leader of the first organized movement that promoted this experience. At Azusa, blacks, whites, Hispanics, and Europeans all met and worshiped together, crossing formerly impossible cultural lines. Although the success of the revival was short-lived, we still enjoy its fruits. Today, Azusa remains a common word within God's household.

> *At Azusa, blacks, whites, Hispanics, and Europeans all met and worshiped together, crossing formerly impossible cultural lines.*

The Azusa Street Mission produced some wild stories. Time was of little concern to these Pentecostal pioneers who would often pray all night for another's deliverance. They believed the Word of God and waited for its manifestation.

In every situation that arose, the seekers made a demand on the Word's authority. If insects tried to destroy someone's crops, believers at Azusa marched out to the field and declared the Word of God over their crops and the insects! In every recorded account, the insects stayed where they were told and didn't cross field borders. If they were destroying a neighbor's crops, they remained about twenty yards away from the believer's crops.

In another story a large group of firemen came rushing into the Azusa Street Mission during a service carrying fire hoses to extinguish a fire. But they never found one! Neighbors of the mission had seen a light that led them to believe the building was engulfed in flames, so they called the fire department. However, what they had actually seen, was the glory of God.

## EYE OF THE TIGER

Centerville, Louisiana, is a southern bayou town only a few miles from the Gulf of Mexico. On May 2 of 1870, a son was born in Centerville to Simon and Phyllis Seymour. They had only been freed from slavery a few years earlier, so William was born into a world of horrible racial violence. The Ku Klux Klan had been on the rampage for years. The Jim Crow Law had been established to prohibit all blacks from any social justices. And segregation was prevalent, even in the Church.

Once freed from slavery, Seymour's parents continued working on the plantation. As Seymour grew, he followed in their footsteps. Undaunted by the lack of formal education, he, like many others, taught himself primarily through reading the Bible.

Seymour found his identity in Jesus Christ, believing that the Lord was the only liberator of mankind. He was a sensitive, high-spirited youth, and hungry for the truth of God's Word. It is said he experienced divine visions, and that early in life began to look for the return of Jesus Christ.[2]

At the age of twenty-five, Seymour finally broke through the mental bondage of his inferiority complex. Then doing what few black men dared, he left the homelands of southern Louisiana and headed north to Indianapolis, Indiana.

According to the U.S. census of 1900, only 10 percent of the black race had ever left the South. But Seymour was determined, so he left. He was determined that man-made shackles would never hold him.

## SAINTS AND SMALLPOX

Unlike the rural South, Indianapolis was a thriving city that offered many opportunities. But many businesses still closed their doors to the black population, so Seymour could only find work as a hotel waiter.

Not long after his arrival, Seymour joined the Simpson Chapel Methodist Episcopal Church. This branch of Northern Methodists had a strong evangelistic outreach to all classes that appealed to Seymour. The church's example helped Seymour to further formulate his beliefs. To him it was becoming ever more evident that there was no class or color line in the redemption of Jesus Christ.

However, it wasn't long before the racial lines hardened in Indianapolis. So Seymour moved to Cincinnati, Ohio. There he continued to attend a Methodist church, but soon noticed that their doctrine was hardening as well. He was an avid follower of John Wesley. Wesley believed in strong prayer, holiness, divine healing, and that there should be no discrimination in Jesus Christ. But it seemed the Methodists were moving away from their original roots.

> **Seymour wrestled with his calling and was fearful to answer.**

In his search for a church, Seymour stumbled upon the Evening Light Saints, which would later become known as the Church of God Reformation Movement. The group didn't use musical instruments. They didn't wear rings or make-up. And they didn't dance or play cards. Even though it seemed like a religion of "nos," the group was extremely happy. They found joy in their faith in difficult times as well as good.[3]

Seymour was warmly received by the Saints. It was in this setting that he received the call to ministry. Seymour wrestled with his calling and was fearful

to answer. In the midst of his struggle, he contracted smallpox, which was usually fatal in that era. He survived three weeks of horrible suffering, but was left with blindness in his left eye and severe facial scarring.

Seymour felt his contraction of the disease was a result of refusing the call of God. So he immediately submitted to the plan of God and was ordained through the Evening Light Saints. Soon he began traveling as an itinerant evangelist and provided his own financial support. In those days, few ministers asked for offerings. And Seymour, like many in his circle, believed that God was his provider. He believed that if God called him, then God would support him.

## SPEAKING IN TONGUES...TODAY?

Seymour left Cincinnati and traveled to Texas, evangelizing along the way. When he arrived in Houston, he found family there, so he decided to make Houston his ministry base.

In the summer of 1905, Evangelist Charles F. Parham was holding crusades in Bryn Hall, which was located in downtown Houston. Each evening after the traffic had cleared, Parham and his helpers would march downtown in spectacular Holy Land clothing carrying their "Apostolic Faith Movement" banner. Newspapers wrote positively about Parham's meetings often giving them headlines.[4]

Houston was a city of cultural variety, so all races were drawn to Parham's meetings. A woman friend of Seymour's, Mrs. Lucy Farrow, attended Parham's meetings regularly, and had developed a pleasant relationship with the revivalist's family. Parham offered her the position of governess with his family if she would accompany them to Kansas where they lived. Farrow was the pastor of a small Holiness church, but her love for Parham's family and her spiritual hunger motivated her to go. Upon her acceptance, she asked Seymour if he would pastor the church in her absence. He agreed to do so until she returned two months later with the Parham family.

When Mrs. Farrow returned to Houston, she told Seymour about her wonderful spiritual encounters in the Parham home – including her experience of speaking in tongues. Seymour was very moved by her experience, but he questioned the doctrine. He would eventually accept it, though Seymour wouldn't speak in tongues for some time himself.[5] The Evening Light Saints didn't approve of Seymour's new theology. So, he left the group, still never having spoken in tongues. Then Charles Parham announced the opening of his Bible school in Houston that December and Mrs. Farrow vehemently insisted that Seymour attend. Moved by her fervency and his own growing interest, Seymour enrolled.

Parham's school in Houston was set up much like the one in Topeka, Kansas. It was a communal-type living arrangement in one house, where the students and their instructor spent days and nights together praying and studying the Word in an informal fashion. The students were not required to pay tuition, but did have to believe God for their own needs. Due to the culturally-accepted practice of the day, it is questionable if Seymour was allowed to stay overnight. Parham was moved by Seymour's hunger for the Word. And it is my belief, though very welcomed by Parham, Seymour was only a daytime student. Though Seymour did not embrace every doctrine that Parham taught, he did embrace the truth of Parham's doctrine concerning Pentecost. He soon developed his own theology from it.

## IN THE BEGINNING

After completing his studies at Parham's school, the events that led Seymour to Los Angeles started to quickly take place. In early 1906, Seymour began making plans to start a new Pentecostal church in which he could preach his new-found doctrine. Then he unexpectedly received a letter from Miss Neely Terry. Terry, who had been visiting relatives in Houston, had attended the church where Seymour pastored in place of Lucy Farrow. When Terry returned to California, she didn't forget Seymour's gentle and secure leadership. In the letter, Miss Terry asked Seymour to come to Los Angeles and pastor a congregation that had broken away from a Nazarene church. Believing the letter revealed his destiny, Seymour packed his bags and left for California in late January. Later he would write:

> **"It was the divine call that brought me from Houston, Texas, to Los Angeles. The Lord put it on the heart of one of the saints in Los Angeles to write me that she felt the Lord would have me come there, and I felt it was the leading of the Lord. The Lord provided the means and I came to take charge of a mission on Santa Fe Street."[6]**

## THE SPIRITUAL CONDITION OF THE CITY

In Los Angeles a spiritual hunger was stirring. There was a deep desire and longing for something to happen.

There was evidence of a spiritual revival even before Seymour arrived. Turn of the century evangelists had spread the fire of God throughout Southern California and many groups of people were praying and witnessing throughout the city door to door. In fact, the entire city was on the verge of a great spiritual happening as many Los Angeles congregations of Christians were earnestly seeking God.

In 1906, Los Angeles was a miniature picture of the world. Racial discrimination was rarely practiced, because every culture, from the Chinese to the Hispanic, flocked to the city.

One particular group, the First Baptist Church of Los Angeles, was waiting for the return of their pastor, Rev. Joseph Smale. He had been on a three-week trip to Wales to sit under the great Welsh evangelist, Evan Roberts. Smale was on fire for God and was hoping to bring the same revival that had visited Wales, home with him to Los Angeles.

Another evangelist and journalist, Frank Bartleman, shared a similar vision and joined with his church in prayer. Bartleman wrote Roberts for revival instructions. One response from Evan ended this way: "I pray God to hear your prayer, to keep your faith strong, and to save California." From these letters, Bartleman said he received the gift of faith for the revival to come. And he went on to believe that the prayers from Wales had much to do with God's outpouring in California, later saying that "The present worldwide revival was rocked in the cradle of little Wales."[7]

In Los Angeles, there was a small black group hungry for more of God, who had formed to worship. The leader of this new group was Sister Julia Hutchinson. She taught sanctification in a way that wasn't in agreement with her church's doctrine. Consequently, the pastor expelled the families involved with her teaching – who would eventually form a group with Seymour as pastor.

The group wasn't discouraged. They quickly banded together in the home of Mr. and Mrs. Richard Asbery, then grew so large that they were forced to rent a small mission hall on Santa Fe Street. Along with this growth came the desire for a change in leadership. The group felt a stranger to the Los Angeles area could be more effective, believing that he would command more respect among them. And Miss Terry, the Asbery's cousin, believed there could be only one man for the job. After praying about it, they all agreed to extend Seymour the invitation.

# BREAKING THE MESSAGE IN

Seymour arrived in Los Angeles where there was already a revival climate, citywide. It seemed to validate his sense of destiny. The large group assembled, eager to hear Seymour's first sermon as he expounded powerfully on the gospel of divine healing and the soon return of Christ. He then began his message from Acts 2:4 on speaking in other tongues. He taught that a person is not baptized in the Holy Spirit unless he or she speaks with other tongues. And he admitted that he had not yet received this manifestation. Nevertheless, he proclaimed it as God's Word.

Seymour was met with mixed reactions. While some agreed with him favorably, others denounced him fervently. A family by the name of Lee, invited him home for Sunday dinner. When returning with him to the mission that evening, they found that Sister Hutchinson had padlocked the doors. She was outraged and declared that she wouldn't permit such extreme teaching in her little mission on Santa Fe Street. And Seymour was denied access to his mission sleeping room.[8]

*When returning with him to the mission that evening, they found that Sister Hutchinson had padlocked the doors. She was outraged and declared that she wouldn't permit such extreme teaching in her little mission on Santa Fe Street.*

Now Seymour found himself with little money and no place to stay. So the Lees felt obligated to take him home, though they did have reservations. While staying with the Lees, Seymour remained behind the closed doors of his room in prayer and fasting. Then after many days, he invited the Lees to pray with him. They accepted his invitation, and began to feel different toward him. Soon other members of the mission began to hear of the prayer meetings at the Lee household. They began gathering with them and Seymour became known as a man of prayer.[9]

Soon Sister Hutchinson learned of those who were joining Seymour. So she arranged a meeting between Seymour and the Holiness clergy to determine the origin of the error. Seymour faced a large, difficult audience of Holiness preachers in his inquisition, but he clung to the Word. He read again from Acts 2:4 and explained that unless the Holiness preachers had the experience that took place in the Upper Room, they weren't baptized in the Holy Spirit. According to Seymour, their problem was with the Word of God, not with him.

One minister who had been against Seymour would later say: "The contention was all on our part. I have never met a man who had such control over his spirit. No amount of confusion and accusation seemed to disturb him. He would sit behind that packing case and smile at us until we were all condemned by our own activities."[10]

## 214 NORTH BONNIE BRAE STREET

The calming leadership of William Seymour was noticed by all. Following his investigation, the Asberys asked him to move into their home on North Bonnie Brae Street and to begin holding regular meetings there. Seymour accepted, and the small group began to meet in late February of 1906. Their meetings consisted of hours of prayer as they sought for the baptism of the Holy Spirit.

As the meetings grew Seymour asked for the assistance of his long-standing friend, Lucy Farrow. He explained to the group that Farrow had an extraordinary ability to present the baptism of the Holy Spirit, and so money was collected to bring her from Houston.

When Sister Farrow arrived, Seymour announced that the group would enter into a ten-day fast until they received the divine blessing of the baptism of the Holy Spirit. The group fasted and prayed through the weekend. Then on Monday, Mr. Lee called Seymour to his home to ask for the prayer of healing. Seymour anointed Lee with oil, prayed for him, and Lee was healed instantly. Then Lee asked Seymour to lay hands on him and pray for the baptism of the Holy Spirit. So Seymour laid hands on him again, and this time Lee broke out speaking loudly in other tongues! The two rejoiced ecstatically for the rest of the day, then walked together to the evening prayer meeting.

When they arrived at the Asbery home on Bonnie Brae Street, every room was packed with people. Many were already praying. Seymour took charge of the meeting, leading the group in songs, testimonies, and more prayer. Then, he began to tell the story of Mr. Lee's healing and his infilling of the Holy Spirit. As soon as Seymour finished, Lee raised his hands and began to speak in other tongues. The entire group dropped to their knees as they worshiped God and cried out for the baptism. Then, six or seven people lifted their voices and began to speak in another tongue. Jennie Evans Moore, who would later marry Seymour, fell to her knees from the piano bench as one of the first to speak in tongues.

Some people rushed outside to the front porch, prophesying and preaching. Others, while speaking in tongues, ran into the streets for all the neighborhood to hear. The Asbery's young daughter rushed into the living room to see what was happening, only to meet her frightened brother running the other way! Then Jennie Evans Moore returned to the piano and began singing with her beautiful voice – in up to six languages – all with interpretation. The meeting lasted until well past 10:00 P.M. when everyone left in great joy and thankfulness.[11]

For three days, they celebrated what they dubbed, "early Pentecost restored." The news spread quickly bringing crowds that filled the Asbery's yard and surrounded their home. Groups from every culture began to find their way to 214 North Bonnie Brae Street. Some would stand outside the windows hoping to hear someone pray in tongues. At times they heard great shouting. At times it was intensely quiet. Many fell "under the power" and lay on the floor – some for three to five hours.[12]

Unusual healings also took place. One person said:

> "The noise of the great outpouring of the Spirit drew me. I had been nothing but a 'walking drug store' all my life, with weak lungs and cancer. As they looked at me, they said, 'Child, God will heal you.' In those days of the great outpouring, when they said God would heal you, you were healed. For thirty-three years, I have never gone back to the doctors, thank God, nor any of that old medicine! The Lord saved me, baptized me with the Holy Ghost, healed me, and sent me on my way rejoicing."[13]

It is said that the Asbery's "front porch became the pulpit and the street the pews" as Seymour would address the people from this home. Eventually, the front porch collapsed because of the weight of the crowd, but it was quickly reinforced so the meetings could continue.

It was during the third night of these meetings that Seymour finally experienced his own encounter with the Holy Spirit. It was late on the night of April 12, 1906, after many had left the meeting, when Seymour himself was filled and began to speak in other tongues. He was kneeling beside a man who was helping him pray for a breakthrough, when at last he received. The long-awaited gift of the Holy Spirit had finally come to the man whose preaching had brought His freedom to so many others.

## 312 AZUSA STREET

Everyone knew another meeting place had to be found quickly. The Asbery home could no longer accommodate the crowds. So on April 14, 1906, Seymour and his elders set out to find the perfect place. They wandered around the city near their area, until they came upon a dead-end street that was about a half a mile long. It was there, in the industrial business section of Los Angeles, that Seymour found what had once been an old Methodist church. After its use by the Methodists, the building had been remodeled for a different purpose. It had been divided in half – the top section of which had been turned into apartments. But a fire had destroyed the floor, and the cathedral-shaped roof had been flattened and covered with tar.

> *The top floor was being used for storage. The bottom floor had been converted into a horse stable. The windows were broken and bare electric light bulbs hung from the ceiling. Seymour was offered the building for eight dollars a month.*

When Seymour acquired the building, the top floor was being used for storage. The bottom floor had been converted into a horse stable. The windows were broken and bare electric light bulbs hung from the ceiling. Seymour was offered the building for eight dollars a month.[14]

As the word got out, people came from everywhere to help restore the building. A. G. Osterburg, the pastor of the local Full Gospel Church, paid several men to help renovate the building. Volunteers swept the floors and whitewashed the walls. J. V. McNeil, a devout Catholic and owner of the largest lumber company in Los Angeles, donated lumber for the cause. Sawdust was placed on the floor, and planks were nailed to wooden barrels for use as pews. Two empty crates were nailed on top of each other to act as Seymour's pulpit.

It was in this humble, skid row-like setting that the new tenants of 312 Azusa Street prepared themselves for international revival.

## BEGINNING STAGES

April 18, 1906 marked the day in U.S. history of the great San Francisco earthquake. The next day, a lesser shock was felt in Los Angeles, causing many out of fear to repent of their sins. Hundreds of them fled to Azusa to hear the Gospel message and to experience the baptism in the Holy Spirit with the evidence of speaking in other tongues. Even the very wealthy came to this lower-class area to hear of God's power.

The seating arrangement at Azusa was very unique. Because there was no platform, Seymour sat on the same level with the rest of the congregation. And the benches were arranged so the participants faced one another. The meetings were spontaneous, so no one ever knew what would happen or who the speaker would be.

In the beginning stages of Azusa, all of the music was impromptu without the use of instruments or hymn books. The meetings began with someone singing a song or giving a testimony. Because there was no program, someone would finally arise, anointed to bring forth the message. The speaker could be any race, age, or gender. And everyone felt that God was responsible for the altar calls which could take place at any point of the meetings.

At Azusa Street, sermons were inspired in English or in tongues with interpretation. Sometimes the services ran continuously for ten to twelve hours. Sometimes they ran for several days and nights! Many said the congregation never tired because they were so energized by the Holy Spirit. Many could be seen after the services ended in the early morning hours congregating under the street lights talking about the Lord.

At Azusa, the services were so anointed that if anyone got up to speak from their intellectual understanding, the Spirit-filled believers would break out in wailing sobs. This has been illustrated well in a story about a woman called Mother Jones. One man arose to speak, apparently not being led by the Spirit. As he stood and preached, Mother Jones is said to have quietly hurried up to the platform, where she sat at the foot of the pulpit, then stared up at the fellow with

*William J. Seymour, 312 Azusa Street*

icy, foreboding eyes. Finally she said, "Can't you see that you aren't anointed to preach?" Because of this incident, Mother Jones quickly earned a reputation that discouraged any unanointed preacher from standing at the pulpit. It is said that all she had to do was stand up, and the unanointed preacher would run from the pulpit!

Soon, all classes of people began attending the Azusa Street meetings. In his book, *Azusa Street*, Frank Bartleman wrote:

> "Many were curious and unbelieving, but others were hungry for God. Outside persecution never hurt the work. We had to fear from the working of evil spirits within. Even spiritualists and hypnotists came to investigate, and to try their influence. Then all the religious sore-heads and crooks came, seeking a place in the work. But this is always the danger to every new work. They have no place elsewhere. This condition cast a fear over many which was hard to overcome. It hindered the Spirit much. Many were afraid to seek God, for fear the devil might get them."[15]

Bartleman also wrote:

> "We found early in the 'Azusa' work that when we attempted to steady the Ark, the Lord stopped working. We dared not call the attention of the people too much to the working of the evil. Fear would follow. We could only pray. Then God gave the victory. There was a presence of God with us, through prayer, we could depend on. The leaders had limited experience, and the wonder is the work survived at all against its powerful adversaries."[16]

I believe this statement of Bartleman may be one of the main reasons that Seymour has been severely criticized as a leader. God was looking for a willing vessel – and He found it in Seymour. God is not looking for those who brag of their status and experience. However, in spiritual terms, Seymour's *limited* experience may have been the cause of his difficulties. I agree that leadership should expound strongly on the truth instead of focusing on that which is false. Deceit can't stand against the authority, strength, and wisdom of prayerful, godly leadership. I'm glad they depended on prayer. Prayer will see you through. But God also gives His leadership a voice. That voice, by the strength of the Holy Spirit, will know how to separate that which is of value from the counterfeit that will tarnish. Strong, godly leadership can separate the gold from the brass.

But despite some spiritual confusion, Azusa began operating day and night. The entire building had been organized for full use. Great emphasis had been placed on the blood of Jesus, inspiring the group to a higher standard of living. And divine love began to manifest, allowing no unkind words to be spoken of another. The people were careful to make sure that the Spirit of God wouldn't be grieved. Both the rich, educated people and the poor, unlearned people sat as one in the sawdust and makeshift barrel pews.

## PACKING THE STREETS, FALLING LIKE TREES

One man at Azusa said, "I would have rather lived six months at that time than fifty years of ordinary life. I have stopped more than once within two blocks of the place and prayed for strength before I dared go on. The presence of the Lord was so real."[17]

It was said that the power of God could be felt at Azusa, even outside of the building. Scores of people were seen dropping into a prostrate position in the streets before they ever reached the mission. Then many would rise, speaking in tongues without any assistance from those inside.[18]

By summer, crowds had reached staggering numbers, often into the thousands. The scene had become an international gathering. One account states that, "Every day trains unloaded numbers of visitors who came from all over the continent. News accounts of the meeting spread over the nation in both the secular and religious press."[19]

> *It was said that the power of God could be felt at Azusa, even outside of the building. Scores of people were seen dropping into a prostrate position in the streets before they ever reached the mission.*

Inexperience may have been prevalent at the beginning, but seasoned veterans of ministry were now arriving to help support Seymour's work. Most came from the Holiness ranks, or were missionaries returning from the nations. The result of this seasoned mixture of people was a wonderful new host of missionaries who were dispatched around the world. Many, newly baptized in the Holy Spirit, would feel a call to a certain nation. So men and women were now departing for Scandinavia, China, India, Egypt, Ireland, and various other nations. Even Sister Hutchinson, who initially locked Seymour out of her mission, came to Azusa, received the baptism of the Holy Spirit, and left for Africa.[20]

Owen Adams of California traveled to Canada from Azusa where he met Robert Semple, Aimee Semple McPherson's first husband. When Adams met

*William J. Seymour and wife, Jennie Evans Seymour*

*William J. Seymour*

*Seymour with F. F. Bosworth (middle), and John G. Lake (bottom right)*

*Daddy Seymour*

*Apostolic Faith Mission, 312 Azusa Street, Los Angeles, California*

Semple, he told him of the miraculous events at Azusa and of his experience of speaking in tongues. Semple then excitedly told his new bride, Aimee, before they went on to China, where Robert Semple would die. But Adam's news had birthed a burning curiosity in the heart of young Aimee. When she returned to America, she would make Los Angeles her ministry base from where her phenomenal ministry would rise.[21]

Though there was much excitement swirling around about the baptism of the Holy Spirit at Azusa, many misunderstood the ultimate purpose of speaking in other tongues. Many felt it was only a divine language for the nation to which they were sent.[22]

At this time, everyone seemed to love William Seymour. When the Spirit moved, he was known to keep his head inside of the top box-crate that sat in front of him, bowed in prayer. He never asked for a salary, so he would very often be seen "walking through the crowds with five and ten dollar bills sticking out of his hip pockets which people had crammed there unnoticed by him."[23]

John G. Lake visited the Azusa street meetings. In his book, *Adventures With God*, he would later write of Seymour: "He had the funniest vocabulary. **But I want to tell you, there were doctors, lawyers, and professors, listening to the marvelous things coming from his lips. It was not what he said in words, it was what he said from his spirit to my heart that showed me he had more of God in his life than any man I had ever met up to that time. It was God in him that attracted the people."[24]**

Missionaries were called from their nations, to come and witness the spiritual phenomena in Los Angeles. Many came, then carried Azusa Street's Pentecostal message around the world. No one could possibly record all the miracles that occurred there.

The members of Azusa all carried tiny bottles of oil wherever they went. They would knock on doors to witness and pray for the sick throughout Los Angeles. They stood on street corners, singing and preaching, and worked as volunteers to clothe the poor and feed the hungry. It was exciting and incredible.

In September of 1906, due to popular demand, Seymour began a publication entitled, *The Apostolic Faith*. Within a few months, the mailing list grew to over twenty thousand names. By the next year, it had more than doubled. In this publication, Seymour announced his intention to restore "the faith once delivered" by old-time preaching, camp meetings, revivals, missions, street, and prison work.[25]

In the first publication, Seymour wrote, "**...multitudes have come. God makes no difference in nationality."[26]**

Then, a few months later, he wrote:

"The meeting has been a melting time. The people are all melted together...made one lump, one bread, all one body in Christ Jesus. There is no Jew or Gentile, bond or free, in the Azusa Mission. No instrument that God can use is rejected on account of color or dress or lack of education. This is why God has built up the work.... The sweetest thing is the loving harmony."[27]

Obviously, these were revolutionary words in a time of such racial division.

## BEGINNINGS OF DECLINE

Persecution outside of Azusa was expected, but it finally began within. Early one autumn morning, some members arrived at the mission to see the words, "Apostolic Faith Mission" written across the top of the building, and started accusing the mission of evolving into just another denomination. This was the name of Seymour's early mentor's movement so the Azusa Mission was now being perceived as a loose offshoot of Charles Parham's ministry. And many feared the mission was becoming just another in Parham's network of churches and Bible schools. One who was there wrote, "From that time, the trouble and division began. It was no longer a free Spirit for all as it had been. The work had become one more rival party and body, along with the other churches and sects of the city...the church is an organism, not a human organization."[28]

By now, Azusa outreach centers had been planted in Seattle and Portland under the direction of a woman by the name of Florence Crawford. And the Los Angeles headquarters was attempting to draw the entire West Coast revival outlets into their organization, but failed. So the revival itself was slowly setting itself up for ultimate failure.

*Up to this point, it had primarily been taught that tongues were for foreign missions. They believed that if a person were to go to the mission field, they would be gifted to preach in the nation's language. Many Azusa missionaries were greatly disappointed when they discovered this was not the rule.*

## "TARRYING" AND TONGUES

The new body of believers also had a misconception of the "tarrying" concept. They would simply wait for hours for the Spirit to come, and restlessness began to surface when they felt many were abusing this time. What they didn't realize was that the Holy Spirit had already come. He was there!

Then there was the confusion surrounding their understanding of speaking in other tongues. Up to this point, it had primarily been taught that tongues were for foreign missions. They believed that if a person were to go to the mission field, they would be gifted to preach in the nation's language. Many Azusa missionaries were greatly disappointed when they discovered this was not the rule. Though it is a biblical and historical fact that tongues will manifest for that purpose, this is not their only use! It would be later, during the growth of the Pentecostal Movement, that tongues would be understood as a prayer language as well. But at Azusa Street, the experience of speaking in tongues was in its "first diaper"!

Azusa members also believed that a person only needed to speak in tongues once to be filled with the Holy Spirit. To the early Azusa members, speaking in other tongues was a sovereign move of God that meant waiting for God to come upon them.

Along with these misunderstandings, accusations of fleshly manifestations that people called the moving of the Holy Spirit began circulating. With this spiritual understanding being so new, can you imagine how it must have been to lead it? It was here that Seymour wrote to Charles Parham, and asked him to come to Azusa to hold a general revival.

## FANATICS, FAKES, AND FRACTION

Though Seymour didn't fully agree with all of Parham's theology, I believe he respected and trusted Parham's leadership experience. Perhaps he felt Parham could present another view and ignite a fresh move of God.

It is said that many others had written letters to Parham begging him to come and determine which manifestations at Azusa were counterfeit and which were real. While there is not documentation of these letters, Mrs. Pauline Parham has claimed that some are in her collections.[29] We do have one letter written by Seymour to Parham that states, "...**we are expecting a general one [revival] to start again when you come, that these little revivals will all come together and make one great union revival.**"[30]

It is true that there were many divisions within the Los Angeles revival. But by previous examples of Seymour's character, I believe he wanted Parham to unite the city instead of discipline it. And it is certain that Parham wouldn't have come to Azusa without an invitation.

When Parham arrived, Seymour introduced him as the "Father in this Gospel of the kingdom.[31]" I believe Seymour was sincere. He needed a spiritual father to help him lead this great movement. But whatever he had expected from Parham, things didn't go as Seymour had planned. After Parham's sermons and private exhortations, Seymour padlocked the mission's door to keep Parham out.

What did Parham say to Seymour? What could have caused him to lock Parham out of Azusa? While it is true that Parham's background in education, leadership, and experience differed from Seymour, their views on the baptism of the Holy Spirit seemed to be the same. Or were they?

Parham sat in the service while looking on in horror at the manifestations around him. In Parham's services, a certain liberality was allowed, but nothing that bordered on fanaticism. Some of Parham's own Bible school students even felt he was too strict in his definition of "fanaticism." And at Azusa, besides the shouting and dancing, the people jerked and shook. It was a highly emotional atmosphere, and there were many genuine, Spirit-filled expressions along with the false. Because of the many cultures represented, Seymour believed that each person should allow their own emotional experience, based on how each individual understood the moving of the Spirit, whether it was right or wrong.

Seymour's theology was to allow the Holy Spirit to do whatever he wanted. But only a few knew enough about the movings of the Spirit to lead the people in it. Seymour felt that if a culture was forced into a certain mode or expression, the Holy Spirit wouldn't manifest Himself among them. I believe Seymour was spiritually sensitive in his leadership, and followed this to the best of his ability. There is a fine line between wounding the human spirit and offending the Holy Spirit.

There is no known written account from Seymour regarding certain hypnotism accounts. But there are from Parham. Here is his account:

> "I hurried to Los Angeles, and to my utter surprise and astonishment I found conditions even worse than I had anticipated...manifestations of the flesh, spiritualistic controls, saw people practicing hypnotism at the altar over candidates seeking baptism, though many were receiving the real baptism of the Holy Ghost.
>
> "After preaching two or three times, I was informed by two of the elders that I was not wanted in that place. With workers from Texas, we opened a great revival in the W.C.T.U. Building in Los Angeles. Great numbers were saved, marvelous healings took place,

and between two and three hundred who had been possessed of awful fits and spasms and controls in the Azusa Street work were delivered, and received the real Pentecost teachings and spake with other tongues.

"In speaking of different phases of fanaticism that have been obtained here, that I do so with all lovingkindness and at the same time with all fairness and firmness. Let me speak plainly with regard to the work as I have found it here. I found hypnotic influences, familiar-spirit influences, spiritualistic influences, mesmeric influences, and all kinds of spells, spasms, falling in trances, etc.

"A word about the baptism of the Holy Ghost. The speaking in tongues is never brought about by any of the above practices/influences. No such thing is known among our workers as the suggestion of certain words and sounds, the working of the chin, or the massage of the throat. There are many in Los Angeles who sing, pray and talk wonderfully in other tongues, as the Spirit gives utterance, and there is jabbering here that is not tongues at all. The Holy Ghost does nothing that is unnatural or unseemingly, and any strained exertion of body, mind or voice is not the work of the Holy Spirit, but of some familiar spirit, or other influence. The Holy Ghost never leads us beyond the point of self-control or the control of others, while familiar spirits or fanaticism lead us both beyond self-control and the power to help others."[32]

Perhaps Parham's perception was right, still, the results may have been different if Parham had been more fatherly than dictatorial. Seymour never changed his theology and neither did Parham. Seymour wouldn't mention the rivalry for some two months. And even when he finally did, his account was discreet, avoiding any direct criticism. Seymour wrote:

**"Some are asking if Dr. Charles F. Parham is the leader of this movement. We can answer, no, he is not the leader of this movement of Azusa Mission. We thought of having him to be our leader and so stated in our paper, before waiting on the Lord. We can be rather hasty, especially when we are very young in the power of the Holy Spirit. We are just like a baby — full of love — and were willing to accept anyone that had the baptism with the Holy Spirit as**

our leader. But the Lord commenced settling us down, and we saw that the Lord should be our leader. So we honor Jesus as the Great Shepherd of the sheep. He is our model."[33]

So in attempting to uphold his doctrine of unity, Seymour remained true to his teachings by not allowing an unkind word to be spoken against any of his accusers.

## THE SANCTIFICATION SLUR

Though Seymour followed John Wesley, he didn't follow his teachings on sanctification. Seymour believed one could lose their salvation if they reacted in the flesh. He taught that sanctification, or sinless perfection, was a separate work of grace aside from salvation. Once you were sanctified, Seymour believed, you acted sanctified all the time. But if you sinned, you lost it.

Can you imagine the trouble and accusations that kind of teaching caused within Azusa? Many overzealous believers got caught up in pointing fingers and judging one another. Their self-righteous behavior resulted in clashes, splits, and controversies. In fact, this is one of the main reasons Seymour never reacted in the flesh to any persecution that came against him. According to his theology, this was necessary to keep his salvation. He said:

> "If you get angry, or speak evil, or backbite, I care not how many tongues you may have, you have not the baptism with the Holy Spirit. You have lost your salvation."[34]

*Seymour believed one could lose their salvation if they reacted in the flesh. He taught that sanctification, or sinless perfection, was a separate work of grace aside from salvation. Once you were sanctified, Seymour believed, you acted sanctified all the time. But if you sinned, you lost it.*

Seymour would padlock an opposing minister, but he would never speak out against him!

## LOVE AND BETRAYAL

In spite of the many accusations, mistakes, and persecutions, Seymour remained faithful in his purpose for revival. It seemed he trusted and believed the best of almost everyone. True to his gentle, almost naive nature, he would later write:

> **"You cannot win people by preaching against their church or pastor...if you get to preaching against churches, you will find that sweet Spirit of Christ...is lacking and a harsh judging spirit takes place. The churches are not to be blamed for divisions. People were hunting for light. They built up denominations because they did not know a better way. When people run out of the love of God, they get to preaching dress, and meats, and doctrines of men and preaching against churches. All these denominations are our brethren.... So let us seek peace and not confusion.... The moment we feel we have all the truth or more than anyone else, we will drop."**[35]

The next spring, Seymour had to decide whether he would purchase Azusa or move to another location. So he presented the option to the congregation and they agreed to make an immediate payment of $4,000 toward the $15,000 needed. Within a year, the remaining balance was paid, far ahead of schedule. By this time, reports of miracles and newly-founded missions poured into Los Angeles from all over the world. Encouraged, Seymour commented, **"We are on the verge of the greatest miracle the world has ever seen."**[36]

During this time, Seymour's thoughts turned to marriage. Jennie Evans Moore, a faithful member of his ministry in Los Angeles, became his wife. She was known for her beauty, musical talents, and spiritual sensitivity. She was a very gentle woman, and was always faithful to stand beside Seymour. It was Jennie who felt the Lord would have them marry, and Seymour agreed. So the couple married on May 13, 1908. After the ceremony, William and Jennie moved into a modest apartment upstairs in the Azusa Mission.

But the news of their marriage angered a small, yet very influential group at the Mission. One of the main antagonists was Clara Lum, the mission's secretary responsible for the newspaper's publication. After learning of Seymour's marriage, she abruptly decided that it was time to leave the mission.

A few believers at Azusa had some very odd ideas about marriage. Lum's group believed marriage in the last days to be a disgrace because of the soon return of Christ and severely denounced Seymour for his decision.

It may have been that Clara Lum was secretly in love with Seymour, and left because of her jealousy. Whatever the reason, she relocated to Portland, Oregon, to join the mission headed by a former Azusa associate, Florence Crawford. And when she did, she took the entire national and international mailing lists with her.

This unthinkable action crippled Seymour's worldwide publication outreach. His entire national and international lists of over fifty thousand names had been stolen, leaving him with only their Los Angeles list. Then when the May, 1908, *Apostolic Faith* was sent out, the cover looked the same, but inside was a column announcing its new address in Portland for contributions and mail. The thousands who eagerly read and sent contributions to the newspaper now started sending them to Portland without questioning the change. By the June issue, no article by Seymour appeared at all. Finally, by midsummer of 1908, all references to Los Angeles were omitted entirely. When it became clear that Lum wouldn't be returning, the Seymours traveled to Portland to confront Lum and ask for the lists. But the lists were never returned. Without this vital information, it was impossible for Seymour to continue the publication, and ended a dramatic era of Azusa.

## THE LAST DIVISION: MAN OR GOD?

Throughout 1909 and 1910, Seymour continued his ministry at Azusa, though the number of people decreased dramatically due to lack of influence and funds. So he left two young men in charge at the mission and departed for Chicago on a cross-country preaching tour. In early 1911 William H. Durham held meetings at Azusa in his place.

Durham's dramatic preaching caused hundreds to flock again to the mission. Many of the old Azusa workers, from various parts of the world, even returned to the mission. They called it "the second shower of the Latter Rain," as the fire began to fall at Azusa once again. In one service, over five hundred people had to be turned away. So between the services, the people wouldn't leave their seats for fear of losing them.[37]

The last conflict at Azusa took place between Seymour and Durham. The two differed greatly in their theology. Durham preached adamantly, and soundly, that people couldn't lose their salvation even if they sinned in the flesh. Salvation was by faith with works involved, not by works alone. Durham preached the needed balance between law and grace that the Pentecostal Movement desperately needed, because the "works" doctrine had led to many divisions.[38] His teaching felt like a cool rain on those who heard. It literally brought the people in droves!

Alarmed by Durham's large following and doctrinal differences, the elders of Azusa contacted Seymour. He returned immediately to Los Angeles for a conference. But Seymour and Durham couldn't come to an agreement in their doctrine. So in May, Seymour used the padlock again, locking Durham out of the mission![39]

Unshaken by this action, Durham and his workers secured a large, two-story building that seated more than one thousand people. The upstairs served as a prayer room, which was open day and night. The crowds from Azusa followed Durham. Thousands were saved, baptized, and healed while the old Azusa Mission became virtually deserted.

> **The crowds from Azusa followed Durham. Thousands were saved, baptized, and healed while the old Azusa Mission became virtually deserted.**

## "TIRED AND WORN"

But the old Azusa Mission remained open to anyone who would come. Seymour remained its leader and kept his doctrine the same, though no one seemed interested in attending. He changed Azusa's meeting schedule to one all-day service to be held on Sunday. And he regularly attempted to increase the meetings, but the interest was not there. In the end, only twenty people remained. And they were mainly those from the original Azusa group. At times, visitors came from the previous "glory days," and of course Seymour was elated in welcoming them. But he spent more and more time reading and reflecting.

In 1921, William Seymour made his last ministry campaign across America. When he returned to Los Angeles in 1922, people began to notice that he looked very weary. He attended many ministry conventions, but was never publicly recognized from the platform.

Finally on September 28, 1922, while at the mission, Seymour suffered a sudden attack of severe pain in his chest. One of the workers ran for the doctor who was only blocks away. Upon examination, Seymour was told to rest. Then at 5:00 P.M. that same afternoon, while dictating a letter, another chest pain clinched him. He struggled for breath, then went to be with the Lord at the age of fifty-two. The cause of his death was officially cited as heart failure.

The revivalist was buried in a simple redwood casket at Evergreen Cemetery in Los Angeles. He was appropriately laid to rest amid the graves of others from many nations and continents. The words on his tombstone simply read, "Our Pastor." Sadly, only two hundred people attended William Seymour's funeral, but they gave many testimonies of God's greatness through this front-line General's ministry.

## SHADOWS AND WOLVES

Following the years after Seymour's death, Mrs. Seymour carried on as pastor of the Azusa Street Mission. Everything continued smoothly for eight years. Then more problems arose in 1931. Through a series of legal battles waged by someone trying to take over the Mission, city officials became annoyed with the group and declared the property a fire hazard. Later that year it was demolished, but not before it was offered to a Pentecostal denomination who replied, "We are not interested in relics."[40] Today only a street sign stands over the property which is now nothing more than a vacant lot.

Five years later, Mrs. Seymour was admitted to the county hospital for terminal care. Jennie died of heart failure and joined her husband in heaven on July 2, 1936.

## THE LEGACY OF POWER

Though the legacy and ministry of William J. Seymour seems heartbreaking, the results of his efforts between 1906 and 1909 produced and exploded the Pentecostal Movement around the world. Today, many denominations attribute their founding to the participants of Azusa. Most of the early Assembly of God leaders came out of Azusa. Demos Shakarian, founder of the Full Gospel Businessmen's Fellowship, said his grandfather was an original Azusa member. The evangelistic efforts of the Valdez family, the Garr family, Dr. Charles Price, and countless others are also linked to this revival.

*William Seymour's Pentecostal ministry increased public awareness to such a degree that it not only turned around a major U.S. city, it also spread throughout the world at an incredible pace.*

Probably everyone in the Pentecostal Movement today can attribute their roots, in some way, to Azusa. Regardless of all the controversy and Azusa's peculiar doctrines, whenever Azusa is mentioned, most immediately think of the power of the Holy Spirit that was poured on their ranks.

## GOD IS NOT A RACIST

Some have tried to make the Azusa Street Revival and the ministry of Seymour a racial issue. Unfortunately, sometimes a pure move of God gets hidden under racial overtones. Perhaps this is one of the main reasons Azusa lasted for only three short years. God won't allow His glory to fall prey to the arguments of men. If that should happen, He leaves – end of discussion.

Some who seem racially influenced get upset that Seymour is called the "catalyst" of Pentecost instead of the "father" of it. According to Webster's Dictionary, a "catalyst" is something that "precipitates a process or event, and increases the rate at which a reaction takes place." That is exactly what Seymour did. William Seymour's Pentecostal ministry increased public awareness to such a degree that it not only turned around a major U.S. city, it also spread throughout the world at an incredible pace. It seems that every continent was touched in some way by the revival at Azusa.

As was mentioned earlier, racial issues were only a small part of the *many* interferences that visited Azusa. I believe a great error is made when this revival is looked upon as primarily a black and white issue. No particular race can claim the patent on a move of God. God has *never* worked according to the color of man; He operates through the heart of man.

As we continue to explore the great Generals of our past and determine to learn from their successes, don't allow yourself to be counted among their failures. Refuse to listen to the voices of yesterday and today who only see appearances. Rather, follow those who press into God's Spirit. Let us go on to maturity and fight for the prize rather than personal glory.

Only eternity will fully reveal the fruit of William J. Seymour's ministry. One thing is clear, he was an able stick of dynamite who God could use to send the explosions of Pentecostal revival around the world. And he did.

## CHAPTER FIVE , WILLIAM J. SEYMOUR
### References

1 A. C. Valdez Sr., *Fire on Azusa Street* (Costa Mesa, CA: Gift Publications, 1980), 87-89.

2 Emma Cotton, *Personal Reminiscences* (Los Angeles, CA: West Coast Publishers, 1930), 2, quoted in "Inside Story of the Outpouring of the Holy Spirit, Azusa Street, April 1906," published in *Message of the Apostolic Faith*, April 1939, Vol. 1, 1-3.

3 James S. Tinney, *In The Tradition of William J. Seymour* 13, quoted from "Father of Modern-Day Pentecostalism," in *Journal of the Interdenominational Theological Center*, 4 (Fall 1976), 34-44, and taken from Dr. Duane Miller, *Autobiography*.

4 Mrs. Charles Parham, *The Life of Charles F. Parham* (Birmingham: Commercial Printing Co., 1930), 112-123.

5 Ibid., Tinney, *In The Tradition of William J. Seymour*, 14.

6 Ibid., 15

7 Frank Bartleman, *Azusa Street* (Plainfield, NJ: Logos International, 1980), 33, 90.

8 C. W. Shumway, "A Critical Study of the Gift of Tongues," A. B. dissertation, University of California, July 1914, 173, and "A Critical History of Glossolalia," Ph.D. thesis, Boston University, 1919.

9 Cotton, *Personal Reminiscences,* 2.

10 C. M. McGowan, *Another Echo From Azusa* (Covina, CA: Oak View Christian Home), 3.

11 Thomas Nickel, *Azusa Street Outpouring* (Hanford, CA: Great Commission International, 1956, 1979, 1986), 5, and Shumway, *A Critical Study Of The Gift Of Tongues*, 175.

12 Shumway, *A Critical Study of the Gift of Tongues*, 175-176, and Cotton, *Personal Reminiscences*, 2.

13 Cotton, *Personal Reminiscences,* 3.

14 Shumway, *A Critical Study of the Gift of Tongues,* 175-176.

15 Bartleman, *Azusa Street*, 48.

16 Ibid.

17 Ibid., 59-60.

18 Tinney, *In the Tradition of William J. Seymour,* 17.

19 Ibid.

20 Nickel, *Azusa Street Outpouring*, 18.

21 Ibid.

22 Shumway, *A Critical Study of the Gift of Tongues*, 44-45

22 Tinney, *In the Tradition of William J. Seymour*, 18.

24 John G. Lake, *Adventures in God*, (Tulsa, OK: Harrison House, Inc., 1981), 18-19.

25 Ibid., 18.

26 *Apostolic Faith,* September 1906.

27 Ibid., November and December 1906.

28 Bartleman, *Azusa Street*, 68-69.

29 Interview with Mrs. Pauline Parham.

30 Parham, *The Life of Charles F. Parham*, 154.

31 Ibid., 163.

32 Ibid., 163-170.

33 *Apostolic Faith*, December 1906.

34 Ibid., June 1907.

35 Ibid., January 1907.

36 Ibid., October 1907 - January 1908.

37 Bartleman, *Azusa Street*, 150.

38 Ibid., 150-151, and Valdez, *Fire on Azusa,* 26.

39 Bartleman, *Azusa Street*, 151.

40 Tinney, *In the Tradition of William J. Seymour*, 19.

# John G. Lake

*"A Man of Healing"*

# "A MAN OF HEALING"

**"I** said to them [scientists], 'Gentlemen, I want you to see one more thing. Go down in your hospital and bring back a man who has inflammation in the bone. Take your instrument and attach it to his leg. Leave enough space to get my hand on his leg. You can attach it to both sides.'

"When the instrument was ready, I put my hand on the man's shin and prayed like Mother Etter prays: no strange prayer, but the cry of my heart to God. I said, 'God, kill the devilish disease by Your power. Let the Spirit move in him; let it live in him.'

"Then I asked, 'Gentlemen, what is taking place?'

"They replied, 'Every cell is responding.' "[1]

If there was ever a man who walked in the revelation of "God in man," it was John G. Lake. A man of purpose, vision, strength, and character, his one goal in life was to bring the fullness of God to every person.

He often said that the secret of heaven's power was not in the *doing*, but in the *being*. He believed that Spirit-filled Christians should *enjoy the same type of ministry Jesus did* while living on earth, and that this reality could only be accomplished by seeing themselves as God saw them.

## THE SHADOW OF DEATH

John Graham Lake lived his life and fulfilled his ministry in the earth with this type of spiritual understanding.

He was born March 18, 1870, in Ontario, Canada. One of sixteen children, he moved with his family to Sault Sainte Marie, Michigan, while still a young boy.

Lake first heard the Gospel preached at a Salvation Army meeting when he was sixteen, and soon after, surrendered his life to the Lord. Though he had lived a morally pure life, his heart was in turmoil until he asked the Lord to save him. Speaking of his encounter Lake would later write:

"I made my surrender to Him. The light of heaven broke into my soul, and I arose from my knees a son of God, and I knew it."[2]

Lake's parents were strong, vigorous people who were blessed with wonderful health. But a spirit of infirmity and death had gripped the rest of their family. Eight family members – four brothers and four sisters – died from illness. **"For 32 years some member of our famiy was an invalid,"** Lake wrote. **"During this period our home was never without the shadow of sickness."** His boyhood was filled with memories of "sickness, doctors, nurses, hospitals, hearses, funerals, graveyards and tombstones; a sorrowing household; a broken-hearted mother and a grief-stricken father, struggling to forget the sorrows of the past in order to assist the living members of the family who needed their love and care."[3]

## WRONG "SCIENCE" – RIGHT ATTITUDE

As a youth, Lake was very interested in the art of science and physics. He enjoyed chemistry and loved to experiment with scientific instruments and equipment. He even took a course in medicine, but later dropped his medical pursuit.

Lake was meticulous in his research both in science and in spiritual matters. He tirelessly investigated the Bible with an eye to not only understand it, but to also prove its accuracy in everyday life. As a result, Lake walked, talked, and breathed in the flow of God's resurrection life.

> *"My boyhood was filled with memories of sickness, doctors, nurses, hospitals, hearses, funerals, graveyards and tombstones...."*

In 1890 when Lake was twenty years old, a Christian farmer taught him about sanctification. The revelation pierced his heart and was solemnly regarded as the crowning work of God in his life. Of this new revelation, Lake said:

**"I shall never cease to praise God that He revealed to me the depth...of the power of the blood of Jesus. A beautiful anointing of the Spirit was on my life."[4]**

One year later, in 1891, Lake moved to Chicago, and was admitted to the Methodist school of ministry. In October of that year he was appointed to a church in Peshtigo, Wisconsin, but he declined the pastorate. He also decided to leave the Methodist school and moved to Harvey, Illinois, where he founded *The Harvey Citizen*, a local newspaper. While living in Harvey, he would meet his future wife, Jennie Stevens of Newberry, Michigan.

## THE GIFT OF "JENNIE"

Jennie was perfect for John Lake. She possessed a wonderful sense of humor, keen judgment, a strong faith in God, and a deep spiritual sensitivity.

The two loved one another dearly and were married February 5, 1893, in Millington, Illinois. God blessed the couple with a marvelous unity in the Spirit, and seven children.

One of Jennie's most important ministries to her husband was prayer and intercession. There were many times throughout the course of their marriage that either of them would be spiritually prompted when the other was experiencing trouble. Lake valued dearly the advice and support of his wife.

But two short years into the Lake's wonderful marriage, sickness and disease crept into their home. Jennie was diagnosed with tuberculosis and heart disease. Her irregular heartbeat would cause her to lapse into unconsciousness, and sometimes Lake would find her unconscious on the floor, or lying in bed.

> *Now Lake was faced with the crises of his life. Where was God's power now? His entire family had been afflicted with illness.*

To combat this she was given increasingly stronger doses of stimulants in an effort to control her heart rhythm, and was eventually forced to use nitroglycerine tablets. For all practical purposes, all of this made her a virtual invalid.

Finally, upon doctors' recommendations, Lake moved his young family back to Sault Saint Marie, Michigan, where he entered into the real estate business. But Jennie's condition continued to worsen until 1898 when the doctors told him there was nothing more that could be done for her.

## LET'S GET RADICAL!

Now Lake was faced with the crises of his life. Where was God's power now? His entire family had been afflicted with illness. His brother had been an invalid due to internal bleeding for twenty-two years. His thirty-four-year-old sister had breast cancer. Another sister was once dying from blood disease. And now the person closest to his heart, Jennie, was close to death.

But Lake had experienced God's healing power before. He had been afflicted with rheumatism in younger years. When the leg distorting pain of his malady finally brought him to a breaking point, he traveled to John Alexander Dowie's Healing Home in Chicago. While there, an older man laid hands on him, the power of God came upon him, and his legs straightened out instantly.

The rest of Lake's terminally afflicted family members had been healed at Dowie's home as well. Following his own healing, Lake brought his invalid brother to Dowie's home where he was healed. When they laid hands on him, his blood disease disappeared and he jumped off his death bed.

Then he took his sister who was dying with breast cancer, to Chicago. When they arrived she had some initial doubts, but once she heard the Word of God preached with such great power, her faith grew – and she was healed. Her pain left instantly, and the large core of cancer fell out within a few days. Then the smaller cancers just disappeared and God restored her mutilated breast.

## DIE? "I WILL NOT HAVE IT!"

Another one of his sisters had remained very ill even after much prayer. He was planning on taking her to the Healing Home too, but before he could, he received a telephone call from his mother. She told him his sister was dying, and that if he wanted to see her, he would have to hurry. When Lake arrived, his sister was unconscious without a pulse and the room was full of mourners. Moved by it all, he looked at his sister's baby lying in the crib and thought, **"She must not die! I will not have it!"** Of this deep compassion he later wrote:

*John, upper left, with the surviving Lake family members. Eight of his original sixteen brothers and sisters died from disease.*

**"No words of mine can convey to another soul the cry
that was in my heart and the flame of hatred for death and
sickness that the Spirit of God had stirred within me. The
very wrath of God seemed to possess my soul!"**

Lake paced the room as his heart cried out for someone with faith to help
them. He could only think of one man who had this kind of faith – Dowie. So
he telegraphed him the following words:

**"My sister has apparently died, but my spirit will not let
her go. I believe if you will pray, God will heal her."**

Dowie's answer came back:

"Hold on to God. I am praying. She will live."

Upon reading these words, Lake waged a tremendously furious spiritual
attack on the power of death, rebuking it fervently in Jesus' name. In less than
an hour, his sister revived totally. Five days later, she joined the family for
Christmas dinner![5]

But that was then, and now his dear wife was suffering, and her condition
was growing worse.

## THE DEVIL REVEALED

On April 28, 1898, when Jennie's final hours seemed to be ticking away, a
fellow minister encouraged Lake to resolve himself to God's will and to accept
Jennie's death. His words weighed heavy, and Lake stiffened in resistance. Still,
the reality of death seemed imminent.

In utter hopelessness, Lake threw his Bible against the fireplace mantle and
it fell to the floor opened to Acts chapter 10. As he walked over to pick it up,
his eyes drifted to verse 38: *"...God anointed Jesus of Nazareth with the Holy
Ghost and with power: who went about doing good, and healing all that
were oppressed of the DEVIL; for God was with him."*

Those powerful words ripped through his thoughts. "OPPRESSED OF THE
DEVIL!" That meant that God wasn't the author of Jennie's sickness, or *any*
sickness! And if Lake was a son of God through Jesus Christ, then God was
*with him*, just as He was with Jesus! Now he was convinced it was the *devil*
who had caused Jennie's illness. It was the *devil* who was stealing the mother
of his children. It was the *devil* who was destroying his life!

## 9:30 A.M.

Then Lake turned to Luke 13:16 and read: *"ought not this woman...whom SATAN HATH BOUND, lo, these eighteen years, be loosed from this bond...?"* Now the realization hit him that not only was Satan the author of sickness and death, but that Jesus Christ – through Lake – could bring healing and deliverance to the afflicted! Through using him, Jesus Christ could conquer the throes of death! There was no doubt in his mind that Jesus died for the healing of his wife, just as He died for her sins. And he determined that absolutely nothing could rob Jennie of that gift.

> *Through using him, Jesus Christ could conquer the throes of death! There was no doubt in his mind that Jesus died for the healing of his wife, just as He died for her sins.*

In a boldness that only the Holy Spirit could have produced, Lake decided to let God, not Satan, have the last say. He marched into the bedroom and declared to the seen and unseen that his wife would be healed at exactly 9:30 A.M.!

Then he contacted Dowie to inform him of what God was about to do at the appointed time. When 9:30 arrived, Lake knelt at his precious wife Jennie's side and called on the living God. When he did, the power of God came upon Jennie and permeated her body from head to foot. Her paralysis left, her heartbeat became normal, her cough ceased, her breathing regulated, and her temperature returned to normal – immediately!

At first Lake heard a faint sound escaping from Jennie's lips. Then she cried out, "Praise God, I'm healed!" totally startling him, because he hadn't heard such strength in her voice for years. Then, Jennie threw back the covers from her bed – and stood up – healed![6] The joyous praise that followed was indescribable as both she and John worshipped God!

## THE LIGHTNINGS OF JESUS

Soon, the story of Jennie's healing became national news inspiring many to travel great distances to visit the Lake home. The newspapers had provoked the nation's curiosity and the Lake's were instantly thrust into a highly sought after ministry. People arrived at their home daily to see God's miracle, and to be prayed for. Many others sent in prayer requests.

One day after praying for a man who suffered from a ten-inch fever sore, Lake received a telegram that read, "Lake, the most unusual thing has happened. An hour after you left, the whole print of your hand was burned into that growth that was a quarter of an inch deep."

Lake would later refer to such power in his sermons as the lightnings of Jesus:

> **"You talk about the voltage from heaven and the power of God! Why there is lightning in the soul of Jesus! The lightnings of Jesus heal men by their flash! Sin dissolves and disease flees when the power of God approaches!"**[7]

Lake would also compare the anointing of God's Spirit to the power of electricity. Just as men had learned the laws of electricity, Lake had discovered the laws of the Spirit. And, as God's _"lightning rod,"_ he would rise within God's calling to _electrify_ the powers of darkness and _solidify_ the body of Christ.

## EXERCISING SPIRITUAL STRENGTH

In 1901, Lake moved to Zion, Illinois, to study divine healing under John Alexander Dowie. Before long he was preaching at night, studying when he could, and working as Dowie's building manager full time during the day.

But in 1904 when Dowie's increasing financial problems began to surface, Lake decided to distance himself and relocated to Chicago. He had invested in Zion's properties while living in the city, but his holdings depreciated leaving him in near financial ruin following Dowie's death in 1907. So he bought a seat on the Chicago Board of Trade. Over the next year he was able to accumulate over $130,000 in the bank, and real estate worth $90,000.

Recognizing his gifts, certain business executives quickly asked Lake to form a trust of the nation's three largest insurance companies for a guaranteed salary of $50,000 a year. He was now a top business consultant to top business executives, and was making hundreds of dollars through commissions as well.

By turn-of-the-century standards, John G. Lake was now making a fortune. But the call of God inside of him continued to grow. For awhile he was able to juggle his great secular success and grow in God. He had learned to walk in the Spirit, in a way he described like this:

> **"It became easy for me to detach myself from the course of life, so that while my hands and mind were engaged in the common affairs of every day, my spirit maintained its attitude of communion with God."**[8]

Some people think that if you are called to the ministry, you must leave your secular job *immediately*. But as was true with Lake, this is not the case. By learning to commune with God from within his spirit, Lake continued to progress toward the perfect timing for his ministry. He didn't venture out ahead of God or cause his family to suffer. Then when the time was right, he was able to sell everything, because he had learned great faith from his years of walking with God as a businessman.

Lake learned early in his ministry training that *"being"* precedes *"doing."* He had learned to follow the divine timing of heaven.

## TONGUES AND THE TIMING OF HEAVEN

While still living in Zion, Lake attended a cottage meeting at the home of his friend, Fred F. Bosworth. Tom Hezmalhalch was preaching, and at the end of the meeting he told Lake, "As I was preaching, Jesus told me that you and I are going to preach together." Lake laughed at Hezmalhalch's proclamation then, but soon surrendered himself to the perfect will of God.[9]

> *Lake learned early in his ministry training that "being" precedes "doing."*

Not long after, in 1906, Lake began to pray for the baptism of the Holy Spirit. He sought the Lord for nine months then quit, thinking it was "not for him." Then one day he went with Tom Hezmalhalch, who was now a close friend, to pray for an afflicted lady. As Lake sat by her bedside he trembled in an unusual yearning for God.

But Hezmalhalch was oblivious to what was happening, and asked Lake to lay hands on the woman. As he did, the lightning of God knocked Hezmolahlach to the ground. "Praise the Lord, John!" he said while picking himself up, "Jesus has baptized you in the Holy Ghost!"[10]

Lake would write later of this:

> **"When the phenomena had passed, the glory of it remained in my soul. I found that my life began to manifest a varied range of the gifts of the Spirit. And I spoke in tongues by the power of God, and God flowed through me with a new force. Healings were more of a powerful order."**

Lake spoke in other tongues often and believed that a lesser degree of infilling could not qualify as the baptism of the Holy Spirit:

"Tongues have been to me," said Lake, "the making of my ministry. It is that peculiar communication with God...[that] reveals to my soul the truth I utter to you day by day in the ministry."[11]

Again, waiting for God's right timing is very important. Our call from God was established before we were born. As we grow in life, we are invited to become aware of it. But just being "aware" of God's calling doesn't mean it is "the time" for that call to be launched into the earth. Divine timing must come before full-time ministry can begin. So don't be discouraged during your time of preparation. And don't compare your call with the call of others. Each call has its own timing and plan. Your faithfulness to the Word of God, along with fervent spiritual preparation determines the timing.

*Lake spoke in other tongues often and believed that a lesser degree of infilling could not qualify as the baptism of the Holy Spirit.*

## AFRICA IS CALLING

After his baptism of the Holy Spirit, Lake's desire to enter full-time ministry increased. So his boss agreed to allow him to take three months off and preach. But he also warned him that, "at the end of three months, $50,000 a year will look like a lot to you, and you will have little desire to sacrifice it for the dreams of religious possibilities." Lake thanked his boss for all he had done for him and left his job. Then once the three months had passed he would boldly declare, **"I am through forever with everything in life but the proclamation and demonstration of the Gospel of Jesus Christ."**[12] He would never return to his job.

In 1907, John and Jennie disposed of their estate, their wealth, and their possessions. In a great move of faith, they determined to be entirely dependent upon God. Now it was time to preach.

While ministering in a northern part of Illinois, the Spirit of God told Lake to, "Go to Indianapolis. Prepare for a winter campaign and get a large hall. Then in the spring, you will go to Africa." When he returned home to tell Jennie, she was already aware of the plan because the Lord had told her as well.

Lake had developed a great interest in Africa when reading about the explorations of Stanley and Livingstone when he was still a boy. As he grew into a young man, he began to experience spiritual visions that seemed to place him more often in Africa than in America. Through the Holy Spirit, Lake was given insight into the geography and people of a land he had never been to. And now that dream was becoming a reality. God said he would go to Africa in the spring!

So Lake moved his family to Indianapolis and joined his old friend, Tom Hezmalhalch. They would stay there for six months as the two formed a powerful ministry team leading several hundred people into the baptism of the Holy Spirit.

Then one morning, Lake felt led to begin a fast. As he sought the Lord over a period of six days He was told that from that point on he would start casting out demons. A special knowing to discern and cast out evil spirits quickly followed, and within a short time, Lake began moving in this area with great precision.

## WALKING ON THE WATER

In January of 1908, Lake began to pray for the needed finances to take the Africa trip. Tom joined with him, and they determined the trip would cost $2,000. They had been praying for a while when Tom got up and slapped Lake on the back, saying, "Don't pray anymore, John. Jesus told me just now that He will send us that $2000, and that it will be here in four days."

Exactly four days later, Tom returned from the post office and threw four $500 drafts on the table. "John, here is the answer!" Tom shouted. "Jesus has sent it. We are going to Africa!"

Just as the Lord proclaimed, in April of 1908, the group left for Africa. The team was made up of Lake, Jennie, their seven children, Tom, and three of his companions. One of Tom's companions had lived in Africa for five years, could speak Zulu, and would serve as interpreter. They bought their tickets, but had no extra money for the expenses of the trip. Now God's one-time millionaire would learn how to fully trust Him. He had only $1.50 in his hand.

And as Lake obeyed, the Lord miraculously provided for the team. The immigration laws of South Africa required each family that arrived to have at least $125, or they wouldn't be permitted to leave the ship. And as they pulled into the port, Lake had no money. So Jennie looked at him and said, "What are you going to do?"

Lake responded, **"I am going to line up with the rest. We have obeyed God this far. It is now up to the Lord."**

As he stood in line, ready to explain his dilemma, a fellow passenger tapped him on the shoulder and called him to the side. He asked Lake a few questions, then handed him two money orders, totaling $200.

"I feel led to give you this to help your work," the stranger said. If you've heard from God, then step out in bold, aggressive faith. He'll be there to meet you every time.

## HOME AWAY FROM HOME

The Lake family had been praying diligently for a home when they reached Johannesburg. As faith missionaries, they had no support from church boards, and no denomination waiting to accept them at their arrival. All they had was their faith in God.

When they arrived in Johannesburg in May of 1908, they noticed a little woman running around the dock area looking at everyone. She was American. Running up to Tom, she said, "You are an American missionary party?" to which Tom replied, "Yes." "How many are in your party?" the lady went on. "Four," Tom answered back. But she shook her head and said, "No, you aren't the family. Is there another?"

Then Tom directed her to Lake. "How many are in your family?" the lady asked. **"My wife, myself, and my seven children,"** Lake said. The lady suddenly looked ecstatic and shrilled, "You are the family!" Then she went on to explain how God had directed her to meet their boat and that on it would be an American missionary family consisting of two adults and seven children. And that she was to give them a home.[13]

That same afternoon, the Lake's were settled into a furnished home in Johannesburg. God had provided it, just as they had asked. The American lady, Mrs. C. L. Goodenough, remained a faithful friend throughout their ministry.

## A SPIRITUAL CYCLONE

Days after Lake arrived, his first ministry door was opened. A South African pastor took a leave of absence for a few weeks and asked Lake to fill his pulpit. He immediately accepted the offer.

Over five hundred Zulus were in attendance his first Sunday in the pulpit. As a result, a great revival broke out among them, and within weeks multitudes from Johannesburg and the surrounding area were saved, healed, and baptized in the Holy Spirit.

The success astounded Lake. Of it, he later wrote:

**"From the very start it was as though a spiritual cyclone had struck."**[14]

The meetings would often last until 4 A.M.

One of the main features of these miraculous meetings were the powerful demonstrations of answered prayer. The prayer of faith would be spoken for someone in another part of Africa with instant results. News of this spread far and wide, and hundreds packed into Johannesburg to be prayed for. After the meetings ended, the natives would follow the preachers to their homes and continue to ask questions to learn about God. Many times, as dawn broke over the African horizon, the group would still be discussing the power of God. Then all through the following day, people could be seen with Bibles in their hands, witnessing about the power of God that was displayed the night before.

> *Wounded, sick, and weak, the people would line up on one side of the platform and would leave the building after they were prayed for, shouting, "God has healed me!"*

There were also many great manifestations of healing. Wounded, sick, and weak, the people would line up on one side of the platform and would leave the building after they were prayed for, shouting, "God has healed me!" The crowd inside the building shouted wildly and cheered as they witnessed the miracles of God.

## JOHN & JENNIE: THE TEAM

If the African people couldn't make it to Lake's meetings, they would travel to "the preacher's" home. At times the throng was so great that Jennie didn't even have time to prepare the family meals. She would usher the people through the front door to be prayed for, then show them through the back door so the room would have space for the others coming in.

Jennie was also John's ministry partner. Lake believed his wife "possessed the spirit of discernment in a more marked degree" than he did. She would often receive a word of knowledge concerning those who were unable to receive healing because of personal difficulty or sin in their life.

The Lakes had a simple way of operating in their healing ministry. As the people passed before John in his office, he laid hands upon them. Those who were instantly healed, were dismissed. But those who continued to suffer, or received a partial healing, were sent into another room. Then when Lake finished with the multitude, he would bring Jennie into the room who would, by the Spirit, personally reveal to each one of them the hindrances of their healing. Upon hearing the inner secrets of their hearts, many would confess and ask God for forgiveness. Then John and Jennie would pray again, and God would heal those who repented. Those who refused to repent, even after acknowledging the truth of what Mrs. Lake had told them, went home suffering in their affliction.

## WHAT WAS HE LIKE?

Lake was a man of action. Once after an inspired altar invitation, the entire congregation ran to the front. In the group was a man who fell to the floor in front of the platform in an epileptic seizure. Immediately, Lake jumped off the platform and was at his side, rebuking the demon in the name of Jesus. After the man was delivered, Lake quietly returned to the platform.

The Spirit of God powerfully rested on Lake during these years. As he shook hands with those entering the services, they would often fall to the ground under the power of God. At other times, people would fall prostrate when they came within six feet of him!

Lake demonstrated his deep compassion by never turning away a cry for help. He never refused to answer the call of a sick person, and was even known to pray for dying animals when called upon. There were times when he needed rest, but the people would find him, then bring him their sick. Lake prayed for them night and day and refused to turn anyone away.

The ministry team was always in great need of food and finances. And true to the practices of that day, Lake never took offerings. But He would often find baskets of food or small pouches of money discreetly left on the family's doorstep.

Perhaps one of the most difficult challenges that Jennie experienced in Africa was adapting to the ministry habits of her husband. It was John's task to bring home the groceries needed for their large family. But if he would happen to meet a widow lady on the way home who had hungry children, he would give everything he had to the widow's family. Also, Jennie never knew whether or not John may be bringing home company for dinner, so she would have to stretch any meal to feed a large crowd. Food always seemed to be in short supply.

## TAG TEAM

From Lake's first meetings held in the pastor's church building, he moved into rented halls. Then when the crowds outgrew them, the ministry team resorted to cottage meetings. Lake and Hezmalhalch were now "team" preachers. Each would speak five or six times during a meeting, and no one could tell where one's message finished and the other's started. It was all harmonized by the Spirit of God.

Lake established the Apostolic Tabernacle in Johannesburg, and in less than a year he had started one hundred churches. The work of overseeing these churches spread throughout Africa and kept him more frequently away from home.

## GOODBYE, JENNIE

> *Lake had become so absorbed in ministering to others that he wasn't aware of what was happening to his own wife.*

Lake was stunned with the most devastating news he had ever encountered on December 22, 1908. While ministering in the Kalahari Desert, his beloved Jennie died. When he returned home twelve hours later, she had already gone to heaven.

Most accounts of Jennie Lake's death attribute it to malnutrition and physical exhaustion. When John was away, scores of sick people would wait on his lawn until he returned. So Jennie would feed them while they waited with what little food she could spare. And she tried to make their stay as comfortable as possible until Lake returned. But in doing so, she physically neglected herself.

Lake had become so absorbed in ministering to others that he wasn't aware of what was happening to his own wife.

One point often ignored in the ministry is that there will always be a "need" to be fulfilled. One ministry can't meet all the needs that will appear, no matter how powerful or anointed that ministry seems to be. So common sense is invaluable to Christian ministry. The natural body and the natural family need attention, and the family unit should always be the core of any ministry.

Understandably, Lake was devastated when he arrived home to find his wife had died. It was a very dark time for him and the agonizing pain stayed with him for many years.

The next year, in 1909, Lake returned to America to gather support for his African ministry and to recruit new workers. And again, God supernaturally supplied the money with one contribution. He was given $3,000 for he and his workers to return.

## THE PLAGUE

As the team landed on African soil in January of 1910, a plague was raging over portions of the nation. In less than a month, one quarter of the entire population had died. In fact, the plague was so contagious that the government was offering $1,000 to any nurse who would care for the sick. Lake and his assistants went to help, free of charge. He and one assistant would go into the houses, bring out the dead, and bury them. But no symptom of the plague ever touched him.

At the height of this horrible plague, a doctor sent for Lake and asked him:

> "What have you been doing to protect yourself? You must have a secret!"

To this Lake responded:

> **"Brother, it is the law of the Spirit of Life in Christ Jesus. I believe that just as long as I keep my soul in contact with the living God so that His Spirit is flowing into my soul and body, that no germ will ever attach itself to me, for the Spirit of God will kill it."**

Lake then invited the doctor to experiment with him. He asked the doctor to take the foam from the lungs of a dead plague victim and put it under a microscope. The doctor did so, and found masses of living germs. Then Lake astounded the people in the room as he told the doctor to spread the deadly foam on his hands and announced that germs would die.

The doctor did so and found that the germs died instantly in Lake's hand. Those who witnessed the experiment stood in amazement as Lake continued to give glory to God, explaining the phenomenon like this:

> **"You can fill my hand with them and I will keep it under the microscope, and instead of these germs remaining alive, they will die instantly."**[15]

This same power constantly flowed through Lake's hands into the bodies of the afflicted bringing healing to the masses. The "lightnings of God" blasted all disease and infirmity.

When the Queen of Holland requested Lake to pray for her problems with conception so she could carry a child to full term, he sent the Queen word that her prayer had been answered. Less than a year later, the Queen, who had miscarried six previous times, gave birth to her first full-term child, Queen Juliana of Holland.[16]

## MINISTRY OF THE SPIRIT

In December of 1910, Tom Hezmalhalch left Lake's ministry. This was a very difficult time for Lake. He had recently lost his dear wife, and now he was losing his best friend and partner. But he drew strength from knowing that he was fulfilling the will of God. And he received much comfort from his American supporters. Encouraging letters came pouring in from many reassuring him of their confidence in his ministry.

Lake spent the rest of 1910-1912 ministering healing as he prayed for the sick. Great miracles were performed that still affect Africa today. And he started two main churches: The Apostolic Faith Mission/Apostolic Tabernacle (not related to the Apostolic Faith Church) and the Zion Christian Church.

Lake and his congregation regularly published a newsletter that was mailed to thousands of people. Before they were mailed, church members would lay hands on them and pray that the pieces of literature would be filled with God's Spirit. They believed the power of God would anoint the newsletter's paper, just as it occurred with the handkerchiefs of Paul. As a result, thousands of letters would pour in from all parts of the world, stating how the Spirit of God came upon the recipients as they opened the paper. One lady said that when she held the newsletter, "she vibrated" in such a way that she could hardly sit in her chair. She was then baptized in the Holy Spirit and spoke in other tongues. Lake simply explained this manifestation by saying:

*They believed the power of God would anoint the newsletter's paper, just as it occurred with the handkerchiefs of Paul.*

**"The ministry of Christianity is the ministry of the Spirit."**[17]

Lake understood how to carry his entire congregation into the presence of the Lord. He trained and matured them out of his spiritual overflow, and as a result, they were able to accelerate with him in the supernatural. In 1912, the congregation was asked to pray for a man's cousin in a Welsh insane asylum that was located some seven thousand miles away. When the spirit of fervent prayer fell on the people, a great consciousness of God came upon Lake. It seemed as if shafts of light were beaming toward him from the intercessors. Then suddenly, he found himself traveling in the spirit at lightning-like speed. Arriving in a place that he had never seen before, he realized it had to be Wales. Then he walked inside the room of this man's cousin who was tied to a cot with her head bouncing back and forth. He laid hands on her and cast the devil out of her. Then, suddenly, he was back in Johannesburg kneeling on the platform. Three weeks later, the report of this woman's compete deliverance had arrived. She had been immediately discharged when physicians found her "suddenly" healthy and whole.

## THE ANOINTED ROVER

By the time John G. Lake would leave Africa to finally return to America, his ministry efforts had produced 1,250 preachers, 625 congregations, and 100,000 converts. The exact number of miracles that occurred in his ministry could never be counted on earth.[18] These statistics are the results of five years of ministry!

Lake returned to America in 1912. The family's first year home was filled with travel and needed relaxation. Then in 1913, John met and married Florence Switzer of Milwaukee, Wisconsin. In the years following they became the parents of five children. Florence was an excellent stenographer and was responsible for recording and preserving many of Lake's sermons.

In the summer of 1914, Lake met with his former railroad financier and friend, Jim Hill. The two had become close when Lake worked in Chicago. Hill was delighted to see Lake and offered his family free railway passes that were good for anywhere his trains traveled.

## THE HEALING ROOMS OF SPOKANE

Lake took advantage of his good friend's offer and began to travel the nation. First, he went to Spokane, Washington, where he would stay and set up "healing rooms" in an old office building. It is estimated that some one hundred thousand healings occurred in those rooms.[19]

The Spokane newspapers consistently published the many healing testimonies of the people. In fact, the results were so unbelievable that the Better Business Bureau decided to verify the authenticity of the healings. So they contacted leaders at the healing rooms for an investigation.

To satisfy the bureau's inquiry, Lake called on the people whose testimonies had appeared in print. All eighteen of them gave testimony to the power of the Lord in front of the bureau. Then Lake gave the investigators the names of those who had been healed throughout the city so they could question them. And after that, he offered to sponsor a meeting the following Sunday at which one hundred people would give their healing testimonies. He asked the bureau to formulate a panel of physicians, lawyers, judges, and educators who could render a verdict.

*John and Jennie Lake and family before leaving for South Africa, 1907*

*Lake and campaign workers*

*Mobilizing the message, Lake on the road*

*Lake and healing home workers in Spokane, Washington, 1915-1920*

*Boy healed at Lake's Spokane Healing Home*

But Lake received a letter from the bureau the Friday before the proposed meeting informing him that their investigations were very positive, and that the Sunday meeting wouldn't be necessary. They also praised him for the work he was doing in their city. Two committee members even visited him privately to tell him, "You didn't tell the half of it."

> *It is said the boy's head was shaped like a yacht, "upside down." Physicians announced there was nothing that could be done for him until he was twelve years old.*

Those interviewed by the bureau included a woman who no longer had her female organs, yet through healing, was able to procreate. She showed her miraculous baby to those investigating the ministry.

Another woman shared about the miraculous healing of her severely broken kneecap. After she received prayer, the bone popped back into place, without pain, in less than an hour. Still another woman afflicted with incurable cancer was totally healed after prayer. And another was instantly healed of rheumatoid arthritis as her bones reshaped and returned to normal. This same woman was also healed of a prolapsed stomach, and the earlobe she was born without miraculously grew into place.

But the most remarkable case at Spokane's Healing Home was that of a small boy. It is said the boy's head was shaped like a yacht, "upside down." Physicians announced there was nothing that could be done for him until he was twelve years old, and then the surgery would be very dangerous. But after prayer, the boy's bones softened, his head expanded, and his skull was restored to normal. His paralysis also miraculously left and he was able to speak like other children.

How did Lake explain these incredible healings? Many times, he liked to use Sister Etter in his illustrations because of her great spiritual influence on his life.

> **"When you see those holy flashes of heavenly flame once in a while in a person's life, as we observe in our Sister Etter; when someone is healed, it is because her consciousness and Christ are one. She is fused into God. I saw a dying, strangling woman healed in thirty seconds as Mrs. Etter cast out the demon. The flame of God, the fire of His Spirit, ten seconds of connection with the Almighty Christ at the Throne of God, that is the secret of it."[20]**

## "STRIVE FOR PENTECOST"

According to government statistics, between the years of 1915-1920, Spokane, Washington, was the "healthiest city in the world," because of the ministry of John G. Lake. The mayor of Spokane held a public commemoration to honor his efforts.

An excellent businessman, Lake made sure his records were always accurate. They showed that up to two hundred persons a day were being ministered to and healed in Spokane's Healing Homes, and that most of them were non-church members.

Lake also founded The Apostolic Church in Spokane that drew thousands from around the world for ministry and healing. He held services six nights a week, twice on Sundays, and made house calls throughout the week.

In May of 1920, Lake left Spokane and moved to Portland, Oregon, where he traveled as an apostle and pastored for a time. Soon, he began another Apostolic Church and healing ministry similar to the one in Spokane.

During Lake's time in Portland, he had a vision in which an angel appeared. The angel opened the Bible to the book of Acts, pointing to the outpouring of the Spirit on the Day of Pentecost. The angel also called Lake's attention to other spiritual manifestations and revelations in the book and said:

> "This is Pentecost as God gave it through the heart of Jesus. Strive for this. Contend for this. Teach the people to pray for this. For this, and this alone, will meet the necessity of the human heart, and this alone will have the power to overcome the forces of darkness."[21]

From that day on, Lake strived to fulfill the Word of the Lord with even greater intensity. He traveled around America for the next eleven years, duplicating his work everywhere he went.

## LAKE'S MISTAKE

In his later years, John G. Lake enjoyed a wonderful balance of the supernatural and natural. But his understanding came at a very heavy price. The price was his family.

Lake's children from his first marriage suffered greatly because of his constant absence. Even when he was present in a room, he would drift away in meditation, being constantly mindful of the ministry and the Lord. Because of this, his children felt greatly neglected.

Remember, it was these same children who saw their mother starve and work to death in Africa. As a result, each of them had developed very hardened attitudes, and they left home very early, between the ages of fifteen and sixteen, to live in Canada. As they grew into adulthood, their lives were characterized by hardened bitterness. However, two of his sons commented while on their deathbeds, "I wish dad were here to pray for me."

Lake grieved over his lack of attention given the children. And he would later write in a letter that the many miracles wrought at his hands were personally unfulfilling and not worth the loss of his family.

> *His children borne by Florence had a different attitude toward him. They remembered him as a man who loved to laugh and enjoy his friends.*

## THE REDEEMING FACTOR

But Lake learned from his experiences, and finally found the key to being a good husband, involved father, and powerful minister. His children borne by Florence had a different attitude toward him. They remembered him as a man who loved to laugh and enjoy his friends.

In his later years, Lake was not "so heavenly minded that he was of no earthly good." He didn't keep his head in the clouds, and people no longer fell into silence when entering his presence because he would lovingly interact with them. Lake had finally learned to enjoy the natural and the supernatural to the fullest extent. The atmosphere in his home was no longer rigid and stiff! He loved to have fun at the dinner table when the family was together. His hearty laugh could be heard echoing down the halls. And he enjoyed symphonic and opera music, so every Sunday evening, he would listen to his favorite radio programs.

Lake also enjoyed a wonderful sense of humor. He loved to read Will Roger's newspaper column, and would later be thought of himself as "a great entertainer." He liked to keep the atmosphere around him light with laughter.

## THE MAGNET OF GOD

At the height of his ministry, the outside world had become so drawn to Lake's understanding of God that they constantly flocked to him. It was his understanding of righteousness that allowed him to take dominion over every situation. He despised the Christian songs that spoke of mankind as a "worm."

When he heard them he would wrinkle his nose and twist his mouth, calling them "lower concept" songs. He felt they were a disgrace to the blood of Jesus. Lake's daughter once described her father as having "a very great conscious-ness of being a king and priest before God, showing a bearing and demeanor of that nobility." This is how he also encouraged others to be viewed. Lake always directed his family to treat all believers as kings and priests.[22]

Lake was the strongest advocate of his day for the supernatural. He often spoke with disgust of educational, medical, and scientific forums that made reference to the weakness of Christianity. One day he would preach, the tables would be turned, and men would flock from everywhere to the – "School of the Spirit" – where they would learn to cooperate and become one with the power of God.

Lake was truly concerned about the world's infatuation with mere psycho-logical power. He tells of once witnessing a man in India who had been buried alive for three days, then came up from the grave well and whole. And of another man who had suspended his body between two chairs in mid-air and had a huge stone smashed on his chest until it broke in two.

He would publicly refute the validity of such manifestations by saying:

> **"These are only on the psychological plane. Beyond that is the spirit plane and the amazing wonder of the Holy Spirit of God, and if God got hold of my spirit for ten min-utes, He could do something ten thousand times greater than that."[23]**

> **"Christianity is one hundred percent supernatural,"** he often said. **"'All Power' language is Christianity vocabulary only."[24]**

He possessed a remarkable ability to encourage faith and revelation in the hearts of others who listened to him. The ministers who sat under his teaching soon found their own ministries of faith which resulted in startling healings. Lake stated:

> **"If he [a Christian] has not the Spirit to minister in the real high sense, he has nothing to minister. Other men have intellectuality, but the Christian is supposed to be the possessor of the Spirit. There should never be any misun-derstanding along these lines."[25]**

To further the supernatural goals, Lake called every believer to the power of Pentecost. Once in doing so he spoke this prophecy:

"I can see as my spirit discerns the future and reaches out to touch the heart of mankind and the desire of God, that there is coming from heaven a new manifestation of the Holy Spirit in power, and that new manifestation will be in sweetness, in love, in tenderness, and in the power of the Spirit, beyond anything your heart or mine ever saw. The very lightning of God will flash through men's souls. The sons of God will meet the sons of darkness and prevail."[26]

*By the end of the talk, his vision was completely restored, and remained that way for the rest of his life.*

## LEGACY OF THE MIRACULOUS

By 1924, Lake was known throughout America as a leading healing evangelist. He had established forty churches throughout the United States and Canada in which there had been so many healings that his congregations nicknamed him, "Dr." Lake.

In December, another significant event took place through his ministry. Gordon Lindsay, founder of Christ For the Nations in Dallas, Texas, was converted while hearing Lake preach in Portland. Lindsay attended his services nearly every night of the week and considered Lake to be his mentor. When Lindsay later contracted deadly, ptomaine poisoning, he was totally healed once he was able to get to Lake's home.

In 1931, Lake returned to Spokane at the age of sixty-one. He was now weak with fatigue, and almost blind. So he decided to have a "talk" with the Lord. He reminded Him of how shameful it would be if he were to go blind after over one hundred thousand people were healed in his ministry in America alone. By the end of the talk, his vision was completely restored, and remained that way for the rest of his life.

## REIGNING IN THE HEAVENLIES

Labor Day came on a hot, humid Sunday in 1935. The Lakes had attended a Sunday school picnic and John returned home from it totally exhausted. So he laid down to rest. Florence encouraged him to stay home while she attended church that night, and when she returned home, she found Lake had suffered a stroke. He remained in poor condition for two weeks, unconscious most of the time. Then on September 16, 1935, John G. Lake went home to be with the Lord. He was sixty-five years old.

During the memorial service honoring Lake's life, many words of praise were spoken about him. But they are best summed up in this eulogy excerpt taken from one of Lake's many Spokane converts:

"Dr. Lake came to Spokane. He found us in sin. He found us in sickness. He found us in poverty of spirit. He found us in despair, but he revealed to us such a Christ as we had never dreamed of knowing this side of heaven. We thought the victory was over there, but Dr. Lake revealed to us that victory was here."[27]

> *If we would just grasp the reality of our position through Jesus Christ, as Lake did, every nation would ring with the praises of God.*

As we close this chapter, I want to challenge you to walk in the revelation of your righteousness in Christ. Righteousness is a *lifestyle* that produces victory in every situation. If we would just grasp the reality of our position through Jesus Christ, as Lake did, every nation would ring with the praises of God. And every demonic regime would crumble under that authority.

John G. Lake proved to us that this lifestyle can be lived and enjoyed by those who pursue it. So don't stop short of what God has given us through Jesus Christ. Allow the Holy Spirit to reveal your heavenly position to you, then take your place and change the nations for God.

## CHAPTER SIX, JOHN G. LAKE
### References

1 John G. Lake, *Adventures in God* (Tulsa, OK: Harrison House, 1981), 30.

2 Wilford Reidt, *John G. Lake: A Man Without Compromise* (Tulsa: Harrison House, 1989), 13.

3 Lake, *Adventures in God*, 73-74.

4 Reidt, *John G. Lake: A Man Without Compromise*, 21.

5 Gordon Lindsay, ed., *John G. Lake: Apostle to Africa* (Dallas, TX: Christ for the Nations, Inc., Reprinted 1979), 12-13, Lake, *Adventures in God*, 77.

6 Lake, *Adventures in God*, 78-80.

7 Ibid., 35-36.

8 Lindsay, *John G. Lake: Apostle to Africa*, 16.

9 Gordon Lindsay, ed., *Astounding Diary of John G. Lake* (Dallas, TX: Christ for the Nations, 1987), 13-14.

10 Lindsay, *Apostle to Africa*, 18-19.

11 Reidt, *John G. Lake: A Man Without Compromise*, 27.

12 Lindsay, *John G. Lake: Apostle to Africa*, 20.

13 Lake, *Adventures in God*, 59-69.

14 Lindsay, *John G. Lake: Apostle to Africa*, 25.

15 Gordon Lindsay, ed., *John G. Lake Sermons on Dominion Over Demons, Disease & Death* (Dallas, TX: Christ for the Nations, Inc., 1949, Reprinted 1988), 108.

16 Lindsay, *John G. Lake: Apostle to Africa*, 36.

17 Lake, *Adventures in God*, 106-107.

18 Lindsay, *John G. Lake: Apostle to Africa*, 53.

19 Ibid.

20 Kenneth Copeland Publications, *John G. Lake: His Life, His Sermons, His Boldness of Faith*, (Fort Worth, TX: Kenneth Copeland Publications, 1994), 442.

21 Reidt, *A Man Without Compromise*, 95.

22 Ibid., 60.

23 Kenneth Copeland Publications, *John G. Lake*, 443.

24 Ibid., 432.

25 Ibid., 27.

26 Lindsay, *New John G. Lake Sermons* (Dallas, TX: Christ for the Nations, Inc., 1976), 19-20.

27 Lindsay, *John G. Lake: Apostle to Africa*, 9.

# Smith Wigglesworth

*"Apostle of Faith"*

# "APOSTLE OF FAITH"

**M**y friend said, 'She is dead.' He was scared. I have never seen a man so frightened in my life. 'What shall I do?' he asked. You may think that what I did was absurd, but I reached over into the bed and pulled her out. I carried her across the room, stood her against the wall and held her up, as she was absolutely dead. I looked into her face and said, 'In the name of Jesus, I rebuke this death.' From the crown of her head to the soles of her feet her whole body began to tremble. 'In the name of Jesus, I command you to walk,' I said. I repeated, 'In the name of Jesus, in the name of Jesus, walk!' and she walked."[1]

Raising the dead was only one amazing facet of the ministry of Smith Wigglesworth. This great apostle of faith walked in such an astounding measure of God's anointing that the miraculous following his ministry was only secondary to it. In his lifetime, this onetime plumber would give new meaning to the word "adventure." Adventure's only requirement? – "Only believe!"

To Wigglesworth, simple obedience to what one believed was not an extraordinary feat – it was simply the fruit of it. His own faith was said to be unflinching and sometimes ruthless. But he was also said to possess an unusual teaching anointing and a keen sense of compassion – the fruit of which produced countless salvations and miracles in his ministry every day.

> *To Wigglesworth, simple obedience to what one believed was not an extraordinary feat — it was simply the fruit of it.*

## THE LITTLE TURNIP PULLER

Smith was born June 8, 1859, to John and Martha Wigglesworth in the small village of Menston, Yorkshire, England. At the time of his birth in 1859 it was already a historic year. The Third Great Awakening had been underway in America for two years, William Booth had distanced himself from organized religion, forming the Salvation Army, and the Church in Wales was praying for revival.[2] That Smith would be counted among the other great Christian leaders such as Booth in John and Martha's day, was the furthest thing from their minds that spring of 1859. But he would. Their son would put God's fire back into a church that had been smoldering for hundreds of years.

Smith's family was poor. His father worked long hours to support his wife, a daughter, and three sons. So the boy began work at the age of six, pulling turnips in a local field. The work was hard. His tiny hands were sore and swollen from pulling turnips morning until night. But it gave Smith his father's solid work ethic of laboring long and hard for reward.

When Smith turned seven he went to work with his father and another at the local wool mill. From then on, life seemed easier for the Wigglesworth family. Their income increased and food became plentiful.

Smith's father was a great lover of birds. At one time he had sixteen song-birds living in their home. So the boy adopted his father's love for nature and often searched for nests. He sometimes caught and sold songbirds at the local market to help sustain his family.

## WHAT'S THE DIFFERENCE BETWEEN US?

Though his parents weren't Christians, there was never a time young Smith didn't long for God. He wasn't taught to pray at home, but he was always seeking on his own. Many times, Smith would ask God to show him where to find a nest of birds. Almost instantly he knew where to look.

His grandmother was an old-time Wesleyan who believed in the power of God. She always made sure Smith attended the meetings with her. As a young boy, he would sit and watch the "old-timers" clap their hands, dance to the Lord, and sing about the "blood." When Smith was eight years old, he got to join in the singing at church. As he began to sing, "a clear knowledge of the new birth" came to him. He realized what Jesus Christ had done for him through His death and resurrection. In later years, Wigglesworth would write of that day:

> "I saw that God wants us so badly that He has made the condition as simple as He possibly could — 'Only Believe.'"[3]

And he never doubted his salvation.

Young Wigglesworth immediately became a soulwinner. The first person he won to Christ was his own mother. When his father discovered the Christian "experience" had come to his family, he started taking the family to the Episcopal church. Smith's father wasn't born again himself, but he enjoyed the parson, as they visited the same pub and drank beer together.

Soon Smith consented to join the church choir with his brother, but because he had to work at such a young age, he was robbed of an education. He was almost ten years old when he was "confirmed." When the bishop waved his hands over the young boy, a powerful awareness of God's presence filled Smith that would remain with him for days. Nothing like that seemed to occur with the others, as Smith would later write:

**"After the confirmation service all the other boys were swearing and quarreling, and I wondered what had made the difference between them and me."**[4]

## THERE'S SOMETHING DIFFERENT ABOUT YOU

When Smith was thirteen, his family moved from Menston to Bradford where he became deeply involved in the Wesleyan Methodist Church. His spiritual life took on a new meaning, and he longed for the Spirit of God. Though he couldn't read well, he never left his house without the New Testament in his pocket.

Later, the Methodists were planning a special preaching meeting, and seven boys were chosen to participate, including Smith. With three weeks to prepare, the teenager "lived in prayer." When the day arrived, he took the platform to preach for fifteen minutes, and afterward had no memory of what he had said. All he could remember was the incredible zeal that clothed him along with hearing the hearty shouts and cheers of the people.

*...he joined the Salvationists when they arrived and would very soon learn about the power of fasting and prayer.*

Smith began to witness the Gospel to everyone he met, but he couldn't understand why so many seemed uninterested. Then, in 1875, the Salvation Army started a work in Bradford. Smith was ecstatic when he heard the news. Finally, he could be with a group of people who shared his desire for the lost! So he joined the Salvationists when they arrived and would very soon learn about the power of fasting and prayer.

The Salvation Army had more results than anyone else at the time, especially in the area of soulwinning. Many times, they would have all-night prayer meetings, lying prostrate before the Lord. The early Salvationists had great spiritual authority and it was manifested in each of their services. At the weekly meetings, the group would join together and claim at least fifty to a hundred people for God, knowing they would reach that number and more. Scores of people found Jesus as their Savior through the branch at Bradford.

When he was seventeen, Smith met a godly man at the mill who taught him the plumbing business. As they worked together, this man explained to Smith the meaning and importance of water baptism.

Eager to fulfill the commandments in the Word, Smith gladly obeyed and was baptized in water shortly afterwards. During this time, he also learned of the message of the second coming of Christ, and believing strongly that Jesus would come by the turn-of-the-century. He was determined to "change the course" of everyone he met.

Believing that the Lord would help him in everything, Smith set out to minister. In 1877, he went to a plumber's home to ask for a job. The plumber advised Smith that he had no need for anyone. So Smith thanked him, apologized for using his time, and turned to walk away. Suddenly the man called him back saying, "There is something about you that is different. I just cannot let you go."[5] And he was hired.

Smith did such excellent work that the plumber couldn't keep him employed – he worked too fast! So he decided to move to Liverpool, taking his plumbing experience with him. With the power of God resting heavily upon him, he began to minister to the children of the city. Longing to help them, he preached the Gospel to them. Hundreds came to the dock shed where Smith ministered. Ragged and hungry, the girls and boys came, and Smith took care of them all. Though he had a good income, he never spent it on himself, using it instead to clothe and feed these children.

Besides his ministry to the children, Smith and a friend would visit the hospitals and ships, witnessing for Jesus Christ. He would fast and pray all day on Sunday, never seeing less than fifty people saved each time he ministered. The Salvation Army constantly invited Smith to preach at their services, and while preaching, he always stood broken as he wept before the people. Though he wished for the eloquence of Charles Spurgeon and other fine preachers, it was his brokenness that caused hundreds to come to the altar longing to know God.

## "WHO ARE THESE SILLY PEOPLE?"

One of the greatest attributes in the life of Smith Wigglesworth was his wife, Mary Jane "Polly" Featherstone. In the lives of many great ministry couples, it seems that when one partner is strong, the other must take a lesser role in order to keep conflict at a minimum. But this wasn't the case with the Wigglesworths! Polly remained equally as strong, if not stronger at certain times, than her husband. She never refused to take a back seat, and Wigglesworth was in agreement with this. He said of her, **"All that I am today I owe, under God, to my precious wife. Oh, she was lovely!"**[6]

Polly Featherstone came from a good Methodist family. Even though her father lectured in the Temperance Movement, he became heir to a large inheritance made through the sale of liquor. However, holding fast to his inner convictions, he refused to touch a "penny" of the tainted inheritance. She watched the lifestyle of her father and echoed his strong character and beliefs of holiness. She was also a woman who said what she thought.

Later, Polly left her socially-affluent surroundings and headed for "fame and fortune" in the city of Bradford. Once there, she accepted service in a large family.

One day, while she was in town, she heard trumpets and shouting. Finding her way to the "noise," she was intrigued by what she saw – an open air meeting! The Salvation Army was a new organization at this time, and she thought, *Who are these silly people?* Curious, she followed the group to a large, dilapidated building. As the Salvationists marched inside, Polly remained on the corner, hoping no one saw her. Finally, overcome with curiosity, she slipped inside and took a seat in the top of the gallery.

*The Wigglesworth family. Top: Alice, Seth, and Harold. Bottom: Ernest, Smith, Mary Jane (Polly), and George*

## "HALLELUJAH! IT'S DONE!"

Gypsy Tillie Smith, sister of the famous evangelist, Gypsy Rodney Smith, was preaching. Hurling her fiery message toward the people, she proclaimed salvation through the blood of Jesus. Polly was deeply moved. Realizing her lost condition, she left the galley and made her way to the altar rail, falling to her knees. She refused any prayer from the workers, until finally, Tillie Smith made her way over to pray with her. With the light of Christ warming her heart, Polly jumped to her feet, threw her gloves in the air, and shouted, "Hallelujah! It is done!"[7] Sitting in the audience, not far from her, a young man watched her intently. That man was her future husband and partner in destiny – Smith Wigglesworth.

> **With the light of Christ warming her heart, Polly jumped to her feet, threw her gloves in the air, and shouted, "Hallelujah! It's done!"**

"It seemed as if the inspiration of God was upon her from the very first," Smith said.[8] The next night, as Polly gave her testimony, Smith felt she "belonged to him." Being allowed to forego the customary period of training, she was eventually given a commission as an officer in the Salvation Army by General Booth himself.

Polly went on to serve the Salvation Army in Scotland for a season, then returned to Bradford. She would eventually leave the army because of conflict surrounding her relationship with Wigglesworth. She was an "officer" and he was a mere "soldier." Though Smith never officially joined the army, the rules were strict regarding any intimate relationship between the two ranks.

After she left, Polly joined the Blue Ribbon Army, but she always remained a true friend to the Salvationists. At this time, Methodist ministers called her to evangelize their churches, and hundreds were converted through her ministry. The power of God rested heavily upon her.

## "SMITH, YOU'RE NOT MY MASTER"

Polly became "Mrs. Wigglesworth" in 1882, at age twenty-two. Smith was one year older than his new wife, and encouraged her to continue her evangelistic ministry, while he was content in the plumbing business. However, he did have a "burden" for an area in Bradford that had no church. So the couple rented a small building and opened it for meetings, calling it the "Bradford Street Mission."

In their thirty years of marriage, the Wigglesworths had one daughter, Alice, and four sons, Seth, Harold, Ernest, and George (who later died in 1915). But before each child was born, the Wigglesworths prayed over them that they would serve God. After their birth, Smith took care of them during church while his wife preached. Following the message, Smith was always at the altar, praying to bring people to Christ. Not at all intimidated by his wife's ministry role, Smith said, **"Her work was to put down the net; mine was to land the fish. This latter is just as important as the former."**[9] He knew the power of a servant's heart.

The winter of 1884 was a severe one for Bradford, and as a result, the plumbers were in high demand. Not only did Smith spend the entire winter working, but remained busy repairing the damage as a result of the elements for two more years.

During those days of heavy work and great prosperity, Smith's attendance in church declined rapidly and his heart grew cold toward the Lord. But as his fire grew dimmer, Polly's grew brighter, and her zeal for God and her prayer life never wavered. Her consistency and diligence in the things of God made Smith's laxity all the more apparent, and he became irritated by her very presence.

*Polly Wigglesworth beautifully illustrated the principle of "stability."*

One night, she came home from church a little later than usual. When she entered the house, Smith remarked, **"I am the master of this house, and I am not going to have you coming home at so late an hour as this!"** Polly quietly replied, "I know that you are my husband, but Christ is my Master."[10] Greatly annoyed, Smith opened the back door and forced her out of the house, locking the door behind her. But in his great annoyance he had forgotten to lock the front door. So Polly walked around to the front of the house and came in through the front door – laughing! In fact, she laughed so much that Smith finally surrendered and laughed with her. In his laughter, a revelation came into his heart and mind, so he decided to spend ten days in prayer and fasting to seek the Lord. In desperate and sincere repentance, he found his way to the road of restoration.

## WHERE DO YOU RATE ON THE RICHTER SCALE?

"The woman is the thermometer of the household," is a true saying. For example, if your wife is in a bad mood, the rest of the members will end up having a negative attitude. On the other hand, if your wife is cheerful, regardless of how bad you feel, everything seems more upbeat.

Polly Wigglesworth beautifully illustrated the principle of "stability." I am sure that her fidelity and joy were severely tested while her husband was backslidden. She was a very popular speaker, holding evangelistic services throughout the city, seeing hundreds come to Christ – while her husband worked or sat at home. No doubt, there were whispers of Smith's spiritual condition, as Polly's ministry was publicly scrutinized, but she never "missed a step." Obviously, the one thing that caused her to triumph was – *her security in Jesus Christ.*

In many cases, when a husband is backslidden, the wife nags and complains thinking she is pushing him into action and repentance, but a repentant heart is a result of the work of the Holy Spirit. The fire of God kept a joyful heart within Polly. As a result, Smith saw his mistake and was drawn back to Jesus. His wife's attitude was directly responsible for his repentance, and eventually, their world-shaking ministry. This is the highest goal of a "help mate," to help (the mate) meet his or her call, whatever it may be. God knows the heart of your mate and what it will take to move him or her to the place he or she belongs. Just keep your own heart right and leave others to God and the Holy Spirit. That way, you will never lose.

## THE FIRST HEALING

In the late 1800s, Smith traveled to Leeds to purchase supplies for his plumbing business. While in Leeds, he attended a church service where divine healing was being ministered. Smith sat in the meeting observing the marvelous healings that took place. His heart was moved and he began to search for the sick in Bradford, paying their expenses to go to the healing meetings in Leeds, never daring to tell his wife what he was doing. He was concerned she would join the other scoffers of that day in labeling divine healing as "fanaticism." But when she found out the truth, she listened intently to his description of the meetings, and, needing healing herself, she accompanied him to Leeds. The prayer of faith was offered for her, and she received an instant manifestation. From that day forward, the Wigglesworths were passionate for the truths in divine healing.

As a result, their church in Bradford grew. So they sought for a larger place and obtained a building on Bowland Street and called the new work, "Bowland Street Mission." They had a huge scroll painted on the wall behind the pulpit that read: "I Am the Lord That Healeth Thee."

Smith's first personal experience with healing came in the early 1900s. A hemorrhoid condition had plagued him since childhood, so a visiting minister prayed and agreed in faith with Smith that this condition would be divinely healed. Up to this point, Smith had used "salts" every day, but being fully persuaded in the will of God, he eventually stopped using them, and found that he was fully healed, remaining so for the rest of his life.

By now, Smith was totally dedicated to the ministry of healing. Being in business for himself, he had the time to take groups of people to the Leeds Healing Home, always paying their expenses. He was known for his great compassion toward the sick and needy. The workers at Leeds would see Smith coming with groups of people and laugh among themselves, because he didn't seem to understand that God could heal the sick in Bradford, just as He did in Leeds.

## "PUSHED" INTO THE PULPIT!

Realizing that Smith needed some "prodding" to get his public ministry going, the leaders of the Leeds Healing Home made a decision.

Knowing they were going to the Keswick Convention, they asked Smith to fill the pulpit in their absence. Smith was hesitant at first, but the ministers assured him that he could do it. So he comforted himself by thinking he would just take charge, and there were any number of people who would agree to preach. When the day came to minister, Smith was in charge, but no one would preach. They all agreed that Smith should do it. Hesitantly, he began to minister and at the close of his message, fifteen people came forward for healing. One man hobbled up on a pair of crutches, and when Smith prayed for him, the man jumped all over the place, without his crutches, instantly healed. There was no one as surprised as Smith!

From this meeting, doors began to open for Smith to minister, and he soon announced he would hold a healing meeting in Bradford. On the first night twelve people came for healing, and each one was healed. One lady had a large tumor that was constantly draining. After the prayer of faith, she went home and reported the next day that only a scar was left.

## PLEASE...SHUT UP!

All too soon, Smith received his first challenge. It was a life or death situation. The wife of a devoted friend was so ill that the doctors expected her to die during the night. Smith's friend said he couldn't believe for his wife, because he didn't know how. Compassion rose up in Smith's heart and he determined to help that family. So he went to a minister who was opening a small church in Bradford, and asked if he would go to pray for the woman. But the minister refused. Smith then went to a friend, who was known for his eloquent prayers. The friend agreed to go with him and the two set out for the woman's home.

> *"Suddenly, the Lord Jesus appeared. I had my eyes open gazing at Him. He gave me one of those gentle smiles.... I have never lost that vision, the vision of that beautiful, soft smile."*

Smith felt encouraged to have someone with him. He exhorted his friend to begin praying as soon as they entered the home, and upon seeing the weakened condition of the woman, the friend took Smith's advice. He began praying – but not as Smith had hoped. This man prayed for "the family that would be left behind" and continued in a rambling, negative tone until Smith cried out for him to stop. Thinking the worst was behind him, he then asked the woman's husband to pray. But he cried out in just as pathetic a fashion. Finally, when Smith could stand it no longer, he cried out so loudly that he could be heard in the street – "**Lord, stop him!**" The husband stopped.

Smith then pulled a bottle of oil out of his pocket and poured the entire bottle over the body of the woman, in the name of Jesus. Then standing at the head of her bed, Smith experienced his first vision. He said, "**Suddenly, the**

*"...all he needed to know was in the Word of God..."*

**Lord Jesus appeared. I had my eyes open gazing at Him. He gave me one of those gentle smiles.... I have never lost that vision, the vision of that beautiful, soft smile.**"[11] And a few moments after the vision vanished, the woman sat up in bed filled with new life. She lived to raise a number of children and outlived her husband.

## "COME OUT, DEVIL!"

As Smith's hunger for the Word of God grew, he never allowed any publications in his home, secular or Christian, except the Bible. He felt that all he needed to know was in the Word of God. Smith said of his wife, "**She saw**

how ignorant I was, and immediately began to teach me to read properly and write; unfortunately, she never succeeded in teaching me to
spell."[12]

Smith's next experience with a life or death situation came in his own life.
One day he was suddenly struck with severe pain and was confined to his bed.
Having agreed previously with his wife that no medications would be in his
house, he left his healing in the hands of God.

The family prayed all night for some kind of relief, but none came. Smith
grew weaker by the hour, and finally, he said to his wife, **"It seems to me
that this is my home-call. To protect yourself, you should now call a
physician."** Brokenhearted, Polly set out for a physician, believing the end
had come for her husband.

When the physician came, he shook his head and told the family that it was
appendicitis and that the condition had been deteriorating for the past six
months. He went on to say that Smith's organs were so damaged that there was
no hope, not even with surgery. As the physician was leaving, an elderly
woman and a young man came into Smith's room. This woman believed in
praying the prayer of faith, and she believed that all sickness came from the
devil. While she prayed, the young man got on the bed, laid both hands on
Smith and cried, "Come out, devil, in the name of Jesus!"

To Smith's great surprise, the "devil came out" and the pain was completely
gone. For good measure, the couple prayed for Smith again, after which he got
up, got dressed, and went downstairs. He said to his wife, **"I am healed. Any
work in?"** As Polly heard his story, she, still in total awe, handed him his job
request. He then set out immediately to remedy the plumbing problem and
was never again plagued by appendicitis.[13]

## "THEY'RE RECEIVING DEVILS"

In 1907 another turning point came in the life of Smith Wigglesworth. He
had heard that a group of people in Sunderland were "baptized in the Holy
Spirit" and "speaking in other tongues." So he determined to see this phenomenon for himself.

Until this time, Smith believed he was already baptized in the Holy Spirit.
He, along with his wife, followed the popular belief of the day that sanctification was the baptism of the Holy Spirit. Smith then recalled an earlier situation
that caused him to repent and begin a ten-day fast. During this fast, Smith had
found his way back to God, and in fact, had experienced a definite change in

his life. It is said that as he prayed and wept before the Lord, he consecrated himself to be wholly sanctified. When the fast was over, he was free from his temper and moodiness to such a degree that some often commented that they wanted the spirit that Smith had. As a result, Smith thought he had been baptized in the Spirit or sanctified.

In writing to his friends in Sunderland regarding the subject of tongues, he was warned to stay away because **"those people were receiving devils."** However, when Smith arrived and prayed with his friends about the matter, they looked at him and said, **"Obey your own leadings."**[14]

He was disappointed as he sat in the meetings at Sunderland, under the leadership of Vicar Alexander Boddy. In Bradford, there seemed to be a mighty move of God. But here, it seemed spiritually dry, with no manifestations. In his frustration, he continually disrupted the meetings, saying, **"I have come from Bradford, and I want this experience of speaking in tongues like they had on the day of Pentecost. But I do not understand why our meetings seem to be on fire, but yours do not seem to be so."**[15]

Smith disrupted the meeting so many times in his desperate search that he was disciplined outside the building.

*"I have come from Bradford, and I want this experience of speaking in tongues like they had on the day of Pentecost. I do not understand why our meetings seem to be on fire, but yours do not seem to be so."*

## BATHED IN POWER & GLORY

Seeking God with all his heart to experience this "baptism in the Holy Spirit," Smith went to a local Salvation Army building to pray. Three times he was struck to the floor by the power of God. The Salvationists warned him against speaking in tongues, but Smith was determined to know God in this realm. Four days he sought the Lord expecting to speak in other tongues, but to no avail. Finally, discouraged in his spirit, he felt it was time to return to Bradford. But before his departure, he went to the parsonage to tell the vicar's wife, Mrs. Boddy, good-bye. He told her that he had to go home and didn't get to speak in tongues. She answered, "It is not the tongues you need, but the baptism."[16] Smith asked her to lay hands on him before he left. She prayed a simple but powerful prayer, and then left the room. It was then that the fire fell. Bathed in the power and glory of the Lord, Smith saw a vision of the empty cross with Jesus exalted at the right hand of the Father. Filled with worship and praise, Smith opened his mouth and began to speak in other tongues, finally realizing that even though he had received an anointing earlier, he was now baptized in the Holy Spirit as on the day of Pentecost.

Instead of going home, Smith went straight to the church where Rev. Boddy was conducting the service. Interrupting, he begged to speak for a moment. When he finished his "sermon," fifty people were gloriously baptized in the Holy Spirit and spoke with other tongues. The local newspaper, the *Sunderland Daily Echo*, headlined the meeting, giving detailed accounts of Smith's experience, including the tongues and the healings. He telegraphed his home, telling them of the great news.

## HOLY LAUGHTER

On returning to Bradford, Smith felt he would have a challenge to face concerning his newfound joy, and he was right. As he came through the door, Polly stated firmly, "I want you to understand that I am as much baptized in the Holy Spirit as you are and I don't speak in tongues.... Sunday, you will preach for yourself, and I will see what there is in it."[17]

She kept her word, and when Sunday came, Polly sat in the very back of the church. As Smith walked up to the pulpit, the Lord gave him the passage in Isaiah 61:1-3. He preached with great power and assurance while Polly squirmed around in the bench saying to herself, *That's not my Smith, Lord. That's not my Smith!*[18]

At the end of the service, a worker stood and said that he wanted the same experience that Smith had. As he sat down, he missed his chair and fell onto the floor! Smith's oldest son stood to say the same and he also missed his chair and fell onto the floor! In a very short while, eleven people were on the floor laughing in the Spirit. The entire congregation became consumed in holy laughter as God poured out His Spirit upon them. This was the beginning of the great outpouring in Bradford, where hundreds received the baptism of the Holy Spirit and spoke in other tongues.

Soon after Polly was baptized in the Holy Spirit, the couple went throughout the country, answering the calls for ministry. Wherever they went, conviction seemed to settle on the people. Once, when Smith entered a grocery store to shop, three people fell to their knees in repentance. Another time, two ladies were working in a field, and when Smith passed by, he called out to them, **"Are you saved?"** Right after he said it they dropped their buckets and cried out for God.[19]

## GOD'S FINANCIAL COVENANT

During the coming days, Smith developed the habit of prayer and fasting. Soon letters from all over the country poured into the Wigglesworth household, begging him to come and pray for their sick. He answered every request he could, and sometimes after a train ride to a city, he would find a bicycle and peddle another ten miles in order to reach the afflicted one.

With such an incredible flood of ministry work, Smith soon saw his personal plumbing business decline. He was called out of town so often that his customers would have to call on another plumber. Each time he returned to Bradford there was less business.

> *With such an incredible flood of ministry work, Smith soon saw his personal plumbing business decline.*

Returning early from a convention, Smith found that most of his customers had called other plumbers to do the work. There was one widow who couldn't find help, so he went directly to her home and did the repair work, as well as the damaged ceiling. When she asked what she owed, Smith replied, **"I won't receive any pay from you. I'll make this an offering to the Lord as my last plumbing job."**[20]

So with that declaration, he paid his accounts, closed his business, and began his full-time ministry. He believed, in spite of the stories of poverty he had heard, that God would abundantly provide as he served Him faithfully. Confident in his partnership with God, he laid down a condition:

> **"My shoe heels must never be a disgrace, and I must never have to wear trousers with the knees out. I said to the Lord, 'If either of these things take place, I'll go back to plumbing.'"**[21]

God never failed to supply all his needs, and he never returned to plumbing.

## "LET HER GO"

One of the greatest sorrows of Wigglesworth's life was soon to follow. While waiting in the train station to leave for Scotland, Smith received devastating news: Polly had collapsed with a heart attack while returning from the Bowland Street Mission.

Rushing to her bedside, he found that her spirit had already departed to be with the Lord. Not settling for this, Smith immediately rebuked the death and her spirit came back, but only for just a short while. Then the Lord spoke: "This is the time that I want to take her home to Myself." So with a breaking heart, Smith released his partner, the one he had loved for so many years, to be with the Lord. Polly Wigglesworth served the Lord until the very last moment of her life, January 1, 1913.[22] It is said by some that after her death, Smith asked for a double portion of the Spirit.[23] From that moment on, his ministry carried an even greater power.

## HERE'S THE SECRET...

Smith immediately started ministering throughout the country traveling with his daughter and son-in-law. It was extremely unusual for the British press to carry stories on religious news. Yet the *Daily Mirror* dedicated their front page to his dynamic ministry featuring four photographs of Wigglesworth in action.[24] Because this newspaper was the most widely circulated paper in the nation, hundreds sought out his ministry. Smith had an incredible revelation on the subject of faith and his teaching on this subject attracted the masses. Wigglesworth didn't settle for hoping that prayer would work. His revelation on faith was concrete, melting the most hardened sinner to the love of Jesus Christ.

Smith's theory on faith was simple: Only believe. He didn't believe that God had favorites. One of his primary examples of this principle came from the New Testament, where John was noted as the apostle whom Jesus "greatly loved." According to Wigglesworth, John's "leaning against Jesus' bosom" didn't make him a favorite. The factor that called attention to John was his relationship and dependence upon Jesus. Smith constantly proclaimed:

"There is something about believing God, that makes God willing to pass over a million people just to anoint you."[25]

Many books have been written attempting to find the secret of Wigglesworth's power, but the answer is very simple. His great faith came from his relationship with Jesus Christ. From that relationship came Smith's every answer to every situation he ever faced. God has no favorites – He works through those who believe Him.

## "I'M NEVER TOO LATE"

Frequently Smith's methods were misunderstood and criticized. He was never moved by the criticism, but he did have compassion on his critics. Instead of retaliation, he would answer, "I am not moved by what I see or hear; I am moved by what I believe."[26]

Preaching the Word

Ministering "in" the Spirit

Later years

God's student

*Four Generations*

*Anointing oil bottle used by Smith Wigglesworth*

The Holy Spirit began teaching Smith the varying degrees of faith. He first taught that *faith could be created* in others.

An example of this concept was a young boy who was seriously ill. The family had sent for Smith, but when Smith arrived, the mother met him at the door, saying, "You are too late. There is nothing that can be done for him." Smith replied, **"God has never sent me anywhere too late."**[27] The boy's condition was so bad, that if he were to be moved, his heart would stop and he would die. Needless to say, the family had no faith and the boy was too sick to believe for himself. Before he could pray for the boy, Smith had to leave for an engagement at a local chapel. But before he left their home, he told the family he would return. He then instructed them to lay out the boy's clothes because the Lord was going to raise him up. When Smith returned, the family had not done what he asked, and when they saw his faith, they were embarrassed and immediately set out the boy's clothes. Smith asked them to put only socks on his feet. Then inside the boy's room, Smith closed the door and told the lifeless boy that something would happen different from anything he had experienced before. **"When I place my hands on you the glory of the Lord will fill the place till I shall not be able to stand. I shall be helpless on the floor."**[28] The moment Smith touched the boy, the power of God filled the room and was so strong that Smith fell to the floor. Suddenly, the boy began to yell, "This is for Your Glory, Lord!" Smith was still on the floor when the boy arose and dressed himself. Opening the door, the boy yelled, "Dad! God has healed me! I am healed!"[29]

> *The moment Smith touched the boy the power of God filled the room and was so strong that Smith fell to the floor. Suddenly, the boy began to yell, "This is for Your Glory, Lord!"*

Such glory filled the house that the mother and father fell to the floor also. His sister, who had been released from an asylum, was instantly restored in her mind. The entire village was moved and revival began throughout their city.

On that miraculous day, Smith learned how to *transfer faith* by the laying on of hands. His ministry would never be the same, for he had learned a new degree of faith. *Faith could be created and transferred into the life of another!*

## "RUN, WOMAN. RUN!"

As his faith began to increase, the Lord showed him another principle of faith: *Faith should be acted upon.*

★ ★ ★ ★ ★<br>214

Until then, the average believer seemed to think that God moved only in a sovereign way. They felt they had no part in it. The ministry of Smith Wigglesworth brought a new light to this dark area. Through his deep relationship with the Lord, Smith began to notice in the Bible that the people who received from God had *acted* upon His Word to produce results. Thus, his ministry began to adopt this operation of faith in every service. At the beginning of his altar calls he would say: **"If you move forward only a foot, you will be blessed; if you move forward a yard, you will get more. If you come up to the platform, we will pray for you, and God will meet your needs with His supply."**[30]

This was the central truth behind his healing ministry regarding faith. A truth that many called, "ruthless." Smith Wigglesworth's actions were a result of strong compassion and a rock-solid faith in God. A Christian must *act* upon what he believes in order to receive the manifestation, and sometimes, Smith had to *initiate* the action for a few individuals. He called this type of ministry **"retail healing,"** mainly because his faith contributed largely to their individual action.

For example, during a meeting in Arizona, a young lady responded to his call for healing. She was greatly distressed with tuberculosis, but as she stepped into the aisle, he said to her, **"Now, I am going to pray for you and then you will run around this building."** He prayed, then shouted, **"Run, woman. Run!"** The woman said, "But I cannot run. I can scarcely stand." **"Don't talk back to me,"** Smith shouted, **"do as I have said."** She was reluctant, so Smith jumped down from the platform, grabbed her, and began running. She clung to him until she gathered speed, then galloped around the auditorium without any effort. [31]

There was another woman in the same meeting. Her legs were locked with sciatica. Smith told her to *"Run!"* She was so reluctant that he pushed her! Then he ran around the building with the woman clinging to him. Finally, the power of God met her action, and she was completely delivered. She walked to the rest of the meetings, refusing the street car, delighted to have the full use of her limbs again.

## "PAPA! IT'S GOING ALL OVER ME!"

Sometimes in his ministry Smith would use another approach to *acting* on faith. He would read portions of Scripture, then act on it himself. Often he held banquets to feed the lame and hungry, with the members of the Bowland Street Mission serving the sumptuous food. He also arranged for healing testimonies to be their entertainment, moving these poor people to tears.

At the first banquet, Smith set a precedent for the other banquets that followed. At the close of the first meeting, Smith announced:

> "We have entertained you tonight. But next Saturday we are going to have another meeting. You who are bound today and have come in wheelchairs...you who have spent all you have on doctors and are none better, are going to entertain us by the stories of freedom that you have received today by the name of Jesus." Then he said, "*Who wants to be healed?*"[32]

Of course, everyone did. A woman in a wheelchair walked home, and an epileptic of eighteen years was instantly delivered and was working within two weeks. A young boy encased in an iron brace was instantly healed when the power of God touched him as he cried, "Papa, Papa, Papa. It's going all over me!"[33]

Week after week, the healing miracles of the previous services went out among the sick and afflicted, bringing them to the banquet service. What a tremendous revival began among them – simply from acting upon the Word of God.

## "I'LL MOVE THE SPIRIT"

> *Smith knew how to draw the Spirit of God. It all stemmed from faith, not arrogance.*

Smith Wigglesworth took Hebrews 11:6 very seriously. He personally believed it was impossible to please God without faith. As a result, he incorporated that faith into every segment of his spiritual life, including the workings of the Holy Spirit. When the slightest breath of the Spirit came upon Smith, he would go off into a room to be alone with God. In developing this relationship, he understood the action of faith as he cooperated with the Holy Spirit.

Once in a meeting, someone commented on how quickly Smith was moved by the Spirit. When they asked him his secret he replied, "**Well, you see, it is like this. If the Spirit does not move me, I move the Spirit.**"[34] Those who didn't understand the principles of faith thought his remark was arrogant and disrespectful. But in reality, *Smith knew how to draw the Spirit of God. It all stemmed from faith,* not arrogance. If the Holy Spirit wasn't moving as a service began, then Smith would begin the meeting in the natural state. By his faith, he would focus the hearers to the Word and power of God and increase their expectancy. As a result, the Holy Spirit would manifest Himself in direct response to their faith. Smith took the initiative and stirred up the gifts within himself by faith. He didn't wait for something to come upon him and spiritually overtake him. To him, every action, every operation, and every manifestation stemmed from one thing – *absolute faith. True faith confronts, and it is ignited by initiative.*

Then Smith Wigglesworth began teaching the body of Christ that they could speak in tongues by *initiative.* To him, faith was the main substance that stirred the human spirit, not sovereignty. J. E. Stiles, a great Assemblies of God minister and author, learned this important principle from Smith Wigglesworth and carried it throughout his ministry.

In a large meeting in California, Smith gave the call for those people who had not received the baptism of the Holy Spirit to stand. Then he asked for all those to stand who had received, but had not spoken in tongues for six months. **"Now, I'm going to pray a simple prayer,"** Smith began, **"and when I'm finished, I'll say 'Go,' and you will all speak with tongues."** Smith prayed. Then he yelled, **"Go!"** The sound filled the auditorium like that of many waters as everyone prayed in other tongues. Then, he told them to do the same thing again, only when he said, **"Go,"** everyone would sing in tongues, by faith. He prayed. Then he yelled, **"Go! Sing!"** The sound was like a vast and glorious choir.

That day, Rev. Stiles said he learned that the Holy Spirit operates by faith. Shortly after this revelation, he launched his international ministry.[35]

## ANOTHER SECRET

*Smith Wigglesworth was a man greatly moved by compassion.* As he received prayer requests from all over the world he would cry out to God and weep on their behalf. Many times, as he ministered to the afflicted, tears ran down his cheeks. He was also very tender with children and the elderly. In his services, when the heat became stifling, he felt great compassion and would call for the babies and the elderly to be prayed for first.

Demonstrating the truths in Acts 19:11-12, thousands upon thousands were healed as Smith prayed and sent handkerchiefs to those he couldn't visit. An intimate friend spoke of the sincerity and compassion portrayed by Smith, saying, "When...the time for the opening of the letters came, we all had to stop whatever we were doing and get under the burden. There was nothing rushed or slipshod about his methods.... Everybody in the house must join in the prayers and lay hands on the handkerchiefs sent out to the suffering ones. They were treated as though the writers were present in person."[36]

## DOG THE DEVIL!

Realizing that the source of all the miracles of Christ stemmed from His compassion, Smith became positively aggressive in undoing the works of evil. His one goal was to heal all those who were oppressed and to teach the body of Christ to deal ruthlessly with the devil.

*He had little patience with demons, especially when they dared to interrupt his meetings.*

Once, while he waited for a bus, he observed how a woman was encouraging her dog to return home, but after several "sweet" attempts, the dog remained. When she saw the bus approaching, she stomped her foot on the ground and shouted, "Go home at once!" and the dog ran with its tail tucked. **"That's how you have to treat the devil,"** Smith responded, loud enough for all to hear. [37]

He had little patience with demons, especially when they dared to interrupt his meetings. Once, he was conducting a meeting and couldn't "get free" to preach, so he began to shout. Nothing happened. He took off his coat, and still nothing happened. Smith asked the Lord what was wrong, and after doing so, the Lord showed him a line of people sitting together on a bench holding hands. Smith knew at once they were spiritualists bent on destroying his meeting.

As he began to preach, he walked off the platform and over to where they were sitting. Then, he took hold of the bench and commanded the devil to leave. The group slid into a heap on the floor, then scrambled to leave the building!

When casting out demons, Smith Wigglesworth was totally confident and secure in his faith. Prayers didn't have to be long; if the prayer carried faith, the answer was sure.

## INTERNATIONAL AUTHORITY

Smith's international ministry, begun in 1914, was in full swing by 1920. Though the persecution against him was strong, it never seemed to be a major issue in his ministry. Unlike some ministries, there is more written about his great strength and miracles than of his troubles and persecution. Perhaps this is due to his extraordinary faith. He brushed off the criticism like dust off his coat, never allowing it a moment of pleasure.

In Sweden in 1920, the medical profession and local authorities thought they would "harness" the ministry of Wigglesworth, prohibiting him from laying hands on the people. But he wasn't concerned. He knew God would answer *faith*, not *method*. After he conducted the meeting, he instructed over twenty thousand people to **"lay their hands on themselves"** and believe for healing as he prayed. Multitudes received instant manifestation. Smith labeled this type of grand-scale healing as **"wholesale healing."**

In the same year, Smith was arrested twice in Switzerland. The warrants were issued for practicing medicine without a license. On a third occasion, the officers came to the house of a Pentecostal minister with another warrant for Wigglesworth's arrest. The minister said, "Mr. Wigglesworth is away now, but before you arrest him, I want to show you the result of his ministry in this place." The minister then escorted the policemen to the lower part of town to the home of a woman they had arrested many times. Upon seeing the manifestation of her complete deliverance and faith in Jesus Christ, the officers were moved. They turned to the minister and said, "We refuse to stop this kind of work. Somebody else will have to arrest this man." And "somebody else" did. But an officer came to him in the middle of the night and said, "I find no fault with you. You can go." To this Smith replied, **"No, I'll only go on one condition; that every officer in this place gets down on his knees, and I'll pray for you."**[38]

## PENTECOST!

Smith's ministry was flourishing by 1921. International ministry invitations flooded his home inviting him to embark on his longest itinerant journey of his life.

Though very popular in Europe and America, no one seemed to notice his arrival in Colombo, Ceylon (Sri Lanka). But within days, crowds packed the building trying to get a seat. Many had to remain outside. When the meeting was over, Smith passed through the thousands of people, touching them and believing God with them. Reports claimed that scores of people were healed as "his shadow" passed by them.[39]

In 1922, Smith traveled to New Zealand and Australia. Some believe that Smith's meetings birthed the Pentecostal churches in New Zealand and Australia. Though he spent only a few months there, thousands were saved, healed, and filled with the Holy Spirit with the evidence of speaking in tongues. Australia and New Zealand experienced the greatest spiritual revival they had ever seen.

## CAN YOU BLESS A PIG?

Dr. Lester Sumrall from South Bend, Indiana, once shared a humorous incident that occurred during his travels with Smith. A dinner had been prepared for them while they were together in Wales. And just as it so happened, the main entree was roasted pig! Smith was asked to bless the food, so with a loud voice, he said, "**Lord, if You can bless what You have cursed, then bless this pig!**" Smith's humor along with his boldness made a great impression on Sumrall. Dr. Sumrall often laughed when he shared that story with me.

*...Smith Wigglesworth prefered to be unattached to any denomination throughout his ministry. It was in his heart to preach all people...*

### AN UNPUBLISHED CONTROVERSY

Though many churches assembled as a result of his meetings, Smith Wigglesworth preferred to be unattached to any denomination throughout his ministry. It was in his heart to reach all people, regardless of their doctrine. He never wanted to be swayed by any particular denomination.

There is a little known controversy that surfaced in the life of Smith Wigglesworth that deepened his belief in independent ministry. In 1915, he had become a member of the Pentecostal Missionary Union. The union's governing council wasn't a denomination, nor did it offer ministerial licenses or ordinations. It was simply designed to be a covering for ministries of like faith. Smith served with the PMU until his forced resignation in 1920.

At the time he was forced to resign, Smith had been a widower for seven years and had developed a friendship with a woman named Miss Amphlett. Smith told her that he felt he had a **"spiritual affinity"** with her. But Amphlett rejected the idea, and she and another woman wrote a letter of complaint to the PMU. It was directed to the attention of Cecil Polhill, who notified the other council members along with the council's secretary, Mr. Mundell.

Though the PMU had very strict views concerning relationships between men and women, Smith Wigglesworth was sure the PMU would stand by him in spite of the accusations. But when the PMU received Amphlett's letter, Mr. Polhill promptly wrote Wigglesworth requesting his resignation from his council position. He went on to say that the council felt he should "abstain for a prolonged season from participation in the Lord's public work, and seek to retrieve your position before God and man, by a fairly long period of godly, quiet living, so showing works meet for repentance."[40]

Smith honored the request for resignation, though he felt the two women in question had joined together to ruin his work. In fact, Smith was so disappointed in Polhill for allowing the situation to be blown so out of proportion, that he wrote directly to the council's secretary, Mr. Mundell. Smith wrote:

"I think that Mr. Polhill has stepped over the boundary this time [they are] making things to appear as if I had committed fornication or adultery and I am innocent of those things. I have done and acted foolishly and God has forgiven me. This thing was settled in the spiritual way and after this at the church and with Mr. Polhill and he ought to of have seen the thing through."[41]

In a separate letter to Mr. Polhill, Smith wrote:

"...God will settle all. The good hand of God is upon me, and I will live it all down. This week, God has rebuked the oppressor through his servant. I shall go forward, dear brother, and ask you to be careful that the Gospel is not hindered through you and ought at this time to do unto me as you would wish one to do unto you. Do not trouble to send anything to sign. I signed my letter to you, that (is) all."[42]

From that point on Smith Wigglesworth was continually on the go answering invitations to minister all over the world. And to guard against any more false accusations of this nature, Smith always traveled with his daughter, Alice. The controversy resulting in his resignation never slowed Smith down. In fact, it seemed to speed him up.

This is often the case when people come out from under the direction of denominationalism. I know the PMU wasn't a denomination. But these kinds of governing committees can sometimes develop an element of control even after they start out in the right spirit. The control can be so slight, but it still affects the flow of ministry. It was better for Smith to branch out on his own. He didn't need the reputation nor the association with the PMU. He had power with God.

## BETTER LIVE READY

Wigglesworth loved the Word of God and was very disciplined in his study of it. He never considered himself fully dressed unless he had his Bible with him. While others read novels or newspapers, he read the Bible. He would never leave a friend's table without reading, as he would say, **"a bit from the Book."**

## AFFLICTION HAD TO BOW

Though the eyes of Wigglesworth had seen many miraculous and instant healings, he himself didn't receive such miracles. In 1930, as Smith was entering his seventies, he was experiencing tremendous pain. He prayed but wasn't relieved. So he went to a physician who, after X-rays, diagnosed his condition as a very serious case of kidney stones in the advanced stage. An operation was his only hope, since according to the doctor, if Smith continued in this painful condition, he would die. Smith responded:

**"Doctor, the God Who made this body is the One Who can cure it. No knife shall ever cut it so long as I live."**[43]

The physician was concerned and dismayed at his response, but Smith left, assuring the physician he would hear of his healing. The pain increased daily, now accompanied by irritation. All night, Smith was in and out of bed, rolling on the floor in agony as he struggled to emit the stones. One by one, the ragged stones passed. Smith thought his ordeal would be short-lived, but it lasted six long and painful years.

> *One by one, the ragged stones passed. Smith thought his ordeal would be short-lived, but it lasted six long and painful years.*

During this time, Smith never failed to appear at scheduled services, many times ministering twice a day. At some meetings, he would pray for as many as eight hundred people while in tremendous pain himself. Sometimes he would leave the pulpit when the pain became unbearable, to struggle in the restroom with passing another stone. Then he would return to the platform and continue with the service.

Frequently, he would arise from his own bed to go to others to pray for their healing. Very few ever knew he was going through the biggest test of his life. Sometimes, he would lose so much blood that his face would be pale and he would have to be wrapped in blankets to give him warmth. After the six years had passed, over a hundred stones had been emitted into a glass bottle.

Smith's son-in-law, James Salter, gave this great tribute to Smith:

"Living with him, sharing his bedroom as we frequently did during those years, we marveled at the unquenched zeal in his fiery preaching and his compassionate ministry to the sick. He didn't just bear those agonies, he made them serve the purpose of God and glorified in and over them."[44]

## "THEIR EYES ARE ON ME"

Two years into the battle with kidney stones, Smith didn't give up. Instead, in 1932, he asked God for fifteen more years in which to serve Him. God granted his request, and during those years, he visited most of Europe, South Africa, and America. His greatest joy was seeing the Word confirmed by signs and wonders, through the faith of the people. His greatest goal was for people to see Jesus, not Smith Wigglesworth. He was saddened in the last month of his life, as he commented:

> **"Today in my mail, I had an invitation to Australia, one to India and Ceylon, and one to America. People have their eye on me."**

Sadly, he began to weep:

> **"Poor Wigglesworth. What a failure to think that people have their eyes on me. God will never give His glory to another; He will take me from the scene."**[45]

## AND HE WAS NOT...FOR GOD TOOK HIM

Seven days later, Smith Wigglesworth journeyed to a minister's funeral. Along the way, he commented to his friends how **"wonderful"** he felt. He pointed out the different landmarks where he and Polly had visited or preached, then would tell of the great miracles that had happened while there.

When he arrived at the church, his son-in-law, James, opened the door and helped him into the vestry where a warm fire was burning. As he entered, he was met by the father of a young girl he had prayed for days earlier. The girl had been given up to die, but Smith had great faith for her healing. When he saw the man, he asked, **"Well! And how is she?"**[46] He was expecting to hear that the girl was completely delivered, but the answer came hesitantly. "She is a little better, a bit easier; her pains have not been quite so bad during the past few days." Disappointed by what he heard, Smith let out a deep, compassionate sigh. Then his head bowed, and without another word or experiencing any pain, Smith Wigglesworth went home to be with the Lord. He left on March 12, 1947.

*Has the power that Smith Wigglesworth walked in left the earth? Did it go with him when he died? Of course not! The same power Wigglesworth operated in is here for us today, we don't need more power.*

## FAITH + COMPASSION = MIRACLES

As I ministered in a prayer line years ago, a man came up to me with tears streaming down his face. He told me of the power he had experienced in the

*Voice of Healing* revival meetings. The power of God in those meetings set him free. Then he said something I will never forget as long as I live: "Isn't there anybody who walks in the power like they did back then? Isn't there anybody who can set me free? Is there anyone like that today?"

Has the power that Smith Wigglesworth walked in left the earth? Did it go with him when he died? Of course not! The same power Wigglesworth operated in is here for us today, we don't need *more* power. We just need to use our faith *and* compassion for that power to operate. Wigglesworth operated in the boldest faith I have ever seen since the book of Acts, but that faith was ignited by *compassion.* Smith took God at His Word and was moved by compassion for the people, and that combination produces miracles.

The challenge now comes to our generation. God has issued the call for men and women to invade cities and nations with the power of heaven. Will you answer the call of God? Will you dare to *only believe?* Is your heart so moved by compassion for the multitudes, that you will take God at His Word and step out? Let it be said of our generation, *"...through faith [they] subdued kingdoms, wrought righteousness, obtained promises, stopped the mouths of lions, Quenched the violence of fire, escaped the edge of the sword, out of weakness were made strong, waxed valiant in fight, turned to flight the armies of the aliens."* (Hebrews 11:33,34.) Stir up the gift within you, and invade your home, your community, and your nation with the power of God. Let the will of heaven be done on earth – through you!

## CHAPTER SEVEN, SMITH WIGGLESWORTH
### References

[1] Stanley Howard Frodsham, *Smith Wigglesworth: Apostle of Faith* (Springfield, MO: Gospel Publishing House, 1948), 58-59.

[2] W. E. Warner, *The Anointing of His Spirit* (Ann Arbor, MI: Vine Books, segment of Servant Publications), 1994), 237.

[3] Frodsham, *Smith Wigglesworth: Apostle of Faith*, 12.

[4] Ibid., 13.

[5] Ibid., 15.

[6] Ibid., 17.

[7] Ibid., 18-19.

[8] Ibid., 19.

[9] Ibid., 22.

[10] Ibid.

[11] Ibid., 35-36.

[12] Ibid., 21.

[13] Ibid., 37-38.

[14] Ibid., 42.

[15] Ibid.

[16] Ibid., 44.

[17] Ibid., 46.

[18] Ibid., 47.

[19] Ibid., 48-49.

[20] Ibid., 53.

[21] Ibid.,

[22] Ibid., 148.

[23] Warner, *The Anointing of His Spirit*, 238.

[24] Ibid.

[25] Frodsham, *Smith Wigglesworth: Apostle of Faith*, 76.

[26] Kenneth and Gloria Copeland, *John G. Lake: His Life, His Sermons, His Boldness of Faith*, (Forth Worth, TX: Kenneth Copeland Publications, 1994), 443.

[27] Ibid., 432.

[28] Ibid., 27.

[29] Gordon Lindsay, *New John G. Lake Sermons*, (Dallas: Christ for the Nations, Inc., 1976), 19-20.

[30] Lindsay, *John G. Lake: Apostle to Africa*, 9.

[31] Ibid., 65-66.

[32] Ibid., 55

[33] Ibid., 56.

[34] Ibid., 126.

[35] George Stormont, *Wigglesworth: A Man Who Walked With God*, (Tulsa, OK: Harrison House, Inc., 1989), 53-54.

[36] Frodsham, *Smith Wigglesworth: Apostle of Faith*, 114.

[37] Ibid., 72.

[38] Ibid., 102-103.

[39] Ibid., 79.

[40] Polhill to Wigglesworth, October 20, 1920, Polhill Letters 1910-1929.

[41] Wigglesworth to T. H. Mundell, October 21, 1920, Letter.

[42] Wigglesworth to Polhill Letters, October 21, 1920, Wigglesworth File.

[43] Frodsham, *Smith Wigglesworth: Apostle of Faith*, 137.

[44] Ibid., 139.

[45] Albert Hibbert, *Smith Wigglesworth: The Secret of His Power*, (Tulsa, OK: Harrison House, Inc., 1982), 14-15.

[47] Frodsham, *Smith Wigglesworth: Apostle of Faith*, 150-151.

# CHAPTER EIGHT

# Aimee Semple McPherson

*"A Woman of Destiny"*

# "A Woman of Destiny"

**S**omebody must have seen her marching up Main Street from the direction of the bank and the barbershop; she was a very young woman in a white dress, carrying a chair.

"Standing on the chair, she raised her long hands toward heaven as if calling for help.... And then she did nothing.... She closed her large, wide-set eyes and just stood there with her arms straight up, like a statue of marble...

"Even with her eyes closed Aimee could feel the critical mass of the crowd when it grew to be fifty spectators gaping and hooting...The young woman opened her eyes and looked around her.

"'People,' she shouted, leaping off the chair, 'come and follow me, quick.'

"Hooking her arm through the back of the chair, she pushed through the crowd and started running back down Main Street. The people chased her, boys first, then men and women.... They followed her right through the open door of the Victory Mission. There was just enough room for all to be seated.

"'Lock the door,' she whispered to the usher. 'Lock the door and keep it locked till I get through.'"[1]

Aimee Semple McPherson has been described as a woman born before her time. Actually, Aimee was the spiritual pioneer who paved the way for the rest of us and should be considered largely responsible for the way we demonstrate Christianity today.

Aimee defied all odds. Her life story portrays her as a woman alive and dramatic. There was nothing mellow about her. To her, a challenge was fair game to be taken and conquered. She rode on the wave of the media, and actually directed its course. If publicity seemed bad, she hyped it further, smiling all the way. If everyone warned her against doing something, she was apt to do

the opposite, refusing to bow to fear. In fact, there was *nothing* too radical for Aimee Semple McPherson. Whatever it took to "get the people" – Aimee did it. She sat with the "publicans and prostitutes," showing up in places where the average Christian was afraid to go. The poor, the common, and the rich all loved her for it, and they showed up at her meetings by the thousands.

> *...there was nothing too radical for Aimee Semple McPherson. Whatever it took to "get the people" — Aimee did it.*

But of course the "religious" hated her. When denominational politics seemed to hinder and wound so many ministers, Aimee rarely gave them thought. She demolished religious seclusion and narrowness, seeming to almost pity those controlled by its grip. Aimee set about building a ministry so vast and so great, that even Hollywood came to take notes.

In a time when women were only recognized as an "accessory," to ministry, Aimee built Angelus Temple to include them. The Temple was built and dedicated during the Depression, and was an elaborate building that could seat five thousand people. When the building filled three times each Sunday, Aimee ventured even further. She built the very first Christian radio station in the world, and founded one of the fastest growing denominations today.

Aimee lived during the height of the Pentecostal Movement that was full of the *"dos"* and *"don'ts"* of religion, when women in general weren't accepted in the ministry. And to make matters worse to the religious mindset of the day, she was divorced.

## A NEW GENERATION IS BORN

Her life began in controversy and scandal. Aimee was born to James Morgan and Mildred "Minnie" Kennedy on October 9, 1890, near Salford, Ontario, Canada. The only daughter of James and Mildred, Aimee Elizabeth Kennedy grew up in a town that roared with gossip because of those who took issue with the circumstances surrounding her birth. Her father, age fifty, married her mother, Minnie, when she was only fifteen years old.

Prior to their marriage, the orphaned Minnie had been a fervent laborer with the Salvation Army. Feeling the call to the ministry, she evangelized day and night in cities throughout Ontario. Then she read in the paper one day about the Kennedys' need for a live-in nurse to care for the ailing Mrs. Kennedy. So she accepted the position and moved in with the family, setting her ministry aside.

After Mrs. Kennedy's death, Minnie remained in the Kennedy home. Not long after, the older man asked Minnie to become his wife. The town roared with gossip, but James Kennedy simply let them talk.

The day after their marriage, Minnie got down on her knees and prayed. She confessed that she had failed in her call to the ministry, and asked God's forgiveness. Then she prayed:

"If You will only hear my prayer, as You heard Hannah's prayer of old, and give me a little baby *girl*, I will give her unreservedly into Your service, that she may preach the Word I should have preached, fill the place I should have filled, and lived the life I should have lived in Thy service. O Lord, hear and answer me...."[2]

Soon Minnie was pregnant. She never doubted that she was carrying a girl, so everything she designed, bought, or received for the baby was pink. Then in answer to her prayers, a little girl was born on October 9 in the Kennedy's Canadian farmhouse near Salford.

The Salvationists came to visit the baby, and brought with them the sad news that Catherine Booth, wife of the great General William Booth, had died. Catherine had been the co-founder of the Salvation Army and one of the visitors suggested that Aimee could very well be her successor.[3]

Whatever plan God had for the child, it was especially clear to Minnie after hearing these words, that Aimee would certainly grow far beyond her expectations.

## BULLFROGS AND SCHOOL SLATES

When Aimee was three weeks old, Minnie dedicated her to the Lord at a Salvation Army service. Her childhood was picture-perfect. She was raised as an only child on a large country farm in a rambling farmhouse with farm animals as playmates. She grew up with the stories of Daniel in the lion's den, Joseph and Pharaoh, and Moses leading the children of Israel out of Egypt. By the time Aimee was four, she could stand on a street corner, in the middle of a drumhead, and draw a huge crowd by reciting Bible stories.

Aimee was a spunky little girl. She was full of headstrong ideas. Nothing intimidated her, except the realization that no matter where she was, God could see everything she was doing.

Once, while sick in bed, a hired man poked his head through her door, asking if he could do anything for her. Aimee sighed in a spoiled way and said, "I would like to hear the frogs sing. Do go down to the swamp and bring me three or four frogs and put them in a pail of water by my bed."

So the man did as he was told, and about an hour later, he came back into her room with a large pail, complete with lilies and frogs. But as he left for work, he failed to hear Aimee screaming for him to retrieve the frogs which had jumped out of the bucket, and were now bouncing around the room! It was Aimee's mother Minnie who had to be the one to catch the slimy intruders![4]

As a young girl in school, Aimee was always in charge. When other children teased her, calling her a "Salvation Army child," Aimee got angry. But instead of fighting back, she would play along with them. In later years, it was just this sort of response that caused Aimee's popularity to soar.

> *As a young girl in school, Aimee was always in charge. When other children teased her, calling her a "Salvation Army child," Aimee got angry. But instead of fighting back, she would play along with them.*

Once when Aimee was made fun of, instead of retaliating against her classmates, she got a box, a ruler, and a red tablecloth. Then she appointed a boy to carry a "red flag," and marched around banging on her box like a drum while singing at the top of her lungs. At first, the boys fell in behind her, making fun of the march, but then they started to enjoy it. Soon, the girls stepped in and joined her lively parade. And from that day forward, no one teased Aimee about the Salvation Army. Her faith always embraced, never repelled.[5]

When Aimee was a young girl, she loved to watch her mother, who was the Sunday school superintendent at the Salvationists' meetings. As soon as Aimee came home from church, she would gather up chairs and set them in a circle in her room. Then she would imitate her mother by preaching to her imaginary crowd.

In her school picture, Aimee, then eight years old, is holding the class slate while sitting in the middle of the other students. The children on either side of the teacher look noticeably angry. They look upset because before the picture was taken, an argument had broken out over who was going to hold the slate sign. But as they bickered, Aimee suddenly jumped into the middle of the group and grabbed it! Then when the others tried to take it from her, the teacher corralled them all and seated them long enough to snap the photo.

The photo serves as somewhat of a prophetic snapshot of Aimee Semple McPherson's future ministry. The children surrounding her sit aggravated by her bold, determined action. And there in the middle, between the protective legs of her teacher sits Aimee – full of joy and confidence in triumphant victory!

# GO FOR THE GOLD!

Throughout her youth, Aimee's dogmatic character began to surface. She had a sportive, playful attitude toward authority. If you were chosen to be a leader over her, you would have to impressively prove you could do it before expecting any submission from her!

Aimee wasn't completely disrespectful or rebellious, and she never truly meant to be a challenge to authority. It was just that her leadership ability was so great, that those around her were automatically challenged and left speechless. Even as a child, when Aimee walked into a room, she would capture everyone's attention without having to speak one word.

Some say Aimee was a spoiled child, and that it was her father, James Kennedy, who spoiled her. James took great delight in his spunky little girl. Others say Aimee simply wore her parents out with her high spirits and creativity. But to them, Aimee Elizabeth was an answer from God, and they treated her like a treasure.

Minnie Kennedy watched over Aimee like a hawk. She was a good mother to Aimee, but learning to stand up to Minnie was no small feat. Just holding her own around Minnie served to groom Aimee for answering the many hard questions that would come her way as a future Christian leader.

Because of her zeal for life and emotional strength, Aimee soon began to enjoy the applause. As a preteen, her dramatic personality became well-known in local village theater productions. And she was a popular orator while in grammar school.

At the age of twelve, Aimee won the silver medal for a speech that she presented at the Women's Christian Temperance Union in Ingersoll, Ontario, Canada. She would go on to compete in London, Ontario, to win the gold medal.

By the time she was thirteen, Aimee was a celebrated, outstanding public speaker. She was invited to entertain at church suppers, various organizations, Christmas auctions, festivals, and picnics. The communities of Ingersoll and Salford soon realized that people would come from miles around to be entertained by this specially gifted girl.[6]

# DARWIN OR JESUS?

But Aimee's training in the Methodist church in Salford would soon cause her some confusion. Though the Methodists encouraged speech and entertainment within their building, they absolutely condemned movie theaters and plays outside of it. In fact, Minnie had been led to believe that "moving pictures" were the most sinful thing ever created. So Aimee grew up in a generation that believed in strict, religious rules. Church authorities and others had solemnly warned her that if she was ever to visit a movie theater, Aimee would end up in hell. Nevertheless, once when she was invited to a movie, she consented to go. And when she did, she recognized several other members from her church. One was a Sunday school teacher. The hypocrisy of it all touched her deeply.

When Aimee entered high school in 1905, the Darwin theory had just been popularized. Suddenly, every new textbook was filled with Darwin's theory that claimed life on earth began from an amoeba, and that man was cousin to the chimpanzee.

> *...in her reading, Aimee finally decided that Darwin's theory had to be true. After all, the church no longer practiced what the Bible said. It seemed the church was only a social gathering for plays and entertainment, and there were no miracles being worked like those she read about in the Bible.*

Aimee was shocked. Though she was not yet a born-again Christian, she had been raised on the Bible, and was truly insulted by Darwin's claims. So she approached her science professor and gallantly questioned him on the matter. As far as he was concerned, "biological research had superseded ancient superstition."[7] But Aimee cornered the poor man to such a degree that he finally had to side step her, then handed her a library list to study.

Aimee accepted the challenge. Not only would she read these secular authors and their theories, but when she was finished no one but those authors would know more on the subject of Darwin's theory than she did. This would become a pattern throughout her life. Aimee was diligent and unbeatable.

But in her reading, Aimee finally decided that Darwin's theory had to be true. After all, the church no longer practiced what the Bible said. It seemed the church was only a social gathering for plays and entertainment, and there were no miracles being worked like those she read about in the Bible. So she began debating with visiting ministers and questioned why they preached if there were no miracles today.

When questioned, one minister cleared his throat and explained how miracles had passed away, describing it as the "cessation of charisma." Then when

Aimee challenged him with other Scriptures, he finally told her that these matters were completely over her head. The man obviously didn't know of Aimee's determination.

Another night after an evening church service, Aimee challenged a visiting preacher in such a manner that her parents were mortified. **"If the Bible is true, why do our neighbors pay good tax money to tear down our faith?"** she asked the trembling minister.[8] Again, Aimee had the last word. But she was miserable, because no one seemed to have the spiritual ammunition to address her confusion.

Aimee finally came to the conclusion that according to her beliefs, if portions of the Bible were no longer true, then none of the Bible could be true. She further reasoned that if there was a leak in one place, the whole thing should be thrown out. So she decided to become an atheist.

Arriving home after this one last searing battle of words with the minister, Aimee sprinted into her room, opened the shutters, and peered out into the night. As she surveyed the magnificence of the stars, Aimee was moved within herself. Someone had to have made the heavens, and she longed to know what, or who. No more stories, and no more hearsay. She wanted facts.

So Aimee prayed, **"O God — if there be a God — reveal Yourself to me!"**[9] Two days later, God would answer her plea.

## THE HOLY ROLLERS ARE HERE!

Aimee was a "study in relaxed determination." At seventeen, she was a beautiful girl who seemed to have everything she wanted. Unlike the other girls of the district, she never spoke of marriage and children. She was very intelligent and her family was financially comfortable. Her tailored clothes were stylish, and her parents adored her. She also had the ability to speak and capture an audience with a sentence or two, and had won every speaking competition she ever entered. She went around to dance halls, finding them full of church members. In fact, the first person who whirled her on the dance floor was a Presbyterian minister. But more than ever, Aimee needed the Lord. And soon she would find Him.

The day after Aimee had prayed for God to reveal Himself, she was driving home from school with her father. As they traveled down Main Street in Ingersoll she noticed a sign in a storefront window that read: HOLY GHOST REVIVAL: ROBERT SEMPLE, IRISH EVANGELIST.

Aimee had heard how these Pentecostal people fell on the floor and spoke in unknown languages. And she had heard the wild stories of their shouting and dancing. She was very curious, so the next evening before Aimee's Christmas program rehearsal, James Kennedy took his daughter to the mission. They sat on the back row.

## EVEN THE BIRDS SMILED

At the meeting, Aimee was all eyes. She was amused as she saw certain townspeople singing and shouting, "Hallelujah" with their hands uplifted. *What a show!* she thought. Had she not been an atheist, Aimee thought she would shout herself! She was thoroughly enjoying this naive show from her intellectual tower. Then, Robert Semple walked into the room.

At that moment, everything changed for Aimee. Semple was about six feet two inches tall, blue eyed, with curly-brown hair, and had a wonderful sense of humor. Years later, Aimee would still affectionately go on about his blue eyes as, **"having the light of heaven."**

*The young evangelist saw no middle ground between serving the world and serving God. If you loved one, then you couldn't love the other. You were either for, or against Him. It was as simple as that. Aimee hung on every word.*

An Irish Presbyterian, Semple left his homeland by boat to sail to New York. He then traveled over land to Toronto, Canada, and then to Chicago, Illinois. It was in 1901 that the Pentecostal manifestation of speaking in other tongues spread from Topeka, Kansas, to Chicago. And it was here in Chicago that Robert Semple first spoke in other tongues. While working as a clerk at Marshall Field's department store in the city, God called him to the ministry. He became a very successful evangelist who was known throughout the northern U.S. and Canada. And now, he had come to Aimee's hometown.

When Semple walked into the little mission, it seemed that Aimee's whole world stood still. Rev. Robert Semple strode up to the pulpit and opened his Bible to the second chapter of Acts. Then he repeated a simple command: "Repent...repent."

Aimee began to squirm uneasily. Every time Semple spoke, his words pierced her heart like an arrow. Later Aimee said, **"I had never heard such a sermon. Using the Bible as a sword, he cut the whole world in two."**

The young evangelist saw no middle ground between serving the world and serving God. If you loved one, then you couldn't love the other. You were either for, or against Him. It was as simple as that. Aimee hung on every word. Then the young evangelist turned his head toward heaven, and began to speak in tongues. As she watched, his face seemed to glow with an inner light.

As Semple spoke, Aimee could understand perfectly what was being said. It was the voice of God, showing Himself to her, answering her prayer:

> **"From the moment I heard that young man speak with tongues, to this day, I have never doubted for the shadow of a second that there was a God, and that he had shown me my true condition as a poor, lost, miserable, hell-serving sinner."**[10]

Three days later, Aimee stopped her carriage in the middle of a lonely road, lifted her hands toward heaven and cried out for God's mercy. Then, suddenly, as she writes it:

> **"The sky was filled with brightness. The trees, the fields, and the little snow birds flitting to and fro were praising the Lord and smiling upon me. So conscious was I of the pardoning blood of Jesus that I seemed to feel it flowing over me."**

Aimee had finally been born again.

## SHAKING WITH THE POWER

Seeking direction for her life, Aimee prayed and received a vision. As she closed her eyes, she saw a black river rushing past with millions of men, women, and children being swept into it. They were being helplessly pushed along by the river's current and falling over a waterfall. Then she heard – "Become a winner of souls."[11]

Puzzled at how in the world *she* could accomplish this task, Aimee began to seek the Lord even further. Women couldn't preach. It was simply not allowed. But Aimee believed that if Peter, a fisherman, could preach, maybe a Canadian farm girl could too. So she searched the New Testament. And as she did, she came to the conclusion that the only requirement necessary for the one called to preach was the baptism of the Holy Spirit. So against her mother's wishes, Aimee started attending "tarrying" meetings that had gone on in Ingersoll, Ontario, for some time.

There were manifestations in abundance at Ingersoll's tarrying meetings. They had been instituted for the purposes of receiving the baptism of the Holy Spirit, and in 1908, were viewed by most as extremely radical. Even the Salvation Army approached Minnie to discuss her daughter's sudden, Pentecostal behavior.[12]

But Aimee never cared what anyone thought. All she really wanted to do, was to please God...and Robert Semple. It was Robert's love for God that caused Aimee to fervently pursue God. She fervently wanted to know Him as Robert did.

Aimee's school grades were now slipping because of spending so much time at the tarrying meetings. One morning, as Aimee passed the house of the woman who held the tarrying meetings, she felt she just couldn't go on to school – she wanted to speak in tongues! In fact, she wanted to speak in other tongues so much, that she turned back from the train and rang the woman's doorbell. Now she was skipping classes to tarry in prayer.

Once Aimee had been invited in and had explained her heart's cry, she and the tarrying group leader started to seek God and pray. Aimee even asked God to delay school so she could continue to tarry there to receive. And when she did, a blizzard hit Ingersoll. The icy blast not only prevented her from traveling to school, it also kept her from going home. Aimee was thrilled! She had been snowed in for an entire weekend to tarry for the Spirit.

Early the next Saturday morning while everyone else was asleep in the house, Aimee arose early to seek the Lord. As she lifted her voice in adoration, her praises came deeper from within her, until at last, there was a thunder that came out of her that vibrated from head to toe.

Aimee slipped to the floor, feeling as if she were caught up in billowy clouds of glory. Then, suddenly, words began flowing out of her mouth in another language – first in short phrases, then in full sentences. By now, the whole house had been awakened by her sounds, and the group came shouting and rejoicing down the stairs. Among them, was Robert Semple. It isn't known exactly how much time Robert Semple spent in Aimee's town. But he must have traveled back and forth because of his being there when Aimee was baptized in the Holy Spirit.

## "ELECTRIC" DANCING

Robert traveled extensively, but corresponded regularly with Aimee throughout the winter. Then in the early spring of 1908, Robert returned to Ingersoll and proposed to her. In fact, he proposed to Aimee in the same house in which she received the baptism a few months earlier. Six months later on August 12, 1908, Aimee married Robert Semple in her family's farmhouse near Salford, Ontario.

Aimee would not finish high school because of her love for Semple. In fact, she left behind everything in order to love, honor, and obey her new husband. Robert was all she needed for a fulfilled and enriching life.

**"He was my theological seminary,"** she would later write, **"my spiritual mentor, and my tender, patient, unfailing lover."**[13]

Before their marriage, Aimee and Robert had convinced her parents that speaking in other tongues was scriptural. But it took much more to convince Minnie of God's will concerning the couple's call to China.

In preparation for their trip, Robert worked in a factory by day and preached by night. Soon, his ministry took them to London, Ontario, where they ministered in homes. Robert would preach while Aimee played the piano, sang, and prayed with the converts. In just a few months, a hundred people had received the baptism of the Holy Spirit, with many more saved. They also saw many remarkable healings.[14]

In January of 1909, the Semples went to Chicago, Illinois, where Robert was ordained by Pastor William Durham. They ministered there for several months in an Italian neighborhood and were very content and happy.

*Robert and Aimee Semple*

Later in the year, the Semples traveled to Findlay, Ohio, with Pastor Durham to work in another mission. It was here that Aimee had her first experience with divine healing. It happened when Aimee broke her ankle after falling down some stairs. The physician who put the cast on Aimee told her that she would never have the use of four ligaments again. And she was told to stay off of her foot for at least one month. But Aimee continued to hobble to the prayer meetings, even though the slightest vibration on the floor would cause tremendous pain.

> *A feeling like a shot of electricity struck her leg, and immediately the blackness left her toes. She felt the ligaments pop into place as her bone mended together, then suddenly, she felt no pain.*

Finally at one meeting, the pain became so intense that she had to return to her room. As she sat and stared at her black and swollen toes, she heard a voice saying, "If you will go over to the (mission) and ask Brother Durham to lay hands on your foot, I will heal it." Recognizing it as the voice of the Lord, Aimee did as she was told.

At the mission, Brother Durham had been walking up and down the aisles, but stopped and placed his hand on Aimee's foot. A feeling like a shot of electricity struck her leg, and immediately the blackness left her toes. She felt the ligaments pop into place as her bone mended together, then suddenly, she felt no pain.

Aimee excitedly asked for someone to cut away the cast. After some debate, they finally agreed to do so. Once the cast was removed, they were shocked to see a perfectly healed foot. Then Aimee put on her shoes and danced all over the church![15]

## DEMONS, CATERPILLARS & BURNING HINDUS

In early 1910, the Semples, who were now expecting a child, set sail for China. The couple visited Robert's parents in Ireland, then stopped over in London where he preached at several meetings. While he was away at one of these meetings, a Christian millionaire asked Aimee to preach in Victoria and Albert Hall. Aimee was just nineteen years old, and had never preached in public before, but she didn't want to turn down an opportunity to serve God. So she nervously accepted.

As Aimee stood before the people crowded in the hall, she opened her Bible to Joel 1:4. Then she began to prophetically teach on the restoration of the Church throughout the ages. In fact, she was so caught up in the moment of it, that after the meeting, she could only remember the tremendous anointing that had inspired the message. She couldn't remember what she said, but she could see the clapping and wiping of eyes of the many who had heard her.

In June of 1910, the Semples arrived in Hong Kong. But Aimee wasn't ready for what she saw. The Chinese diet of caterpillars, bugs, and rats revolted her, and their apartment was very noisy, so they got very little rest. They eventually discerned their little apartment was "haunted" by demon spirits that were making some of the noises heard day and night.

One day, the Hindus burned a man alive outside their kitchen window. This, along with everything else, had Aimee living on the edge of hysteria most of the time. She had grown to hate the mission. And soon, because of their poor living conditions, she and Robert both contracted malaria. Robert's case was worse than hers, and on August 17, only two months after they had arrived, Robert Semple was dead.

Aimee was now left alone to fend for herself in this strange and foreign land. Her grief was unbearable and she was pregnant with Robert's child. One month after Robert's death on September 17, 1910, she gave birth to a small, four pound baby girl, naming her Roberta Star.

But Robert's death had flooded Aimee's life with grief. Nothing could describe her misery as she laid in her hospital bed overcome with the horror of the reality of carrying on alone. At times she would turn toward the hospital walls and scream into them.[16]

Aimee's mother, Minnie, sent her the money to finally travel home. As the forlorn missionary widow steamed home across the Pacific, the tiny baby she was holding was the only thing that brought her any hope.

## HOME SWEET HOME

Once home, Aimee mourned the loss of Robert for over a year, but she also continued to search for God's will in her life. She went to New York and then on to Chicago, hoping to minister in the churches Robert had left. Then the baby's health suffered, and she returned to her childhood home. But Aimee's grief wouldn't allow her to sit still for long, and she eventually returned to New York.

While in New York Aimee met Harold McPherson, who would soon become her second husband. McPherson was from Rhode Island, and was described as a solid, clear-thinking man, great in strength, and very kind.

On February 28, 1912, Aimee and Harold were married. Aimee nick-named Harold, "Mack." Roberta would call him Daddy Mack. They moved to Providence, Rhode Island, to settle into a small apartment where Harold got a job in a bank and Aimee stayed home as a housewife. And by July of 1912, Aimee was expecting her second child.

According to Aimee, the only real problem that she and Harold had to contend with in their marital relationship was in the area of their vastly different goals. She described the three years following their wedding as being much like the story of Jonah. Aimee had run from God, and as a result, was suffering from depression. She was plagued with illnesses, and finally experienced an emotional breakdown.

*With hope almost gone, the interns moved Aimee from her room to a ward where they took the dying. It was then that Aimee began speaking out of the lifelessness of her coma. She was calling the people to repentance — and she was hearing the voice again: "WILL YOU GO?"*

## "WILL YOU GO?"

Then Rolf, her only son, was born on March 23, 1913, and as a mother, she began to realize that an emotional maturity and stability was being built within her that would benefit her future. Not long after his birth, Aimee began to hear the voice of the Lord telling her, "Preach the Word! Will you go? Will you go?" She would hear the voice especially when she was cleaning the house.[17]

The sensitivity to the voice of God's Spirit that Aimee developed in those years would eventually shake a sleeping nation. It has been said that she tenderly spoke to the thousands in her ministry like a mother would speak to her children.

In 1914, Aimee worked around the community, preaching and teaching in Sunday schools, but this didn't satisfy the call that by now had begun to boom, "DO THE WORK OF AN EVANGELIST! WILL YOU GO?"

But it was also in 1914, that Aimee became gravely ill. After several surgeries, she grew no better and became despondent to the point of begging God to let her die.

The physicians called Harold's mother and Minnie to inform them of Aimee's approaching death. But as Minnie listened to their report, she vividly remembered praying to God for her little girl. And she remembered her vow – that Aimee would fulfill the call Minnie had rejected herself. She held on to God's promise, refusing to let Aimee die. The nurses wept as they watched Minnie standing over Aimee's body, crying and renewing her promise to God.

With hope almost gone, the interns moved Aimee from her room to a ward where they took the dying. It was then that Aimee began speaking out of the lifelessness of her coma. She was calling the people to repentance – and she was hearing the voice again: "WILL YOU GO?" She mustered up the energy to whisper that she would. Then she opened her eyes, and all the pain was gone. And within two weeks, she was up and well.

## "I WAS ON MY BACK IN THE STRAW"

By now, Harold had a good job and wanted Aimee to be like other women – clean the house and cook in the kitchen. But Aimee felt she could not remain so confined and be able to fill the call to go. So in the spring of 1915, after Harold left for work, Aimee bundled up Roberta and Rolf, along with their belongings, and left for Toronto.[18]

She wired Harold before leaving to attend her first Pentecostal camp-meeting, **"I have tried to walk your way and have failed. Won't you come now and walk my way? I am sure we will be happy."**[19]

Minnie agreed to take care of the children so Aimee could start the ministry. Harold responded to Aimee's wire many months later. By then they were so far apart, Harold could not catch up to her. After months of trying to work out their differences, they faced up to the inevitable.

With her future now committed, Aimee was concerned she would never again operate in the power that she did while married to Robert. She feared God's anointing had left her. But her fears ended when she was welcomed by her friends at the campmeeting warmly. She was inspired when she heard all their hearty praise and sensed God's fire ignite within her.

Still, she felt the need to confess her laxity to the Lord, and at the camp meeting's first altar call, she was the first one down. When she knelt at the altar, she felt God's grace and acceptance.

**"Such love,"** she recalled, **"was more than my heart could bear. Before I knew it I was on my back in the straw, under the power."**

Aimee would remain at this camp meeting for weeks. She washed dishes, waited tables, and prayed for people. It had been a long time since she had been this happy.[20]

## A RIPPED TENT & SPIRITUAL POWER

Soon Aimee began preaching on her own. She would use any method to draw a crowd, and people would travel from all over the countryside to hear her. In 1915, one of her meetings drew more than five hundred people. She had

become a novelty. Besides her dramatics, she was a woman, and women preachers were hard to find in those days. So everyone was curious to see and hear her. The townspeople collected $65 for her at one of her meetings. With the offering she was able to purchase a much needed $500 tent. Thrilled at obtaining the bargain, Aimee unrolled the seasoned canvas to set it up. But unfortunately, it wasn't a bargain. The canvas had been ripped to shreds in some places. So Aimee quickly assembled her volunteers and sewed holes with them until their fingers were stiff and sore. By sunset, the patchwork tent was up.

Once, looking out over the crowd, Aimee saw Harold. He had traveled to one of her meetings to see her preach. Before the night was over, he was filled with the Holy Spirit and joined her briefly in the meetings.

There was a natural empathy in Aimee that accentuated her ministry mannerisms and drew huge crowds of people from every walk of life. People could relate to her, because after all, everyone had a mother. And those who came would experience the power of God through amazing manifestations. Many would come just to sense the presence of God, and thousands received the baptism.

## THE ROLLING CHURCH

For the next seven years, Aimee crossed the United States six times. Between the years of 1917 and 1923, she preached in more than one hundred cities with meetings ranging in duration from two nights to a month.

Her first ministry experience with divine healing took place with a woman afflicted by rheumatoid arthritis. The woman's neck was so twisted that she was unable to look at the evangelist. But immediately following the prayer of faith, she turned her neck and looked into Aimee's face. God had healed her, and how Aimee knew it, as she looked at her eye to eye.

Aimee stated emphatically that she never sought a healing ministry, and hardly relished the idea of one.[21] But healing came with her evangelistic call, and after hearing of the unusually successful results in answer to her prayers, people came in droves for prayer.

In one meeting, the offerings were large enough to buy a 1912 Packard touring car. It would soon become her rolling church. Aimee would stand in the back seat and preach eight to ten meetings a day. Then between meetings, she would pass out tracts and handbills, inviting all to come.

Though Aimee conducted her meetings with grace, she was also very strong. She had developed a great deal of strength from hauling her tent, and from hammering its stakes into the ground during setup. In fact, she was louder and stronger than most men.

## BURNS, BLISTERS, & MARDI GRAS

As discussed earlier, Aimee was noted for her affectionate preaching. She would often treat her audiences as a mother would her child. She was never condemning or threatening, always encouraging her listeners to fall in love with the grace and mercy of God.

But, like a strong mother, Aimee wasn't weak. Once, a lamp exploded in her face, covering her with flames. She quickly plunged her head into a bucket of water, but not before blisters developed on her neck and face. To make matters worse, all of this happened as hecklers were watching and jeering. The tent was full the night this occurred, so she exited behind it, being in great pain. One of the hecklers jumped on the platform and said, "The lady who preaches divine healing has been hurt. She burned her face, so there will be no meeting tonight."

> *"The lady who preaches divine healing has been hurt. She burned her face, so there will be no meeting tonight."*

But right after he said it, Aimee furiously rushed in through the tent flaps and leapt on the platform. She was in agony, but was able to draw enough strength to sit down at the piano and cry out, **"I praise the Lord who heals me and takes all the pain away!"** Then within two to three stanzas of the song, the crowd witnessed a miracle: Aimee's face went from lobster red to the color of normal flesh![22]

Aimee used every opportunity to draw a crowd, so while in a town during a Mardi Gras parade, she felt her efforts would be feeble if she didn't come up with a plan. She noticed the many parade floats being entered with the themes of different states and local businesses. So she quickly turned her 1912 Packard into a floating church! Her staff helped her quickly cover the top, making it appear to be a hill with a tent on its summit, then decorated it with green palms and Spanish moss. On the sides, she painted, "Jesus is coming soon," and "I am going to the Pentecostal camp meeting. R.U.?" Then inside, Aimee played her baby organ, while Harold drove the car into the parade line, unnoticed by the policeman. The crowd loved it and shouted their approval with raucous laughs and cheers! And that night, they packed the tent! **"The**

**very audacity of the thing which we had done,"** Aimee recalled, **"seemed to appeal to them."**[23]

## FROM HAROLD TO MINNIE

It was around this same time that Aimee started publishing *The Bridal Call*. The publication began as a four-page newspaper, but within three months, had grown to a sixteen-page magazine complete with photos, sermons, poems, and a subscription price. Aimee's intentions in publishing it were to reshape the Church, by taking "away the damnation and sin to take on the tone of a celebration, a happy wedding."[24]

> *Minnie immediately took charge of the crowd phenomenon. ...She believed evangelism was more than faith — it required organization!*

Aimee's reputation for freedom in the Holy Spirit attracted people from many different backgrounds. Soon every sort of thrill seeker, rover, and thug in the area would show up at her tent. When the meetings were small, she could control them. But when they grew to over a thousand in attendance, the only way she could calm their emotional outbursts was to resort to music and singing, and she did it very masterfully. Before long, she was incorporating narrative and drama into her preaching.

Aimee found herself at ease among the black culture. She loved visiting in their homes, usually finding herself much poorer than any of them. They knew she loved them also. They thronged her in the South as she visited and worked with them in the cotton and tobacco fields.

Now the crowds were soaring in numbers. But Aimee's personal life began to suffer again as she and Harold disagreed about the ministry. He didn't like the vagabond life they were leading, nor did he understand her vision for the future. So finally, after an all-night confrontation, Harold packed his belongings and left.

Several years later, Harold filed for divorce, claiming that Aimee had deserted him. But she countered the suit, stating the opposite. Harold would go on to remarry and live a much more normal family life.

Minnie now joined Aimee's ministry and brought along with her Aimee's daughter, Roberta. Roberta was now seven and hadn't seen her mother in two years. But now that she was with her, she was quickly filled with the excitement of her mother's ministry and loved to watch her preach.

Minnie immediately took charge of the crowd phenomenon. Aimee had drawn multitudes of people. As the thousands thronged her meetings, Aimee desperately needed someone to help manage them. And Mother Kennedy was a natural for this. She believed evangelism was more than faith – it required organization! Minnie's meticulous detailing was up to the task of Aimee's anointing, and it would eventually take her daughter from tents to coliseums.

## STRETCHED SHOES AND A BOTTLE OF CLOUDS

Amid all the frenzy and obsession of the ministry, Aimee's children said they always felt secure with their mother on the road. They loved traveling with her. Some accused Aimee of making life difficult for them. But the truth of the matter was, both were greatly disappointed when they couldn't go with her!

Rolf and Roberta both have wonderful memories of their mother. Roberta remembers the stories her mother told her as they drove down the highway. Once, Roberta wanted to catch a cloud after her mother had described one so beautifully. So Aimee promptly steered to the side of the road, grabbed an empty bottle, and got out of the car. Then she held the empty bottle up in the air until the mist and fog surrounding her formed tiny droplets on the bottle's inside. When she brought it back to the car, she presented it to Roberta with a genuine cloud.

Rolf remembers how badly he once needed shoes, and how he received a pair as a gift. When the box arrived, the family was excited. But when Rolf tried to put them on, they wouldn't fit. Disappointment set in until Roberta asked, "Mother, what did the Israelite children do for shoes in the wilderness?...their feet must have grown." Then without thinking Aimee quickly replied, **"God must have stretched their shoes."** Roberta then asked if God would do the same for Rolf's shoes, so Mother Aimee said, **"I don't know, but let us kneel and ask Him."** Then Rolf tried the shoes on again, and this time – they fit perfectly!

There was another time when Rolf was playing barefoot in the tall grass of a campground when he injured his foot by stepping on a hidden rake. His foot was deeply pierced and was bleeding dark red blood.

When Aimee learned of Rolf's accident she quickly rushed to his side and carried him to his cot in their little tent. Rolf fondly remembers how his mother held his foot while kneeling in prayer to ask God for his healing. After she prayed for God to heal her son, then almost immediately, Rolf fell asleep.

Many hours later Rolf was awakened by the distant roar of the masses in the tent meeting. When he sat up he saw the blood stains on his bed, and he grabbed his foot. When he did, he looked at the bottom where the rake had pierced him, but there was no sign of a wound. Thinking he had looked at the wrong foot, he grabbed the other, but it was also smooth. Elated by the sight, he realized his foot was completely healed!

## DRESSING THE PART

The only early Pentecostal belief Aimee was ever known to have taken a stand against was the doctrine of sanctification as a second work of grace. She strongly felt that those who claimed or pursued "Christian perfection" often turned their backs on the people of the world, creating a religious isolationism.

Aimee wanted the Gospel to fit everyone. And she didn't want anyone to feel intimidated about coming to hear about God's Word. She was burdened by the eliteness she had seen in the Church that kept needy sinners away. She called sin, sin, inviting everyone to repentance:

**On the way to the West Coast, Aimee drove into Indianapolis just as they had lifted the influenza ban. It was then that she met Maria Woodworth-Etter. It was the thrill of her life to finally meet this woman who had so inspired her — and to hear her preach!**

"**Whatever fancy name you give it, sin is sin....God looks on the heart and as for holiness, why, without holiness no man shall see the Lord. We must be saved, we must be sanctified, but 'tis all through the precious atoning blood of Jesus Christ.**"[25]

In 1918, when World War I was raging in Europe, and America was plagued with a deadly outbreak of influenza, Aimee was viewed as a ray of hope because of her doctrine. One of her major thrusts of ministry appreciated by everyone was that of servanthood. To demonstrate this, the Lord directed Aimee one day while she was out looking for a new dress to actually make a purchase:

"You are a servant of all, are you not? Go upstairs and ask to see the servants' dresses," the Lord said.

So Aimee obeyed and bought two servants dresses for $5. And from that time on she was always seen in her distinguishing white servant's dress and cape.[26]

# I DID PROMISE YOU A ROSE GARDEN

One afternoon, when Roberta was suffering with influenza, she asked her mother why they didn't have a home like everyone else. As Aimee prayed for Roberta's healing, God spoke to her and proclaimed that He would not only raise up her daughter, but would also give them a home in sunny Southern California. She even received a vision of their new home, seeing a bungalow with a rose garden.

When Roberta recovered, the group set out for California. Roberta would later say they had no idea of how much of a miracle the house really was because, "When mother told us something would happen, it was like money in the bank."[27]

The trip was no small exploit. Road maps were few, towns were far apart, and the conditions of the roads were questionable. But none of this hindered Aimee.

On the way to the West Coast, Aimee drove into Indianapolis just as they had lifted the influenza ban. It was then that she met Maria Woodworth-Etter. It was the thrill of her life to finally meet this woman who had so inspired her – and to hear her preach!

When she finally arrived in Los Angeles in late 1918, Aimee's fame had preceded her. By now, the Azusa Street Mission was just a memory. Its members had scattered throughout the city, but they were waiting for the person whom God would use to pull them back together. And when Aimee arrived, they believed it was her.

Two days after she arrived, Aimee preached a message to seven hundred people entitled, "Shout! For the Lord Hath Given You the City." By early 1919 the aisles, floors, and window sills of the Philharmonic Auditorium were packed with people to hear her.

The people of Los Angeles couldn't do enough for Aimee and her family. Less than two weeks after she arrived, a woman stood up in one of her meetings, saying the Lord had impressed her to give the evangelist some land on which she could build a home. Others stood and pledged their labor and the material. Even the rose bushes in her vision would be donated, and by April, the house with gabled porches and a fireplace was a reality.

## A COAT OF MANY COLORS

By now, Aimee could see that a permanent place to preach was a great need. So between the years of 1919-1923, she traveled across the U.S. nine times, preaching and raising money for the building of Angelus Temple. And everywhere she traveled, people loved her.

Aimee's preaching tone could change from "baby talk" and girlish stories, as she would often like to do in delighting older audiences, to the solemn, deep-toned demeanor of a dynamic, soulwinning prophetess. God gifted her in her delivery to accommodate many different situations.

The press discovered Aimee in 1919. And when they did, they were invited into what was to become in later years one of America's most celebrated media love/hate relationships ever on record. Aimee loved them, but they were never sure of what she was doing to them! They weren't accustomed to anyone taking advantage of their methods, and would try to trip her up with trick questions such as, "Aimee, are silk stockings evil?" In response, she would gracefully cross her legs and reply, **"It depends altogether on how much of them is shown."**[28] This sort of coverage lent itself to making Aimee a national phenomenon.

In Baltimore, Maryland, the first auditorium Aimee preached in seated three thousand people. But people were turned away for lack of seating space. So she rented another auditorium that seated sixteen thousand. It was here that Aimee

*On the road*

shocked the Baltimore masses through her pointing out of the demonic behavior in an overly-demonstrative worshipper. Up until then, it was considered unethical to confront someone who was "ecstatic" for God. But Aimee rebuked her and called for a choir member to retain her in a smaller room.

After prayerfully observing the woman, Aimee challenged the leadership ethics of her day and would call the Church to spiritual maturity:

> **"The woman proved to be a maniac who had been in an asylum....Yet this was the kind of woman many of the saints would have allowed to promenade the platform — fearing lest they quench the Spirit."[29]**

While Aimee was in Baltimore a national healing campaign began. Incredible and highly unusual miracles occurred. The headlines screamed the results of each meeting.

It has been said that when Aimee would enter the hall before a meeting, there were often throngs of desperately ill people seeking to touch her. And that when she saw them, she would run back overwhelmed into her dressing room to pray for God's help.

Everywhere Aimee went, crowds pressed in to touch her. She would watch in regret as the police were forced to bolt the doors in trying to protect her.

After a while, when she closed her eyes at night, all she could see was the seventeen hundred people who were packed into a place that was built to hold a thousand. She would see the altars and basements overflowing with the sick and would wake up thinking of how Jesus had dealt with all this:

> **"Wouldn't you just realize how Jesus had to get into a boat and push away from land, in order to preach to the people?"[30]**

In 1921 Aimee held a three-week meeting in Denver, Colorado, at which sixteen thousand people filled the Municipal Auditorium two and three times each day. One night, eight thousand people were turned away.

## "MINNIE" — NOT A MOUSE

During these great days of ministry, Minnie aggressively guarded her daughter's health. She considered it the highest of priorities, because if Aimee's health were to fail, so would the ministry. They were more like sisters than mother and daughter, but would never truly bond spiritually.

Minnie was an incredible organizer. She ran Aimee's ministry from the rafters to the basement, keeping their finances in the black. She was tough, and sometimes only slept two hours a night. She screened every sick person before the service to weed the troublemakers out. And she spent long hours with the invalids before the service began.

> *If anyone ever got too close to Aimee, Minnie would harass her daughter until that particular relationship was broken. Many employees quit or were fired because of Minnie.*

Minnie would never sit down to a meal. She would grab food at the oddest of moments between registering invalids, greeting delegates, and organizing the ministry of helps. She worked diligently to establish a business foundation for the ministry. But she never grasped the fullness of Aimee's call. And she never really understood why Aimee did what she did.

If anyone ever got too close to Aimee, Minnie would harass her daughter until that particular relationship was broken. Many employees quit or were fired because of Minnie. Perhaps this was the one reason Aimee never had a close friend for very long. Their mother-daughter relationship had always involved much stress. And in the years to come, Aimee's feeling of being "owned" and "controlled" would eventually cause them to part.

In 1921, Aimee was weary from her time on the road and began searching for the land on which they could build Angelus Temple. She found it adjoining Los Angeles' prestigious Echo Park area that was surrounded by abundant grass, picnic grounds, and a beautiful lake.

## A "FIRST" – FROM THE KKK TO HOLLYWOOD

Aimee was a "first" in many areas. While building the Temple, the Oakland Rockridge radio station invited her to be the first woman to ever preach on the air. This would ignite another fire within her, and in time she would build her own radio station. But first, she would build the Temple.

Everyone contributed to the building project. Mayors, governors, gypsies – even the Ku Klux Klan were quick to give. Though Aimee didn't agree with the KKK, they loved her. But it was this "love" for her, that caused them to commit a crime.

After another meeting in Denver in June of 1922, Aimee was in a side hall with a woman reporter when someone asked her to pray for an invalid outside. She took the reporter outside with her because she wanted her to witness the prayer. But when they walked out the door, the two were abducted, blindfolded, and driven to a meeting of the KKK.

As it turned out, all the KKK wanted was a private message from the evangelist. So she gave them a message out of Matthew 27 on "Barabbas, the man who thought he would never be found out." After she preached, Aimee listened politely as the Klan pledged their national and "silent" support for her. To them, this simply meant that wherever Aimee went in the U.S. she could depend on them to observe and protect her. Then they blindfolded the two once again and took them back to the hall in Denver.[31]

The reporter published a great story about the kidnapping that hurled Aimee to even greater heights and brought more money in for the Temple.

In late 1922, Aimee's five thousand seat temple was finally completed. Its dedication took place in an extravagant service on New Year's Day of 1923. Those who couldn't attend saw its likeness on a flower-covered float that was ridden by singing choir members in Pasadena's Tournament of Roses parade. This carried away the first prize of its division.[32]

The New York Times gave the dedication full coverage, and from then on, Angelus Temple's five thousand seats were filled four times each Sunday.

*Angelus Temple, Los Angeles, California*

The Temple had perfect acoustics. It was said that many Hollywood producers were hoping Aimee would fail so they could simply acquire the building to turn it into a theater. But Aimee wouldn't fail, and she would eventually have it transformed into a theater herself. It was a theater for God.

According to Aimee, the entire Bible was a sacred drama that was meant to be preached and illustrated dramatically. And it was here that she believed denominational churches had lost their cutting edge. Aimee truly believed the Church had grown too cold and formal, while the world's love for entertainment brought them encouragement, joy, and laughter. She also felt this to be the reason that so many Christians were hungry for entertainment.

> *Most of Los Angeles knew attending a service at Angelus Temple was quite a major event.*

In July of 1922, Aimee named Angelus Temple, THE CHURCH OF THE FOURSQUARE GOSPEL because of a vision she received while preaching from the first chapter of Ezekiel. The first signing day of her new association produced one thousand pastors.

Two meetings were set aside each week at the Temple to pray for the sick. Though she had twenty-four elders on staff, Aimee would personally conduct most of these meetings until her passing in 1944.

The healing results in Los Angeles were astounding, but they were less observed by the general public than they had been in Aimee's national campaigns. In the Temple's larger services, the focus was on soulwinning, and on the training of soulwinners.

## SOME TEMPLE TALES

Without question, Angelus Temple was a very busy place. Aimee had a prayer tower that was manned twenty-four hours a day. She also formulated a one-hundred-voice choir and a brass band of thirty-six people. The sanctuary was filled with music in every service. And she purchased costumes, props, and scenery to accent her sermons in Hollywood. Most of Los Angeles knew attending a service at Angelus Temple was quite a major event.

Aimee had a remarkable sense of humor, and though there were many flaws in her early illustrated sermons, she always made the best of them. Once, to give her Garden of Eden scene some life, she ordered a macaw from a visiting circus. But she didn't know of its coarse, vulgar language learned while working with the show. And in the middle of her oratory, the macaw turned to her and said, "Oh, go to hell."

The five thousand in attendance froze in disbelief. Then, as if the bird wanted to be sure that *everyone* had heard it, it repeated itself again! But Aimee was not to be outdone! She made the best of the mistake – as she did every blooper – by proceeding to "witness" to the bird, encouraging it to respond. Then when it did respond with the very same words, the audience was hysterical! She finally "persuaded" the rented bird of the true Christian way by promising it a bird perch in heaven for its part in her show.[33]

Of course, certain ministers persecuted Aimee for her methods. But she would respond to them publicly by saying:

> **"Show me a better way to persuade willing people to come to church and I'll be happy to try your method. But please...don't ask me to preach to empty seats. Let's not waste our time quarreling over methods. God has use for all of us. Remember the recipe in the old adage for rabbit stew? It began, *first catch your rabbit.*"[34]**

## TWINKLING STARS, BIBLE SCHOOL & RADIO

Many Hollywood stars were interested in what Aimee had to say. Frequent attendees at the Temple were Mary Pickford, Jean Harlow, and Clara Bow. Charlie Chaplin was able to slip into a few of her services, and would later become good friends with the evangelist. In fact, Chaplin would later help Aimee with the Temple's staging for her illustrated sermons – and Aimee would show him the truth of life.

Also, Anthony Quinn played in Aimee's band. Quinn was with Aimee before his great debut as an actor. While Quinn was a teenager, Aimee took him as her translator on a Spanish crusade. The world renowned actor would later say that one of the greatest moments of his life was when Aimee noticed him. And, he would write:

> "Years later, when I saw the great actresses at work, I would compare them to her...Ingrid Bergman...Katharine Hepburn... Greta Garbo...they all fell short of that first electric shock Aimee Semple McPherson produced in me."[35]

In February of 1923, Aimee opened her school of ministry that would eventually become known as L.I.F.E. (Lighthouse of International Foursquare Evangelism) Bible College. Aimee was an avid instructor.

At the school, "Sister," as the movement called her, served as a teacher and openly revealed her weaknesses as well as her strengths to the student body. Her favorite Christian authors were Wesley, Booth, and a Canadian revivalist by the name of Albert Benjamin Simpson. Aimee often quoted these men and taught from their writings.

Sometimes she would test the students by leaving early and ask them to remain and pray. Then she would hide in a hallway. As the students left she would watch for those who left frivolously, and for those who were attentive enough to pick up a piece of planted, paper trash. The attentive ones would receive her praise because of her belief that attention to detail produced a valuable, sensitive minister.

In February of 1924, Aimee opened Radio KFSG (Kall Four Square Gospel), with the first FCC license ever issued to a woman. It was also the first Christian radio station ever operated.

## IS AIMEE DEAD?

By 1926, Aimee was in need of a good vacation, so she traveled to Europe and the Holy Land. She ended up preaching during most of it. Then upon her return in 1926, the greatest scandal and controversy of her ministry took place. On May 18, while enjoying an afternoon at the beach with her secretary, Aimee made some final notes on a sermon to be given that night. She asked her secretary to call the information back to the Temple, but when her secretary returned, Aimee was gone. Thinking Aimee had gone for a swim, the secretary scanned the water, then notified the authorities.

*The next thing she knew, someone was holding her head back, and the woman pushed a chloroform-soaked pad into her face.*

Over the next thirty-two days, Aimee's disappearance became the hottest news story in the world. Los Angeles' beaches were combed, and its outlying waters were searched for any trace of her. But nothing was found.

In the meantime, a ransom letter for $25,000 was received at Angelus Temple. Minnie threw it away with the rest of the crazy mail that was now pouring in. Then another letter came from a different source demanding $500,000, and the press went wild. "Aimee sightings" were the order of the day. Once she was reportedly seen sixteen times on the same day, from coast to coast.

# KIDNAPPED!

A memorial service was finally scheduled for Aimee at Angelus Temple on June 20. Then three days after the service, Aimee walked into Douglas, Arizona from the desert at Agua Prieta, Mexico.

When questioned about her whereabouts, Aimee told the world that a man and a woman approached her to pray for their dying child that day at the beach after her secretary left. She said the woman was crying, and that the man brought a cloak to cover her swimsuit in the hopes that she would consent. She then agreed to help the couple and followed them to their car. Aimee explained how she had done this many times in her ministry, and thought nothing much of it.

But when the three of them arrived at the car, Aimee noticed it was running. She said there was a man at the wheel, and that the woman posing as the mother stepped into the car before her. Then she was told by the supposed father to get inside as he roughly pushed her in. The next thing she knew, someone was holding her head back, and the woman pushed a chloroform-soaked pad into her face.

When Aimee awoke, she was being held in a shack by a woman and two men. She said they threatened her, cut off a piece of her hair, and burned her fingers with a cigar. She also said that when they moved her to another place, the two men left, and that she was able to make her escape when the woman went shopping. The woman had tied Aimee up with bed cloths before she left, but Aimee was able to cut through them with the jagged edge of a tin can. Once she was free, Aimee left through a window, then walked through the desert for hours until she came upon a cabin in Douglas, Arizona.

When she finally received cooperation from the police once they believed her "claimed" identity, Aimee phoned Minnie in Los Angeles. But even Minnie didn't believe her until she revealed a secret that only Aimee could have known about their private life.

# WHAT DO YOU THINK?

Following a night in the hospital, some fifty thousand people welcomed Aimee back to Angelus Temple. But her ordeal had just begun.

Aimee had accused and described her kidnappers, but they were never to be found. And when the police accompanied her in an attempt to retrace her desert footsteps, there was no shack matching her description anywhere to be found.

Then Los Angeles District Attorney, Asa Keyes, accused Aimee of lying and went to great lengths to discredit her. She had been reportedly seen in a

*Flying the Foursquare colors*

*Angelus Temple*

*Everyone say, "Praise the Lord!"*

*Los Angeles Times Photo*

*Five thousand seats*

*Aimee and choir presenting one of her many operas in Angeles Temple*

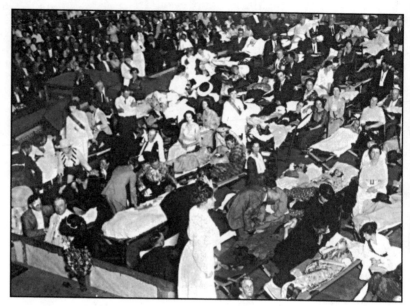

*"Stretcher Day" at a revival*

*Thousands lined up at Aimee's funeral*

Carmel bungalow with her radio producer, Kenneth Ormiston, and Keyes produced many witnesses in an attempt to confirm the fact.

So far as possible kidnappers were concerned, it is true that Aimee had
made many enemies in the underworld. Gangsters had a huge network of pros-
titution, drug-trafficking, loan sharking, and bootlegging in the Los Angeles
area. And Aimee had won several of their key people to the Lord.

It's also true that Aimee regularly opened the airwaves of her radio station
to allow new converts to give salvation accounts. But when these former
underworld converts broadcasted their testimonies, they would often give not
only their salvation accounts – they would expose the criminal deeds of their
former associates – many times calling them by name.

Aimee's kidnapping story never varied. In fact, her's was the only story that
never changed. Reporters, detectives, and prosecutors all changed their
accounts time and time again. Even the witnesses who testified against Aimee
changed their testimony. And when they did, her charges of corruption of
public morals, obstruction of justice, and conspiracy to manufacture evidence
were finally dropped.

Some interesting side-notes concerning Aimee's scandal include the facts
that District Attorney Keyes would eventually be sentenced to San
Quentin. And Aimee's attorney would later be found dead. Incidences have
suggested to many that the mob was really involved.[36]

## DID SHE BREAK MINNIE'S NOSE?

Following her return to the ministry, Aimee would wear the robes of a true
apostolic evangelist. She would show up at night clubs, dance halls, pool halls,
and boxing matches to announce her meetings during intermissions. Managers liked the publicity, and their clientele adored her.

Aimee wasn't afraid of the world's sinners and now would seek with even
greater fervor to bring Jesus to where they were. She thought it funny that so
many Christians set boundaries as to where-or-where-not the Gospel should
be preached.

But in the latter part of 1926, lawsuit after lawsuit was assaulting her, and her
promoters were involving her in all kinds of business ventures. When their plans
failed, the blame and unpaid bills always fell on Aimee. Attorneys only seemed
to make matters worse. And now more than ever, Aimee desperately needed a
friend. She needed someone she could trust. It seemed that everyone she had
ever been close to was either betraying her or withering under the criticism.

Even Minnie, Aimee's mother, was now wavering back and forth in her support for her daughter. Minnie kept crossing back and forth between her role of the devoted, helping mother, and the malevolent overseer of a ministry that she didn't understand. She was always quick to criticize her daughter when she saw things differently. And soon she would do so publicly.

> *Minnie kept crossing back and forth between her role of the devoted, helping mother, and the malevolent overseer of a ministry that she didn't understand.*

Aimee had always honored her mother in public, but when Minnie went public with her antagonistic jabs, things reached a breaking point. Now that Aimee's own mother was fighting her in the public square, she felt totally betrayed. And the church started to split. Those serving under Minnie were torn in their loyalty, while the Temple's Board of Elders sided with Aimee. In fact, when the end came, the elders would help work out Minnie's "permanent retirement plan."

Miraculously, in the midst of all of this, Aimee would compose her first opera in 1931 and name it, *Regem Adoratge*, or, *Worship the King*. This was followed by another visit to the Holy Land. But she was reluctant to come home this time because of the growing difficulty with her mother. And her apprehensions proved to be well founded, because when she did get home, she and Minnie would finally have it out.

It was a well-known fact that when Minnie got angry at Aimee, her words were cruel and vicious. But following this final round of their famous disagreements, it was made known in the press that Minnie ended up with a bruised and bandaged nose. The headlines accompanying her front-page picture deceitfully read, "MA SAYS AIMEE BROKE HER NOSE!"

But things were not as they seemed. In fact, Minnie had just undergone plastic surgery on the eve of their argument, and would later deny the whole thing.[37] All the same, that was it. Minnie was finished. Now she was gone.

Following Minnie's forced "retirement," a series of managers would file through to take her place. Coupled with the expense of settling with her mother, the depression, and lawsuits, Aimee's debts quickly mounted up. In fact, it would take the next ten years to settle all the lawsuits and to pay her debtors off. And when it finally happened, there was a celebratory notice placed atop the Temple.

## SHE'S NOT BIONIC

But the strain of it all had simply turned out to be more than Aimee could bear. And in 1930, she suffered a complete emotional/physical breakdown, and was confined to a Malibu beach cottage under a physician's constant care.

Following this ten-month ordeal, Aimee would return to Angelus Temple, and would recover to some extent. But she would never regain the vim and vigor that she formerly enjoyed. Aimee's physician explained her problem by simply stating she "could not get her needed rest."[38]

By the time 1931 arrived, Aimee was very lonely. The price of fame was high, she had no close friends, and she dearly wanted companionship.

Rolf would marry a Bible school student in the middle of that year, and Aimee was elated. Then on September 13, 1931, she would marry again. This time, to her third husband, a Mr. David Hutton. It has been said that because of Aimee's loneliness, and her desperate need for love and protection, that she imagined all sorts of virtues in this man. But in reality, they simply weren't there.

> *Aimee was sued by disgruntled employees, associate pastors, and whoever else thought they could make a dollar on her.*

Not long after they were married, Hutton was sued by another woman he had promised marriage to. The court proceedings lasted a year, and the ruling went against him.

But Aimee carried on in her calling around the nation. She experienced tremendous success in New England, as thousands came to hear her. Due to her health, on April 22, 1927, she offered to resign as pastor of Angelus Temple. This offer was refused. Then in January she set sail for Europe, in accordance with her doctor's advice. And again, thousands crowded her meetings. While she was away, Hutton, amid scandal, filed for divorce.

## THE QUIET WAR QUEEN

The years between 1938 and 1944 were very quiet years for Aimee. There was very little said about her in the press.

Aimee was sued by disgruntled employees, associate pastors, and whoever else thought they could make a dollar on her. So she hired a new business manager, Giles Knight, who kept her out of the public eye. Every reporter had to go through him to see her, and everyone was refused. Aimee would keep

Knight informed of her whereabouts, then stay away to live a halfway anonymous life.

Rolf McPherson still speaks highly of Knight for the service rendered his mother that brought so much peace into their house.

Much of Aimee's efforts during these years was given to pastoring, training future ministers, establishing hundreds of churches, and sending missionaries around the world. But in 1942, she also led a brass band and color guard into downtown Los Angeles to sell war bonds. She sold $150,000 worth of the bonds in one hour, so the U.S. Treasury awarded her a special citation for her patriotic endeavor. She would also organize regular Friday night prayer meetings at Angelus Temple for the duration of World War II, gaining the expressed appreciation of President Roosevelt and California's governor for doing so.

## A GREAT ONE IS RESTING

By 1944, Aimee's health was very poor. She was suffering from tropical infections that she had contracted during her missionary trips. So in February of that year, she named Rolf as the new vice president of the ministry. Rolf had proven his faithfulness and served his mother well over the years. In fact, he was the *only* person who stayed with her through both good times and bad.

Then in September of 1944, Rolf flew to Oakland with his mother to dedicate a new church. There was a blackout in the city because of the war, so Aimee and Rolf spent the evening together in her room for some ministry and family talk. Huge crowds and the work of the ministry always exhilarated Aimee, so she was in high spirits. When the evening drew to a close, Rolf kissed his mother goodnight and left the room.

Aimee had always been plagued with insomnia. She was taking sedatives from her physician, and she had obviously taken a couple on this night to sleep. She probably didn't know how many it would take, and she was scheduled to preach the next day. So she must have decided she needed more to fall off to sleep.

According to the physicians, it was about dawn when Aimee must have known something was wrong. But instead of calling Rolf, she placed a call to her physician in Los Angeles. He was in surgery and didn't respond. So she called another physician, who referred her to a Dr. Palmer in Oakland, California. But before she could make this third call, Aimee lost consciousness.

At 10:00 A.M. Rolf tried to wake his mother and found her in bed, breathing hoarsely. Unable to revive her, he called for medical assistance. But it was too late, and on September 27, 1944, Aimee Semple McPherson, went home to be with the Lord. She died at the age of fifty-three.

Aimee's body laid in Angelus Temple for three days and three nights as sixty thousand people filed by to pay their last respects. The stage on which her open casket rested, the orchestra pit, and most of the Temple's aisles were filled with flowers. Five car loads of them had to be turned away.

Then on Aimee's birthday, October 9, 1944, a motorcade of six hundred automobiles drove to Forest Lawn Memorial Park where this front-line General of God's Christian army was finally laid to rest. The cemetery admitted two thousand people, along with seventeen hundred Foursquare ministers whom Aimee had ordained.

> *What Aimee was literally telling us to do when she said to, "stay in the middle of the road" was this: Being excessive might sky-rocket you, but you will eventually explode and plummet to earth. The Christian faith is a way of life, so run it like a marathon — not a sprint.*

The complete story of Aimee Semple McPherson could never be told in just one chapter. As with God's other great Generals, only heaven will reveal everything she accomplished. But for our purposes here, let me say that in her lifetime, Aimee composed 175 songs and hymns, several operas, and thirteen drama-oratories. She also preached thousands of sermons and graduated over 8,000 ministers from L.I.F.E. Bible College. It is estimated that during the Depression, some one and a half million people received aid from her ministry. And today, the Foursquare denomination is continuing to expound the truths of God's Word as they were revealed to Sister McPherson, in her revealed Foursquare Gospel's original Declaration of Faith. The four squares are: "Jesus is Savior, Jesus is healer, Jesus is baptizer in the Holy Spirit, and Jesus is coming King."

## DIRECT YOUR DESTINY

In conclusion, I want to focus on an important point that Aimee would always make with her Bible school students:

**"Stay in the middle of the road."**

From all you have now read about her, it should be clear that this statement is not referring to compromise. Sister Aimee was talking about the strength it takes to stand firm in one place. And the statement had a twofold meaning to her.

First, she would say, *be bold in the mainstream of life,* but don't allow the secular world to clone you in their mold. Be uninhibited and freely demonstrate the love and freedom that Jesus brought to the earth. And stand firm in the face of pressure, never flinching in the face of fear. Also, be bold to perform the plan of God for your life in the strength of what heaven has called *you* to do.

Second, be passionate in the gifts of the Spirit, *but never be excessive.* Don't intimidate the crowd just because you have the power. Aimee often used the example of an automobile and its power to make this point. Although it could easily go eighty miles an hour, one would have to be very foolish to rev it to that speed in the middle of a crowd. She would point out that such power from the Holy Spirit was always there, but that it was meant to be used over the long haul of ministering God's service to others.

What Aimee was literally telling us to do when she said to, "stay in the middle of the road" was this: Being excessive might skyrocket you, but you will eventually explode and plummet to earth. The Christian faith is a *way of life,* so run it like a marathon – not a sprint.

Now take the torch Aimee has passed to us, never settling for the mediocrity of a "religious" life. Shake your world for God with the freedom, boldness, and wisdom that God has given you. And stand strong in the "middle of the road," as you fulfill your personal destiny in the call of God.

## CHAPTER EIGHT, AIMEE SEMPLE MCPHERSON
### References

[1] Daniel Mark Epstein, *Sister Aimee: The Life of Aimee Semple McPherson* (Orlando, FL: Daniel Mark Epstein, reprinted by permission of Harcourt Brace and Company, 1993), 3, 80-81.

[2] Ibid., 10.

[3] Ibid., 11.

[4] Ibid., 21.

[5] Ibid., 22-23.

[6] Ibid., 28.

[7] Ibid., 30-31.

[8] Ibid., 36.

[9] Ibid., 39.

[10] Ibid., 41-47.

[11] Ibid., 48-49.

[12] Ibid., 50.

[13] Ibid., 55.

[14] Ibid., 57.

[15] Ibid., 57-59.

[16] Ibid., 67.

[17] Ibid., 73.

[18] Ibid., 75.

[19] Ibid., 76.

[20] Ibid., 77-78.

[21] Ibid., 111.

[22] Ibid, 119.

[23] Ibid., 120.

[24] Ibid., 122.

[25] Ibid., 134.

[26] Ibid., 144.

[27] Ibid., 145.

[28] Ibid., 159.

[29] Ibid., 172.

[30] Ibid., 201.

[31] Ibid., 241-243.

[32] Ibid., 248.
[33] Ibid., 256-257.
[34] Ibid., 259.
[35] Ibid., 378.
[36] Ibid., 312.
[37] Ibid., 340.
[38] Ibid., 343.
[39] Ibid., 417.

# Kathryn Kuhlman

## "The Woman Who Believed in Miracles"

# "THE WOMAN WHO BELIEVED IN MIRACLES"

**66** **H**undreds have been healed just sitting quietly in the audience without any demonstration whatsoever. None. Very often not even a sermon is preached. There have been times when not even a song has been sung.

"No loud demonstration, no loud calling on God as though He were deaf. No screaming, no shouting, within the very quietness of His presence. There were hundreds of times when the presence of the Holy Spirit was so real that one could almost hear the rhythm as thousands of hearts beat as one."[1]

In this rapt silence a voice speaks, "I–ah...belieeeeeeeve–ah – in–ah merrrrrrricals–ah!" Suddenly the applause is deafening as thousands watch a tall, slim figure emerge from the shadows in a white, frothy gown. She glides to center stage, and another Kathryn Kuhlman miracle service is underway.

In her international ministry, Miss Kuhlman laid a foundation for the workings of the Holy Spirit in the lives of countless thousands throughout the world. Her unique ministry shifted the focus of the body of Christ from the outward show of the supernatural gifts of the Holy Spirit back to the GIVER of the Gifts, the Holy Spirit.

A prophetic tone in her ministry set the pace for what the Church would be like in times to come. Her ministry was literally a forerunner for the Church of the future.

Though she called herself **"an ordinary person,"** Kathryn was unique. Many have tried to imitate her voice and her theatrical mannerisms, but to no avail. Others have tried to translate her special anointing into techniques and methods without success.

I thank God for Kathryn Kuhlman. She was an example of one who fearlessly paid the price to walk in the service of God. I am grateful for the lessons I have learned through her life. And in this chapter I want to share some of those lessons with you, many from her own words.

## RED HAIR AND FRECKLES

Concordia, Missouri, was settled by German immigrants who began arriving in the late 1830s. Kathryn's mother, Emma Walkenhorst, married Joseph Kuhlman in 1891. According to her permanent high school record, Kathryn Johanna Kuhlman was born May 9, 1907, on the family farm about five miles from Concordia. Kathryn was named after both of her grandmothers. She never had a birth certificate since one was not required by Missouri law until 1910.

When Kathryn was two years old, her father sold their 160 acre farm and built a big house in town. This was the house that Kathryn always called "home."

A childhood friend described young Kathryn as having: "...Large features, red hair, and freckles. It couldn't be said of Kathryn that she was pretty. She wasn't dainty or appealingly feminine in any sense of the word. She was taller than the rest of 'our gang' (five feet eight), gangly and boyish in build, and her long strides kept the rest of us puffing to keep up with her."

As a young girl, Kathryn was also noted for her "independence, self-reliance and a desire to do things her way."[2] She managed to twist her "papa" around her little finger, getting almost anything she wanted from him. According to Kathryn,

*Kathryn in front of childhood home*

the discipline was always left to her mother, a harsh woman, who never praised Kathryn or gave her any affection. Yet Kathryn never once felt unloved or unwanted. Her papa gave her all the love and affection she ever needed. In fact, she so adored her papa that even thirty years after his death, tears would come to her eyes as she talked about him.

Once, when Kathryn was about nine years old, she wanted to do something nice for her mother's birthday. So she decided she would give her a surprise birthday party.

> *As a young girl, Kathryn was also noted for her "independence, self-reliance and a desire to do things her way." She managed to twist her "papa" around her little finger, getting almost anything she wanted from him.*

Well Kathryn never thought about her mother's birthday falling on a Monday. So she went around to all the neighbors, telling them *all* to show up with a cake.

Mondays were wash days at the Kuhlman household. Every other day of the week, Emma Kuhlman would dress from head to toe in her best clothes. One never knew when an unexpected guest might come by, and she dreaded the idea of anyone seeing her groomed poorly.

So Monday came and Emma Kuhlman was dressed for wash day. As she labored over a hot tub, her hair hung down wrung in the sweat, her clothes were damp and soiled, and she was bare-legged. There was a knock at the door, and when she opened it – there stood the neighbors all dressed up in their finest attire. And there stood Emma, totally wilted and fatigued from her wash day! Her pride ruined, Emma vowed to Kathryn under her breath that she would take care of her later.[3]

And take care of her she did! In fact, Emma Kuhlman made Kathryn stand and eat every one of the birthday cakes the neighbors brought!

Kathryn's father taught her the principles of business. He was a stable owner. She loved to go with him as he collected bills, and in later years would give him credit for everything she knew about organization and business.

## "PAPA! JESUS CAME INTO MY HEART!"

Kathryn was fourteen years old when she was born again. She told the story many times during her life of how she answered what seemed to be a sovereign wooing directly from the Holy Spirit Himself, not from any person. She came from a "religious" background rather than a spiritual one, so the churches she attended never gave altar calls to receive salvation.

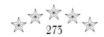

Of this, Kathryn would later write:

"I was standing beside Mama, and the hands of the church clock were pointed to five minutes before twelve o'clock. I can't remember the minister's name or even one word of his sermon, but something happened to me. It's as real to me right now as it was then — the most real thing that ever happened to me.

"As I stood there, I began shaking to the extent that I could no longer hold the hymnal, so I laid it on the pew...and sobbed. I was feeling the weight of (conviction) and I realized that I was a sinner. I felt like the meanest, lowest person in the whole world. Yet I was only a four-teen-year-old girl.

"...I did the only thing I knew to do: I slipped out from where I was standing and walked to the front pew and sat down in the corner of the pew and wept. Oh, how I wept!

"...I had become the happiest person in the whole world. The heavy weight had been lifted. I experienced something that has never left me. I had been born again, and the

*The Kuhlman family — Kathryn wearing ribbon*

**Holy Spirit had done the very thing that Jesus said He would do (John 16:8)."**[4]

Kathryn's father was standing in the kitchen when she came running home from church that day to share with him her good news. It was her custom to tell Papa everything.

In her words, she rushed up to him and said, **"Papa...Jesus has just come into my heart."**

Without any emotion, he just said "I'm glad."[5]

Kathryn recalls how she was never really sure whether or not her father understood what she meant. She would eventually choose to join her father's Baptist church rather than her mama's Methodist church. But even then, she had a mind of her own.

Kathryn says she was never sure if her father was born again. At times, she would speak convincingly that he was. But privately, she sometimes expressed frustration at not knowing for sure.

Kathryn did know, however, that her father had a strong aversion to preachers. Actually, she said that he despised preachers! If Joseph Kuhlman saw a preacher coming down the street, he would cross over to the other side to keep from speaking to him. He thought all preachers were "in it for the money." And the only time he attended church was on holidays or for special services at which Kathryn was giving a recitation. As far as she knew, he never prayed or read the Bible.

## THEIR FIRST EMBRACE

According to Kathryn, church attendance was just as important as going to work. At first she attended the Methodist church with her mother. It was there, in 1921, that she was born again. But from 1922 on, the entire family was listed as members of the Baptist church. Though she came from a denominational background, her ministry in later years would become ecumenical as she freely moved through all churches from the Pentecostal to the Catholics. No denomination barred the ministry of Kathryn Kuhlman. She refused to be a part of a denomination and gave no organization any credit for her ministry. She gave credit only to God.

> *According to Kathryn, church attendance was just as important as going to work.*

Throughout Kathryn's teenage years, her mother taught the Epworth League for young people in the Methodist church. A neighbor said Mrs.

Kuhlman was an "excellent Bible teacher, and Kathryn and her sisters and brother must have received some very fine teaching and training at home." The neighbor also talked of hearing someone in the Kuhlman family singing in the evening and someone else playing the piano.[6]

Even though her mother was called an excellent teacher in the Epworth League at church, she was not actually born again until 1935 during one of Kathryn's meetings in Denver.

Kathryn had invited her mother to the meeting. After the close of the first service, Kathryn went into the prayer room behind the pulpit to pray for those who answered the invitation to receive salvation. Later, her mother walked into the prayer room, saying she wanted to know Jesus as Kathryn knew Him.

Kathryn, now choked with tears, reached out and laid her hand on the back of her mama's head. The moment her fingers touched her mother, Mama began to shake, then cry. It was the same kind of shaking and crying that Kathryn remembered when she had stood beside Mama in that little Methodist church in Concordia. But this time, there was something new. Mama lifted her head and began to speak, slowly at first, then more rapidly. But the words weren't English, they were clear, bell-tone sounds of an unknown tongue.

"Kathryn fell to her knees beside her, weeping and laughing at the same time...when Emma opened her eyes, she reached out for Kathryn and held her tightly. It was the first time that Kathryn could ever remember being embraced by her mother."[7]

Her mother didn't sleep for three days and two nights after that. She was a new person, and for the rest of her life in Concordia, Emma Kuhlman had a wonderful, sweet communion with the Holy Spirit.

## THE EVANGELISTIC MAID

One characteristic of those greatly used by God is their willingness to drop everything and follow His leading. In 1913, Kathryn's older sister Myrtle married a young, good-looking evangelist who was just finishing his course at Moody Bible Institute. So Myrtle and her new husband, Everett Parrott, began an evangelistic tent ministry. About ten years later, in 1924, she and Myrtle persuaded their parents that it was God's will for Kathryn to travel with them.

At that time, the Parrotts, whose headquarters were in Oregon, were acquainted with Dr. Charles S. Price, who had a healing ministry. He had introduced them to the baptism of the Holy Spirit. However, wonderful as this experience was, the Parrott's marriage had not been a happy one, and now financial strains were adding to the problems.

It would have been easy for Kathryn to slip into self-pity because of these circumstances. Instead, she busied herself around the Parrott house, taking over the washing on Monday and the ironing on Tuesday.

## A PORTION OF HER CHARACTER

During this time, along with earning the lessons of patience in adversity, Kathryn also learned not to give way to self-pity. Later many of her messages flowed out of her personal spiritual growth in these areas. Self-pity and self-centeredness were the same to Kathryn. Obviously, she determined as a teenager not to allow either of these have a place in her life, regardless of what happened to her.

> "Be careful of the person, whether they're a member of your family, whether you work with them, whether they are an employee, be careful of a person who can't say, 'I am sorry.' You will find that person very self-centered.
>
> "That is the reason you have heard me say ten thousand times that the only person Jesus can't help, the only person for whom there is no forgiveness of sins is the person who will not say, 'I'm sorry for my sins.'...Such a self-centered person usually draws disease to themselves like a magnet."[8]

*Kathryn learned early in life that self-centeredness, along with all the other "self" sins, such as self-pity, self-indulgence, or even self-hatred, causes a person to judge or condemn himself. And that this hinders the Holy Spirit's working in his or her life.*

Kathryn learned early in life that self-centeredness, along with all the other "self" sins such as self-pity, self-indulgence, or even self-hatred, causes a person to judge or condemn himself. And that this hinders the Holy Spirit's working in his or her life.

Kathryn always said that anyone could experience the operation of the Holy Spirit in his life if he was willing to pay the price.

"Paying the price" is not a one-time experience. It begins with an initial commitment, a determination to follow God each day of your life.

There were many times and places where Kathryn could have chosen not to submit to the correction of the Holy Spirit. But, fortunately for the present-day body of Christ, she made the right choices and is an example for us to follow.

## THERE'S NOTHING LEFT TO PREACH!

Kathryn spent five years with her sister and brother-in-law, preparing the foundation for her own ministry. She worked in the household to ease any burden her presence might have brought, and spent many hours reading and studying the Word.

In 1928, the Parrotts arrived in Boise, Idaho. By this time they had acquired a tent and a pianist by the name of Helen Gulliford. But their marital problems continued to grow. So they decided that Everett would go on to South Dakota while they would leave Myrtle, Kathryn, and Helen in Boise to conduct a meeting there.

After two weeks, the offerings collected weren't enough to pay the rent on the building, their small apartment, or to buy food. They lived meagerly on bread and tuna.[9]

Myrtle soon felt that her only recourse was to rejoin her husband. Kathryn and Helen couldn't see any hope for their future by continuing to travel with the Parrotts. So like Paul and Barnabas in the New Testament church, they decided to part company. A local pastor in Boise offered them a chance to preach in a small pool hall that had been converted into a mission – and that was the beginning of The Kathryn Kuhlman Ministry!

From the "pool hall" mission, they went to Pocatello, Idaho, where Kathryn preached in an old opera house. The building was filthy and had to be cleaned before they could use it. You can guess who did the cleaning – the evangelist, of course. From there, they went to Twin Falls, Idaho, in the dead of winter where Kathryn slipped on the ice and broke her leg. Though the doctor had told her to not put her foot down for two weeks, she immediately continued to preach with her foot in a cast. She never allowed her flesh to cause her to compromise the will of God.

Kathryn once said,:

**"From that first sermon I preached in Idaho – Zacchaeus up a tree, and God knows if anyone was up a tree, I sure was**

— one thing I knew, I was sold on the things of God. Jesus was real to me. My heart was fixed."[10]

After preaching four or five sermons, she would humorously say:

"...I wondered, 'What more can I preach about?' There isn't anything else in the Bible. I have absolutely exhausted the supply of sermons. For the life of me, I can't think of anything else to preach about."[11]

## STABLE AND STRONG IN THE TURKEY HOUSE

Many times in those early years, their accommodations were meager, to say the least. On one occasion, the family with whom she was scheduled to stay didn't have a place for her – until they scrubbed out the turkey house. Kathryn often said she would have gladly slept on a straw stack, because her need to preach was so strong within her. Years later she would often laugh and tell how she would lock the doors and not let anyone out until she was sure they were all saved! That was her joke; however, she would also stay at the altar until the wee hours of the morning praying with anyone who lingered.

Other places Kathryn stayed might have been cleaner than the turkey house, but they weren't as warm. In those days guest rooms weren't heated. Later she would tell how she snuggled under great piles of covers until she got the place warm where she lay. Then she would turn over on her stomach and study the Word of God for hours at a time.

*What keeps a person devoted to their call? Kathryn's answer was "loyalty."*

Her heart was "sold out" to the Lord. That was the secret of her ministry. Her heart was *fixed* on Jesus. She determined to be loyal to Him and to avoid grieving the Holy Spirit.

In Kathryn's early years of ministry, two other characteristics were developed – dedication, and loyalty to God and His people. Kathryn expanded and developed her spiritual understanding from the foundation of character that she developed early in life.

## KATHRYN'S "LOYALTY"

What keeps a person devoted to their call? Kathryn's answer was "loyalty."

"The word *loyalty* has little meaning in these days because there's so little of it being practiced...Loyalty is something that is intangible...It's like love. You can only understand it as you see it in action...*Love is something you do,* and that's also true of loyalty. It means faithfulness. It means allegiance. It means devotion.

"...My heart is fixed. I'll be loyal to Him at any cost, at any price. Loyalty is much more than a casual interest in someone or something. It's a personal commitment. In the final analysis, it means, 'Here I am. You can count on me. I won't fail you.'"[12]

In other words, true loyalty for those called into the ministry would be expressed by their decision never to deviate from God's call. Do not add to it or take from it – just do it. According to Kathryn, when people begin to do their own thing, their loyalty changes from God, to themselves.

## I WANT IT B-I-G!

After preaching all over Idaho, Kathryn and Helen moved into Colorado. Following a six-month revival in Pueblo, they arrived in Denver. A businessman, Earl F. Hewitt, had joined her in Pueblo as her business manager. That year of 1933 the Depression was in full swing. Businesses were closed down, millions of people were out of work, and churches were struggling to stay open.

Kathryn was a traveling evangelist without the financial backing of any denomination, yet her belief was in a big God whose resources weren't limited. She believed if you were serving a God of *limited* finances, then you were serving the wrong god. She lived by the principle of faith and trusted in God.

She told Hewitt to go into Denver and act as if they had a million dollars. When he pointed out that in reality they had only $5, she said:

"He [God] is not limited to what we have or who we are. He can certainly use our five dollars and multiply it just as easily as He multiplied the loaves and fishes...Now go on up to Denver. Find me the biggest building you can. Get the finest piano available for Helen. Fill the place up with chairs. Take out a big ad in the *Denver Post* and get spot announcements on all the radio stations. This is God's business, and we're going to do it God's way – big!"[13]

Hewitt took her at her word and followed the instructions. The building had been a Montgomery Ward Company warehouse. The meeting lasted five months, during which time they moved to yet another warehouse. The first night, one hundred twenty-five people were present, the second night, over four hundred people attended. From then on, the warehouse filled to capacity every night. After five months, Kathryn announced that the meeting was over, but the people wouldn't hear of it. One man offered to make the down payment on a permanent building and erect a huge neon sign over it which would read, "Prayer Changes Things."

People were hungry for the Word of God. However, her main message in those years was salvation. From time to time, pastors were born again at her invitation to receive Jesus as Savior and Lord. Kathryn's was a ministry of hope and faith. During this time, Helen had developed a choir of one hundred voices and composed much of the music they sang.

Because the response to Kathryn's ministry was so great, she agreed to stay in Denver. Everything seemed to be flawless, so they began to search for a permanent building. Then suddenly, out of nowhere, tragedy struck.

*Early ministry years*

## PAPA IS GONE

Kathryn experienced the first real trauma of her life in late December of 1934, when her beloved father was killed in an accident. She learned much later that he had fallen on an icy street and had been struck by a car that swerved to try to miss him in a snowstorm.

Because of the storm, it was hours before a friend could reach Kathryn in Colorado. Upon receiving the news that her father was near death, she started home, driving in blizzard conditions from Denver across Kansas toward Missouri. She said only God knew how fast she drove on icy roads and in near-zero visibility.

On December 30, Kathryn had made it to Kansas City. From there she called home to tell her father that she was almost home, only to find that he died early that morning.

She arrived home to find Papa laid out in his casket in the living room with the mourners keeping the traditional vigil. The trauma was almost more than Kathryn could bear. Hate welled up inside her toward the youth who drove the car that struck her father.

**"I had always been a happy person, and Papa had helped to make me happy. Now he was gone, and in his place, I was battling unfamiliar strangers of fear and hate.**

**"I had the most perfect father a girl ever had. In my eyes, Papa could do no wrong. He was my ideal."**

Kathryn had left home more than ten years earlier, visiting only a few times in between. Now her Papa would never be able to hear her preach. Later, she related that the hatred for the young man who killed her father seethed within her, and she spewed out this venom about the accident to everyone – until the day of the funeral.

*"Sitting there in the front row of the little Baptist church, I still refused to accept my father's death. It couldn't be."*

"Sitting there in the front row of the little Baptist church, I still refused to accept my father's death. It couldn't be ...One by one, my family rose from their seats and filed by the coffin. My two sisters. My brother. Only I was left in the pew.

"The funeral director walked over and said, 'Kathryn, would you like to see your father before I close the casket?'

"Suddenly I was standing at the front of the church, looking down – my eyes fixed not on Papa's face, but on his shoulder, that shoulder on which I had so often leaned ...I leaned over and gently put my hand on that shoulder in the casket. And as I did, something happened. All that my fingers caressed was a suit of clothes ...Everything that box contained was simply something discarded, loved once, laid aside now. Papa wasn't there.

"...This was the first time the power of the risen, resurrected Christ really came through to me. Suddenly, I was no longer afraid of death....as my fear disappeared, so did my hate. Papa wasn't dead. He was alive."[14]

## RENEWED AND SMILIN'

Kathryn returned to Denver with a new understanding and compassion. Upon her return, a building was found and renovation began in February of 1935. On May 30 of that year, the Denver Revival Tabernacle opened with a huge neon sign over it, as promised – "PRAYER CHANGES THINGS." The auditorium held two thousand seats and the name of the Tabernacle could be seen from a great distance. Thousands of people from the surrounding areas attended Kathryn's meetings over the next four years. Services were conducted nightly except on Monday.

> *...the romantic involvement became publicly known between Kathryn and Waltrip, whom she nicknamed, "Mister."*

The revival center soon developed into an organized church. There was no denominational affiliation. Ultimately a Sunday school was begun, and buses were in operation to bring people to the services. There were outreaches to prisons and nursing homes. Later on Kathryn began a radio program called, "Smiling Through."

In 1936, many musicians and preachers ministered at the Denver Revival Tabernacle. One of those was Raymond T. Richey, a prominent evangelist, who spent three weeks at the church. Richey had been a leading pioneer in America's earlier healing revivals.

Kathryn labeled the trauma of her father's death as her "deepest" valley experience, but there was another valley experience that would prove to be nearly as deep.

## WHAT A "TRIP"

In 1935 an evangelist named Burroughs A. Waltrip from Austin, Texas, was invited to speak at the Tabernacle. He was an extremely handsome man and eight years older than Kathryn. Soon they found themselves attracted to each other.

The only problem was that he was married and had two little boys. Kathryn seemed to ignore the promptings of the Holy Spirit within her telling her that this relationship was a mistake. Shortly after his first visit to Denver, Waltrip divorced his wife and told everyone that his wife left him. However, his ex-wife, Jessie, said Waltrip believed that if you didn't love your spouse at the time of marriage, then there was no covenant, making a person free to divorce and remarry. After Waltrip left his wife, he never returned home to her, and his two little boys never saw their father again.[15]

## MISTER IS SPELLED M-I-S-T-A-K-E

After leaving his family, Waltrip moved to Mason City, Iowa, representing himself as a single man, to begin a revival center called Radio Chapel. He was known to be a dramatic and sensational evangelist and began daily radio broadcasts from the Chapel. Kathryn and Helen came into town to help him raise funds for his ministry.

Soon, the romantic involvement became publicly known between Kathryn and Waltrip, whom she nicknamed, "Mister." Helen and other friends from Denver sincerely advised Kathryn not to marry the handsome evangelist, but she reasoned that his wife had left him, making him free to marry.

It should be noted that the details of Waltrip's separation from his wife and the timing of Kuhlman's involvement are not clear. Those who loved and appreciated her ministry kept these things quiet. Obviously, they felt that God had forgiven Kathryn of any mistakes in this relationship, so the details weren't important.

On October 16, 1938, Kathryn announced to her Denver congregation that she planned to join the ministry with "Mister" in Mason City, Iowa. Two days later on October 18th, almost sixteen months after Waltrip's uncontested divorce, Kathryn and Burroughs were secretly married in Mason City.

## WHAT IS THE ISSUE, ANYWAY?

Let me make a point here. Divorce was not the issue. Of course, it is an issue with religious people and their self-righteous denominations, but it is not an issue to God. He lays it out very simply. According to the New Testament, there are two scriptural reasons for divorce. One spouse being involved in repeated immorality is one reason. And the other comes into play when one spouse leaves the marriage. If either one of these things happen to a person, that person is free before God and blessed to remarry. If you made a decision regarding divorce that didn't line up with the Word of God, there is forgiveness and restoration and a new and clean beginning waiting for you. Self-righteous people and certain denominations may not give you a new beginning, but God can help you if you seek Him.

Kathryn found herself in a situation where there were lying and deceiving spirits in operation. Waltrip left his wife in Texas and divorced her, which was his first mistake. Then, he tried to cover it by embracing a deceiving doctrine and lied about it to those around him. The Kuhlman-Waltrip marriage was *totally wrong* from the start!

## SHE ALMOST DID IT...

Kathryn chose to believe this man's story that his wife left him. However, her heart was constantly troubled throughout their wedding plans. She found no peace in her spirit. Most people say that "Mister" didn't love Kathryn at all. Instead, he loved her ability to draw a crowd and raise money. He was well-known for his greed and extravagant lifestyle. When he married Kathryn, people in eight different states were "hounding" him for money.

Even "Mister's" mother begged Kathryn not to marry her son. She had hoped he would come to his senses and re-unite with his wife and sons. You may ask, then *why* did Kathryn go ahead with the marriage?

Before the scheduled marriage in Mason City, Kathryn discussed the issue with her friends, Lottie Anthony and Helen. Lottie remembers Kathryn saying, **"I just can't seem to find the will of God in this matter."** The women tried to convince Kathryn to wait and follow the peace of God. But she would not listen to them.

When the three women arrived in Des Moines on the way to Mason City, Helen announced to Kathryn that she wouldn't go through with it. She remained at their hotel. Lottie agreed with Helen and also refused to attend the wedding.

But Kathryn found another friend to witness the marriage between her and Waltrip. Kathryn fainted during the ceremony. Waltrip helped to revive her so that she could finish the vows. The deliberate decision to step out of the will of God obviously weighed heavily upon her.

As the newlyweds drove back to Des Moines from the ceremony, Kathryn did an odd thing. After the couple checked into their hotel, Kathryn refused to stay with her new husband. Her close friend Lottie Anthony states that Kathryn jumped in the car and drove to her and Helen's hotel.

Kathryn sat in their hotel room, weeping and admitting she had made a mistake with the marriage and would get an annulment. Lottie called Waltrip, informing him of Kathryn's plans. As Waltrip complained of losing his wife, Lottie snapped, "She was never yours in the first place!"

The three women left Des Moines, hoping to explain the situation away to the Denver congregation. But the congregation never gave her a chance. They were furious with her for taking the situation so lightly and for the secrecy of the marriage. Lottie said that the Denver congregation "drove her back into Waltrip's arms."[16]

> *In spite of the looks, the whispers, and the wholesale rejection, it took great faith and dogged determination to restore Kathryn's ministry.*

## THE SHATTERED DREAMS

The work Kathryn had so diligently built over the previous five years quickly disintegrated. Hewitt bought out Kathryn's share of the building, and Helen went to work for a smaller church in Denver. The "sheep" scattered. Because of this grievous mistake, Kathryn lost her church, her close friends, and her ministry. Even her relationship with God suffered because Kathryn put "Mister" and his desires over her passion for God.

Kathryn Kuhlman, the woman some had worshipped as a "perfect madonna," was actually a human being, subject to human temptations. She was a great woman of God, but *what made her great was her choice and action to recover from her mistake*. In spite of the looks, the whispers, and the wholesale rejection, it took great faith and dogged determination to restore Kathryn's ministry. It is said that her own mistakes produced the powerful revelation behind her sermons of temptation, forgiveness, and victory.

But this action and revelation didn't come overnight. Kathryn spent the next eight years in oblivion as far as major ministry was concerned. Six years were spent in the marriage and the next two she spent trying to find her way back to full-time ministry. Friends who traveled to Mason City the year Kathryn lived there said she would sit on the platform behind her husband and weep while he preached.

When the people of Mason City learned that Waltrip had lied about his first marriage, they stopped attending, and Radio Chapel soon closed. The few times Waltrip allowed Kathryn to minister alone were in places where no one knew she was married. At least once, a series of meetings were canceled at the last moment after the pastor who invited her was told by a member of his congregation of Kathryn's marriage to a divorced man.[17]

## THE PAIN OF DYING

Kathryn left Waltrip in 1944 while they were living in Los Angeles, but he didn't get a divorce until 1947.

On one of the rare occasions when she would talk of those years and what happened, she said:

> **"I had to make a choice. Would I serve the man I loved, or the God I loved? I knew I couldn't serve God and live with Mister. No one will ever know the pain of dying like I know it, for I loved him more than I loved life itself. And for a time, I loved him even more than God. I finally told him I had to leave, for God had never released me from my original call. Not only did I live with him, I had to live with my conscience, and the conviction of the Holy Spirit was almost unbearable. I was tired of trying to justify myself."[18]**

In one of her final appearances, in a question and answer session, a young man asked her how she "met her death." He had heard her speak of this death several times.

She answered:

> **"It came through a great disappointment, a great disappointment, and I felt like my whole world had come to an end. You know, it's not what happens to you, it's what you do with the things after it happens. And that goes back to the will of the Lord.**
>
> **"At that time, I felt that which had happened to me was the greatest tragedy of my life. I thought I would never rise again, never, never. No one will ever know — if you've never died — what I'm talking about ...Today, I feel it was a part of God's perfect will for my life."[19]**

Kathryn commented several times how she suffered for the sake of the ministry. But actually, there were other people who suffered also. There was a wife who had been left in Texas with two small boys, needing an explanation of why they would never see their dad again. The ordeal brought great heartache to everyone who knew and loved the couple.

## BOTH SIDES OF THE COIN

But from the moment she made her decision, Kathryn Kuhlman never wavered from answering the call on her life, never deviated from the path God had set for her, and never saw "Mister" again. She bought a one-way ticket to Franklin, Pennsylvania, and never turned back.

Kathryn was totally restored in her life with God. Though this was a difficult time for Kathryn, the blessings of God soon followed her. But the fate of Waltrip was uncertain. He simply dropped out of sight, not even contacting his family. According to his ex-wife Jessie, it was years later that his brother, James Waltrip, sadly discovered that Burroughs had eventually met his death in a California prison, convicted of stealing money from a woman.[20]

> ...*Kathryn came out of her "wilderness" and moved into the "Promised Land" of her real ministry.*

## OUT OF THE CAVE

No one ever seemed to know why Kathryn picked Franklin, Pennsylvania, to begin her "comeback." Franklin was a coal-mining city, settled by German immigrants. Perhaps she felt at home there. Perhaps it was because they accepted her there. Whatever the reason, it worked!

From Pennsylvania she went through the midwestern states and the south into West Virginia, Virginia, and the Carolinas. In some places, she was quickly accepted, in others, her past surfaced quickly and the meetings were closed. In Georgia, a newspaper took hold of the story concerning her marriage to a divorced man and printed it. Kathryn then took a bus back to Franklin.

In 1946, Kathryn came out of her "wilderness" and moved into the "Promised Land" of her real ministry. After an unsuccessful tour of the South, she was invited to hold a series of meetings in the fifteen hundred seat Gospel Tabernacle located in Franklin, Pennsylvania. The Tabernacle had been famous in circles since Billy Sunday preached there. And Kathryn's meetings were so glorious in this building that it was as if the last eight years never existed.

## THE MANY VOICES

Not too long after she opened her meetings at the Tabernacle, she began daily radio broadcasts from WKRZ Radio in Oil City, Pennsylvania. Response had been so great, that within a few months, she added a station in Pittsburgh. Instead of being shunned, Kathryn was now being inundated with mail. The Oil City station finally had to bar visitors from the studio because they hindered the staff's work.

World War II had just ended, and many luxuries were still scarce. One day, Kathryn casually mentioned over the air that she had made a run in her last pair of stockings, and soon afterwards the station was deluged with packages of nylon stockings.

The Holy Spirit moved in the days surrounding the end of the war to restore the body of Christ through the gift of healing. The great healing revivals were in full swing, and great healings were manifested through the ministries of such men as Oral Roberts, William Branham, and the late Jack Coe. The late Gordon Lindsay, founder of *The Voice of Healing* magazine and Christ for the Nations Bible School, published the news of these great revivals in *The Voice of Healing* magazine.

At this time, Kathryn was still praying mainly for people to receive salvation. But she was beginning to pray and lay hands on people who came for healing. Though she despised the term "faith healer," she attended the meetings of these ministers hoping to find out more about this phenomenon of God. Kathryn didn't have the slightest idea that a "healing ministry" would bring her international fame.

As she observed various tent meetings, Kathryn walked away with greater understanding. Though she always had unanswered questions about divine healing, she did establish a standard for her ministry:

> **"In the early part of my ministry, I was greatly disturbed over much that I saw occurring in the field of divine healing. I was confused by the many methods that I saw employed. I was disgusted with the unwise performances that I witnessed, none of which I could associate in any way whatsoever with either the action of the Holy Spirit or the nature of God.**
>
> **"...To this very day, there is nothing more repulsive to me than the lack of wisdom.... There is one thing I can't**

stand, and that is fanaticism – the manifestations of the flesh that bring a reproach on something that is so marvelous, something that is so sacred."[21]

Kathryn went on to speak of her heartache while watching these meetings. For the rest of her life, she exhorted the people to focus and concentrate on Jesus, and nothing else. After attending a tent meeting in Erie, Pennsylvania, she said:

"I began to weep. I couldn't stop. Those looks of despair and disappointment on the faces I had seen, when told that their lack of faith was keeping them from God, were to haunt me for weeks. Was this the God of all mercy and great compassion? I left the tent, and with hot tears streaming down my face, I looked up and cried, 'They have taken away my Lord, and I know not where they have laid Him.'"[22]

> *The moment Kathryn saw in God's Word that healing was provided for the believer at the same time as salvation, she began to understand the Christian's relationship with the Holy Spirit.*

It is interesting to note that Kathryn Kuhlman chose not to associate her ministry with Gordon Lindsay's *Voice of Healing* publication. The publication was the promotional outlet for the healing evangelists of that era, and Kuhlman chose not to be a part of it. Many of these evangelists were sincere and honest, but others turned to sensationalism and used questionable methods in their ministries.

## HERE COME THE MIRACLES!

The moment Kathryn saw in God's Word that healing was provided for the believer at the same time as salvation, she began to understand the Christian's relationship with the Holy Spirit. In 1947 she began teaching a series on the Holy Spirit. Some of the things she said during the first night of her teaching were revelations even to her. Later she spoke of being awake all that night, praying and reading more in the Word.

The second night of her meeting was a momentous occasion. A unique testimony had been given by someone who was healed in a Kathryn Kuhlman meeting. A woman stood up and told of having been healed while Kathryn preached the night before. Without anyone laying hands on her and without

Kathryn even being aware of what was happening, this woman was healed of a tumor. The woman had gone to her doctor to confirm her healing before the evening service.

On the following Sunday, the second miracle occurred. A World War I veteran who had been declared legally blind from an industrial accident, had 85 percent of his vision restored in the permanently impaired eye, and perfect eyesight restored to his other eye.

## SHARK, SHERIFF, AND GLORY

Once the healings and miracles began to take place, the crowds at the Tabernacle were even larger than those brought in by Billy Sunday. God began to prosper Kathryn's ministry greatly, but the devil's adversaries had now stepped in, attempting to undermine the working and flow of the Holy Spirit in Kathryn's ministry.

The attack came through M. J. Maloney and the Tabernacle trustees. Maloney insisted that he receive a certain percentage of all the ministry revenue, including that which came from the radio broadcast and mailouts. Kathryn balked and Maloney threatened to sue her.

The activities surrounding this "showdown" included Maloney's locking her out of the building. A fight ensued between Kathryn and her coal miner followers and Maloney's men, ending in Kathryn's partisans breaking off the padlocks so services could continue. It only ended when Kathryn's supporters raised $10,000 and purchased an old roller skating rink in nearby Sugar Creek. They named that roller rink Faith Temple. It was twice the size of Maloney's building and was packed from the first service.

Ironically, during this hectic and crucial time of 1947, another amazing thing happened. One night, Kathryn heard a knock on the door of her apartment. When she opened the door, there stood the sheriff dressed in street clothes. He proceeded to tell her that "Mister" had filed for divorce in Nevada and his office had received the papers that morning, naming her as the defendant.

Kathryn looked down and saw the papers in his hand. Her head remained bowed. Seeing her shame and disappointment, the sheriff reached out and touched her arm, for he had been attending Kathryn's services and knew she had been sent by God to their area. Knowing that names of famous persons on divorce papers were often given to the media for press release, the sheriff made sure the papers remained private by delivering them personally.

The sheriff went on to reassure Kathryn that no one but the two of them would ever know of this legal action. Kathryn told the sheriff she would be grateful to him for the rest of her life.

His goodness saved Kathryn from great heartache. Seven years later reporters did find out about it, but by that time, Kathryn's ministry had so advanced, it was not affected by old news.

*...signs from heaven would urge Kathryn to move to Pittsburgh.*

Great healing services continued at the renovated roller rink, and additional services expanded into neighboring towns and to Stambaugh Auditorium in Youngstown, Ohio. The Holy Spirit had found a ministry that wouldn't try to take the credit for His deeds, nor the glory from the results of His operations.

A former secretary remembered:

> "Miss Kuhlman was so tender toward God. I was standing in the Tabernacle after a service and could see into the radio room. There Miss Kuhlman, unaware that anyone could see her, was on her knees praising God for the service."[23]

As her ministry developed, she put less emphasis on faith, and more emphasis on the sovereignty of the Holy Spirit. In her meetings, there were no prayer cards, no invalid tents, and no long lines of sick people waiting for her to lay hands on them. She never accused people who failed to receive healing of being weak in their faith. It seemed that the healings took place anywhere throughout the auditorium while the people sat in their seats, looking toward Heaven and focusing on Jesus.

## THE ROOF FELL IN!

At her first meeting in the Carnegie Hall in Pittsburgh, the custodian told her that even opera stars couldn't fill it, but she insisted that enough chairs be set up to fill the auditorium. It was a good thing she did, because every chair was filled.

The first service was in the afternoon, and the hall was packed. A second meeting was held that evening to accommodate the throng. Jimmy Miller and Charles Beebee ministered in music at these services, and remained in ministry with Kathryn until the end.

The radio ministry continued to expand, and by November of 1950, the people began to urge Kathryn to relocate to Pittsburgh permanently. Even Maggie

Hartner, the woman who became her "right arm" agreed they should move. Kathryn was reluctant, feeling committed to the people in Franklin who had stood by her and supported her, and had taken her in and loved her when no one else would.

But signs from heaven would urge Kathryn to move to Pittsburgh.

In response to pleas that she move, Kathryn announced:

**"No! The roof on Faith Temple literally would have to cave in before I'd believe God wanted me to move to Pittsburgh."**

On Thanksgiving, 1950, the temple's roof fell in under the weight of the greatest snowfall in area history.[24]

Three weeks later, Kathryn moved to the Pittsburgh suburb of Fox Chapel, where she lived until her death.

## "I WANT TO BE LIKE AIMEE"

In 1950, a worldwide ministry began to develop. In later years, Kathryn said that God didn't call her to build a church, maintaining that her ministry was not to be isolated to any one building. Some may be called to build buildings, but she wasn't one of those.

The fact that she did build churches was largely overshadowed by the publicity of the miracle services. The Kathryn Kuhlman Foundation, established in Pittsburgh, financed more than twenty churches in foreign mission fields with nationals as pastors.

Many call her "pastor" out of love and respect, but Kathryn was never ordained to the office of pastor. After her stay in Denver, she never pastored a church. Kathryn said she was not called to a five-fold office, i.e., Ephesians 4:11. She walked in the simplicity of being "a handmaiden" of the Lord.

It is said by those closest to her, that Kathryn announced at the very beginning of her ministry, that she would be the next Aimee Semple McPherson, founder of the Four Square denomination. Aimee was definitely Kathryn's role model. When the flamboyant "Sister" built Angelus Temple in Los Angeles, Kathryn was present during its highest popularity. It is said that Kathryn attended Aimee's Bible school, and sat in the balcony of her church, taking in every aspect of the anointed messages and theatrics of "Sister". Unlike the other L.I.F.E. Bible School students, Kathryn chose not to stay with the Four Square denomination. She chose an independent route. It is interesting to note that Rolf McPherson, Aimee's son, doesn't remember Kathryn being a student at the school.[25]

Though she never met Aimee personally, the effects of her ministry rubbed off on Kathryn. There was a major difference between the two: Aimee taught people to seek for the baptism in the Holy Spirit; Kathryn thought to "seek for it" was a devisive practice. Kathryn was Pentecostal but didn't make an issue of it. People had always compared Kathryn with Aimee, but it was six years after Aimee's premature death before Kathryn made the national headlines.[26]

## A MEDIA CHURCH

Kathryn's messages were heard all over the United States and various places overseas, via short-wave radio broadcast. It seemed that America could hardly wait to hear that warm, pleasant voice ask listeners at the beginning of her program, **"Hello, there, and have you been waiting for me?"**

*If it looked like she wouldn't have freedom, or if questionable people were present who might taint her ministry, she canceled. It has been said that even "those in charge were not in charge" when Kathryn was present.*

Her radio program was not religious or stuffy. Instead, the program made a person feel as though Kathryn Kuhlman had just dropped by for coffee. She ministered to the needs, concerns, and hurts of her audience, and her encouragement changed lives. She frequently chuckled, making the listener feel as though they had just had a heart-to-heart talk with her. If she wanted to cry – she cried; if she wanted to sing – she sang. Kathryn had the ability to minister over radio just as she ministered in public. Not many could do that, but Kathryn did. By popular demand, the Kuhlman Foundation was requested to supply her old-recorded radio tapes to the radio stations for six years after her death!

For more than eight years before her death, her weekly television program was aired nationwide. At the time, her program was the longest running half-hour series produced in the CBS studios, though it didn't air on the CBS network.

## IT HAD TO BE "KATHRYN'S" WAY

Her meetings were moved from Carnegie Hall to the First Presbyterian Church in Pittsburgh, and for years these sessions were attended by some of the most elite Bible scholars in Pittsburgh. For the last ten years of her life, she held monthly services at the Shrine Auditorium in Los Angeles, where she ministered to countless thousands, and hundreds were healed. She also spoke at large churches, conferences, and international meetings. She especially enjoyed ministering at the Full Gospel Business Men's Fellowship International, a laymen's organization founded by Demos Shakarian in Los Angeles.

It was several years before Kathryn would consent to integrate the miracle services with other conferences. She felt the confinements of a general conference, with schedules and time limits, might restrict the liberty of the Spirit that was so a part of her meetings.

If another group wanted Kathryn to speak for them, they had to adjust their program to fit her style. She knew that God had called her to minister a certain way, and there would be no changes. If it looked like she wouldn't have freedom, or if questionable people were present who might taint her ministry, she canceled. It has been said that even "those in charge were not in charge" when Kathryn was present.[27]

## SHE DIED A THOUSAND TIMES

Kathryn never preached against smoking or drinking alcoholic beverages. She didn't advocate their use, but she refused to alienate people. Also, she didn't like the way that some of the healing evangelists ministered. Kathryn felt it was "rough," and she would not support that type of ministry.

She never taught that sickness was from the devil. She avoided the subject, pointing instead to how big God is. She felt if she could turn the eyes of the people toward God, then everything would fall into place. Early in her ministry, she encouraged people to leave their denomination. In her later years, Kathryn encouraged them to return and be a shining light and a healing force.[28]

It is said that Kathryn's life was a prayer. Traveling constantly, she didn't have conventional times of devotion, so she learned to make wherever she was her prayer closet. Before her meetings, Kathryn would be seen "pacing back and forth, head up, head down, arms flung into the air, hands clasped behind her back." Her face would be covered in tears. It seemed she was pleading with the Lord, saying, **"Gentle Jesus, take not Your Holy Spirit from me."**[29]

Though this depth of prayer would seem to be a personal thing, it wasn't so with Kathryn. Many times, she would be interrupted with a question, which she would answer, then she would resume the same depth of prayer at the point of interruption. Oral Roberts described her relationship with the Spirit this way:

"It was like they were talking back and forth to each other, and you couldn't tell where Kathryn started and the Holy Spirit left off. It was a oneness."[30]

> *Though there were thousands upon thousands of miracles, the greatest miracle to Kathryn was when a person became born again.*

People from all walks of life and denominations came to her meetings: Catholics, Episcopals, Baptists, Pentecostals, drunkards, the sick, the dying, the deeply spiritual and the unconverted. And Kathryn knew she was the vessel who would point them to God. In some way, she could cross every barrier and bring them all to the same level of understanding. How could she do this? I believe it was because she lived in such surrender to the Holy Spirit. She always said, **"I die a thousand deaths before every service."**[31]

Being an ecumenical evangelist, Kathryn never permitted the spiritual gifts of tongues, the gift of interpretation, or prophecy to operate in her services. If someone repeatedly spoke in tongues loudly enough to disturb, she discreetly had them removed from the service. Kathryn believed in all the gifts of the Spirit, but didn't want to do anything that would hinder or distract the uninitiated from a simple belief in God.

However, she did allow people to be "slain in the Spirit." Many came to believe in the awesome power of God from witnessing this manifestation alone. Kathryn offered this simple explanation:

> **"All I can believe is that our spiritual beings are not wired for God's full power, and when we plug in to that power, we just can't survive it. We are wired for low voltage, God is high voltage through the Holy Spirit."**[32]

She never left the platform, even when a musician or soloist ministered. She usually stepped to the side, but always remained in the view of the audience, standing, smiling, and lifting her hand to God.

Kathryn was always aware that she would, one day, stand before the Lord and give an account for her ministry. She never believed she had been God's first choice for the ministry. She believed a man had been called to do it, but was not willing to pay the price. She was never quite sure if she was even second choice or third choice, but she did know that she had answered **"yes"** to the Lord. Her ministry stands out as one of the leading ministries, if not *the* leading ministry, of the Charismatic Movement.

✫✫✫✫✫

## TOO MANY TO NAME...

What were some of the outstanding miracles? Though there were thousands upon thousands of miracles, the greatest miracle to Kathryn was when a person became born again. On one occasion a five-year-old boy, crippled from birth, walked to Kathryn's platform without assistance. On another, a woman, who had been crippled and confined to a wheelchair for twelve years, walked to the platform without aid from her husband. A man in Philadelphia, who had received a pacemaker eight months earlier, felt intense pain in his chest after Kathryn laid hands on him. Returning home, he found the scar gone from his chest where the pacemaker had been implanted, and he couldn't tell if the pacemaker was functioning. Later, when the doctor took X-rays, he discovered the pacemaker was gone and the man's heart healed!

It was common for tumors to dissolve, cancers to fall off, the blind to see and the deaf to hear. Migraine headaches were healed instantly. Even teeth were divinely filled. It would be impossible to list the miracles that the ministry of Kathryn Kuhlman witnessed! God alone knows.

*Screen stars were coming to her meetings. Even comedienne Phyllis Diller recommended one of Kathryn's books to a dying fan.*

Kathryn was known to weep for joy as she watched the thousands being healed through the power of God. Some even remember her teardrops falling on their hands.

It is also said that Kathryn would weep as she watched the people leave who remained sick or in wheelchairs. She never tried to explain why some received their healing and some did not. She believed the responsibility remained with God. She liked to refer to herself as in sales, not management. Whatever Management decided to do, she would have to oblige. But she did say it would be one of the first questions she would ask God when she got to heaven!

## NORTHERN EXPOSURE

In August of 1952, Kathryn preached to over fifteen thousand under Rex Humbard's tent in Akron, Ohio. On the pre-dawn hours before Kathryn's first Sunday service, the Humbard's were awakened by a loud knock on their mobile home door. It was a policeman who said, "Reverend Humbard, you're gonna have to do something. There's nearly eighteen thousand people out at

*Rushing for seats at a Kuhlman meeting*

*Seattle, Washington, 1974*

*Laying hands on the sick*

*Ministering to the lame*

*Emptying more wheel chairs*

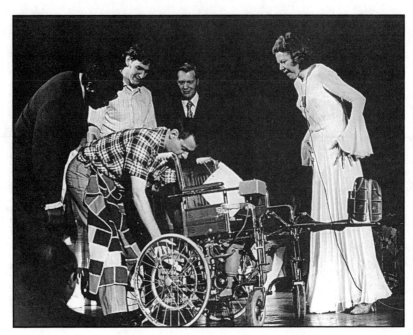

*"Rise and push!"*

*Kathryn with Oral Roberts*

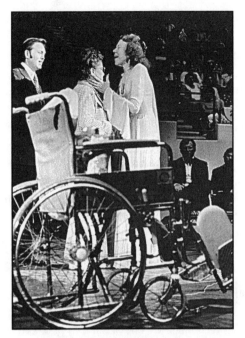

*"Be set free in Jesus' name!"*

*"Don't you just love Him, honey?"*

that tent." It was 4:00 A.M. in the morning, and the service was not scheduled to start until 11:00 A.M. that morning.

Kathryn, being used to crowds of people who couldn't all fit under one roof or into one tent, told Humbard there was only one thing to do, they would have to start the service at 8:00 A.M. And that's what they did! Maude Aimee, Rex's wife, remembered that Kathryn ministered until 2:30 P.M. that afternoon.

After these meetings, the Humbards parked their mobile home in Akron and subsequently built one of the largest churches and television ministries of that era – the 1960s and 1970s. Kathryn and the Humbards also built a life-long friendship as a result of their Akron experience.

Around this time, Kathryn was diagnosed with suffering from an enlarged heart and defective mitral valve. Yet, she kept going, remaining entirely dependent upon the Holy Spirit.

## GLITTER AND THE FALLING STARS

By now, Kathryn had become a celebrity figure in the Christian as well as the secular world. Screen stars were coming to her meetings. Even comedienne Phyllis Diller recommended one of Kathryn's books to a dying fan.[33] The Pope granted Kathryn a private audience in the Vatican, and gave her a pendant engraved with a dove. The largest cities in America were presenting her with the "key" to their cities. Even the nation of Viet Nam gave her a Medal of Honor for her contributions to the hurting.

Of course, in the midst of honor came attacks. Some she was able to ignore. But there were others that wounded her deeply. Among those were the betrayals of her employees, Dino Kartsonakis and his brother-in-law, Paul Bartholomew.

In short, Dino and his brother-in-law demanded a high pay increase in their contracts after they discovered the Kuhlman Foundation had signed a multimedia contract.

Kathryn had greatly enjoyed Dino's company. No doubt many of her crusade audiences remember how she fondly introduced him, saying with a great sweep of her arms, **"And now, heeere's DeeeeNo!"** Kathryn had taken Kartsonakis out of obscurity and launched him into an international ministry. It was said that she dressed him in the finest of clothes and exalted his name constantly before the media.

But Dino seemed to have fallen under the influence of his brother-in-law, Paul Bartholomew. Though Bartholomew had been the highest paid person on staff, he wanted more, and eventually sued Kathryn for an outrageous sum of money. And when Kathryn didn't approve of Dino's publicized relationship with a secular show-girl, he became bitter and also demanded more money. As a result, Kathryn fired them both. But not before they made many public accusations concerning her character that were heard around the world.[34]

In her later years, Kathryn didn't spend much time analyzing the character of her staff members. Instead, she chose people she simply enjoyed, but often the enjoyment she received was short-lived and heartache followed. It is possible that her mistakes in hiring came from her physical and mental exhaustion. Her schedule was tremendously hectic. Though she was warned that the hiring of Bartholomew and Kartsonakis was a mistake, Kathryn hired them anyway, resulting in the foregoing fiasco.

Though there may have been mistakes made in judgment, lack of understanding, and mistakes made through the people around her, she never allowed flesh to participate in any of the movings of the Holy Spirit, and she never took any of the credit. Kathryn Kuhlman always gave the glory to God.

With the ministry continuing in full swing, major denominations gave Kathryn credit for having the purest ministry of the Holy Spirit in their time. Kathryn had no hidden agendas and no ulterior motives, what you saw was what you got. She never pretended to have answers that she didn't have, and she was always concerned that she might grieve the Holy Spirit. She remained committed, submitted, honest, and sincere as long as she lived.

## HOW CAN YOU MISS THE BLEACHERS?

In 1968, Kathryn ministered for Pat Robertson and his associate, Jim Bakker, to a crowd of over three thousand people. Shortly after the meeting began, a row of bleachers broke loose and fell back against the wall. Many fell to the floor or were suspended in the air. The emergency squad arrived and carried some away on stretchers. Folding chairs replaced the bleachers, and the meeting finally returned to normal – yet, Miss Kuhlman oblivious to it all, was half-way through her sermon!

*Was it possible that Kathryn knew she would never return to the platform? Was it possible that, at that moment, she said good-bye to her earthly ministry?*

During 1968, Kathryn traveled internationally to Israel, Finland, and Sweden. She was guest on *The Johnny Carson Show, The Dinah Shore Show,* and many others. Though Kathryn was very diplomatic and accepted among all kinds of people, she still manifested the power of the Holy Spirit in her life on all of these media programs. It was said that the employees of the CBS studios always knew when Kathryn entered the building, because the whole atmosphere seemed to change.

In 1975, though now in her late sixties and weakened from her physical ailment, Kathryn made a ministry trip to Jerusalem to speak at the Second World Conference on the Holy Spirit. Despite her age and ailments, she was still spunky when it came to ministry.

> *Kathryn Kuhlman was a special treasure. Her ministry pioneered the way for us to know the Holy Spirit in our generation. She attempted to show us how to fellowship with Him and how to love Him. She truly had the ability to reveal the Holy Spirit to us as our Friend.*

Kathryn had heard that Bob Mumford was going to be a featured speaker there, and threatened to cancel her appearance because of it. She said his teachings on discipleship were complete heresy and she wouldn't participate. In the end though, Kathryn went to Israel and helped many of the Middle Easterners experience the ministry of the Holy Spirit.

## IT IS WELL WITH MY SOUL

The last miracle service of Kathryn Kuhlman's ministry was held at the Shrine Auditorium in Los Angeles, California, on November 16, 1975. As she left the building, an employee in Miss Kuhlman's Hollywood office saw something she would never forget.

As everyone left the auditorium, Kathryn walked quietly to the end of the stage. She raised her head and slowly scanned the balcony, as if she was gazing at every seat. It seemed like an eternity. Then, Kathryn dropped her gaze to the second balcony, following every row and every seat with her eyes. Then, she looked at the ground floor, studying every seat.[35]

We can only imagine what was going through Kathryn's mind, the memories, the victories, the healings, the laughter, and the tears. Was it possible that Kathryn knew she would never return to the platform? Was it possible that, at that moment, she said good-bye to her earthly ministry?

In just a little over three weeks from that November date, Kathryn lay dying in the Hillcrest Medical Center of Tulsa, Oklahoma, after open-heart surgery.

By now, Kathryn had given complete control of her ministry to Tink Wilkerson, formerly in the automobile business in Tulsa, Oklahoma. Wilkerson is the son of the late Jeannie Wilkerson, who was a true prophetess of the Lord.

Wilkerson was with Kathryn for only a short ten months. She trusted Wilkerson. He was the one who chose where she would have the heart surgery. After her death, she left the majority of her estate to him. When the former Kuhlman staff was questioned about him, there was division. Some felt Wilkerson deceived Kathryn, others felt he was sent by God for her final hour. However, the media ran rampant with questions of why Wilkerson received so much of Kathryn's estate, and Maggie Hartner, her associate for years, received so little.

In 1992, Wilkerson was convicted in two U.S. district courts in Oklahoma for fraud in a former auto business. He was scheduled for release from prison in the summer of 1993 at which time he planned to write a book on his and his wife's friendship with Kathryn.[36] Wilkerson has kept quiet for all these years, possibly out of respect. I believe he has a story that needs to be told.

## "I WANT TO GO HOME"

Oral and Evelyn Roberts were among a few of the visitors permitted to see Kathryn in Hillcrest Medical Center. As they walked into her room and went to her bedside to pray for her healing, Oral remembers a significant occurrence. "When Kathryn recognized that we were there to pray for her recovery, she put her hands out like a barrier and then pointed toward heaven." Evelyn Roberts looked at Oral and said, "She doesn't want our prayers. She wants to go home."

Kathryn's sister Myrtle received the same message from Kathryn. She told Wilkerson, "Kathryn wants to go home."[37]

The wonderful red-headed lady who introduced the ministry of the Holy Spirit to our generation and thrilled the hearts of millions, finally received her heart's desire. It was said that the Holy Spirit descended upon her one more time and her face began to shine. The nurse in her room noticed a glow that enveloped her bed, creating an indescribable peace.[38] At 8:20 P.M. on Friday, February 20, 1976, Kathryn Kuhlman went home to be with Jesus. She was sixty-eight years old.

Oral Roberts presided over her funeral at Forest Lawn Memorial Park in Glendale, California. Kathryn was buried in the same cemetery a half mile from Aimee Semple McPherson's vault. Oral had a vision, at Kathryn's death, that God would raise up and spread similar ministries throughout the world, making the magnitude of God's power greater than He did through Kathryn's life.

Kathryn Kuhlman was a special treasure. Her ministry pioneered the way for us to know the Holy Spirit in our generation. She attempted to show us how to fellowship with Him and how to love Him. She truly had the ability to reveal the Holy Spirit to us as our Friend. So no one can close this chapter as well as she:

> **"The world called me a fool for having given my entire life to One whom I've never seen. I know exactly what I'm going to say when I stand in His presence. When I look upon that wonderful face of Jesus, I'll have just one thing to say: 'I tried.' I gave of myself the best I knew how. My redemption will have been perfected when I stand and see Him who made it all possible."**[39]

## CHAPTER NINE, KATHRYN KUHLMAN

### References

[1] Roberts Liardon, *Kathryn Kuhlman: A Spiritual Biography of God's Miracle Working Power* (Laguna Hills, CA: Embassy Publishing Company, 1990), 68.

[2] Helen Hosier, *Kathryn Kuhlman: The Life She Led, the Legacy She Left* (Wheaton, IL: Tyndale House Publishers, 1971), 38.

[3] Jamie Buckingham, *Daughter of Destiny: Kathryn Kuhlman... Her Story* (Plainfield, NJ: Logos International, 1976), 17-18.

[4] Hosier, *Kathryn Kuhlman: The Life She Led*, 32-33.

[5] Buckingham, *Daughter of Destiny*, 23.

[6] Hosier, *Kathryn Kuhlman*, 44.

[7] Buckingham, *Daughter of Destiny*, 70-71.

[8] Sermon by Kuhlman, "Not Doing What We Like, But Liking What We Have To Do."

[9] Buckingham, *Daughter of Destiny*, Chapter 3.

[10] Sermon by Kuhlman, "Guidelines for Life's Greatest Virtue."

[11] The Kathryn Kuhlman Foundation, *Heart to Heart with Kathryn Kuhlman*, 58.

[12] See Footnote 10.

[13] Buckingham, *Daughter of Destiny*, 57.

[14] Hosier, *Kathryn Kuhlman*, 60-64.

[15] Wayne E. Warner, *Kathryn Kuhlman: The Woman Behind the Miracles* (Ann Arbor, MI: Vine Books, segment of Servant Publications, 1993), 84, Footnote 5, 263.

[16] Ibid., 93-94.

[17] Buckingham, *Daughter of Destiny*, Chapter 5.

[18] Ibid., 88.

[19] Sermon by Kuhlman, "The Ministry of Healing."

[20] Warner, *Kathryn Kuhlman*, 104.

[21] Sermon by Kuhlman, "The Secret of All Miracles in Jesus' Life."

[22] Buckingham, *Daughter of Destiny*, 101-102.

[23] Warner, *Kathryn Kuhlman*, 120.

[24] Buckingham, *Daughter of Destiny*, 118-119.

[25] Personal Interview with Rolf McPherson, February 1996.

[26] Warner, *Kathryn Kuhlman,* 203-205, 276, Footnote 4.

[27] Ibid., 210.

[28] Ibid., 162.

[29] Buckingham, *Daughter of Destiny,* 147.

[30] Warner, *Kathryn Kuhlman,* 234.

[31] Ibid., 212.

[32] Ibid., 220.

[33] Ibid., 164.

[34] Ibid., 186-189.

[35] Ibid., 236.

[36] Ibid., 242.

[37] Ibid., 240.

[38] Buckingham, *Daughter of Destiny,* 305.

[39] "A Tribute to the Lord's Handmaiden," quoted from the *Abundant Life Magazine* (Tulsa, OK: Oral Roberts Evangelistic Association, May 1976), cover.

# William Branham

## "A Man of Notable Signs and Wonders"

# "A MAN OF NOTABLE SIGNS AND WONDERS"

"'You are of the devil, and deceiving the people,' he shouted, 'an imposter, a snake in the grass, a fake, and I am going to show these people that you are!' It was a bold challenge and everyone in the audience could see that it was not an idle threat.... It appeared to be an evil moment for the little figure on the platform, and most of them must have felt exceedingly sorry for him. Certainly they could see there was no room for trickery. The man on the platform would have to have the goods or else take the consequences.

"The seconds passed.... Presently it appeared that something was hindering the challenger from carrying out his evil designs. Softly but determinedly the voice of the evangelist...could be heard only a short distance.... 'Satan, because you have challenged the servant of God before this great congregation, you must now bow before me. In the name of Jesus Christ, you shall fall at my feet.'

"Suddenly he who a few minutes before had so brazenly defied the man of God with his fearful threats and accusations, gave an awful groan and slumped to the floor sobbing hysterically. The evangelist calmly proceeded with the service as if nothing had happened as the man lay writhing in the dust."[1]

William Branham was a humble, soft-spoken man familiar with tragedy, heartbreak, and poverty. Semiliterate by worldly standards, Branham was educated through supernatural occurrences. Gordon Lindsay, founder of Christ For the Nations, was a personal friend of Branham's, and his official biographer. He said Branham's life was "so out of this world and beyond ordinary" that if it had not been for documented truths, a person could, under normal circumstances, consider the stories of his life and ministry "far-fetched and incredible."[2]

Simple in his reasonings and poor in his command of the English language, Branham became the leader in the Voice of Healing revival that originated in the late forties. There were many healing revivalists who came to the forefront during this era and each had his or her own uniqueness. But none were able to combine the prophetic office, the supernatural manifestations, and divine healing as William Branham did.

> *Simple in his reasonings and poor in his command of the English language, Branham became the leader in the Voice of Healing revival that originated in the late forties.*

Sadly though, the final phase of his ministry carries a shadow. As this Branham chapter progresses, what is written will be shocking to some, and sad to others. Understand that the details are for instruction. Branham's life is a tragically sad illustration of what happens when one does not follow the times and seasons of heaven. However, the beginning of Branham's life and ministry is a tribute to the supernatural influence of God in the earth. If there is any "religious" tradition in you, the early life and times of William Branham will, no doubt, send a shock wave through your system.

## A WHIRL OF LIGHT

Just as morning dawned on April 6, 1909, a small, five-pound baby boy was born in the hills of Kentucky. Pacing the dirt floor of the old cabin, the eighteen-year-old father was dressed in his new overalls for the occasion. The baby's mother, barely fifteen years old, held her new son as they decided his name: William Marrion Branham.

With the light beginning to break through the early morning skies, the grandmother decided to open a window so the Branhams could better see their new son. It was here the first supernatural occurrence happened to young Branham. In his own words, he tells the story as it was described to him:

**"Suddenly, a light come whirling through the window, about the size of a pillow, and circled around where I was, and went down on the bed."**[3]

Neighbors who witnessed the scene were in awe, wondering what kind of child had been born to the Branhams. As she rubbed his tiny hands, Mrs. Branham had no idea those same hands would be used by God to heal multitudes, and lead one of the greatest healing revivals to date.

Two weeks later, little William Branham had his first visit to a Missionary Baptist church.

## DIRT FLOORS AND PLANK CHAIRS

William Branham's family was the poorest of the poor. They lived in the back hills of Kentucky, with dirt as their floor and planks as their chairs. These people were totally uneducated, as far as worldly standards go. So reading the Bible, or any book, was nearly impossible.

Living conditions were poor and there was little emphasis on serving God. The Branham family had a general knowledge of God, and that was about it. Theirs was a rugged environment, and they gave all their effort to survival. The Branhams went to church mainly as a moral duty, or occasionally as a social event.

When you understand Branham's background, it is easier to see why God used sovereign and supernatural signs to speak to William Branham. He didn't know how to read or study the Bible for himself. Branham didn't know how to pray, and throughout his youth, he never heard anyone pray.

*Branham's cabin/birthplace near Berksville, Kentucky*

If you do not know how to read, then you can't hear from God through His Word.

If you do not pray, then you can't hear from your inner voice, or spirit.

*God is not limited to the confines of educational theology. He is God — and sometimes, He will call a person like William Branham to come along and break our religious molds. Religion wants us to forget that the word "supernatural" describes God's presence. It makes some people nervous when God breaks through the confines of their "religiosity."*

If no one around you knows God, then there is no one to teach you.

In these kinds of situations God is left to convey His message to a person through signs and wonders. It is rare, but God is not limited because of ignorance and poverty. It happened then, and it can happen today. God will get His message to an individual, one way or another.

In the Old Testament, a donkey spoke to Balaam. It was the only way Balaam would hear the Word of the Lord.

God spoke to Moses through a burning bush. In the book of Acts, signs and wonders empowered believers to turn a dark, "religious" world upside down.

God is not limited to the confines of educational theology. He is God – and sometimes, He will call a person like William Branham to come along and break our religious molds. Religion wants us to forget that the word "supernatural" describes God's presence. It makes some people nervous when God breaks through the confines of their "religiosity."

It was God working through signs and wonders that caused Branham to know God, to understand God's call on his life, and eventually to walk in it.

## SAVED FROM A FREEZING DEATH

The providence of God was with Branham from his birth. His father, working as a logger, had to be away from home for long periods of time. When Branham was only six months old, a severe snowstorm blanketed the mountains, trapping the young child and his mother inside their cabin. With firewood and food supply gone, death seemed certain. So Branham's mother wrapped herself and her baby in ragged blankets, and then they laid hungry and shivering in the bed to face their fate.

But "fate" cannot change God's plan. He was watching over them through the eyes of a neighbor. This neighbor, concerned that smoke was not coming from their chimney, trudged through the heavy snow to their cabin and broke through their door. Quickly he gathered wood for a warm fire and waded through the heavy snow back to his own cabin to get food for the Branhams. This man's goodness and alertness saved their lives.

Soon after this ordeal, Branham's father moved his family from the backwoods of Kentucky to Utica, Indiana, where he went to work as a farmer. Later, the family moved to Jeffersonville, Indiana, which would become known as the hometown of William Branham.

Although the family had moved to Jeffersonville, a moderately sized city, they remained extremely poor. At age seven, young Branham didn't even have a shirt to wear to school, only a coat. Many times he sat sweltering in the heat of the small school, embarrassed to take his coat off because he had no shirt underneath. God never chooses between the rich and the poor. God looks upon the heart.

## THE WIND FROM HEAVEN

School had just ended for the day, and Branham's friends were going to the pond to fish. Branham wanted to go with them, but his father told him to draw water for that evening.

Branham cried as he drew the water, upset that he had to work instead of going fishing. As he carried the heavy bucket of water from the barn to the house, he sat down under an old poplar tree to rest.

Suddenly, he heard the sound of wind blowing in the top of the tree. He jumped up to look, and he noticed that the wind was not blowing in any other place. Stepping back, he looked up into the tree, and a voice came saying, "Never drink, smoke, or defile your body in any way, for I have a work for you to do when you get older."

Startled by the voice and shaking, the little boy ran home crying into the arms of his mother. Wondering if he had been bitten by a snake, she tried to calm him. Failing to soothe him, she put him to bed and called the doctor, fearful that he was suffering from some strange sort of nervous disorder.

For the rest of his childhood, Branham did everything he could to avoid passing by that tree.[4]

As strange as that experience may have been to Branham, he found that he could never smoke, drink, or defile his body. Several times, as a result of peer pressure, he tried. But as soon as he would lift a cigarette or drink to his lips, he would again hear that sound of the wind blowing in the top of the tree. Immediately, he would look around to see, but everything else was calm and still as before. The same awesome fear would sweep over him and he would drop the cigarette or the bottle and run away.

As a result of his strange behavior, Branham had very few friends as he was growing up. Branham said of himself, **"It seemed all through my life I was just a black sheep knowing no one who understood me, and not even understanding myself."** He often commented that he had a peculiar feeling, **"like someone standing near me, trying to say something to me, especially when I was alone."**[5] So Branham spent the years of his youth searching and frustrated, unable to answer or understand the call of God upon his life.

## NO PLACE TO RUN

Although Branham had received supernatural manifestations in his life, he was not yet born again. When he was fourteen, he was injured in a hunting accident that left him hospitalized for seven months. Still, he didn't receive the urgency of God's call that pressed upon him. He had no idea what was happening to him. His parents weren't familiar with God, so he had no encouragement from them. All he had was his own limited knowledge, so he resisted the call of God.

At the age of nineteen, Branham made a decision to move, hoping that a new location would relieve him of this pressure. Knowing that he would meet with disapproval from his mother, he told her he was going to a campground that was only fourteen miles away from his home, when actually he was going to Phoenix, Arizona.

With new surroundings and a different way of life, Branham secured a day job on a local ranch. At night, he pursued a professional boxing career, and even won a few medals. But try as he might, Branham couldn't run from God even in the desert. As he looked out upon the stars at night, he would again sense the call of God upon him.

One day, he received news that his brother, Edward, who was closest to him in age, was seriously ill. Branham felt that, in time, everything would be all right, so he continued working at the ranch. Just a few days later, Branham received the heartbreaking news that his brother had died.

The grief was nearly unbearable for Branham. **"The first thing I thought of was,"** Branham recalled, **"whether he was prepared to die....Then again God called me, but as usual I tried to fight it off."**[6]

As Branham traveled home, tears ran down his cheeks as he thought of their childhood together. Remembering how hard things were for them, he wondered if God had taken Edward to a better place.

The death was very hard on the family, because no one knew God, and it was impossible for them to find peace. As a matter of fact, it was at his brother's funeral where Branham remembered hearing his first prayer.[7] It was here that he decided to learn to pray. After the burial, Branham intended to return to Arizona, but his mother begged him to stay at home. Branham agreed and found a job at the Gas Works in New Albany.

## IN THE FACE OF DEATH

About two years later, while testing gas meters, Branham was overcome with the gas. The entire lining of his stomach was coated with chemical acid, and he suffered for weeks before seeking medical help from specialists.

The doctor diagnosed Branham with appendicitis and placed him in the hospital for surgery. Because he wasn't experiencing pain, Branham asked for a local anesthetic only. Then he could remain conscious and watch the surgery. Even though he was not yet born again, Branham asked a Baptist minister to go into surgery with him.

After surgery, Branham was moved to his room, where he found himself growing weaker and weaker. As the beating of his heart became fainter, he felt death upon him.

Gradually, the hospital room grew dark to Branham, and in the distance he heard the sound of wind. It seemed as if it were blowing through a forest, rustling the leaves of the trees. Branham remembered thinking, **"Well, this is death coming to take me."**

The wind came closer – and the sound grew louder.

**"All at once, I was gone,"** Branham said. **"I was back again a little barefoot boy standing in the same lane, under the same tree. And I heard that same voice, 'Never drink or smoke.' But this time the voice said, 'I called you and you would not go.' The words were repeated the third time.**

**"Then I said, 'Lord, if that is You, let me go back again to earth and I will preach Your Gospel from the housetops and street corners. I'll tell everyone about it!'"**

Suddenly Branham awoke and saw that he was in his hospital room. He was feeling better, but the surgeon thought him to be dead. When he came in and saw Branham, he said, "I'm not a church-going man,...but I know God visited this boy."[8]

A few days later, Branham was released from the hospital, and true to his vow, he immediately began to seek the Lord.

## HEALED! AND PROUD OF IT!

Branham searched from church to church, trying in vain to find one that preached repentance. Finally, in desperation, he went out to the old shed in back of his house and tried to pray. He had no idea of what to say, so he simply started talking to God as he would talk to anyone.

Suddenly, a light came and shown on the wall of the shed, forming a cross. Branham believed it was the Lord, as it seemed "a thousand pounds were lifted off him." It was there by that old shed that Branham was born again.

The accident he had suffered with chemical acid left Branham with strange side effects, and when he looked at anything too long, his head would shake. Branham told the Lord that if he was to preach, he would have to be fully healed. So he found a small, independent Baptist church that believed in healing, went forward for prayer and was healed instantly. Seeing the power this

*Branham in his early years*

church exhibited, Branham began to pray and seek God for that kind of power in his life. Six months later, he received his answer.

After accepting the call to preach, Branham was ordained an independent Baptist minister. Securing a small tent, he immediately began to minister with great results.

## THERE'S THAT LIGHT AGAIN!

In June, 1933, at the age of twenty-four, Branham held his first major tent revival in Jeffersonville. As many as three thousand people attended in one night.

He conducted a water baptism service on June 11, immersing one hundred thirty people in the Ohio River. As he baptized the seventeenth person, another supernatural occurrence took place. In Branham's own words he describes it:

> *That autumn, the people who had attended his meetings built a tabernacle, calling it "Branham Tabernacle."*

**"A whirl came down from the heavens above, here come that light, shining down...it hung right over where I was at...and it liked to a-scared me to death."**

Many of the four thousand on the river bank who saw the light, ran in fear, some remained and fell in worship. Some claimed to hear an actual voice, others didn't.[9]

That autumn, the people who had attended his meetings built a tabernacle, calling it "Branham Tabernacle." From 1933 to 1946, Branham was the bivocational minister of the Tabernacle while he worked at a secular job.

## HIS WONDERFUL "HOPE"

It was during this happy time of the 1930s that Branham met a wonderful Christian girl. Her name was Hope Brumback. She met Branham's requirements; she never smoked or drank, and he loved her greatly.

After several months, Branham decided to ask Hope to marry him. But being too shy to speak with her, he did the next best thing and wrote her a letter. Fearing her mother would get the letter first, he hesitatingly slipped the letter in her mailbox. But Hope got the letter first and promptly answered, "Yes!"

The two were married shortly afterward, and Branham recalled, **"I don't believe there was any place on earth that was any happier than our little home."** Two years later, a son, Billy Paul, was born to the Branhams. As he described that moment, Branham said, **"When I first heard him cry in the**

**hospital I seemed to know that he was a boy, and I gave him to God before I even saw him."**[10]

## A NEW DOSE OF POWER

The Great Depression of the 1930s soon hit the Branham Tabernacle, and times became a little hard. Soon Branham began to preach without compensation. He continued to work in a secular job to support his family. After saving some money, he decided to take a fishing trip to Michigan. All too soon, he ran out of money and started back home.

On the return trip, he saw a great group of people gathering for a gospel meeting and wondered what kind of people they were, so he stopped and had his first experience with "Pentecostalism."

The gathering was a "Oneness" camp meeting. (The Oneness people were a denomination of people who believed, as they explained it, in "Jesus only.") Branham was impressed with their singing and clapping. The longer he stayed, the more he realized there was something to this power they talked about.

That night, Branham drove his Model "T" into a cornfield and slept in the car. He was eager to return the next day. He had introduced himself as a minister, and that very day the leader announced that the group would like to hear from the next to the youngest minister there, William Branham.

Branham was so shocked, that he ducked in embarrassment. He didn't want anyone to know he was there. He had used his good trousers for a pillow the night before and was wearing an old pair of seersuckers.

The speaker again asked for William Branham to come to the platform, but Branham sat still, too embarrassed to respond. After all, no one knew who he was anyway, so he thought he was safe.

Finally, a man leaned over to him and asked, "Do you know who William Branham is?" Branham replied, **"It's me,"** but explained that he couldn't preach before these people appearing as he did. The man said, "They care more about your heart than how you look." The man stood up and pointing to Branham, yelled, "Here he is!"

Branham reluctantly walked up and took the platform, and as he began to preach, the power of God engulfed him and the meeting lasted two hours. Afterwards, pastors from all over the country approached Branham, asking him to come to their churches to conduct a revival. When Branham left, his calendar was filled for the year. These Oneness people had no idea they had just asked a Baptist to conduct weeks of meetings in their churches!

## "TRASH" AND TRAGEDY

Branham raced home. As he pulled into their driveway, Hope ran out to meet him. Branham, excited from his experience, told Hope of the camp meeting and the meetings he had scheduled. She seemed as excited as he, but family and friends were not as jubilant. The main opposition came from Branham's mother-in-law who was adamant in her opposition. She exclaimed, "Do you know that's a bunch of holy rollers?...Do you think you'd drag my daughter out amongst stuff like that?....Ridiculous! That's nothing but trash that the other churches has throwed out."[11]

Influenced by his mother-in-law, Branham cancelled his meetings for the Oneness Pentecostals. Later, he regretted it as the greatest mistake of his life. If he had gone on to hold those meetings, his family would not have been in the great Ohio flood of 1937.

The winter of 1937 was severe. As heavy masses of snow began to melt, it caused the Ohio River to swell over its natural boundaries. Even the dikes and levees couldn't hold back the great swell of water.

The flood couldn't have come at a worse time for the Branhams. Hope had just had another baby, and this time they were blessed with a baby girl, whom they named Sharon Rose. Because of childbirth, Hope's immune system had not been completely restored, and as a result, she contracted a serious lung disease.

> *The main opposition came from Branham's mother-in-law who was adamant in her opposition. She exclaimed, "Do you know that's a bunch of holy rollers?..Do you think you'd drag my daughter out amongst stuff like that?... Ridiculous! That's nothing but trash that the other churches has throwed out."*

It was during Hope's convalescence that the levee on the Ohio River gave way to the force of water, which quickly flooded the area. The sirens blared out the warning that all must evacuate for their own safety. Hope was in no condition to be moved, yet there was no choice. Despite the cold and the rain, she was transported to a makeshift hospital on higher ground. Also, during this great flood of 1937, both Branham babies became seriously ill with pneumonia.

## "WHERE'S MY FAMILY?"

As much as he wanted to stay with his loved ones, Branham knew he must help the town fight the rising flood. So he joined the rescue squad, only to return to the hospital four hours later and find that flood waters had broken down the walls, and his family was gone.

Frantically, Branham searched for his family throughout the night. Finally, he was told they were placed on a train and sent to another town. Feverishly, he attempted to make his way to them, but the floodwaters trapped him. For two weeks he was marooned and unable to leave or hear any word regarding his family.

As soon as the waters went down, he left in his truck to search for his family. He didn't know if they were dead or alive. When he arrived at the next town where he supposed they were sent, no one knew of a hospital, much less about his family.

Totally despondent, Branham walked the streets with his hat in his hands, walking, praying, and crying out for his family. Someone recognized him and told him where his family had been sent, but the flood waters had cut off any travel to that city. Branham thanked the man and continued his search.

Suddenly, as if it were an act of God, he ran into a friend who told him that he knew where his family was, and that Branham's wife was near death. The two men searched until they found a way to bypass the flood waters, and by evening Branham and his friend pulled into the town and found his family.

## "I WAS ALMOST HOME..."

The Baptist church in this town had been turned into a makeshift hospital. When Branham found Hope, he knelt down beside her bed, only to learn that the X-rays had shown tuberculosis creeping deeper and deeper into her lungs. Branham spoke with Hope softly, and she told him the children were with her mother. When he found them, their health was deteriorating as well.

Branham determined he would work and make whatever amount was necessary to see Hope and the children recover. One day while working, he received a call from the hospital. The doctor told Branham that if he wanted to see his wife alive, he needed to come right away.

Racing to the hospital, Branham ran through the door, where the doctor met him and took him straight to his wife's room. The sheet was already pulled over her face. Nevertheless, Branham grabbed her and shook her, crying, **"Honey! Answer me!...God, please let her speak to me once more."** And suddenly, Hope opened her eyes. She tried to reach out to Branham, but she was too weak.

She looked at her husband and whispered, "I was almost home. Why did you call me?" Then in her weak, faltering voice, she began telling Branham about heaven. She said, "Honey, you've preached it, you've talked of it, but you can't know how glorious it is."

Tearfully, she thanked Branham for being a good husband, then she began to grow quieter....Branham finishes the story this way: **"She pulled me down to her and kissed me good-bye....Then she went to be with God."**

As Branham drove home, alone in the darkness, everything he saw reminded him of Hope. His grief seemed unbearable. At home, thinking of his motherless babies, he fell asleep, only to be awakened by a knock at the door.

## THE SADDEST NIGHT ON EARTH

"Billy, your baby is dying now," were the words from the man at the door.

Feeling that his life was at its very end, Branham got into the man's pick-up truck, and they transported baby Sharon to the hospital, but to no avail. X-rays showed the baby had spinal meningitis.

The hospital moved Sharon into the basement where they kept isolated cases. The fatal disease had twisted her little leg out of normal position, and the pain caused her eyes to cross. Unable to see her in such agony, Branham laid his hands on Sharon and prayed, asking God to spare her life. Sadly, Branham thought God was punishing him for not going on the Oneness revivals. Shortly after his prayer, baby Sharon joined her mother in heaven.[12]

In just one night, Branham had lost two of the three most precious people on earth to him. Only Billy Paul was left.

*The next five-year period was a "wilderness experience" for Branham. No one seemed to understand. His Baptist church seemed to grow impatient with him, calling his visions demonic.*

Two days later, a heartbroken man buried his daughter in the arms of her mother. It seemed his grief was too great to be endured. Yet, in the coming years, the remembrance of those feelings would cause the tears of compassion to flood his cheeks as William Branham prayed for the sick.

## THE WIND RETURNED

The next five-year period was a "wilderness experience" for Branham. No one seemed to understand. His Baptist church seemed to grow impatient with him, calling his visions demonic. They even suggested that the light which

appeared at his birth probably indicated the presence of a demon in his life. They went on to warn Branham to stop the visionary experiences, or his ministry "would fall into disrepute."[13]

During these years, Branham married again. He said many times that he would have never done so, but Hope had asked him to, for the children's sake.

He continued to preach at the Branham Tabernacle, working as a game warden on the side. On May 7, 1946, a very beautiful spring day, Branham came home for lunch, and a friend came over. The two men were outside under a large maple tree when, according to Branham, **"It seemed that the whole top of the tree let loose...it seemed like something came down from that tree like a great rushing wind."**

His wife came running out of the house to see if he was all right. Trying to get control of his emotions, Branham sat down and told her the story of the past twenty years. At that point, he made a decision that he was going to find out, once and for all, what was behind this "wind." He said, **"I told her (his wife) and my child good-bye and warned her that if I didn't come back in a few days, perhaps I might never return."**

## THE ANGEL OF THE LORD CAME

Branham went to a secluded place to pray and read the Bible. So deep was his travail that it seemed his soul would tear out of his body. **"Will You speak to me some way, God? If You don't help me, I can't go on,"** he cried.

That same night about 11:00 P.M., he noticed a light flickering in the room. Thinking someone was coming with a flashlight, he looked out the window, but saw no one. Suddenly, the light began to spread across the floor. Startled, Branham jumped up from his chair when he saw a ball of fire shining on the floor. Then he heard someone walking. As he looked, he saw the feet of a man coming toward him. As he continued up from the feet, he saw a man that appeared to be about two hundred pounds in weight, clothed in a white robe.

As Branham trembled in fear, the man spoke, "Fear not. I am sent from the presence of Almighty God to tell you that your peculiar life and your misunderstood ways have been to indicate that God has sent you to take a gift of divine healing to the peoples of the world."

## THE ANGEL CONTINUED...

"If you will be sincere, and can get the people to believe you, nothing shall stand before your prayer, not even cancer."

Branham's first response was like Gideon's, of old. He told the angel that he was poor and uneducated, thus, he felt no one would accept his ministry or listen to him.

But the angel went on to tell Branham that he would receive two gifts as signs to vindicate his ministry. First, Branham would be able to detect diseases by a physical vibration in his left hand.

Some have made fun of this physical manifestation, or labeled it demonic. To comprehend the Word of the Lord, we must grasp the law of righteousness and the law of the Spirit, then formulate the principle. It is possible that the "vibration" can be accurately explained this way: When the unclean disease in the afflicted person met with the supernatural power of God through Branham, it would set off a physical reaction, or, a vibration. When the unclean meets the clean, *there is going to be a reaction!*

> *When the unclean disease in the afflicted person met with the supernatural power of God through Branham, it would set off a physical reaction, or, a vibration.*

In later years, Gordon Lindsay witnessed this supernatural phenomenon. He said that the "electric, current like" vibration was so strong at times, it would instantly stop Branham's wristwatch. Lindsay went on to say that after the spirit was cast out of the person, Branham's "red and swollen" hand would return to normal condition.

The angel continued to instruct Branham, that when he felt the vibration, he was to pray for the person. If the vibration leaves, the person is healed. If not he was to "just ask a blessing and walk away."

## THERE WILL BE A SECOND SIGN

Branham responded to the angel, **"Sir, I'm afraid they won't receive me."** The angel responded: "Then it will come to pass that you'll know the very secret of their heart. This they will hear."[14]

In connection with this second sign, the angel made this statement: "The thoughts of men speak louder in heaven than do their words on earth." Any sin in a person's life that was under the blood was never revealed. But if the sin was unconfessed or covered, it would be brought to light through this spiritual gift, the word of knowledge. When this occurred in his prayer line, Branham would step away from the microphone and speak privately with the person, leading him to an immediate repentance.

Was this a true visitation from God? Yes. How do we know? Because angels are sent to minister to the heirs of salvation (see Hebrews 1:14). Angels announced the birth of Jesus and ministered to Him throughout His life on earth. Throughout the Bible angels ministered, proclaiming the Word of the Lord to mankind.

The angel of the Lord will never reveal anything that is contrary to Scripture. He never adds anything to or takes anything away from the Word of God. In other words, the angel of the Lord neither invents an additional Bible nor does he distort Scripture. The Word of God is always the standard.

During his visit, the angel of the Lord went on to tell Branham many other things concerning his ministry. First, he said that Branham, an unknown preacher, would soon stand before thousands in crowded arenas. Second, He told him if he would be faithful to his call, the results would reach the world and shake the nations. The visitation lasted about half an hour.[15]

## NO TIME WASTED

After the visitation from the angel, Branham returned to his home. The following Sunday evening, he told the people in the tabernacle of his visitation. Ironically, they fully believed his revelation.

The word of the Lord came to pass quickly. While Branham was speaking, someone came in and handed him a telegram. It was from a Rev. Robert Daughtery, asking Branham to come to St. Louis and pray for his daughter to be healed. He had exhausted the aid of physicians and felt that prayer was the only answer.

Branham had no money to make the trip. So the congregation quickly took an offering, collecting enough money for a round-trip train fare. He borrowed a suit of clothes from one of his brothers, and a coat from another. At midnight, members of the congregation escorted him to the train bound for St. Louis.

## THE FIRST MIRACLE

The little girl in St. Louis lay dying from some unknown malady. The church had fasted and prayed for her, but to no avail. The best physicians of the city had been called, but were unable to diagnose her case.

Tears rolled down the cheeks of Branham as he walked toward the little girl. She was skin and bones and lay in bed, clawing at her face like an animal. She had become hoarse from screaming in pain. She had been in torment this way for three months.

Branham joined his prayer with the rest of them, but to no avail. He finally asked for a quiet place to be alone and seek the Lord. This became his pattern in his early ministry. In seeking the Lord, he would often see the answer through a vision. He would wait until the conditions were exactly as he saw in the vision, then he would act on what he had seen. The results were always immediate when he followed this pattern.

After a while, Branham marched confidently back to the house. He asked the father and the others, **"Do you believe that I am God's servant?"** "Yes!" they cried. **"Then do as I tell you, doubting nothing."** Branham proceeded to ask for several things, then prayed for the child, according to the vision the Lord had given him. Immediately, the evil spirit left the girl and she was healed. She lived to see a normal, healthy childhood.

When news of the healing spread, the people flocked to see Branham, but he withdrew from them, promising he would return later. He did return within a few weeks.

## THE DEAD ARE RAISED

In June of 1946, Branham returned to St. Louis and conducted a twelve-day meeting to preach and pray for the sick. The tent was packed with many people standing outside, even in the torrential rains. Tremendous manifestations took place as the lame walked, the blind saw, and the deaf heard. A minister who had been blind for twenty years received his sight, a woman who rejected the Spirit of God fell dead outside the tent from a heart attack. Branham went out to her and prayed. She arose and found salvation in Jesus Christ. The healings multiplied and grew beyond count. Branham often stayed until 2:00 A.M., praying for the sick.

From St. Louis, he was asked to hold a revival in Jonesboro, Arkansas, where some twenty-five thousand people attended the meetings.[16] During this meeting, Branham slipped out of the service to go inside an ambulance where an elderly woman had died. After praying a simple prayer, the woman sat up and hugged her husband. There were so many people standing against the back door of the ambulance that it

> *Branham proceeded to ask for several things, then prayed for the child, according to the vision the Lord had given him. Immediately, the evil spirit left the girl and she was healed.*

could not be opened for Branham to leave. So the ambulance driver held his coat over the front window so Branham could leave through the front door.[17]

One woman, who had driven hundreds of miles, made a tearful attempt to describe to others the humility, compassion, and meekness of Branham. When she looked at Branham, she said "all she saw was Jesus," adding that "You will never be the same after seeing him."[18]

## LET'S SPREAD OUT

In Arkansas, Branham acquired his first campaign manager, W. E. Kidson, an editor for *The Apostolic Herald*. This was the newsletter that had published the results of Branham's ministry. Kidson, being a die-hard pioneer of the Oneness doctrine, had introduced Branham to that denomination, and took him around to several small churches.

The year 1947 is remembered as a high-profile time for the Branham ministry. *Time* magazine published the news of his campaigns, and his ministry team took their first tour of the western states.

T. L. and Daisy Osborn were greatly influenced by his meetings in Portland, Oregon. They had just returned from India, where they had served as missionaries. They were defeated in vision and purpose, and nearly ready to quit the ministry.

The story is told that T. L. was present as Branham turned a little cross-eyed girl around to face the audience. As Branham laid his hands on her, T. L. watched as her eyes gradually straightened. It is said that T. L. heard these words, "You can do that! You can do that!" After the Branham meeting, the Osborns were refreshed, rekindled, and focused. They finally found the answer for which they were searching. The result was an incredible international missionary and healing ministry through the Osborns to the nations of the world.

It was also in 1947 that Branham met and joined with Gordon Lindsay. Jack Moore was a Oneness minister who had been traveling with Branham when they joined with Lindsay. Although Lindsay was a Trinitarian, the two men formed a coalition that proved imperative to Branham's success.

When Lindsay realized that an unprecedented divine move of God had begun, he urged Branham to take his ministry beyond the boundaries of the Oneness circles and into the Full Gospel circles. Realizing that Lindsay was being used to fulfill the words that came during his angelic visitation, Branham agreed. Lindsay was a master in organization, an attribute that Branham lacked. So Branham gave Lindsay the liberty to organize and promote one of the greatest healing revivals to this day.

Moore and Lindsay formulated the first Union Campaign in the fall of 1947. These meetings were to bring the Oneness and Trinitarian believers together in one great meeting. Held in the northwestern states and parts of Canada, the Union Campaign was well received because Branham's messages avoided doctrinal differences. The people attending experienced "their greatest religious experiences ever." Oftentimes, according to reports, as many as fifteen hundred people were born again in a single service. W. J. Ern Baxter joined the healing team in Canada, and wrote that as many as thirty-five thousand healings were manifested during that year of ministry.[19]

## "VOICE OF HEALING" IS BORN

In an effort to give voice to this message of healing throughout the land, the Branham team devised a new method of publicity. They decided that a new publication should be created, which would circulate outside of the isolated Oneness congregations and into every realm of Christianity. Realizing again that this fulfilled the word of the Lord concerning him, Branham agreed. However, Kidson, his editor, didn't agree, so Branham relieved Kidson of his duties and appointed Lindsay and Moore as editors, and himself as publisher. Together, the team conceived *The Voice of Healing* magazine.

Originally, only one magazine was to be published, introducing Branham. But the demand was so great, the pilot magazine was reprinted several times. The team finally decided to publish *The Voice of Healing* on a monthly basis.

From that point on, Branham made it a key issue never to discuss doctrinal issues. He said:

> "God didn't put His endorsement upon one particular church, but He revealed that the pure in heart would see God," Branham often added: "Let the fellow believe whatever he wants to about it. These things don't amount to very much anyhow. Be brothers, have fellowship with one another."

Branham often said that believers should be able to **"disagree a million miles on theology,"** but if they ever came to the place where they couldn't embrace one another as brothers, then they should feel **"backslid."**[20]

> *Originally, only one magazine was to be published, introducing Branham. But the demand was so great, the pilot magazine was reprinted several times. The team finally decided to publish* The Voice of Healing *on a monthly basis.*

329

## EARLY TROUBLE

In 1948, Branham's ministry came to an abrupt halt when he suffered a nervous breakdown. He was physically and mentally fatigued from overwork in the ministry. Before hiring Lindsay as his campaign manager, he would pray until the early morning hours for those in the healing lines, totally exhausting himself. He did not know when to stop. His weight dropped considerably, and rumors began to circulate that Branham was dying.

As a result, Lindsay, administrator of his campaigns, cut Branham's ministry time to one hour or less each evening, and visitors were no longer allowed in Branham's hotel room. Lindsay expanded Branham's meetings, but wisely cut down on the interruptions and excesses.

When Branham experienced his breakdown, he began to point fingers at those he blamed for the illness. He accused Lindsay of overextending him. Then he informed Lindsay and Moore that in the future *The Voice of Healing* magazine would be their sole responsibility.

Lindsay was shocked at Branham's accusations. He had just planned an extensive healing campaign for Branham, and felt deserted when *The Voice of Healing* magazine was dropped in his lap. But he continued to publish the magazine, expanding the articles to cover other healing ministries. Although they continued to work together, Lindsay and Branham's close relationship never quite recovered from that point on.

During this time, other healing evangelists began to surface. Oral Roberts, who had entered the ministry one year after Branham, requested that everyone pray for Branham's restoration. Six months later, Branham suddenly appeared back on the scene, claiming he was miraculously healed. His return was greeted by his followers with great excitement.

Branham held his first major crusade after his illness in 1950. It was at this time that F. F. Bosworth, the great healing evangelist from the 1920s, had now joined the Branham team. Crowds of over eight thousand people came to a single service.

It was here that the most famous photo of Branham's ministry was taken. It is known as the "halo" photo. A Baptist pastor had challenged Branham to a debate on healing. Branham accepted. The Baptist hired a photographer to capture the event. It was one of the pictures taken there that featured a halo of light resting over Branham's head. Lindsay immediately had the photo authorized and documented as an original, certifying that no make-overs or touch-ups were performed on either the photo or negative.

## SHAKING NATIONS

In April of 1950, Branham traveled to Scandinavia, making him the first Voice of Healing evangelist to travel to Europe.

Before going to Europe, Branham had a vision of a little boy being hit by a car and being raised from the dead. He told this vision throughout America.

While in Finland, Branham's car was behind a car that had struck two small boys. Branham's party picked up one boy and proceeded to the hospital. Realizing his pulse and circulation had stopped, Branham knelt on the floor of the car and prayed for God's mercy. The boy came back to life and began to cry. He was released from the hospital three days later. The next day, Branham received a vision showing him that both boys would live.

*Realizing his pulse and circulation had stopped, Branham knelt on the floor of the car and prayed for God's mercy. The boy came back to life and began to cry.*

The associate who was traveling with him wrote Branham's first vision about the boy on a piece of paper at the time the vision occurred, and placed the piece of paper in his wallet. After the incident happened, it is said the associate pulled the paper out of his wallet and read it to Branham. It was the exact vision Branham had told throughout America.

He had also received many prayer requests from Africa, some of which were accompanied by a plane ticket. In the fall of 1951, Branham and his ministry team traveled to South Africa. They held campaigns through December. It is reported that the meetings were the greatest ever in South Africa, with crowds estimated to be fifty thousand in number, with thousands turned away.

The city of Durban had a population of well over two hundred thousand people. Every bus in the city was put to work, and still all the people could not be transported to the Branham meetings. The results were so incredible, that a book entitled, *A Prophet Visits South Africa,* was written to describe it.

## HOW DID HE OPERATE?

Branham's personality was captivating. He didn't have a charismatic, exuberant personality, but was best remembered for his humility and humble origins. He often apologized for his lack of education and cultural abilities. Branham couldn't speak well before crowds. When he did speak, it was usually with a very quiet and stuttering voice. Branham usually left the preaching to Bosworth and others, then he ministered divine healing to the multitudes.

Everything about his ministry was geared toward the supernatural. He refuted any person who was led by intellectualism, and would not permit them to be on the platform with him. His entire ministry team focused on creating an atmosphere in which divine healing could manifest. Baxter and Bosworth preached in the morning and afternoon services. Baxter preached in his evangelistic role, while Bosworth gave special instructions for receiving and maintaining healing. Lindsay, the coordinator of the campaigns, would handle the altar calls. Though Branham insisted his primary role was praying for the sick, he always spoke in the evening services.

Since the demand for a Branham campaign was so great, his meetings became limited to a few nights in each city. To handle the flow of people, Lindsay devised and authored a small booklet, *Divine Healing in the Branham Meetings*, that was widely distributed in a city before the team came to town. Unlike the earlier healing evangelists, Branham couldn't spend weeks instructing the people on healing before he prayed for them. This booklet served as a teaching tool for those seeking healing. As a result, they came ready to receive and Branham was able to pray for them during the first night of his campaign.

Branham avoided all personal interviews prior to the night services. Most of the time, he spent three days of prayer and fasting before each campaign.

Branham would not pray for people until he sensed his angel standing at his right side.

"Without this consciousness," Bosworth said, "he seems to be perfectly helpless. When he is conscious of the angel's presence, he seems to break through the veil of the flesh into the world of the Spirit, to be struck through and through with a sense of the unseen."

A few witnesses claimed they had seen the angel standing beside Branham. However, the majority that noticed the presence, usually described it as a "heavenly light." Bosworth wrote that in the 1951 South African campaign, a light was seen over the heads of the people whose faith had reached the necessary level. While under the anointing, Branham would recognize that light.[21]

When Branham prayed for the people in a prayer line, he directed them to line up on his right side as well. This way, he felt the people received a double dose of power because they passed by the angel and Branham. The Branham team used the popular "prayer cards," where each person was given a card with a number on it, and the numbers were randomly called during the service. Branham also prayed over handkerchiefs to be carried to the afflicted (see Acts 19:12).

## HIS DOCTRINE IN THE EARLY DAYS

Branham believed that healing was the finished work of Calvary. He also believed that all sickness and sin were caused by Satan. **"What doctors call 'cancer,' God calls it a devil,"** Branham preached.[22]

Branham also had a strong deliverance ministry. Along with sin and sickness, he identified insanity, temper tantrums, disbelief, and lustful habits as the work of demons. Branham didn't believe that deliverance healed a person, but he did believe it cleared a pathway for healing to have entrance.

Before Branham would cast out demons in his services, he would stop and tell the skeptics present that he couldn't be responsible for what "evil fate befell them."[23]

If a person desired healing in his meetings, the person must do two things: (1) believe and confess that Jesus died for his healing and (2) believe that Branham was the prophet of God sent to administer healing.

Branham believed that faith was a sixth sense. To him, faith was believing what God has revealed. People lost their healing because they quit believing what had been revealed to them. **"As faith kills it [disease], unbelief resurrects it,"** Branham reasoned.[24] A person didn't have to be a Christian to be healed, but they must become a Christian to remain healed, according to Branham.

While Branham supported the work of physicians, he also believed their work was limited. He felt that medicine merely "kept the body clean while God performed the healing." Branham asserted, **"There's not one speck of medicine ever did cure any sickness."** It is said that Branham would "bristle" when one described divine healing as fanaticism. He would respond by stating that **"medicine was never defined as fanaticism when a person died from incorrect medical treatment."**[25]

Branham was also against the prosperity of Christians, especially ministers. He often claimed that he could have been a millionaire from the revenue of his ministry, but chose not to be, refusing great gifts of wealth by stating, **"I want to be like the people who come to be prayed for."** When he finally accepted a Cadillac as a gift, he kept it in his garage for two years, out of embarrassment.[26]

## HE BEGAN TO SLIP...

Branham remained very influential in the ministry of divine healing for nine years. During this time, healing evangelists began to surface all over the country, operating through great signs and wonders. In 1952, at one of the heights in the Voice of Healing revival, forty-nine prominent healing evange-lists were featured in *The Voice of Healing* magazine. The revelation of divine healing had reached an all-time peak across the world. But from that year on, the healing revival fires began to dwindle. By 1955, Branham began to experience difficulties, and his ministry took on a radical change.

## LOST LINDSAY

Gordon Lindsay was one of the greatest things that could have happened to the ministry of William Branham. Lindsay had the Word and Branham had the gift. Lindsay also had the organizational skills that would enhance Branham's gift and ministry. Obviously, they were a ministry team made in heaven.

But Branham refused to acknowledge the worth of Lindsay. Instead, he pointed fingers at him, accused him, and abandoned him to some degree. I firmly believe the Lord had ordained Lindsay to help Branham, because Branham couldn't make it by himself. Therefore, I also believe that Branham's dis-association with Lindsay was a great mistake, and that Branham plunged into doctrinal error because of it.

## SURROUNDED BY "YES" MEN

Due to Branham's coolness toward him, added to the fact that his own ministry was growing, Lindsay left the Branham team after four years. The men who replaced Lindsay were far from his caliber in character and integrity.

Branham was unable to match the wits and sophistication of those who came to take subtle advantage of him. It was a widely publicized fact that Branham had no business sense and could really care less about it. With the hedge of protection that came with Lindsay's management gone, many felt that Branham's managers took advantage of him and his ministry funds by using them for themselves and their own wealth. During Lindsay's management, Branham's ministry had always excelled financially, but under new administration, the ministry was hurting for money. It became so bad, that Branham thought he would have to leave the ministry and go to work at a secular job.

Branham's crowds were down in number, and soon the ministry took on a $15,000 deficit. Branham's mail count had dropped from one thousand letters a day to approximately seventy-five.

In the height of the revival, Branham's carelessness in financial matters didn't seem to show. But now that things were tight, his carelessness brought the attention of the Internal Revenue Service. In 1956, a tax-evasion suit was brought against the evangelist. Despite his objections, Branham incurred a $40,000 out-of-court settlement, a debt he carried for the rest of his life.[27]

Eventually, Branham found that a cult had formed around his personality. As other healing evangelists began to come to the forefront, these men would pacify Branham's ego. They encouraged Branham in his weird visions, claiming him to be the new Elijah, the forerunner of Christ's return, and the head of the seventh Church age. They claimed that only Branham could carry this calling of the Laodicean messenger, no one else would be able to impersonate it.

By 1958, there were only about a dozen prominent healing evangelists. It was evident to everyone that the glory days of the Voice of Healing revival had come to a close. It was now time to seek the Lord and find the roles to be played in the next move of God.

## HE DID NOT STAY IN HIS CALLING

Branham didn't take the change well, in fact, he never made the transition at all. Instead of seeking the Lord for his place of ministry in the next move of God, he turned to radical doctrine and sensationalism. Branham took on the office of the teacher by his own will, not by the command of God.

It is possible that through his prophetic gift, Branham saw the awakening of the teaching gift that would move on the earth through the Word of Faith Movement, which began in the late 1970s. He obviously jumped ahead of its timing, perhaps hoping to regain his status as the leader of it. Branham failed to realize that he was already an undeniable leader in the Church world, he just needed to get back into his calling.

God didn't call Branham to be a teacher, because he didn't know the Word. As a result, disturbing doctrines were taught and emphasized through his ministry. Everything he had stood for in the former days of ministry seemed to have escaped him.

> *Eventually, Branham found that a cult had formed around his personality. As other healing evangelists began to come to the forefront, these men would pacify Branham's ego. They encouraged Branham in his weird visions, claiming him to be the new Elijah, the forerunner of Christ's return, and the head of the seventh Church age.*

Without a doubt, this great mistake caused his life to end early and continues to overshadow his ministry today.

✦✧✦✧✦

*Oral Roberts attended the Branham campaign in Kansas City in 1948. The above is a rare photograph showing, from left to right, Young Brown, Jack Moore, William Branham, Oral Roberts, and Gordon Lindsay*

*The Voice of Healing Convention of leading evangelists in December of 1949, which Brother Branham attended. Back row, left to right: Orrin Kingsriter, Clifton Erickson, Robert Bosworth, H. C. Noah, V. J. Gardner, H. T. Langley, Abraham Tannenbaum.... Middle Row: Raymond T. Richey, William Branham, Jack Moore, Dale Hanson, O. L. Jagger, Gayle Jackson, F. F. Bosworth, Gordon Lindsay....Front row: Mrs. Erickson, Mrs. Kingsriter, Mrs. Lindsay, Miss Anna Jeanne Moore, Mrs. Bosworth, Mrs. Jackson, and Mrs. Langley*

*Preaching the Word!*

*Branham in South Africa*

*Branham with F. F. Bosworth*

*Ministering in a Spanish church, Phoenix, Arizona, 1947*

*Gordon Lindsay, William Branham, and
W. V. Grant in Dallas, Texas, 1964*

*The famous halo photo*

## HE DID IT HIS WAY

Branham claimed to have strange spiritual visions that seemed to make him ever-searching and driven for their fulfillment. Throughout the 1960s, he lamented his decline in popularity, noting that other evangelists had surpassed him.[28] It had become a competitive race to him.

Branham tried to push his popularity through doctrinal teaching, which, according to him, was given by prophetic revelation. By abusing his gift, the prophecies became warped. Instead of using his prophetic ability to call the hearts of men back to God, he tried to predict international events.

## BRACE YOURSELF...

When you read a sample of these doctrines, you will understand why it was such a great mistake for Branham to allow Lindsay to leave. If Lindsay had remained, all the other mistakes would have been sorted out of Branham's life. Here is a sample of the shocking "prophetic" doctrines Branham taught until the end of his life.

## NO ETERNAL HELL

Introduced as new revelation, Branham taught that there was no eternal hell. He said that hell was forever, but not for eternity. Forever, to him, meant a period of time. After this period of time, those in hell would be annihilated.[29]

## SEED OF THE SERPENT

He also taught that women weren't a created product of God, but were merely a by-product of man. He even suggested that animals were a higher rank of species than women because they were created from nothing. Their secondary status, according to Branham, marked women as **"the most easily deceived and deceitful beings on earth."**

Branham also taught that women carried the seed of the Serpent. This doctrine taught that Eve and the Serpent had sexual relations in the Garden and created Cain. Branham said that God had meant for multiplication to come from the dust of the earth, as occurred with Adam, but Eve's action with Satan altered that plan. Because of Eve and her sexual relationship with Satan, the inferior method of procreation came about. According to Branham, every woman carries the literal seed of the devil.

Branham once said:

> "Everytime that a funeral goes down the street, a woman caused it...Everything that's wrong, a woman caused it. And then put her head of the church...shame on her."[30]

Because of this hereditary and disgraceful act with Satan, Branham argued that women weren't qualified to be preachers. He also taught that Eve's supernatural offspring, Cain, built great cities where scientists and intellectualism were born. Therefore, to Branham, every scientist and every intellectual person who rejects the supernatural nature of the Gospel, is from the seed of the Serpent.[31]

> *Branham taught that denominationalism was the mark of the beast, that the Protestants were the harlots and the Catholics were the Beast.*

## DIVORCE

According to Branham, since women introduced men to sex, polygamy was brought about. Women had to be punished. So men could have many wives, but women only one husband. Branham taught that when Jesus spoke on divorce, He was speaking to the woman, not the man. A woman couldn't remarry under any circumstances. But a man could divorce whenever he wanted to and remarry a virgin.[32]

## MARK OF THE BEAST

Branham taught that denominationalism was the mark of the beast, that the Protestants were the harlots, and that the Catholics were the Beast. From a vision, he insinuated, (though never formally acknowledged) that he was THE end-time messenger, and THE Laodicean prophet, who could reveal the seventh seal in the book of Revelation. He predicted that the destruction of the United States would begin in 1977.[33]

## HIS MOUTH HAD THE POWER

Branham felt that there would come a day in his ministry where the "spoken Word" from his mouth would change physical bodies into glorified bodies for the Rapture. This tremendous power would be unleashed because Branham's words would restore God's original name of JHVH. Previously, the name had never been pronounced correctly, however "Branham's mouth was specially formed to say it."[34]

## ONENESS

Although he denied it at the beginning of his ministry, Branham now openly declared the Oneness doctrine. However, Branham criticized the "Jesus Only" churches, citing that **"there were many people named 'Jesus,' but there is only one Lord Jesus Christ."** He would teach one day that Trinitarians weren't born again, then on other days, he would declare that only some were. He even prophesied stating that **"Trinitarianism is of the devil,"** then commanded everyone listening to the tape of that message to be baptized in the name of Jesus Christ.[35]

He often changed in his salvation doctrine as well. At times, he would say that **"anyone could be saved."** Then, he would be heard speaking in line with Calvinistic doctrine. He would say, **"There was millions that would do it if they could, but they can't. It's not for them to have it."**[36]

A following was born out of this group of disciples. They called themselves "The Messengers." Today, they are also known as "The Branhamites." These churches are not affiliated with any denomination, since Branham detested that form of organization. They are followers of Branham, believing him to be the Laodicean messenger for this church age. To this day, a large portrait of Branham hangs in the church, introducing him as their "pastor."

The Messengers, or the Branhamites, are a worldwide movement. In fact, the fourth largest church in the nation of Zaire is of this group.[37]

## THE STORY OF HIS DEATH

Branham preached his last message during Thanksgiving week of 1965 at Jack Moore's church. Though Moore disagreed with Branham's doctrine, he remained friends with him throughout his ministry.

On December 18, 1965, while traveling back to Indiana via Texas, Billy Paul Branham was driving the car in front of Branham and his wife. A drunk driver swerved and missed Billy Paul, but crossed the middle line and hit Branham's car head on.

Turning his car around, he headed to the scene of the accident. Jumping out of his car, he noticed that Branham had gone through the windshield and back again.

Checking his father, Billy Paul noticed that his bones were broken, but there was a pulse. In checking Mrs. Branham, there was no pulse. She was obviously dead.

Suddenly, Branham stirred. Upon seeing his son, he asked, **"Is Mom okay?"**

Billy Paul answered, "Dad, she's dead." Then Branham said, **"Just lay my hand on her."**

Billy Paul picked up Branham's bloodied hand and placed it on Mrs. Branham. Instantly, a pulse returned and she revived.[38]

William Branham remained in a coma for six days before dying December 24, 1965. Mrs. Branham lived.

Though saddened by his death, the Pentecostal world was not surprised. Gordon Lindsay wrote in his eulogy that Branham's death was the will of God. He said, **"God may see that a man's special ministry has reached its fruition and it is time to take him home."**[39]

I think it is interesting to note that Lindsay had accepted the interpretation of the young evangelist, Kenneth E. Hagin, from Tulsa, Oklahoma. God had told Hagin of Branham's death two years before it happened. In a prophetic word spoken through Hagin, the Lord said that He was "removing the prophet" from the scene. Branham died exactly when the Lord told Hagin he would.

Hagin was conducting a meeting when the news came of Branham's accident. Hagin called the saints to the front of the altar to pray. As Hagin himself knelt to pray, the Spirit of the Lord spoke to him saying, "What are you praying for? I've told you that I'm taking him." Hagin got up, unable to pray any further.

Because of Branham's disobedience to his call and the creation of doctrinal confusion, Hagin believed that God had to remove the "father" of the healing revival from the earth.

Four times the Holy Spirit had told Lindsay that Branham was going to die, and that he was to tell him. But Lindsay couldn't get through the barrier of "yes" men that surrounded Branham.

Finally, he got through the barrier, and slipped through to Branham unannounced. He attempted to reason with Branham. He asked Branham, "Why don't you function where God wants you and manifest the gift God's given you? Stay there! Don't try to get over into this other ministry."

Branham said simply, **"Yeah, but I want to teach."**[40]

Branham had an incredible healing gift. But having no Bible knowledge to match it, he turned into a doctrinal disaster. Ignorance is not bliss, especially

> *Branham had an incredible healing gift. But having no Bible knowledge to match it, he turned into a doctrinal disaster. Ignorance is not bliss, especially when you affect the multitudes with your words.*

when you affect the multitudes with your words. God had given Branham a great gift, He couldn't take it back. That gift was misleading people, causing them to follow Branham's doctrine, so God practiced His sovereign right in 1 Corinthians 5:5; "To deliver such an one unto Satan for the destruction of the flesh, that the spirit may be saved in the day of the Lord Jesus." Actually, it was an act of mercy on God's behalf. It is believed that He saved Branham from hell.

## UNABLE TO RESURRECT

Although the funeral was held December 29, 1965, Branham's body was not buried until Easter of 1966. All sorts of rumors were circulating. One was that his body was being embalmed and refrigerated. Many of his followers were believing Branham would be raised from the dead. Whatever the reason, the official statement came from his son on January 26, 1966, at a Memorial Service.

It was said that Mrs. Branham had requested the delay in burial because she was trying to make a decision whether to move to Arizona or remain in Indiana. She wanted his body buried where she chose to live. Until she decided, Branham's body remained in the attic of the funeral home.

Still, there remained great hope among The Messengers that Branham would be raised on Easter Sunday. Branham's son affirmed that his father claimed Easter to be the time of the year that the Rapture would take place.

Reluctantly, and with great disappointment, William Branham was buried on April 11, 1966. His grave monument is a large pyramid with an eagle on top. (Unfortunately, the eagle keeps being stolen.) Branham is memorialized as being the only person to open the seventh seal, as the head of the seventh church age.

Branham's followers refuse to see him as a human being, and rumors of his return continued to circulate even through the 1980s. Each year, Branham Tabernacle continues to have a special Easter Service, in which the followers listen to Branham's taped sermons. Some of them still secretly hope for his return at that time. It is said that the current pastor does not encourage speculation of Branham's resurrection, however, the Branhamites have never accepted his death.[41]

## LEARN THE LESSON

The story of William Marrion Branham was not written for criticism. believe it contains a lesson more powerful than this one chapter can hold.

The lesson here is this: Do what God says to do, nothing more and nothing less. There is no game here. There is one move, and it belongs to God. Your job is to follow it.

In this generation, heaven must determine the timing of your life and your church as a whole. You are either in the will of God, or out of it. Your call must stay with the timing of heaven.

All Branham wanted was to be a voice. If he had remained in the plan of God, Branham could have been one of the greatest voices that had ever lived. His greatness in the ministry is never to be forgotten or discounted, his gift was legitimate. *But we must understand that great error comes from not having both the Word and the Spirit working together in our lives.*

Many of us weren't yet alive when these men and women of God had their great ministries. As a result, we didn't have the opportunity to watch and study their lives. And this is the reason I wrote this book. So study what you have read, and learn from it. Cry out to God to help you in the things you are unsure of. Ask Him to train you and teach you how to operate through His Spirit and within His timing. Follow His exact plan all the days of your life, and never deviate from it because of your own ideas, or pressure from others. Your anointing will only come when you follow the plan that God has outlined for you. So embrace that plan, and hold to it tightly. Then, run strong with it and do mighty exploits, in Jesus' Name.

### CHAPTER TEN, WILLIAM BRANHAM
References

[1] Gordon Lindsay, *A Man Sent From God* (Jefferson, IN: William Branham, 1950), 23-25.

[2] Ibid., 11.

[3] C. Douglas Weaver, *The Healer-Prophet, William Marrion Branham: A Study of the Prophetic in American Pentecostalism* (Macon, GA: Mercer University Press, 1987), 22.

[4] Lindsay, *William Branham*, 30-31.

[5] Ibid., 31.

[6] Ibid., 38-39.

[7] Weaver, *The Healer-Prophet*, 25.

[8] Lindsay, *William Branham*, 39-41.

[9] Weaver, *The Healer-Prophet*, 27.

[10] Lindsay, *William Branham*, 46.

[11] Weaver, *The Healer-Prophet*, 33.

[12] Lindsay, *William Branham*, 52-63.

[13] Weaver, *The Healer-Prophet*, 34.

[14] Lindsay, *William Branham*, 76-80 and Weaver, *The Healer-Prophet*, 75.

[15] Lindsay, *William Branham*, 75-79.

[16] Ibid., 93.

[17] Ibid., 94.

[18] Ibid., 102.

[19] Weaver, *The Healer-Prophet*, 46-47.

[20] Ibid., 54.

[21] Ibid., 72, 74.

[22] Ibid., 62.

[23] Ibid., 63.

[24] Ibid., 65.

[25] Ibid., 66-67.

[26] Ibid., 109.

[27] Ibid., 94.

[28] Ibid., 96.

[29] Ibid., 118-119.

[30] Ibid., 110-113.

31 Ibid., 113.

32 Ibid., 112.

33 Ibid., 116.

34 Ibid., 138-139.

35 Ibid., 120.

36 Ibid., 121-122.

37 Ibid., 152-153.

38 Personal interview with Billy Paul Branham.

39 Weaver, *The Healer-Prophet*, 105.

40 Kenneth E. Hagin, *Understanding the Anointing* (Tulsa, OK: Faith Library Publications, 1983), 60-61.

41 Weaver, *The Healer-Prophet*, 153-155.

# Jack Coe

## *"The Man of Reckless Faith"*

# "THE MAN OF RECKLESS FAITH"

66 I went before the judge and he asked me if I was guilty of disturbing the peace. I replied, 'Whose peace?'

'Well,' he replied, '...you folks clap your hands and shout, and other such things as that.' 'Judge, is it not true that people at the ball game make a lot of noise, and do I not hear them yell, shout, and clap their hands also?'

"He answered, 'Well, their hand clapping doesn't seem to bother anyone, but when you folks do it, people just can't sleep.'

"I asked, 'Judge, do you want to know what the difference is?' He answered, 'Yes, I'd like to know.'

"'The difference is that the Holy Ghost is in our shout, and it bothers the neighbors, keeping them awake...and it causes the beer joints to close their doors.'"[1]

Jack Coe was a large, domineering man with a tactless sense of humor in the healing tent. And he was a loving, compassionate "father" figure to the orphans in his children's home. As one of the main leaders in the Voice of Healing revival, Coe was either greatly loved, or greatly despised. He was raised without a father, so he learned as an adult to make God his Father. As a result, he had no problem putting men – no matter how high their denominational title – in their place, that is, if they tried to override the voice of God. The revivalist's dynamic personality left little room for a lukewarm response!

Coe was considered a radical evangelist because he, along with others, was doing much to combat racial prejudice in the Church. At a time when society was calling for segre-

> *Coe was considered a radical evangelist because he, along with others, was doing much to combat racial prejudice in the Church. At a time when society was calling for segregation, Coe strongly encouraged all races and cultures of the community to participate in his meetings.*

gation, Coe strongly encouraged all races and cultures of the community to participate in his meetings.

## A DESOLATE CHILDHOOD

Jack Coe was born on March 11, 1918, to Blanche and George Coe of Oklahoma City, Oklahoma. He was one of seven children. Blanche had been raised a Baptist, but when Jack was born it isn't certain that she was born again. It is believed that his father was born again at a Billy Sunday meeting, but George never attended church afterwards.

Coe's grandparents were Christians, so his father had been raised in a good home. Besides the positive atmosphere, his grandparents were also excellent providers, and left a considerable inheritance for Coe's father. But their solid principles of stewardship never seemed to rub off on his father, George. He had a bad habit of gambling and drinking. His mother tried to attend church for awhile, but since George wouldn't go with her, she stopped going too. Coe always believed things would have gone differently for his family if his mother would have continued in church and sought to pray for his father.

When Coe was five years old, a moving van backed up to their home. When he saw it, he got all excited, thinking something new was being delivered. He watched as the men approached his mother and spoke to her. Then he watched his mother turn pale and break out in tears. As he watched the men, young Coe realized that nothing new was coming out from that truck. Instead, these men were removing from their home what furniture they had! George had left them all after gambling away every possession in their home – and these men were coming to collect!

As the van pulled away, his mother was left to face the future with her seven children, having no one to turn to. So she knelt on the porch and began to pray. It was the first time Coe saw his mother pray!

Things got worse. The next day, a man came to see their house. Thinking he came to buy it, Blanche informed him that it wasn't for sale. "I didn't come to buy the house," the man said, "it's already mine! I'm very sorry, but you'll have to move out." It was unbelievable. His father had also gambled away their home.[2]

## "NO DICE, MR. COE!"

Blanche Coe moved her children to Pennsylvania, where she tried to make a life for them. They lived in a basement. As Coe's older sister watched after the children, Mrs. Coe worked doing laundry by day and went to nursing school by night. It was a terrible struggle for all of them.

Then one day, Coe's father showed up at their door. He pleaded with Blanche to come back to him, and he promised to quit gambling. Feeling that life had been too difficult by herself, she reunited with him, and George took his family back to Oklahoma. The gambling started all over again, and this time, Blanche Coe left George for good. But she kept her daughter and left Jack and his brothers with their father.

## NO ONE WANTED HIM

The young boys were often left alone as their father went to gamble. Many times they had nothing to eat. It wasn't long until Mrs. Coe returned for the boys and took them with her.

By the time Coe was nine years old, his mother felt overwhelmed by the responsibility of caring for her children alone. So she took Coe and his brother to a large home. Then after talking to the people and saying her good-byes, she turned and walked away, leaving young Coe and his brother standing on the steps of an orphanage.

Of this experience Coe would later write:

"I thought to myself, dad didn't want me, and now mother...the only friend I've ever had...she's turned her back on me and left me. I thought my heart would break within me as I saw her going down that walk. For a long time I stood and cried."[3]

*When he turned seventeen, he started to drink and carouse, and before long, he too, like George, had become an alcoholic.*

He didn't know that his mother also cried for days.

Coe's brother, who was three years older than him, would later run away from the orphanage. After hopping railroad cars and stealing a bicycle, he was hit by a car on the highway and was killed instantly. At the funeral, young Jack felt even more alone.

## NO FRIEND IN THE BOTTLE

Coe remained at the orphanage for eight years. During this time, he knew very little about God. When he turned seventeen, he started to drink and carouse, and before long, he too, like his father, had become an alcoholic.

There were times during his alcoholic enslavement when Coe sought to know God. But everyone who went to the church he attended occasionally, lived uncommitted lives. They didn't have his answers. So, he sank more deeply into sin.

Soon, Coe's health began to suffer. He had developed ulcers in his stomach due to the alcohol, and his heart was beating twice as fast as the normal rate. He had nearly drank himself to death, and the doctor cautioned him that the next drink could kill him.

So Coe tried to make a new resolution to help himself. But still not knowing God, he wondered who could help him keep this commitment. This led him to move to California. His mother lived there, and if anyone could help him, she certainly could.

Upon his arrival, his sister invited him to a dance. But soon, Coe found himself at the bar while the others danced. He was brought home that night in a drunken stupor, without his mother knowing about it.

## "GOD, GIVE ME UNTIL SUNDAY!"

The next evening, Coe thought he was dying. He was very weak, and could hardly walk. He was picked up in an ambulance, taken to a hospital, and examined. He sat in the chair and raised his hands pleading, **"Oh God, don't let me die, please give me one more chance. I don't want to go to hell."**[4] Then suddenly, Coe got better. His weakness left and so did his symptoms. He didn't know what happened to him at the time, but he was glad!

After this, Coe decided to leave California. So he took his mother with him, and the two left for Fort Worth, Texas. There, Coe obtained a job as a manager for the Singer Sewing Machine Agency. He soon forgot about the promises he had made to God and came home one evening in another alcoholic stupor. But this time, when he fell into his bed, he couldn't sleep, tossing to and fro over the conviction of God. Finally, he got up and drank another pint of whiskey just so he could pass out. Then in a few days a unique experience happened that changed Coe's life forever.

He had just returned home from drinking. It was about 3:00 A.M., and he was trying to go to sleep. But he couldn't, and as he reached for another pint of whiskey, he heard someone in the room!

Startled, Coe noticed that his heart was bothering him. It would start, then stop. Start, then stop. Then he heard a voice. "This is your last chance," the voice said. "I've called you several times, and I'm calling you now for the last time."

At this, Coe jumped out of his bed and fell to his knees, crying, **"Oh God, give me until Sunday. If You'll just give me until Sunday, I'll get right with You."**

## "HOT DOG, I'VE GOT IT!"

Sunday came, and Coe had no idea of where to go. As a youth, he had been baptized in several places, but nothing had ever changed his life or answered his questions. Because church started much later in the evening in those days, it wasn't until later in the afternoon that he began to seriously wonder about where to go. He simply had no idea. So at 5:00 P.M., he finally went to his office to look at the telephone book. Coe had heard about people opening their Bible to whatever verse their thumb fell on, taking that to be a message from God. So he thought he would try it with the phone book.

Coe picked up the big book and let it fall, and when he opened his eyes, he saw the name and address of a Nazarene church. He arrived in the parking lot two hours before the service began. When the doors finally opened, he jumped from the car and found a seat at the back. Then after the sermon, when the preacher asked if there was anyone who wanted to go to heaven, saying, "We have a born-again experience for you," Coe ran to the altar, shouting, **"That's what I want! That's what I want!"** A little gray-haired lady prayed with him. Then suddenly, Coe felt something he had never felt before. Not knowing the "Christian lingo," he found himself running all over the church, shouting, **"Hot dog, I've got it! Hot dog, I've got it!"** Later, when Coe recalled the moment, he would say, **"I didn't know what 'Glory, Hallelujah' meant. I had to let something out – there was something within me!"**

> *...Coe ran to the altar, shouting, "That's what I want! That's what I want!" A little gray-haired lady prayed with him. Then suddenly, Coe felt something he had never felt before. Not knowing the "Christian lingo," he found himself running all over the church, shouting, "Hot dog, I've got it! Hot dog, I've got it!"*

Coe returned to his home at 4:00 A.M. He had stayed at the church all that time, praying and praising God.

## "WHAT HAVE THEY DONE TO YOU?"

For the next six months, Jack Coe was a "hungry" man. He went to church every night and would stay there into the early morning hours. He devoured his Bible, and often imagined himself in the place of certain Bible characters. His mother watched his behavior, and was quite concerned about it. Finally one night, she asked if he was going to church. Of course, he was. So his mother said, "We're going with you tonight to find out what they've done to you." At the end of the message, his mother made her way to the altar. She didn't know how to pray, so she just said, "Oh God, give me what Jack's got." Then suddenly, she came up with tears rolling down her cheeks, "Jack! I've got it! I've got it!" As they sat on the bench, Coe and his mother hugged each other, praising God.

On the way home, late that night they stopped at a grocery store to buy some food. Very few people were shopping and neither Coe nor his mother could contain their joy. So they ran up and down the aisles, shouting, laughing, and praising God. The store butcher said, "You must have just gotten saved." As they talked with the man, tears began to roll down his cheeks, and before long he too was down on his knees, asking God to save him![5]

## "THEY'LL PUT A SPELL ON YOU!"

About a year and a half after he was saved, Coe learned of his first "holy roller" meeting. So out of curiosity, he and his sister went to check it out. He actually felt the meeting was a lot like his Nazarene church, except these people spoke in other tongues. And when people went to the altar, they would fall down under the power. At first he thought they were fainting.

Finally, the preacher spotted Coe. Pointing at him, he asked, "Are you a Christian?" After Coe answered positively, the preacher asked, "Have you received the baptism in the Holy Ghost? Did you speak in tongues?" Coe replied, **"No sir, I haven't, and I don't want to, either."**

Then the preacher asked Coe another question, "Will you go home and read everything there is on the baptism of the Holy Ghost? Then get down on your knees and pray that if it's for you, you'll get it, if not, there's nothing to it?"

Coe answered, **"Sure, I know there is nothing in the Bible about tongues."** To that the preacher said as he walked away, "That's fine, go home and read the Bible."

Every place Coe searched in Acts, he found the term, "other tongues." So the next evening, he went to the house of his Nazarene pastor. As Coe showed him the passages about tongues in Acts, the pastor replied, "If God ever wants you to speak in tongues, He'll let you do it after He calls you to be a missionary, so that natives can understand you." It made sense to Coe. And as he turned to leave, the pastor warned, "Stay away from those holy rollers, or they'll put a spell on you."

## "I'LL DIE IF I DON'T GET IT!"

That night, Coe refused to go to the meeting with his sister. In fact, he told her the meetings were of the devil. To this she responded, "Then, why do they quit their lying and stealing, and other wrong things?" and went without him.

Coe tossed and turned in bed that night, then finally jumped out of bed, got dressed, and went to the meeting. When he arrived, the preacher pointed to Coe again. And again, Coe told him that he didn't want to speak in tongues. So the preacher said, "We'll make you a special case. If God wants to fill you without speaking in tongues, it will be all right with us."

**"If that's the case, I'll come,"** Coe replied. Then he went to the front, but the people that gathered around him sounded like they were contradicting each other as they cried out – "Turn loose!" "Hold on!" "Empty him!" "Fill him!" After a few minutes of this, Jack jumped up from the altar and ran for the door.

Outside, he breathed deeply and managed to regain his composure. He straightened the wrinkles from his pants and managed a tight smile as he said to himself, *I sure proved there wasn't anything to it.* Then God immediately spoke to his heart, "You want it so bad you don't know what to do. You know it's for you; you know it's real." After that, Coe whined, **"God...if I don't get it, I'm going to die."** All the way home, he cried, **"Praise God for the glory!"**

> *The brighter the light became, the more Coe seemed to fade away. The more he praised God, the brighter the light. Finally, a hand reached out and took hold of his hand.*

The next night came and Coe made a run for the service. And when the altar call was given for the baptism of the Holy Spirit, he jumped to the front. The same people surrounded him, but this time he stayed. Suddenly, he saw a bright light. The brighter the light became, the more Coe seemed to fade away. The more he praised God, the brighter the light. Finally, a hand reached out and took hold of his hand. It was Jesus, and the two of them walked and talked together for quite some time.

When Coe came to, he was lying in sawdust. It was 4:00 A.M. and he found himself speaking in another tongue. In fact, all he could do for three days, was to speak in tongues! He had to write English words on paper. During those days, he lived in a heavenly atmosphere as all of creation seemed to praise God.[6]

## BIBLE SCHOOL, JUANITA & THE ARMY

From 1939 to 1940, Coe attended Southwestern Bible Institute, an Assemblies of God Bible college. P. C. Nelson was college president at the time.

While there, he met a girl named Juanita Scott. Their meeting would prove to be more than mere coincidence.

In 1941, after Japan bombed Pearl Harbor, Coe joined the army. At first, he was a little embarrassed to pray and act like a Christian around his fellow soldiers. But once he realized these crude men had no shame with their behavior, he decided to behave like a believer. And he suffered great persecution for it. But the persecution didn't stop him. In fact, Coe could be as rough as these men. The only difference was, he would listen to the voice of God. So he continued to preach at every opportunity.

While stationed at the 130th Bomb Squadron in Walter Boro, South Carolina, Coe was able to receive a pass to go whenever he wanted. He was located, "in the middle of nowhere," and the closest church was forty-five miles away. So every night he would walk five miles, then hitchhike the rest of the way to attend church! He didn't care if it was raining. He never missed church. This went on for six months.

Then one day his sergeant told him to gather his belongings. He was being sent to the dispensary. From there he was sent to the hospital. Coe protested the whole affair, especially after he realized he had been sent to the psychiatric ward! After the psychiatrist interviewed him, Coe told him that anyone who disobeys the Bible is the one who is crazy, not the other way around. So they locked him up.

## LIFE IN THE "PSYCH" WARD

*Private Coe*

Coe wanted to fast and pray, but in doing so, he simply convinced them even more of his "craziness." After he had been confined for nine days, Coe began to cry out to God. He opened his Bible to the book of Acts and read about how God sent an angel to rock Paul and Silas' prison cell, opening their jail doors when they sang their way out of prison. Feeling ashamed of his weak attitude after reading this, Coe began to lift his voice in song.

Suddenly, he heard a knock at his door. The ward boy walked in with tears in his eyes blubbering, "Preacher, I've stood it as long as I can. I come out here every night, and have to listen to you pray and cry and seek God all night long. I'm going to lose my mind if I don't get what you've got. My daddy was a Pentecostal preacher, but I never did get saved. Will you pray for God to save me?"

Coe knelt down with the boy, cried with him, and prayed, and the boy was gloriously saved. After the prayer they shouted so loud that the other inmates woke up and started yelling too!

Overcome with gratitude, the boy told Coe, "I don't know what I can do for you, but I'll try." The next morning, Coe was released. The doctor begrudgingly told him that he was suffering from a serious condition (psychoneurosis – or, religious fanaticism), but that he wasn't dangerous.

Coe changed companies seven times while in the army. And each time, sooner or later, they put him in the psychiatric ward for a while, because they didn't know how to handle him![7]

## BE A...WHAT?

After serving in the army for fifteen months, Coe's heart burned to preach the Gospel. He would lie in his bed at night and imagine preaching to the multitudes. During the day, he would preach to himself.

Finally, he decided to visit the Church of God pastor in town hoping for an opportunity to preach. The pastor invited him to get involved with prayer at the altar and other altar work. This wasn't what Coe wanted to hear, so he turned to walk away. But as he started to leave the Lord spoke to Coe's heart to tell the pastor he would do anything he was asked to do.

"Well, I'm glad to hear that," the pastor said. "Our janitor recently left and I would appreciate it if you could take over and clean the church."

Coe felt insulted and informed the pastor that he was called to preach – not to be a janitor, then turned and walked out. But the Lord continued to deal with Coe, and after another sleepless night, he returned to the church to be their new janitor!

> *Coe felt insulted and informed the pastor that he was called to preach — not to be a janitor, then turned and walked out. But the Lord continued to deal with Jack, and after another sleepless night, he returned to the church to be their new janitor!*

## SPIRITUAL BOOT CAMP

Coe would later say that this pastor was the toughest inspector he had ever worked for. He would run his hands over the wood that had been polished,

making sure it was clean. After a season of this the pastor invited Coe to begin teaching Sunday school. Coe was elated! He would finally get to preach. That is, until he found out he would be teaching the "beginners'" class. Coe was in shock. At first he resisted, then he reluctantly accepted. The class ranged from toddlers to three year olds.

After a while, Coe was promoted to song leader, then to youth minister, then to associate pastor. Then when the pastor was called to another church, the congregation asked Coe to fill in as pastor. Finally, he was ready to preach to someone![8]

## MARRIAGE AND A VISION

While Coe was at this church he heard that Juanita Scott was traveling the country with a singing group. Coe and Juanita had written each other through the years, but their relationship had never swung toward the romantic. After the Church of God hired a new pastor, Coe decided to start a church of his own. He wrote to Juanita's singing group, the Southern Carolers, asking them to come to town to help him raise the new work. But by the time the group came to town, Coe's plans had fallen through. He had been restricted to his army post, and couldn't carry on with regular meetings.

Coe located other revival work for Juanita's singing group and would meet them after services. During these times, he and Juanita grew closer. Soon, they were married, and Coe found them government housing. Having no money, they slept on a concrete floor with army blankets and fasted for three days, until they could buy some food. But before long, the Coes had three rooms of furniture, a car, and a thousand dollars in the bank. He was good with his hands, so he fixed a broken radio and sold it for $60. He also tripled his investment on the sale of some hens. And he was blessed with a car for helping a friend.

Also during this time, Coe began to pray and seek for an understanding of divine healing. He had heard of people being healed, but knew nothing about it. One day while reading a book by P. C. Nelson on healing, Coe fell asleep. He dreamed that his sister was dying in a hospital room. Then suddenly, a bright light filled her room, as she jumped up and ran, shouting, "I'm healed! I'm healed!"

The next day, Coe found out that the dream was a reality. His sister had double pneumonia and was given up to die. He immediately got leave to see her.

As Coe entered her hospital room, he found the surroundings were identical to his dream. He also learned that after a series of critical events that were against all odds, God healed and saved his sister – at the last possible moment. It was a total miracle that powerfully affected his life.[9]

## READY TO DIE

When Juanita was expecting their first child in 1944, Coe fell ill. He had contracted tropical malaria at the age of twenty-six and his weight had now dropped from 230 to 135 pounds. He was literally skin and bones. Once his fever shot up to 106 degrees, then remained there for fifty-four hours. His spleen and liver swelled to twice their normal size, producing pain so great that Coe would bite his tongue until it bled.

Finally, when the fever broke enough for Coe to understand conversation, the doctors told him of his condition. They saw there was nothing they could do for him, so after a few days, he was discharged and sent home to his family. **"Now, God, what shall I do?"** was his earnest prayer. The Lord's answer was, "I've called you to preach the Gospel. Go out and preach it!"

For a while, Coe would appear to be well, then another malaria attack would bring him down. Strong chills and a high fever brought the man to his knees. It was difficult for him to maintain a normal life. The intense pain in his spleen and liver was almost unbearable. Juanita would sit with him for hours, applying ice packs to comfort him.

Finally, Coe thought he could stand it no more. Feeling it was her husband's time to die, Juanita left their trailer in tears. It was then that Coe began to repent as the Lord showed him different things. This went on for some time, and Coe began to feel inwardly free. **"All right Lord, I'm ready to go now,"** were his words toward the end of this time. A voice spoke back to his heart, "You're ready to go, but you don't have to." Then suddenly, Coe felt as if he were covered with warm oil from head to toe as the Lord spoke, "You are healed now."

Coe jumped out of bed. He grabbed his wife, who by this time, was asleep near him and shouted, **"Honey! Honey! I'm healed! I'm healed!"**

The next night, despite harassing thoughts from the devil, Coe dressed and preached on the street. Three people were saved. Later that same year, the Assemblies of God ordained him into the ministry.[10] Coe would never have another attack of malaria – God had truly healed him!

## OH NO! A BLIND PERSON?

In 1945, Coe went to Longview, Texas, where he continually studied and prayed on the subject of divine healing. He asked God for a special manifestation of His power, then decided to announce a healing meeting. **"God's going** to open the eyes of the blind and cause the lame to walk, and the deaf to hear. He's going to do it right here in this church tomorrow night," was his bold confession of faith.

> *Desperate, Coe prayed, "Lord, that woman is almost to me now. What am I going to do?" But the Lord quickly rebuked saying, "Son, whatever made you think that you could open the eyes of the blind, anyway? Do what you are supposed to do and I will do what I am supposed to do."*

The next night, the church was packed. After Coe preached, the people lined up. The ailments didn't seem too bad. There were a few stomachaches, headaches, and other minor ailments. But then suddenly Coe looked up – and there she stood – a blind woman. "Oh Lord, what in the world am I going to do with her?" he asked, then began worrying about what people would say if she didn't receive her sight.

When the blind woman stepped up for her turn to be prayed for, Coe sent her to the back of the line. He was hoping by the time she came to him again, he would have enough faith! And soon, she was nearing her turn again. Desperate, Coe prayed, "Lord, that woman is almost to me now. What am I going to do?" But the Lord quickly rebuked saying, "Son, whatever made you think that you could open the eyes of the blind, anyway? Do what you are supposed to do, and I will do what I am supposed to do."

Coe repented, then prayed and anointed the woman with oil. Her eyes were opened and she could see something moving in the back of the church, but not clearly. So remembering that Jesus had prayed for someone twice, Coe prayed again. And this time, she began to cry out, "I can see! I can see!"[11]

## AWAY WE GO!

News of her healing saturated the town, and Coe's faith skyrocketed. A pastor from Oklahoma asked him to come and hold a three-day meeting. After the first night, they had to rent the high school gymnasium to hold the people because deaf ears and blind eyes were opened, and people got up from stretchers and walked.

At that time, Coe thought he had to stay and pray for everyone who came up. He would often be found still ministering to the people at 5:00 A.M. the next morning. As he began traveling throughout Oklahoma, praying for the sick, he got very little sleep.

In different towns, he would stay in private homes. When he did, people would come to that home for prayer. If he was asleep, they would wait until he woke up. If there were very many of them, they would wake him up to pray for their needs. Sometimes, this would happen four or five times a day.

Soon, Coe's body began to break down. He was only sleeping an hour or so each night. But the needs of the people were so great and demanding that he would always pray for them whenever they came. In those days, healing campaigns were still new and there were many practical ministry principles people didn't understand. Finally, God told Coe that he needed to use wisdom and get proper rest. So he obeyed and was revitalized to pursue a stronger ministry to the sick.

## SAY GOOD-BYE TO THE HOUSE

In 1946, Coe merged his editorial efforts with Gordon Lindsay's *The Voice of Healing* publication, and was named a co-editor. Then in 1947, Coe and his wife made a dramatic decision that affected the rest of their lives. The couple had purchased a small home, and Juanita was very proud of it. She had furnished it nicely, and worked on the lawn to keep it immaculate.

But after returning home from a church service one day, Juanita began to cry. She knew God was speaking to them to sell all they had to enter into the ministry full time, so they decided to sell. Before Coe awoke the next morning, someone was at his door to buy it. A few days later, Coe purchased an old tent, a new truck and house trailer.

The Coes were ready to go, and the first place they would go to would be Chickasha, Oklahoma. The second night of this meeting, they experienced their first real ministry challenge. A storm blew in and tore the canvas off the top of the tent, leaving only its ropes. After the storm, their pastor challenged them to really know whether or not they were in the will of God. To this, Juanita responded, "If everything we have is gone, I still believe we are in the will of God." So as he turned to go, their pastor said, "If you've got that much faith in God, I've got enough faith to help you." Then he handed them $100.[12]

By the time this first meeting had closed, the Coes had enough money to re-canvas their tent and to buy a larger truck to carry it.

## TENT TALES

In 1948, Coe headed for Redding, California, for his next meeting, having been specifically directed to this city. Before hearing God's Word of direction,

*Healing the sick*

*Jack and Juanita Coe*

*The Big Top*

Jack Coe

Behind bars

Under the Big Top

he had never even heard of Redding. Once there, the devil went about his business of blocking the meetings. The fire marshall told Coe that his tent wasn't fireproof and that he wouldn't allow him to set it up. The cost of fireproofing it was $1,700, and the tent only cost $400.

Coe bought the fireproofing solution himself, then dipped each part of the tent in it until the entire canvas was covered. But the make-shift solution failed the fire marshall's inspection. Utterly frustrated, Coe began to cry. And when he did, the fire marshall told him that if it meant that much to him, he could go ahead with his meetings and set the tent up.

> *Once there, the devil went about his business of blocking the meetings. The fire marshall told Coe that his tent wasn't fireproof and that he wouldn't allow him to set it up. The cost of fireproofing it was $1,700, and the tent only cost $400.*

The first few nights, crowds were small. But Coe was faithful to pray for the sick. One lady came wearing a brace and using crutches. She was totally healed. That night, for the first time in years, she knelt down to pray beside her bed. She prayed until the sun came up, then walked to the next meeting. Her testimony stirred the entire city. She shared that the doctors were preparing to amputate her leg.

Coe aired the testimony on radio and the lady who managed the radio station was saved. A prominent Catholic lady arrived at his meeting that night in a chauffeur-driven Cadillac. The lady was saved and immediately closed all the drinking establishments she owned. She would come into the meetings with her hands raised and leave the same way.

Up to this time, the offerings had been very small. Creditors had threatened to take his truck, so Coe stood up in front of the people and told them he needed $740 badly. When he did, one lady walked up to him and wrote out a check for the entire amount. Two nights later, he said, **"I sure would like to have a Hammond organ or some kind of music for this tent,"** and the same lady bought him an organ. Coe's revival team would stay in Redding for seven weeks, and would receive enough money to fund the next crusade.[13]

After a much needed vacation, the Coes continued ministering in California. In Fresno, he was arrested for disturbing the peace. Coe pleaded "not guilty," and the court case came to trial several months later. But it was thrown out due to lack of evidence and was never mentioned again.

## THE MAN AND THE MINISTER

Coe was a very boisterous man who brilliantly played to the crowds. He was said to be saucy, angry, flippant, humble, and always nervy. It was also said that he loved controversy and attracted lots of it. He appeared to enjoy a good fight. Of him, Gordon Lindsay wrote, "In growing up it was root hog or die. For that reason, he tangled."[14]

Coe's faith was "reckless and challenging," but no one seemed to mind when they walked away healed! He was often seen hitting people, slapping them, or jerking them. But, again, they all walked away healed. Some didn't even feel it when he hit them. He was also the first evangelist to attract, and welcome, large numbers of the black community into his services. He preached bluntly, and called things as he saw them. He was a preacher with a sting. Once, a group of young people were standing on the chairs in the tent, and he shouted out at them, **"Those are my chairs! I wouldn't do that at your house!"**[15]

Another time the highway patrol approached Coe to tell him that his crowd was blocking the highway, and to get the people off of it. He responded by telling the highway patrol that he didn't have anything to do with the highway, and that it was up to them to arrest the people if they wanted them off. He then proceeded with his meeting, undisturbed by their demand.[16]

By 1950, Coe seemed to always be in competition with other preachers. He competed by ordering larger and larger tents. And still his team would have to turn away thousands every night.

In 1951 Coe visited an Oral Roberts meeting. He measured the length of Roberts' tent and ordered one slightly larger. Then in July of that year, he ran a notice in *The Voice of Healing* magazine that said:

> "A letter from the Smith Manufacturing Company, Dalton, Ga., declares that according to his measurements the Coe tent is by a slight margin, the largest gospel tent in the world. Since Oral Roberts has a prayer tent 90' x 130', Brother Roberts has the largest amount of tent equipment. Both the Coe and Roberts tents are larger than the Ringling Brothers [circus] big top."[17]

## "THE FRECKLED FACE" VISION

One night in a Lubbock, Texas, meeting, a little freckled-face boy approached the revivalist. Locking his arms around Coe's legs, the boy said with a lisp, "Pleathe, mithter, let me go home with you." Then a woman dragged him away, as Coe stood watching. But the impression stayed with Coe the entire night. The next day, he looked for the boy, but couldn't find him.

Coe had always felt he would someday provide a home for other homeless children, as he had been a homeless child himself. But he also knew that if God was speaking to him that He would speak to Juanita as well. He couldn't escape the memory of this little boy's freckled face.

Finally, while driving home after a meeting, Coe asked his wife, **"Honey, what would you say if I told you that God had been speaking to me about starting a children's home?"** It looked financially impossible. But Juanita said, "I always thought that I should work in a children's home, so maybe this is it. You go ahead and obey God!"[18]

## PIECE BY PEACE

In obedience, the Coes put a small down-payment on a lot in Dallas, and continued on with their healing crusades. In every meeting, Coe let the people know of his children's home plans, and soon, people began to donate lumber and supplies. The Coes put their own home up for sale. It sold the same week, and they used the proceeds to help pay the workers. Then they moved into a portion of the children's home still under construction and lived there until it was finished.

> *Coe had always felt he would someday provide a home for other homeless children, as he had been a homeless child himself. But he also knew that if God was speaking to him that He would speak to Juanita as well.*

There was no running water and the heater couldn't sufficiently heat the room. As a result, their baby fell ill with pneumonia. They put the child's health in God's hands and left for their next meeting. After they had traveled about fifty miles, the baby's fever broke, and the baby was playing in the car – instantly healed!

Little by little, God made the finances available for the children's home. People began to donate draperies, blankets, and clothing, and before long, the Coes were able to hold their "Open House." The home was ready and children were received.

One day as Coe sat watching the children play, a little boy walked up to him and said, "You'll be my daddy now." Then several others locked their arms around him, wanting his love. Of this, Coe said, **"It seemed that my dream had at last, been fulfilled."**[19]

# GOD SAID, "NO."

Bob Davidson was a young boy in the children's home. His own father had been crippled, and could not take care of his family. Although Coe was a national evangelist, Davidson said he was like a "compassionate father" when he was at the home. Coe was remembered by some as always being happy. He was a fun-loving man, who enjoyed playing jokes on people. Even so, Coe heard from God concerning the children, and knew when to draw the line.

Once, after being at the home for several years, Davidson had wanted to go to a State Fair with some of his friends. When he went to ask Coe for money to go, Coe told him that if he finished his chores, he could go.

Davidson worked hard to complete his duties in time to go. Running to meet Coe, he shouted that he had finished all his work. About that time, the guys he was going to the Fair with pulled in front of the home in a brand new Plymouth Fury. They waved to Davidson, telling him to hurry and get in the car so they could go.

Watching the scene, Coe gave Davidson money for his chores, but changed his mind about the boy going to the Fair. Coe told him, **"God said not to let you go."**

Of course, Davidson didn't understand. He cried and yelled at Coe, "You lied! You lied!" Then he ran to another part of the home.

After a while, Coe found Davidson and said, **"If you really want to go to the Fair, I'll take you myself. But God said you could not go with those boys. I didn't feel right about letting you leave."**[20]

So Davidson dried his face and left for the Fair with Coe. As they traveled down the road, an ambulance and a sheriff's car passed them at high speeds, heading straight ahead of them.

Driving up ahead, nothing could match the horror of what they saw. There in the ditch, was the brand new Plymouth Fury, crushed and mangled. Beside it, scattered along the ground, were the broken bodies of Davidson's friends – all of them dead. Coe and Davidson stood by the road, holding one another, and crying.

# DRESSED LIKE ROYALTY

Davidson has never forgotten how Coe cared enough to hear God for him. He feels that he owes his life to the strict compassion of Jack Coe.

Sometimes, seventeen children would be in the home. Davidson remembers it reaching one hundred children at one point. Some of the children came so dirty, their hair would have to be washed four or five times just to see their scalp. Most of the children had been left alone, some starving. Neighbors of the abandoned children would report the condition to authorities. Then the children's home would take what it could hold.

Coe always told the donors, "**Don't send me worn out clothes for the kids in my home. My kids are going to be dressed as good as yours.**" It was said that after Coe took the kids, that even the governor of the state would have been proud to claim them. They were all taught to pray, led to Christ, and taken to church regularly. Most all of them spoke in other tongues.

Eventually, Coe was able to purchase two hundred acres outside of Dallas for the home. This was enough room for a self-sustaining farm and four large dormitories. Coe targeted two hundred children as his goal. God honored his efforts, and abundantly supplied the needs of the children's home.

*"Well, the 'holy rollers' are going. What's the matter? Where's your faith in God?" So Coe yelled back, "That's just the reason we're leaving. We've got faith in God, and God told us to go!"*

## THE BIG TOP

By now, Coe had purchased and sold several tents, working his way toward owning the largest tent in the nation. Finally, he succeeded. He now bragged that his new tent was "bigger than the big top." Storms had destroyed others, but Coe was believing for this one to be supernaturally sustained by the hand of God.

Coe didn't just have small, confined tent meetings. His meetings were huge! One of his largest meetings was held in Little Rock, Arkansas, where the governor estimated over twenty thousand people were in attendance! Deaf ears were unstopped, blind eyes were opened, and crippled persons walked as God miraculously healed them. Thousands were also born again.

Finally, another dreaded storm swirled around Coe's gospel tent. On this night, the wind blew so hard, the revivalist himself could hardly stand outside. There were thirty-five hundred people still inside the tent when the worst of the storm passed through, when lightning struck the electrical system and all the lights went out. When this happened, Coe ran into his trailer and began to pray. As he did, the wind suddenly subsided and the storm calmed.

Coe went back inside to see how the people were, and a woman was lying on the ground with an apparent heart attack. He could hear the rattle of death in her throat. Someone suggested they call an ambulance, but Coe said, **"We'll pray and believe God. God will heal her."** Within a few minutes, she was back to normal praising the Lord with the rest of the people![21]

## A PRESENT-DAY FLOOD STORY

Coe was also present when the greatest flood in U. S. history struck Kansas City. Before he had arrived in the city, he dreamed of a great flood, closing in on every side. But it didn't keep him from coming. He had raised his big top on the Kansas side. And God was speaking judgment in the meetings through the gift of prophecy. But most of the people ignored the warnings. Some of them, laughing and jeering, even left the meetings. It rained every night, soaking the ground as thousands answered the altar calls. But Coe remained troubled in his spirit. For two nights, he was unable to sleep.

The next day, he turned to his wife and said, **"Would you think I were crazy if I took that tent down? Something tells me to take the tent down."** As he began putting action to his words, he walked out to find that his trucks were stuck in the mud, and that the dampness had affected the batteries – they wouldn't start. After working on them feverishly the crew was finally able to start the trucks late that afternoon.

As Coe moved to strike the big tent, people began to question his motives. "What are you doing?" "You're not having service tonight?" "I don't think you have anything to worry about." "The most the water would do if the river flooded, would run under your chairs." "There's no danger of the water coming over the dikes." "Don't let the devil defeat you." Nevertheless, God had spoken clearly to Coe: "Get the tent out of here."

But by 7:30 P.M. that night, the crew had made no progress. So he organized them, urging them to hurry. They were just getting ready to lower the top, when another minister approached Coe and said "Don't take the tent down. God can take care of this tent." To this Coe responded, **"I know God can take care of this tent, and that's the reason I'm moving. God told me to move it, and I'm going to move it."**

Finally, three hours later, as they were pulling out the last stake, the puller locked and refused to give another inch. At that very moment, every whistle and siren in town began to blast and shrill. "The dikes are breaking!" came the call.

Coe was ready to go, but he couldn't get all the canvas in the trucks, and the men were running off. So he stood on a large box and pleaded with them, **"Men, don't leave me now. The tent is rolled up, don't leave me!"** By this time, the bridge leading out of their area was snarled as panic-stricken people fought one another to cross. The men would look at the congestion, then look at Coe. Finally, one said, "We ought to be men enough to stay here and help him. If he isn't afraid of drowning, I'm surely not." With that, forty men came alongside of Coe to help him load the canvas. Once loaded, they headed out of town.

As Coe's trucks left Kansas City, some of the people who refused to leave sat on their porches and jeered at him. "Well, the 'holy rollers' are going. What's the matter? Where's your faith in God?" So Coe yelled back, **"That's just the reason we're leaving. We've got faith in God, and God told us to go!"** Others stood on their porches and laughed too. They never thought the flood would destroy everything they had, but for many it did.

On his way out of town, Coe stopped to help Pastor Barnett move his furniture and belongings to the church. (This was Tommy Barnett's father. Today, Tommy Barnett pastors one of America's largest churches located in Phoenix, Arizona.) But their moving party proved to be too little, too late as Barnett watched with Coe from the truck as the flood waters crashed through the windows of the church. Losing everything he had, Barnett made a fresh commitment to stay in Kansas City.

Barnett and Coe attempted to save many people from the disaster. But in the process they witnessed the drowning of many. After they had done everything possible, they started out over the bridge to safety, and as Coe looked behind them, he saw that the water level where the tent had stood was now standing at around twenty feet. The tent would have been completely destroyed, and only a small part of Barnett's church building still showed.[22]

> *Here the sick would be allowed to remain until they received their healing. Prayer and classes on healing would be offered daily.*

The two men turned their backs, thanking God in their hearts for His absolute provision and deliverance.

## EMBARRASSED? WHAT ELSE IS NEW?

In 1952, Coe went throughout the South holding massive healing crusades. Two years earlier he had started publishing, *The Herald of Healing*, and by 1951, its circulation had reached 35,000. The masthead boasted that it was one of the nation's fastest growing magazines, with 100 percent renewal each year. By 1956, the circulation had reached 250,000.[23]

In August of 1952, Coe went on the radio with the Gospel. His broadcasts eventually grew to one hundred different stations a week. Thousands were saved and healed as a result of his program. It was around that time that creative miracles – the miraculous appearance of missing body parts – also began taking place in his meetings.

When Coe finally held a meeting in Springfield, Missouri, the Assemblies of God began to oppose him. They weren't comfortable with divine healing and deliverance ministries. But Coe had a volcanic personality, especially when it came to someone trying to dictate or control his call. He tried to cooperate with their suggestions and criticisms, and even sponsored the *Pentecostal Evangel* (the official Assemblies of God publication) at one of his meetings, receiving one hundred twenty new subscriptions for it. He also took up a large offering for their missions program.

> *No medicine was ever offered or permitted in the building, and patients were taken nightly to the Dallas Revival Center.*

But Coe wasn't a denominational man. As much as he tried, he couldn't stand for all the restraints and regulations placed upon him. He felt the Assemblies of God leaders no longer believed in the miraculous. So he wrote a bold letter, suggesting they replace their present leadership with men who believed in the miraculous power of God. The General Council found his letter offensive.

Finally, in 1953, Coe was expelled from the Assemblies of God. They had become frustrated by his "extreme independence" and embarrassed by some of his methods. A bitter feud followed. It has been said that Coe even thought of establishing a split-off group called the Fundamental Assemblies of God, but decided to pursue his own call, instead.[24]

## NEW CHURCH, NEW HOME, NEW UNDERSTANDING

Soon Coe began grasping the vision for his own independent church. It would be a revival center where evangelists could come and hold continuous campaigns. It would provide accommodations large enough to hold the people their ministries drew. And it would eventually be duplicated around the nation in every major city. Coe realized he would be highly criticized for this move, but he decided to pursue the dream regardless of persecution, and in 1953 he started the first one, the Dallas Revival Center.

In the spring, Coe began to ask God why people weren't healed. Though he had seen thousands healed, he had also seen thousands walk away without their healing. After a season of prayer, God revealed to Coe that many didn't understand how to receive healing and that they needed instruction in His Word concerning His will and His power. This was a tremendous revelation in that day! Up until then, most of the Voice of Healing evangelists depended upon the anointing of their healing gift, and many knew little about what the Word of God had to say on the subject.

So in an effort to strengthen the faith and dispel the doubts of those who were seeking healing, Coe built a faith home. Here the sick would be allowed to remain until they received their healing. Prayer and classes on healing would be offered daily. Finally, after months of struggling through the city's resistance to his building plans, Jack Coe's Faith Home opened next door to his Herald of Healing Children's Home in the summer of 1954. In September, Coe's Faith Home received its first full-time patient. From there, the numbers grew. No medicine was ever offered or permitted in the building, and patients were taken nightly to the Dallas Revival Center.

In July of that year, Coe experienced the greatest tent revival in the history of his ministry. He had taken the big top to Pittsburgh, Pennsylvania, where it is estimated that thirty thousand people were born again. One night was devoted to "stretcher cases" only. More than 75 percent of those on stretchers got up and walked. A local television station broadcast the revival meetings, drawing even greater crowds. Though great winds ripped the big top while he was in Pittsburgh, this month-long meeting was the high point in Coe's life.

*Ironically, it seems that the Voice of Healing generation didn't understand the stewardship of the physical body as we do today.*

Throughout 1953, his church, the Dallas Revival Center, continued to grow. Meetings were held in a large rented theater, which he and another pastor had renovated for nightly attendance. Coe's love for children moved him to develop a full Christian school at the Dallas Revival Center, where children were taught and loved by Spirit-filled teachers.

The church balcony and lower floor were packed every night, and by the fall of that year, the congregation had grown to the point where they were able to construct their own building.

In January of 1954, Coe opened the new Dallas Revival Center Church. It was beautifully and simply built, with a huge white cross gleaming across its front. The center provided a place to attend church every night of the week. Bus service picked up those who had no way to get there, and an ambulance provided free service to anyone who wished to come from the hospital, or home, for prayer.

## SEVERAL TRIALS — MINISTRY & LIFE

Coe continued to evangelize around the nation, trying to raise money for a television program. But in 1956, he was arrested in Miami, Florida, for practicing medicine without a license.

Let me make a point here. At this time, the city of Miami was known for its persecution of ministers. Especially those who preached on divine healing. When the persecutions broke out, most evangelists would usually just pack up and leave town. But not Coe! He stayed to fight. Remember, Coe loved a good fight. As a result, the Miami police arrested him and threw him in jail. He was later released on a $5,000 bond.

Because of his incarceration, Coe began admonishing other healing evangelists to come to Miami and stand up for what they believed. And when his case came to trial, it was evident that his words had been heard. Many prominent healing evangelists came to testify on his behalf. In fact, it is recorded that these evangelists had healing miracles manifest – while they were on the stand! God turned the situation around for his good, and in the end the judge dismissed the case.

Coe's Miami incident had proven to be a great victory. But a turning point was soon to come in his ministry. In December, while preaching in Hot Springs, Arkansas, the healing evangelist became critically ill.

*If we fail to be good stewards over our flesh, our bodies die early and our spirits have to leave.*

It was a known fact that Coe had terribly neglected his health. Coe maintained an extremely rigorous schedule, holding three meetings a day, that lasted four to six weeks at a time. The overwork, the stress, and a lack of proper rest soon took its toll. Because of the tremendous wear and tear on his body, it was said that Coe inwardly possessed the body of a ninety-year-old man.

Today, the Coe family says the Lord told him of his death one year before the time, and that Coe accepted that he was soon to die. They also say he believed the coming of the Lord would follow shortly after his death. Because of these two things, Coe worked relentlessly to spread the Gospel – even to the extreme.

Besides Coe's brutal schedule, his eating habits were irregular and unhealthy. Many times after a crusade, Coe would eat a heavy meal at 3:00 A.M. As a result, he was extremely overweight.

Ironically, it seems that the Voice of Healing generation didn't understand the stewardship of the physical body as we do today. We must understand that the physical body is the only thing holding our spirit on the earth. We must practice a healthy maintenance of our eating habits, mental attitudes, and general well-being. Otherwise, our physical "house" – our bodies – will break down and die. Then our spirits will have to leave the earth and go to heaven.

I like to compare our physical bodies to a space suit. If you go to the moon, the only thing that will hold your body to the surface of the moon is your space suit. Such a suit contains an oxygen supply, a body shield, and is heavy enough to walk upright in the weightlessness of space. But if you were to harm that space suit, your oxygen supply would be cut off, your shield would be broken, and your body would float away from the surface of the moon. Why? Because you need such a space suit to remain on the moon.

The same is true with our physical bodies. If we fail to be good stewards over our flesh, our bodies die early and our spirits have to leave. Therefore, if you don't take care of your physical body, your life and your ministry will come to an end.

## AN UNTIMELY DEATH

At first, Coe thought he was suffering from exhaustion, but soon he was diagnosed with polio. His wife wanted him admitted to the hospital, so Coe consented for her peace of mind.

*One of the great things about Jack Coe, is that he never allowed his past to hold him back. His past might have influenced his attitude, but it never stopped him or caused him to withdraw.*

In the hospital, Coe remained unconscious most of the time. There were a few times when he would regain his ability to speak and make his desires known. According to his wife, the Lord spoke to Coe and told him that He was going to take him home.[25] Then early in 1957, Jack Coe went home to be with the Lord.

Juanita Coe was scolded by many evangelists for not allowing them to pray for her husband. But Gordon Lindsay said his death must have been the will of God, or "providence would have allowed someone to pray for him. His ministry had simply been fulfilled."

There is a story that says Coe had been warned of his impending death, due to some health habits, personal habits, and his rigorous schedule. The story says that the Lord had spoken several times to one minister in particular. This prophetic man of the time is said to have heard the warning of the Lord for Jack Coe. And it is said that he obeyed God and went to Coe.

As the story goes, Coe was told to judge himself in three areas: (1) his love of the brethren; (2) his weight problem; and (3) the love of money. The prophet reportedly told Coe that if he would not judge himself in these areas, he would die early. And Coe did die early. He was only thirty-eight years old when he died.

It is important to note that the Coe family strongly refutes that this particular prophet ever spoke to Coe. The family maintains that a member of the Coe family approached the prophet to confront him about this widespread report. According to the Coe family, this prophet said that he never spoke to Coe directly, although he was told by God to do so.

## THE MINISTRY CONTINUES

After Coe died, Juanita Coe announced that she and the department heads would continue her husband's ministry. She served as assistant pastor of the Dallas Revival Center, and for a time, continued to conduct healing campaigns. There were many that felt she could have gone on to have her own major revival ministry, but she chose to let that phase of the ministry end. More and more Juanita Coe directed her energies toward foreign missions and the Herald of Healing Children's Home. Even after Coe's death, the *Herald of Healing* had a circulation of 300,000 readers. It was only when Juanita decided to taper off that phase of ministry, that her husband's popularity dwindled.

Today, both of Coe's sons, Jack Jr. and Steve, are in the ministry, pastoring their own churches, and Mrs. Coe is still active in the church. The Coes are continuing to preach and teach Jesus Christ to this generation and to the next, carrying on the plan of God for their individual lives.

## LIVE PAST YOUR PAST

One of the great things about Jack Coe, is that he never allowed his past to hold him back. His past might have influenced his attitude, but it never stopped him or caused him to withdraw.

As a child, he was terribly hurt by his home condition, but it never caused him to sit in a corner and feel sorry for himself. Instead of pushing him under, those hard times built an awareness in him of a need for deliverance. He knew that he couldn't depend on others to find it for him. He was a fighter. And it is true that he sometimes fought in the flesh. But he was determined to do something with the hunger in his heart! He was determined to take control of his horribly disadvantaged life instead of allowing it to continue controlling him.

As a result, Coe was hurled headfirst into his place as one of the leaders in the Voice of Healing revival. He had the kind of "independence" that it takes to keep you on the cutting edge. It is when we base our lives and faith on the words of men, or on the horrors of our past, that we are defeated. But when we pursue and run after the cry of our hearts, God will meet us every time and manifest His glory.

Another important lesson to be drawn upon from Coe's life is this: Understand that you don't have to exaggerate the facts or compete with someone else to show your worth. This is the only place where I can see that the ministry of Jack Coe bears reproach. Sometimes, if insecurity prevails in a ministry, the person will either withdraw or go overboard to prove his worth. When we go the way of the flesh, we have to rely on our own strength, and we wear out before our time.

Your past will never determine your future, that is, unless you give it the power to do so. There is a whole new future in faith. It is clean, untouched, waiting for you to pioneer with it by the dream in your heart. Keep God as your number one passion, and the desire of your heart will surely follow.

## CHAPTER ELEVEN, JACK COE
### References

1  Jack Coe, *The Story of Jack Coe*, (Dallas, TX: Herald of Healing, Inc., 1955), 78-79.

2  Ibid., 5-6.

3  Ibid., 12.

4  Ibid., 15.

5  Ibid., 16-20.

6  Ibid., 21-26.

7  Ibid., 29-34.

8  Ibid., 42-44.

9  Ibid., 48-54.

10  Ibid., 55-59.

11  Ibid., 60-62.

12  Ibid., 68-69.

13  Ibid., 72-75.

14  David Harrell Jr., *All Things Are Possible*, (Bloomington: Indiana University Press, 1975), 58-59.

15  Interview with Pastor Gary Ladd who attended Coe meetings in Tyler, Texas, in 1949.

16  Coe, *The Story of Jack Coe*, 79-80.

17  Harrell, *All Things Are Possible*, 59-60.

18  Coe, *The Story of Jack Coe*, 86.

19  Ibid., 90.

19  Ibid.

20  Interview with Bob Davidson on July 25, 1995.

21  Coe, *The Story of Jack Coe*, 98.

22  Ibid., 99-106.

23  Harrell, *All Things Are Possible*, 60.

24  Ibid., 61.

25  Personal comments from the Coe Family, April 1996.

# CHAPTER TWELVE

# A. A. Allen

*"The Miracle Man"*

# "THE MIRACLE MAN"

Before we get into A. A. Allen's story, I would like to make a few comments that I feel will help your perspective in this story.

Everyone has a personal preference when it comes to ministry gifts. There are certain ministries that you enjoy more than others, but not every ministry gift is going to fit into your personal mold.

Some of us might be surprised to find that our idea of ministry, or how a ministry should operate, wasn't Jesus' idea at all. I like to describe "preference" as more of an idea in your mind than a revelation in your spirit.

Our personal preferences are just that – preferences. They are not rules. Therefore, we must be very careful not to judge the call or ministry gift of another according to our personal preferences. Surrounding yourself with ministries that satisfy your preferences only – could cause you to miss out on something important.

I have great compassion for A. A. Allen. Sure, he made mistakes. Every General did, and every future General will. Personally, I also feel there are things Allen did in the "flesh" that he called "Spirit."

But when you consider Allen's disastrous background, you must take note of how he triumphed over it all to affect the world for Jesus. Very few people, if any, have overcome what Allen did to successfully answer the call of God. His story should speak to every generation. Consider this as you read.

## A LITTLE MILK, A LOT OF WHISKEY

Asa Alonzo Allen was born on a stormy Easter morning, March 27, 1911. His parents, Asa and Leona, decided to name him after his father and his father's uncle, a Presbyterian minister. His name was the only connection to God that his parents gave him, and they certainly didn't think he would end up a preacher. But Asa Alonzo would arise from out of their little known region of Sulphur Springs, Arkansas, to become one of the most sensational revivalists of modern time.

*He was severely criticized for his dramatics and sensationalism...*

It is true that A. A. Allen drew more controversy than any other of the Voice of Healing evangelists. He was severely criticized for his dramatics and sensationalism, and he was totally denounced for his personal habits. The media scorned him to the fullest, and denominational leaders banished him while ordering others to distance themselves from him. Nevertheless, some consider him to have been one of the most important revivalists to emerge during the Voice of Healing revival.[1] It is also important to note that those who criticized Allen were far less productive in the ministry than was Allen.

> *Nevertheless, some consider him to have been one of the most important revivalists to emerge during the Voice of Healing revival.*

Allen was born into a troubled home in which "turmoil" was a household word. At the time of his birth, Allen had two brothers and four sisters. As a young boy, his sisters brought him the only joy he knew; they loved him, played with him, and treated him like a little prince. But his parents were drunkards and raised the children in total poverty. Even Allen's first pair of shoes were bought for him by a total stranger.

Allen's parents also made home brew liquor behind their shack. His mother drank heavily while she was pregnant with Allen, and being as poor as they were, a new baby was hardly anything to be joyful about.

A favorite pastime of his parents was to give Allen and his sisters some of their home brew liquor until they were drunk. Then they would sit back and laugh at their children's drunken antics until they would either fall down or pass out.[2] Allen's mother repeatedly filled his bottle with liquor to keep him from crying, and he would go to bed nightly with a baby bottle filled with the home brew.

Tobacco was also plentiful in the household. Being home grown, it was very strong, yet, Allen learned to smoke before he was old enough to go to school. He always took a few puffs of his mother's cigarettes when he lit them for her.[3]

His father was a talented musician, and though he wasn't a Christian, the local church asked him to lead their choir and perform with them. He usually did so while drunk. Young Allen caught hold of those talents and sometimes stood on the street corner singing to the crowd. It must have been a sight, hearing that baby voice sing hymns he had learned from his drunken father. Young Allen would sing the church hymns over and over because the crowd tossed pennies, nickels, and dimes to him. He stepped into the entertainment world at an early age, and it seemed he was born for it.

# A BUCKET OF BEER 'N' TROUBLE

Allen's parents were always fighting, throwing furniture, and threatening one another with weapons. Finally, when he was four years old, his mother left his father. She took the children with her to Carthage, Missouri.

Soon after his mother left, she married again, but the turmoil was the same. In drunken rages, his mother and stepfather would fight to such an extreme that the young children would run out of the home in terror. By the time Allen was six years old, he was carrying tin buckets of beer home from the saloon to his stepfather.

Allen recalled:

> **"Every one of us grew up with a taste for liquor. I had only two brothers. One of them died when I was just a tiny lad. I hardly remember him at all. But my oldest brother died a drunkard. My father filled a drunkard's grave. My mother quit drinking before I was grown, but my four sisters and I were well started on the road to a drunkard's hell."[4]**

In addition to the drinking problem, his mother had fits of jealousy. She had married a younger man, and as Allen's stepfather would go to work, she would watch him with binoculars to see if he stopped to talk with any women. They lived very close to his work, so she watched everything he did and made him give account for it on payday. If the paycheck seemed less than usual, she accused him of spending it on another woman. His stepfather finally had all he could take and left, and so had young Allen.

At eleven years old, Allen ran away from home, determined to go back to Arkansas and find his father. But he wasn't sure of the way, and once he left the weather turned bad, so he returned home to his mother. Carefully plotting his next attempt, he decided that the next time he wouldn't fail.

When he was fourteen, Allen was as large as a grown man, so he ran away again. This time, he decided he would do whatever it took to make it, so he hitched rides in vehicles and empty freight cars and traveled over a large portion of the South. While traveling with several other vagabond friends, he picked cotton, worked in gins, and dug ditches; and he still ended up in jail for stealing corn.

## "RUN HIM OUT OR KILL HIM!"

Everywhere he went, Allen was known as the life of the party. He had a beautiful tenor voice and a great sense of rhythm. He was always singing, dancing, drinking, and smoking. Though his energy seemed boundless, Allen said later that he was miserable. Many times, he would leave the party and go into the woods to weep bitterly.

By the time he was twenty-one years old, Allen was a nervous wreck. When he lit a cigarette, he had to hold his wrist with the other hand because he shook

> **By the time he was twenty-one years old, Allen was a nervous wreck. When he lit a cigarette, he had to hold his wrist with the other hand because he shook so badly.**

so badly. It was said that he couldn't even hold a cup of coffee without spilling it. His chest burned, he was racked with a deep hacking cough, and his memory was slipping. In short, by the early prime of his life, Asa Alanzo Allen was dying.

With nowhere else to turn, Allen went home to his mother. Thinking that farm life and regular meals would be good for him, he hoped for the return of his health.

But once back home, he returned to his old ways. In their rugged, country setting, Allen and his mother built a bootleg still to make their own liquor. In addition to the still, they turned their place into a dance hall every Saturday night, and soon, attracted large groups of rowdy people who were eager for entertainment.

Just down the road, another man who was called Brother Hunter was opening his home for a different reason. Though unlearned, he was born again and filled with the Holy Spirit. So, he decided to form a church and become the pastor. But he was uneasy about the dance hall down the road.

Brother Hunter sought out the young people, but most of them were too mesmerized by the Allen "Dance Hall and Still" to be interested in church. So the preacher decided that if the community was ever going to see revival, the dance hall would have to be shut down. A group gathered together and began praying. They cried out:

"God, close up that Allen dance hall! Save him if you can. But if he won't yield to God, either run him out of the neighborhood or kill him. But close down that dance hall, one way or another!"[5]

Well, thank God, a portion of their prayer was graced!

## THE LADY IN THE WHITE DRESS

In June of 1934, things began changing when one of Allen's rough friends asked him to accompany him on an errand. As they traveled, they passed by a country Methodist church. The lights were blazing, and inside there was a celebration of loud singing, clapping, and dancing.

Allen was amazed, these people were enjoying themselves! He thought church was to be solemn and mournful, so he asked his friend to stop.

When he went in to investigate, he found an even greater surprise. The preacher was a woman, dressed in white, and as she talked, Allen thought she must be an angel. He didn't want this woman to notice him because she seemed so pure. So every time she came near to him, he would hide behind the stove pipe. For the first time in his life, conviction seized him. But before the altar call was made, he and his friend quietly slipped out.

All through that night and the next day, he struggled with God and his heart. He longed for the joy and peace he had seen on the faces of those people at the country church. So deciding not to fight it any longer, he went back to the service the following night.

As the meeting started, Allen listened carefully to every song and testimony. The sermon was about the blood of Jesus and how it washed away every sin, and as soon as the call for salvation was given, his hand shot straight up!

The lady evangelist knew of him, and thought he was only there to cause trouble, so she asked those who were serious to stand. Without a second thought, he stood.

She became fearful because she felt he was there to cause a scene, but she decided to continue. She asked those standing to come down to the front if they were really serious, and Allen was the first one down the aisle. In fact, he was the only one who had stood to actually walk down to the front. Thinking he was still there for trouble, the lady asked him, "Do you *really* want to be saved?"

**"Certainly, that's what I came down here for,"** Allen said.

To her great surprise, he fell to his knees and asked Jesus to be the Lord of his life. From that moment on, there was a new A. A. Allen. No more dances. No more bootlegging. His old friends laughed, but that didn't change Allen back to his old ways. He was a new creation.[6]

## "THEY'RE OF THE DEVIL!"

In an old trunk in the attic, Allen found a Bible that his sister had won in a contest. It had never been read, so he took the little Bible and read it from cover to cover. He took it to the fields and read it, and would read it before every meal. According to Allen, it seemed he just couldn't read enough of the Bible.

In the meantime, there was great rejoicing in Brother Hunter's Pentecostal church down the road! "That Allen boy" was born again! Their prayers had been answered, and it even seemed that many of the young people who used to attend Allen's Dance Hall were now stopping by the church because they were curious about the singing and worshipping. The biggest surprise of all was when Allen himself slipped into one of their services. After he left, the congregation prayed that God would fill him with the Spirit and use him to win souls.

The morning after he attended the Pentecostal meeting, he visited with a Methodist pastor who warned him to stay away from the Pentecostals saying they were of the devil because they spoke in tongues.

**"After that, I just couldn't wait to go back,"** Allen said. **"I was curious to hear them talk in tongues!"**[7]

> *The morning after he attended the Pentecostal meeting, he visited with a Methodist pastor who warned him to stay away from the Pentecostals saying they were of the devil because they spoke in tongues.*

A few services later, the gift of tongues and interpretation operated in one of the meetings, and as Allen sat and listened, he could tell that this was from God. Now he really wanted what these people had.

The next day, he met with the Methodist pastor again. He shared his experience with him and showed him Scripture to prove that speaking in tongues was for today. The pastor declared, "You can't have it! No one is getting that kind of an experience today!"

**"Well, I'm going to have it,"** answered Allen. **"And Pastor, that is just what you need."**[8]

The pastor left in a rage, and Allen severed ties with the Methodist church.

Soon after this, one of Allen's sisters was born again. And not long after that, Allen would finally receive the baptism of the Holy Spirit. He received and spoke in tongues at a Pentecostal camp meeting in Oklahoma that he and his sister attended together.

Those days were like heaven on earth to him. The night he was filled with the Spirit, he wore his only change of clothes – a solid white shirt and solid white pants! He fell to the ground which was covered with saw dust, but he didn't care. All Allen wanted was God. Soon, he felt as though electricity was slowly inching its way down his fingertips, until it covered his entire body. Then it happened. Allen was aware of nothing but the presence of God. He stood up and shouted out in other tongues! His white suit had been ruined, but Allen had the desire of his heart!

## COLORADO & LEXIE = LOVE

Drought hit Missouri hard in 1934, and there was no work anywhere. Then one day, Allen received a letter from an old friend who invited him to Colorado to work on a ranch.

So in September of 1934, Allen found himself walking through the Colorado plains, tired and thirsty and feeling a little alienated from the lack of Pentecostal fellowship. Though he was going to a new place to work, he was concerned there would be no Christians who shared his new belief. As he walked along, the wind blew a sheet of paper into his pathway. Bending down he picked it up. And seeing what it was, he smiled broadly. It was a page of the Foursquare publication, *Bridal Call*. He knew then that somewhere, someone on these plains believed in the power of God as he knew it.

As soon as he arrived at the ranch, he asked if anyone attended the Foursquare Church. His friends told him that a girl who lived up the road possibly did. They said: "She even thinks she's called to preach."[9]

Soon afterwards, Allen introduced himself to Lexie Scriven, who was called to preach and had just returned home from traveling with some evangelist friends. The two quickly became friends, studying the Bible together daily, searching Scripture and seeking answers to questions. Lexie was challenged and refreshed as she listened to Allen, who regularly challenged the religious tradition that she held to. He was never raised with tradition, so he felt he saw things more clearly than she did. She was soon persuaded to his way of seeing the Scriptures, and they began attending church together. They seemed inseparable, but it was nothing more than mutual friendship.

Soon, Allen returned to Missouri to help his mother move her belongings to her new home in Idaho. Lexie left to attend Central Bible Institute in Springfield, Missouri, but every day, the letters came from Allen. They both began to realize they were in love with each other. So he wrote to her, proposed, and the couple married on September 19, 1936, in Colorado. Their marriage was later blessed with three boys and one girl.

## THE THANKSGIVING OPOSSUM

The Allens began their new life together with one hundred dollars, a few wedding gifts, and an old Model A Ford. They had no jobs and no promise of any, but they knew they were called of God to preach.

They saved what money they could to enroll at Central Bible Institute that September and then left Colorado, heading for Missouri, with plans to stop and visit his mother. But they found her very sick, with no income and no one to care for her. So immediately, the couple bought her food and necessities, cared for her home, and paid the bills. Soon, they found their money was gone and so was their hope to enter Bible college.

When his mother's health improved, the couple continued on their way, searching for jobs and a place to live. During this search, someone suggested they hold a church meeting in a local home. So God provided Allen's first chance to preach, and before the meeting was over, they left that home with plans made for the first A. A. Allen revival meetings.

*The Allens began their new life together with one hundred dollars, a few wedding gifts, and an old Model A Ford. They had no jobs and no promise of any, but they knew they were called of God to preach.*

But there was one problem – no money and none expected coming in, so the couple began chopping wood and selling it during the day. The money they made bought gasoline for their preaching trips. For two weeks, they chopped and hauled wood, stopping only to write down thoughts God would give them for preaching that evening.

Allen's heroes were Dwight L. Moody and Charles Finney. The first sermon he preached was based on the sermons of these men.

At their first Thanksgiving dinner, instead of turkey, they ate opossum, which they gladly accepted from the congregation. Lexie stuffed it and prepared it just as she would a turkey. The congregation took an offering at the end of two weeks to surprise the preacher, and collected thirty-five cents.

## BEANS AND BACKWOODS

When the last meeting ended, they were given an invitation to conduct another one, but that posed a problem – the location was too far from their home to drive to in one day, so they would have to find another place to stay near their new meeting location. The only place vacant was a two-room cabin being used as a granary, but the kind old man who owned the building agreed to remove the grain and allow them to stay. There were huge cracks in the floor, the windows were broken out, and the back door had disappeared. However, they made the best of it by hanging a blanket in place of the door, draping cloth over the windows, and using cushions out of their car for a bed. Lexie used old orange crates covered with tea towels for chairs and a table, and for weeks, they lived on beans and cornbread, relying totally on the Lord to supply their needs. In their diary, they recorded special offerings with amounts like "five cents."

During these meetings, the Allens learned the power of prayer. After one prayer session, everyone who attended the following revival meetings was born again with a total of thirty people saved in two weeks, many of them having walked six miles just to attend the meeting. After holding a baptismal service, they set out on the road again.

If there had been jobs at this time, Allen would have taken secular employment, but there were none to be had, so he worked at studying the Bible and praying. The rest of his time was spent visiting people and praying for their needs.

## "LIKE A WHIRLWIND, I HEARD HIS VOICE"

In the late 1930s, just weeks after their first son was born, Allen accepted a pastorate with the Tower Memorial Assembly of God, in Holly, Colorado. While there, Allen was licensed by the Assemblies of God.

Determined to find the secret of God's power, Allen began to fast and pray and seek the Lord. Fasting was new to him and so he encountered considerable trouble. Just as he would start to seek the Lord, he would smell the food his wife was cooking for her son and herself. But try as he might to be committed, the spirit was willing but the flesh was weak. He would finally give in, emerge from his prayer closet and join the family meal.

Then one day, just as he had taken a bite of food, he was immediately convicted. Dropping his fork, he announced to his wife that he wasn't coming out of his prayer closet until he heard from the Lord, and even instructed her to lock him in the closet. She laughed and told him that he would be pounding to get out within an hour.

But hours passed, and he didn't knock to get out. Wrestling with his flesh, he found the victory inside of his prayer closet, and in his own words, he tells of his experience with the Lord:

> "...I began to realize that the light that was filling my prayer closet was God's glory!...The presence of God was so real and powerful that I felt I would die right there on my knees....Then, like a whirlwind, I heard His voice. It was God! He was speaking to me! This was the glorious answer that I had sought so diligently and for which I had waited since my conversion at the age of twenty-three....It seemed faster than any human could possibly speak, faster than I could follow mentally, God was talking to me....God was giving me a list of the things

which stood between me and the power of God. After each new requirement was added to the list in my mind, there followed a brief explanation, or sermonette, explaining that requirement and its importance.... As God spoke to me, I wrote them down."

## THE PRICE TAG FOR MIRACLES

> *"...It seemed faster than any human could possibly speak, faster than I could follow mentally, God was talking to me. ...God was giving me a list of the things which stood between me and the power of God."*

"...When the last requirement was written down on the list, God spoke once again, and said: *This is the answer. When you have placed on the altar of consecration and obedience the last thing on your list, you shall not only heal the sick, but in My Name shall you cast out devils, you shall see mighty miracles as in My Name you preach the Word, for behold, I give you power over all the power of the enemy.'*

"God revealed to me at the same time that the things that were hindrances to my ministry...were the very same things which were hindering so many thousands of others.

"At last, here was the price I must pay for the power of God in my life and ministry. THE PRICE TAG FOR THE MIRACLEWORKING POWER OF GOD!"[10]

Here are the thirteen things A. A. Allen said the Lord told him. He would see the miracle-working power of God, if he understood and did these things:

1. He must realize he couldn't do greater quality miracles than Jesus.
2. He could walk as Jesus walked.
3. He must be blameless like God Himself.
4. He must measure himself to Jesus alone.
5. He must deny his fleshly desires with fasting.
6. After self-denial, he must follow Jesus seven days a week.
7. Without God, he could do nothing!
8. He must do away with sin in his body.

9. He must not continue in shallow, pointless discussions.
10. He must give his body wholly to God forever.
11. He must believe all of God's promises.

The remaining two guidelines were "pet sins" that God had pointed out by name. Allen never felt he could share them with anyone.[11]

## HEAVEN'S VISIT — THE FIRST MIRACLE

Finally, Allen began pounding on the closet door for his wife to let him out, and as soon as she saw his face she said, "You've got the answer!"

**"Yes...God has paid me a visit from heaven, and here is the answer."**

Written on a piece of cardboard were the thirteen requirements from the Lord. The couple sat at their old kitchen table. They both wept as he told her the story and went over the list.

Shortly after that visitation from God, the Allens resigned from their church, feeling called to the evangelistic field and so, by invitation, set out for Missouri. It was there that the Allens saw their first miracle service.

An old coal miner who was totally blind as a result of a mine explosion years earlier began attending the services. Night after night, he sat and listened to the Word of God, and finally, in response to an altar call, came forward for healing.

The Allens were shocked by his faith, and both admitted later that it would take more faith than they had for this man to receive his healing! They prayed for everyone who came forward and placed the blind man at the end of the line. People who had headaches, colds, and deaf ears were healed and went on their way rejoicing, but the blind man remained.

Suddenly, Allen called for everyone who had faith for the healing of this blind man to come up and pray with them. Then he said, **"There is unbelief in this room. I can feel it!"** And with that, a man got up and stomped out the door.

*A. A. Allen*

God answered their prayer. When the prayer was finished, the blind man could name the color of Allen's tie and point to objects around the room![12]

## WOMAN — THE COAT OF MANY COLORS

For the next four and a half years, Allen traveled as an Assemblies of God revivalist. Though he held a prestigious position, his pay was very low, and financially, life remained hard during the first half of the 1940s, especially now that they had four children. Lexie stayed at home to care for the young babies. Allen was away sometimes for three consecutive months at a time.

> *Lexie had to cope with the frustrations of not seeing her husband regularly, while having to deal with her own call.*

Lexie had to cope with the frustrations of not seeing her husband regularly, while having to deal with her own call.

Though she longed for the stability of a normal home life, she learned a valuable ministry lesson. She was called into the ministry, but her ministry also consisted of being a mother. She realized there was a timing to all things. Motherhood and a stable home were to never be sacrificed for the other half of her ministry call, because those days would come again for her, and then she would have fulfillment, knowing that every facet of her call had been completed.

Years later, as the children grew older, Allen continued to evangelize alone. Lexie looked around her community and found a section without a Full Gospel church. So she started a church and became the pastor! When Allen was financially able to take her and the children on his trips, she eventually resigned the church and turned it over to another pastor![13]

## HEAVEN ON EARTH — TEXAS!

Then, in 1947, Lexie received a phone call from Allen, telling her to get ready to move to Corpus Christi, Texas. He had been asked to pastor one of the largest Assemblies of God churches in the area, and was very excited, thinking of the stability this would provide his family. He told Lexie that they would probably stay there until Jesus came again.

The Allen family loved Corpus Christi and the church there, but in a city of over one hundred thousand people, there were only a handful of Full Gospel churches.

The Allens came at the time of the church's building program, and where some would have been overwhelmed, Allen's spiritual appetite was only whetted. He threw himself into this new phase of work, dreaming of a church that would operate in the gifts of the Spirit, evangelize, and progressively move forward in the things of heaven. This church seemed to be his answer. The church members heard him preach for two weeks before asking him to be their pastor. He preached hard, holding nothing back from what he believed, and they still wanted him!

He gave every area of that ministry his utmost attention, with each worker being selected and given special training. The attendance grew, and they soon ran out of space.

## A DEADLY BLOW

Now, the church was reaching a few hundred people, but Allen was considering how to reach the city through radio. So he began to lay plans for an effective radio ministry and even attended a radio seminar in Springfield, Missouri.

He returned home, thrilled and filled with energy, so he called a special board meeting and carefully explained his radio plans to reach the city, knowing the men of the board would catch his vision.

*Allen had tried to compromise his heavenly call for earthly security, which is understandable, because he wanted to be a dad to his children.*

But one of the men proceeded to inform him that the board didn't approve of what he was doing, and that he was wearing them out! The board member went on to say that Allen had helped them build one of the finest churches in Texas, but they needed time to recover from that, and that they couldn't keep up the pace.

Then another stood and called attention to the tremendous cost and burden it would be on the church. The general opinion was that enough had been accomplished for the time being, and no further advances needed to be made for some time.[14]

Allen was absolutely crushed, and he quickly dismissed the meeting.

A point here: It was Allen's *call* that energized him to move forward. His call wasn't to the pastorate, but to evangelize the nations. Allen was spiritually built for this kind of thrust; it came with his call. Lay people are not automatically built that way, and there is nothing wrong with this. It is just a fact. God gave us the fivefold ministry gifts in order to step up the spiritual process so we can all keep the timing of heaven. We need lay people, and we definitely need pastors. But just as importantly, we *need* everyone to stand in the office of their calling and operate in the heavenly anointing.

Sadly though, Allen innocently tried to disguise and confine his call to that of a pastor. Can you imagine how it must have felt to try to restrict the call of an evangelistic revivalist? When the board vetoed Allen's thrust, they unknowingly killed a large portion of his being by bridling his life and snuffing out a portion of his destiny.

Allen had tried to compromise his heavenly call for earthly security, which is understandable, because he wanted to be a dad to his children. But soon, Allen would see that the price was too great. It would have been better, though possibly harder, to seek God and find another way of making it work.

## BLACKNESS, TORMENT, HELL: THE BREAKDOWN

When Allen returned home, he said nothing to his wife, trying to act as if nothing had happened. He even discussed a vacation with her.

But during the night she awoke to hear Allen sobbing in the next room. She thought he was interceding for someone until he came into the bedroom, still sobbing deeply.

Startled, she questioned him. It was then that he told her what happened at the board meeting, and she saw he was more than disappointed, he was devastated. There was no bitterness, no anger, no blame – just a broken heart.

Allen offered his resignation and felt he could never preach again. But the church really loved him, and they offered him several months of vacation with full salary. They even insisted that additional offerings be given to him to take care of any expense he incurred on the trip.

It was apparent Allen was suffering from an emotional breakdown. The church thought he was overworked, but his wife aware of his strength and his zeal, knew that wasn't possible. She knew the breakdown came from a broken heart. A portion of his being was held captive, and he thought he had lost it forever.

Lexie took him on an extended vacation, but he was so tormented, he could find only a partial rest as they traveled, and as his condition grew worse, it became impossible for either of them to rest. After only a week in the mountains with no relief, he wanted to go home, thinking he would never return to normal.

## "COME OUT OF HIM!"

Lexie began to seek the Lord desperately. Suddenly, it came to her! They had not failed...God wasn't through with them! The call and purpose of God for A. A. Allen was just as it had always been! When she finally realized that Satan had taken advantage of his deep hurt, she began to pray against the attack. Soon Allen also saw that he was being tormented by a demon that was taking advantage of his emotional hurt. He realized he was being attacked by a tormenting spirit.

While driving back to Texas, Allen pulled the car to the side of the road and asked his wife to lay hands on him. According to Allen, the second Lexie said, "Come out of him, I command you to GO," the evil spirit left him, and they rejoiced together as he actually felt a physical release and lightness replace the heaviness he had felt. Then suddenly, he began to get sleepy, and before Lexie could pull onto the road, he was asleep, never remembering getting home, nor getting into his own bed. He slept like a baby for three days straight, and when he woke up, he was fully recovered.

## "YOU FAILED TO PAY THE PRICE"

By fall of 1949, the Allens began to hear stories about miraculous healing meetings that were taking place. The evangelists conducting the meetings weren't necessarily outstanding preachers. In fact, many preachers were more eloquent in their sermon delivery than these evangelists, but when these healing evangelists prayed for the sick, miracles happened so quickly, no one could count them. The Allens refused to believe half of the stories they were told, but their curiosity was aroused.

> *...when these healing evangelists prayed for the sick, miracles happened so quickly, no one could count them.*

One day, a friend gave Allen a copy of *The Voice of Healing* publication. After reading it, Allen said, **"As I read its pages, I laughed in ridicule. *Fanatics,* I thought, as I closed the magazine and laid it away in my study."**[15] Some of his church members came from these tent meetings with glowing reports, but Allen discounted them and felt they were drifting into fanaticism.

Personally, I don't believe that was his true heart in the matter. He might have spoken those words, but I believe he was incredibly stirred inside, because he knew this was his own call being manifested before his very eyes.

*However, you can become so backslidden in your calling that the things you once held as precious and attainable, are now a distant memory.*

Not long after this, some minister friends persuaded Allen to go to Dallas and attend an Oral Roberts tent revival. Along the way, he remembered the experience he had with God in his prayer closet many years ago, recalling the thirteen things that stood in his way of walking into the miraculous. Being out of his spiritual office and trying, instead, to be a pastor had caused him to shelve the vision God gave him.

As he approached Dallas, he became more and more aware that there he would witness the very thing God had called him to do. **"But I had never paid the price for God's miracle-working power in my life,"** he added.[16]

He was captivated by the tent meeting and by the power of God being displayed through Roberts, feeling as though he was living in the book of Acts. Miracle after miracle took place as he watched, but it wasn't fanaticism; it was God's miracle working power.

As he sat watching the prayer line, he again heard the voice of God say:

"My son, eleven years ago you sought My face.... Eleven years ago I called you into the same ministry.... But you failed to pay the price and to make the consecration. Therefore, you have failed to do this thing which I have called you to do." With tears streaming down his face, Allen lifted his hands and cried out, **"Lord, I'll do it!"**[17]

## GOING, GOING...GONE!

Two Sundays later, he resigned his pastorate. He would have left the first Sunday after his return, but his wife asked him to wait and make sure he was doing the right thing.

Immediately, pastors from all over the nation called for his services as an evangelist, and in less than a month, a new pastor occupied the pulpit. The Allens kept the Corpus Christi church as their home base and traveled out from there.

They moved all their possessions into a house trailer, and in less than three months after his "breakdown," A. A. Allen was on the revival trail.

Allen began studying the list of thirteen requirements the Lord had given him eleven years earlier. He couldn't believe all the time that had been lost. Eleven years! As he studied the list, he noticed that numbers twelve and thirteen had not been accomplished in his life, but that every other item had been marked through. Finally, with great determination, he was able to mark through the last two. After that, noticeable miracles began to take place through his ministry.

In May of 1950, Allen sent his first report to *The Voice of Healing* magazine, the result of a great campaign in Oakland, California. Of the meeting he writes:

> **"Many say this is the greatest revival in the history of Oakland.... Night after night, the waves of Divine Glory so sweep over the congregation that many testify of being healed while sitting in their seats."**[18]

In 1951, Allen made a great leap. He decided to purchase a tent and advertise himself as a "healing" revivalist. He heard of a tent for sale, equipped with lighting, seats, a platform, and a public address system, all for $8,500!

But he only had $1,500, so he called the minister and made the offer of $1,500 as a downpayment. The owner told him that another preacher had just called and offered the full price, but he would pray about the matter and call him the next day.

The next day when Allen called the man, he wasn't surprised to learn that the owner decided to give the tent to him with a $1,500 downpayment. The rest was to be paid in $100 payments, as Allen could afford, so the tent was his!

On July 4, 1951, the A. A. Allen Revival Tent went up for the first campaign in Yakima, Washington.[19]

## FINALLY — RADIO!

In November of 1953, Allen finally saw his dream come true, when he began the nationally known radio broadcast, *Allen Revival Hour*, on nine stations and two superpowered stations. By 1955, Allen was on seventeen Latin American stations and eighteen American ones.[20] Soon, he had to set up a permanent office to take care of the flood of mail coming in. He began conducting yearly services in Cuba and Mexico. Many responded to the altar calls by denouncing witchcraft and destroying their idols on the platform. These revivals continued from 1955 until 1959 when Castro took power.

*Allen seemed to thrive on persecution and pressure. Described as a short, "jowly" man, his face would contort into a scowl as he loudly roared one minute and whispered the next.*

Allen seemed to thrive on persecution and pressure. Described as a short, "jowly" man, his face would contort into a scowl as he loudly roared one minute and whispered the next. He was an "old-time religion" preacher, complete with foot-stomping, shrieks, sobs, cries of **"Glory to God!"**, loud tongues, and wild, dramatic dancing. He would sometimes hop up and down while pounding on a tambourine, and during his meetings you were likely to see someone turning cartwheels down the aisle, "jerking" across the front of the platform, and several people dancing ballet style throughout the crowd.

Allen was never influenced by the changing fads, but he felt it was his job to preach this way. He didn't mince words when he preached, and he seemed to always turn adversity into his advantage. He said what he thought, and that is what the people came to hear.

> *...Allen told his friends that he had been kidnapped and knocked unconscious. When Allen awoke, one friend said he was in a "smoke-filled room, and some-body was pouring liquor down his throat."*

## HARD KNOCKS IN KNOXVILLE

In 1955, accusations began surfacing, each one more serious than the previous one, each affecting Allen greatly.

The charge that Allen drank abusively always seemed to follow his ministry. Whether people believed the charges or not depended on whether people listened to his enemies or his friends.[21] Some never believed that he was able to overcome the excessive abuse of alcohol that was so much a part of his youth.

But his greatest crisis came in the fall of 1955 while conducting a revival in Knoxville, Tennessee. Allen was arrested for drunken driving, but the case never came to trial because Allen failed to appear in court, so he forfeited his $1,000 bail and left the state.[22]

The entire incident is hazy. But Allen maintained that the Knoxville media was notorious in their slander of evangelists, and he stated that he was even shown a list of preachers who paid certain newspapers to slander him. According to one close associate, Allen told his friends that he had been kidnapped and knocked unconscious. When Allen awoke, one friend said he was in a "smoke-filled room, and somebody was pouring liquor down his throat." However, word had already spread that Allen had confessed the charge to prominent ministers of Knoxville.[23]

# WITHDRAW? NO WAY!

In 1956, upon hearing of the charges and the controversy, Ralph M. Riggs, superintendent of the General Council of the Assemblies of God, sent Allen a letter asking him to withdraw from public meetings until things cleared up. Allen felt this request was impossible, and felt his organization had deserted him when he needed them the most, in order to save their reputation. He sent Riggs a searing letter reminding him how he had ministered with him for **"eighteen years with no question being raised at any time concerning my integrity,"** and then turned in his ministerial credentials to the Assemblies of God, stating that in doing so there was **"no great loss."** He told Riggs that **"a withdrawal from public ministry at this time would ruin my ministry, for it would have the appearance of an admission of guilt."**[24]

The accusation also caused great problems in the Voice of Healing association. Though Lexie assured the leadership of the Voice of Healing association that the charges weren't true, Gordon Lindsay felt that those who belonged to the group must make a strong stand on ethics, so Allen resigned from that group as well.

Allen's daughter felt that the Voice of Healing was really an Assemblies of God organization of evangelists, stating that they were trying "real hard to work within the framework of the Assemblies." If the rules weren't obeyed within the general denomination, a minister could possibly have trouble with the Voice of Healing network.[25]

# R. W. SCHAMBACH SPEAKS

One of the greatest evangelistic ministries in our generation is that of R. W. Schambach from Tyler, Texas. When Schambach was just starting out in ministry, he joined Allen's revival team and soon became his right-hand man. Being a man of character and integrity, he knew what it meant to pay the price for revival.

Recently, Schambach and I were in the same town, attending the same meeting, when I shared my views with him concerning the importance of preserving history for the generations to come.

He agreed to tell me his side of the A. A. Allen story, so as we spoke, he shared with me some very interesting things. Schambach told me how he joined the A. A. Allen revival team the night before the Knoxville incident. Then, he made a startling statement, contrary to every other written account of A. A. Allen.

Schambach said that Allen *wasn't* drunk. "I know," he stated, "because I was with him in the car!" He said the entire incident was a conspiracy to ruin Allen's ministry, and after the Knoxville trouble, he saw the extreme persecution that Allen suffered. It was here that Schambach began to learn how to pay the price for revival. No matter what kind of accusation was hurled at Allen, Schambach knew the man's innocence, because he was with him all the time. So, Schambach remained faithful to serve Allen in his ministry. For the six years that Schambach was his associate, he went on every crusade with the evangelist.

> *"There was not a jealous bone in his body," Schambach smiled. "If I would get started on a point, he'd yell out, 'Go ahead Schambach, you've got it!'"*

"He was a man of God," Schambach remembered. "I was with him all the time, like a hand in [a] glove. When we had to travel together, I even slept in the same room with him! He never did one thing contrary to the Word. He was a man of prayer and a man of miracles. That's how I knew him."

Schambach also described Allen as a "very touchable" man, accessible to the people at all times. "There was not a jealous bone in his body," Schambach smiled. "If I would get started on a point, he'd yell out **'Go, ahead Schambach, you've got it!'** Then he would sit back and let me preach, no matter where we were." Schambach humorously compared Allen's clothes and personality to a "cross between James Cagney and Spike Jones."

As Schambach and I walked outside of the hotel to continue our discussion, we noticed a fire truck in the parking lot.

"Oh, that reminds me of another story, Roberts."

Schambach said that the story about the fire on top of the tent during the Los Angeles meeting really happened! It seemed that the fire trucks went rushing up and down the streets searching for the fire but could never find it. They knew that a fire was coming from somewhere because they could see the smoke. Finally, the fire trucks went in the direction of the tent, but once they arrived, no fire was to be found.

"God wanted everyone to know that we were in town," he smiled. "So He put His holy fire on the top of that tent just to let the folks know we were there."

What about the "miracle oil" that appeared in the palms of people's hands?

"That was real, too. I even had an element of it on my own hands," Schambach answered.

In Los Angeles, at one of the Allen meetings, "Everyone got the oil on their hands but Allen," Schambach smiled. "I believe God allowed that just to prove that it was true and not a hoax."[26]

Schambach left A. A. Allen to begin his own ministry in 1961. But Schambach stood faithfully by Allen for the rest of his life. If there is anyone who operates similar to the ministry of A. A. Allen, it is the great evangelist, R. W. Schambach.

## FORWARD! FOR A WHILE

So, Allen had turned in his license with the Assemblies of God and broken his ties with the Voice of Healing association, and became an independent evangelist. Many said it suited him well, and history books note the same.

Most evangelists do work well independently, as long as they stay "hooked up" with those who understand their call and can scripturally speak into their lives. They can call a church their "home church," but that local church must give them the freedom to pursue their individual call. It is sometimes difficult for their methods to meet with the approval of an organized establishment because the two are so different. Evangelistic revivalists are fast, wild, dramatic, and have the strength of an ox. If a pastor understands the call of an evangelist, the two can work well together, but if the pastor tries to control an evangelist to fit within needs of the local church, there will be trouble.

The year of 1956 seemed to be a time when ministries were changing. But Allen found a way to thrust forward when many were pulling back. He had a great ability to raise money, and at this time, was still attempting to stay within his call.

So Allen progressed forward by starting his own publication, *Miracle Magazine*. It consisted of his messages on healing and deliverance and featured many healing testimonies. By the end of 1956, it had a paid subscription list of over two hundred thousand people.

By the fall, Allen had started the Miracle Revival Fellowship, an independent organization to license ministers and to support missions. He firmly denied any charges that it was "denominationally minded." Allen reported five hundred ministers in its first ordination.[27]

## SENSATIONALISM, CONTROVERSY, AND MIRACLES

After the Knoxville incident, Allen became an extremely controversial figure, and the media followed him everywhere hoping for a story. Wild and sensational occurrences were reported to have happened at the Allen revivals, but much of these reports were aimed at discrediting his ministry. Lexie said that during this time, Allen's enemies did all they could to destroy him. It did seem that whenever persecution would attack him, he would retaliate with some unusual miracle or occurrence, going to the extreme in an attempt to prove his call.

> *In Los Angeles, it was reported that a cross appeared on Allen's forehead, and a flaming fire appeared over his tent...*

In Los Angeles, it was reported that a cross appeared on Allen's forehead, and a flaming fire appeared over his tent, as R. W. Schambach mentioned earlier in the chapter. According to Allen, this was a sign. As proof, he cited Ezekiel 9:4, which says an angel was sent from heaven to place a mark on the foreheads of all the people who cry out for the Lord because of evil in the earth. The sighting on Allen's forehead and the flame over the tent were reported by the media.

Allen's cameraman, R. E. Kemery, took a picture of a man who had nail scars appear in his hands. At another meeting, "miracle oil" reportedly began to flow from the heads and hands of those attending the Allen revivals. Allen answered those who questioned this occurrence by referring to Hebrews 1:9 that stated, the reward for hating evil and loving righteousness was to be anointed with the oil of gladness.

He was also criticized for selling a recording that captured the sounds of a demon-possessed woman, and he also sold a booklet that contained eighteen drawings of demons, drawn by a demon-possessed, insane person.

Some of the healings were sensational, and in one meeting near Los Angeles, a five hundred pound woman lost two hundred pounds instantly when Allen laid hands on her. People testified to seeing her body shrink.

A Full Gospel pastor who had "alligator scales" on his arms for nearly fifty years, was healed as he sat on stage behind Allen. The scales dried up, fell off, new skin appeared, and the pastor was able to wear short sleeve shirts for the first time.

Another man was driving down the highway, and as he listened to the *Allen Radio Hour* he was moved in his heart. So he pulled the car over, laid his hands on the radio, and prayed with Allen asking God to "put all the parts back." He had his right lung, three ribs, and a chest bone removed by surgeons, plus he was missing his second toe on the left foot because of disease. That night, the man's toe grew in complete with the toenail, and his physician was amazed when the X-rays showed that what he had removed had returned in its proper place.

When Allen submitted an advertisement to the *Akron Journal* in 1957, he was refused. Instead, the paper published a front page "slander account" of this ministry warning the city of his revival. Allen announced that he had received $25,000 worth of front-page advertising, absolutely free.[28]

In the mid-fifties, he unleashed an all out attack on denominationalism and "man-formed religion." While many things he said and wrote concerning denominationalism were true, it was apparent he was speaking from hurt and frustration. When he tried to open lines of communication again with the Assemblies of God headquarters, according to Allen, they banished him and urged others to ignore him as well. While the General Council denied his charge, they did state that his ministry "threw a shadow."[29] In other words, if someone associated with Allen, that person's own character would be in question.

## MIRACLES FROM THE VALLEY

Even with all the controversy, Allen's ministry continued to grow, and he began the International Miracle Revival Training Camp for ministers. Here, he taught ministers the principles of prosperity, healing, casting out demons, and various other topics.

And in January of 1958, while holding a revival in Phoenix, Arizona, God impressed him to build a Bible school there. That same morning, twelve hundred fifty acres of land a few miles from Tombstone, Arizona, were given to him. He called the land "Miracle Valley," and began building his headquarters and training center. He doubled the acreage, and many Native American tribe members were born again as a result of his ministry. Christians in the area were fervently revived, and the area became a thriving city by the 1960s.

> *He preached the same message with the same fervency to each audience, and never changed the text to fit the class of people.*

The year of 1958 became a time of crisis for the Voice of Healing revival, but it didn't seem so for Allen. That year, he announced a five-pronged program for his ministry in Miracle Valley – tent revivals, the *Allen Revival Hour* radio program, overseas mission programs, the Miracle Valley Training Center, and a publications department.[30] It was dur-

*Anatomy of a miracle*

*"The Lord is here to set you free!"*

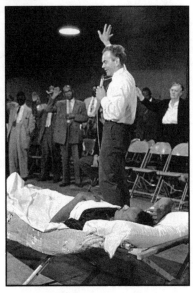

*"We ask you now God to heal!"*

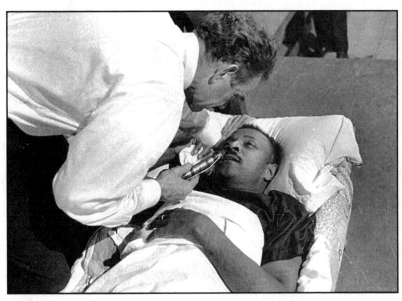

*"What would you like Jesus to do for you?"*

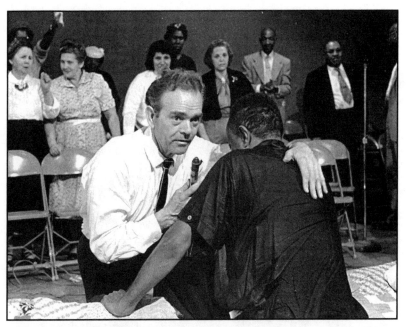

*"If you believe God is healing you, rise up now in faith."*

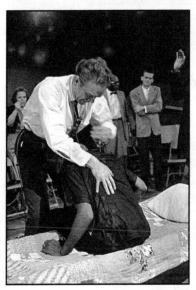

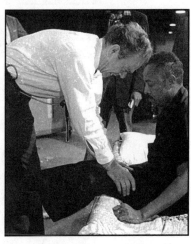

*"Now do something with those legs you couldn't do before."*

*"That's it..."*

*"Healed in Jesus' name!"*

*"Let's walk a while."*

ing this time that he began teaching prosperity according to the Bible. In fact, most everything he taught connected in some way with financial prosperity.

People from every social strata attended his meetings. He preached the same message with the same fervency to each audience, and never changed the text to fit the class of people. Everything from mink coats and pearls, to bare feet and overalls could be seen at his meetings. When people walked through the parking lot, they would see everything from polished Cadillacs, to car hoods tied down with rusted wire.

But in 1960, during the heat of racial tension, the Ku Klux Klan threatened to disrupt an Allen meeting where white and black people were present. They succeeded in blowing up a nearby bridge with dynamite hoping to scare Allen and his group, but both the worship service and the baptismal service continued without a hint of fear.

It was also in 1960 that Allen built a church in Miracle Valley that seated four thousand people. He had great plans for this city and wanted to build private homes, recreational facilities, and media centers.

## A TRAGIC ENDING

Something happened during the last few years of Allen's life and ministry. Though the details are sketchy, Allen was sued for $300,000 in back taxes. And in 1967, Allen and his wife, Lexie, separated. Details about this incident are unclear, but close friends of the family state the couple never divorced.

The few details available report that before their separation, each were totally engulfed in serving the Lord until their deaths, with Lexie, a journalist, spending her time at home and Allen traveling extensively, rarely at home. Some believe if Allen had not died a short time after the separation, that he and Lexie would have reunited. Upon their deaths, they were buried side by side, sharing the same gravestone, on the grounds of Miracle Valley.

In 1969, Allen was a sick man suffering from a severe arthritic condition in his knee. He spent much time recalling his humble beginnings. According to him, that year the *Miracle Magazine* had a circulation of 340,000, with mail received from ninety nations.

But the arthritic condition soon worsened, so Allen submitted to surgery on his left knee. He suffered from so much pain that Don Stewart, a young man, full of zeal, began to fill in during the crusades.

On June 11, 1970, Allen traveled to San Francisco and checked into the Jack Tar Hotel (now named the Cathedral Hills Quality Hotel). He checked in at

12:56 P.M. He was scheduled the next day for a 9:00 A.M. doctor's appointment at the University of California Medical Center in San Francisco, to discuss whether a second surgery needed to be performed on his knees.

Sometime before 9:00 P.M. the same evening, Allen made a phone call to his close friend, Bernard Schwartz. The exact conversation is unknown, but Schwartz was alarmed and proceeded to the hotel. When Schwartz arrived at Allen's room, the door was locked and he didn't answer. Schwartz told the assistant manager of the problem and Allen's door was opened with a pass key.

At 9:15 P.M., Allen was found dead by Schwartz and the assistant manager. The Coroner's Report states Allen was sitting in a chair in front of his television. He was officially pronounced dead at 11:23 P.M. on June 11, 1970. A. A. Allen was fifty-nine years old.

*...when Schwartz arrived at Allen's room, the door was locked and he didn't answer.*

## WHAT HAPPENED? THE CORONER'S REPORT

There are some details about A. A. Allen and his death that are very important. Though not widely known, he was suffering from a severe arthritic condition. In fact, it is documented that his personal physician, Dr. Seymour Farber, prescribed Percodan, Seconal, and Valium to ease the pain and for insomnia brought on by the severity of the pain.

Here are the facts: The Coroner's Report, Case #1151 for Asa Alonzo Allen recorded the blood alcohol concentration in Allen's body measured .036 percent – a very high and concentrated level of alcohol in the blood system. The cause of death on the coroner's report was stated as "acute alcoholism and fatty infiltration of the liver."

At first, it would seem that Allen died a chronic alcoholic, but upon further investigation, I believe the opposite. Here is my opinion of what I believe happened.

## HOLD ON! LET'S INVESTIGATE

First of all, his personal physician knew Allen very well. Though chronic alcoholics can deceive a novice, they cannot deceive their personal physician; especially if their personal physician sees them as many times as Dr. Farber saw Allen and tested him. Dr. Farber wouldn't have prescribed such highly addictive drugs as Percodan, Valium, and Seconal to a chronic alcoholic. It would have been a death sentence, because the mixture of alcohol and prescribed barbiturates and narcotics could lead to death. When Allen's blood scan was performed and reported by a laboratory toxiology department, there was no trace of drugs found in his system, though there were plenty of prescribed pills at the death scene.

His closest personal friends say that Allen detested, even hated prescribed medications. He continually stated that he wouldn't take the medications and preach, as the drug effects lingered with him and he couldn't think clearly.

Understanding how Allen was raised, I believe we are dealing with a position of attitude. Allen was in severe, arthritic pain – in fact, so much pain he could barely move.

Medical personnel who work with arthritic patients say it isn't unusual for the patients to use alcohol in a medicinal sense. Many turn to it instead of developing an addiction to prescribed drugs. I am not offering an excuse, but I am presenting a reality.

It should be recognized that the coroner's report stated Allen died of "acute" alcoholism, not "chronic" alcoholism. There is a distinct difference in the medical verbiage.

"Acute" means rapid onset or sudden, but "chronic " means ongoing; or in other words, an alcoholic. The coroner's report said Allen died of a sudden onset of alcohol, *not* of alcoholism.

Here is another fact. According to the autopsy report, fatty tissue found within the liver is consistent with alcoholic binge drinking.

We must also understand that there is a medical difference between chronic and habitual drinkers. Chronic drinkers have drunk for a long period of time, staying drunk most of the time whether you can tell it or not. A habitual drinker could have only been drinking for a few weeks, or, they are also called social drinkers.

*...there is no evidence whatsoever that Allen was an alcoholic, as the condition of his liver proved.*

In discussing this autopsy diagnosis with several prominent physicians and specialists throughout the country, they explained to me that this liver condition *was not* cirrhosis. Cirrhosis of the liver comes from chronic alcoholism and is a death of the liver tissue that spreads gradually over a period of time. If the fatty tissue throughout the liver remains intact from habitual drinking, it could lead to cirrhosis.

Habitual drinking of alcohol produces fatty tissue. After several days, if no further alcohol is ingested, the tissue dissolves and returns to normal. Allen had the liver of someone who, for a period of weeks or months, had been binge drinking, which means simply he was drinking to the point of drunkenness.

Throughout the coroner's report, the majority of the discussion centers around Allen's arthritic condition; not the alcoholic content found in his blood. In fact, there is no evidence whatsoever that Allen was an alcoholic, as the condition of his liver proved. Instead, there is much more evidence that the alcohol was taken medicinally.

That is what I believe as well. Allen wasn't an alcoholic, but I think he periodically binged on alcohol for medicinal relief, and to be honest, I really don't believe Allen saw much of a difference between alcohol and prescribed drugs. He hated prescribed drugs and their lingering effects. Alcohol can dissipate quickly and the effects were probably less severe with him. He might not have always chosen the alcohol over the drugs; but we medically know that at least for a few weeks, he did.

It is easy to think clearly if your body is free from pain, but attitudes are sometimes different in someone who is experiencing constant and excruciating pain.

It is my opinion that on the night of his death, Allen was in excruciating pain. This seems especially clear because he had flown to San Francisco for a doctor's appointment the next day.

From the facts that I have researched, it is my opinion that on this particular evening of June 11, 1970, in a desperate attempt to stop the pain, Allen literally drank himself to death.

## THE VALLEY OF SHADOWS

Though some of the ministerial details at the end of his life are vague, his former banking department head, Mrs. Helen McMaines, has a great love and respect for Allen, saying he was "one of a kind." According to Mrs. McMaines, he was up front and honest with all the financial gain his ministry received, and she remembered how he would bring the love offerings to her and plop the heavy bags down on the counter. **"Put it all back into the ministry, Helen,"** she remembers Allen saying, **"This all belongs to God."** McMaines said that he worked day and night for the people, never seeming to tire.

"Nothing was put in his name; not the house or anything in Miracle Valley," Mrs. McMaines stated. "According to him, when he died, all of the property should go to God." Mrs. McMaines sadly reiterated that she believed there has never been another minister like A. A. Allen. "He was not afraid to fight the devil," she proclaimed, "and when you are not afraid to fight the devil, all kinds of persecution will rise up against you." The McMaines are a charming couple, and still maintain a close relationship with Allen's son, James. According to them, James Allen highly respects the ministry of his father and mother.[31]

In spite of Allen's fervency, it does seem that his charismatic personality and ministry direction did change in the later years, by publishing violent renunciations of certain churches, and focusing heavily on vows and financial prosperity. Did the extreme hurts, betrayals and denominational conspiracies against him push him into this type of ministry? Did God remove Allen's focus on the miracle ministry of divine healing? Whatever the reasons, I feel that the ministry of A. A. Allen ended sadly, much like the ministry of John Alexander Dowie.

Just like Dowie's Zion City, there is no longer a spiritual purpose for Allen's Miracle Valley.

Today, Miracle Valley is just twelve hundred fifty acres of land. Recently, I was informed that a farmer had purchased the acreage with plans to cultivate it. The buildings have all been torn down or rented.

I sponsored a group to go to Miracle Valley and search for memorabilia on Allen. What they found was shocking.

In a huge pile outside of a building, the group found hundreds of testimony letters, personal notebooks, letters, financial diaries, ministry photos, original text of the *Miracle Magazine*, film footage, undeveloped negatives, and a priceless notebook of healing testimonies with photos. The testimonies consisted of hundreds of healings: deafness, allergies, migraines, lung disease, ulcers, cancer, arthritis, bone deficiencies, blindness. It was all there, and whoever threw these things in the dumpster had obviously made one final attempt to destroy all traces of A. A. Allen's ministry.

But God had other plans.

Today, these items are registered in the historical museum of the Reformers and Revivalists Library, in Irvine, California. They will be safely preserved for this generation and the generations to follow. Here, not only can you study spiritual history, but you can see it and witness it as well.

## LET'S GO FURTHER

I know Allen made mistakes. I have no problem with that. But in spite of the mistakes, he made an attempt to show how to pay the price for spiritual power. In fact, R. W. Schambach learned how to pay the price by observing him.

Allen overcame a horrendous background to pursue the call of God, and that is a great credit to him and his ministry, because he almost succeeded. But he didn't go far enough. We must go further than Allen did to succeed.

What does it take? It seems like a broken record, but I will say it again: *Stay in your call.* Don't venture out to satisfy a suggestion of someone else or the personal desire of your own and don't allow persecution and criticism to push you into a corner.

> *What does it take? It seems like a broken record, but I will say it again:* **Stay in your call.**

What else does it take? Begin to build an immunity to the things that affect you negatively. How? Guard your heart; let God lead you with His Word until there is no trace of withdrawal *or* self-propulsion within you, and soon, the persecution in that area of your life will not even affect you. Then if you begin to feel another "hit," or something begins to bother you, start building the immunity in that particular area as well. Find Scriptures that pertain to that area, according to your call. Then, speak them over your heart *until it saturates your being and becomes a part of you;* that's how you develop an immunity. Then, when that thing tries to capture you, you will walk right through it, and the Word will guard your heart. You will have built a spiritual strength in that area.

Be daily filled with the ministry of the Holy Spirit. Allow Him to impart the oil of joy and gladness into your life. His joy is what gives you the strength to succeed.

Don't try to stand alone, but keep yourself surrounded with people who know your call and are filled with the strength of the Word and the Spirit. If you don't have this operating in your life and ministry, then ask God to bring you those *divine* connections and relationships. These aren't "yes men" who pamper and encourage you in every decision you make, right or wrong, but are *divine relationships* with people who know how to stand strong in the Spirit because of their personal experience. If they keep themselves clean, they will be equipped to speak into your life and help you when a crisis comes your way.

*Don't search the Scriptures to find retaliation against your accusers.* If you do that, you will have a harsh and embittered ministry. At times, it is tempting, but God is the One who vindicates His own! So let God do His thing, and you do yours. Search the Scriptures for yourself *first.* And when God's Word heals you, you build an immunity through the Word, and are daily filled with the Holy Spirit, then you can take on the next level of ministry. But if you stop to point fingers, you will remain there. If you remain in one level too long, you will grow stagnant and search for other avenues of ministry. Or, you may search for other "highlights" within your current ministry. Some have remained in a position of stagnancy for so long they can't find their way back.

There is nothing new under the sun. What happened to these great men and women of the past, could happen again, so learn from their lives, and build strength in your inner man. It takes spiritual strength to fulfill the will of God. *Determine* that your life and ministry will be a spiritual success in heaven and in the earth, to the glory of God!

## CHAPTER TWELVE, A. A. ALLEN
### References

1 David Harrell Jr., *All Things Are Possible* (Bloomington, IN: Indiana University Press, 1975), 66.
2 Lexie E. Allen, *God's Man of Faith and Power* (Hereford, AZ: A. A. Allen Publications, 1954), 55.
3 Ibid.
4 Ibid., 56.
5 Ibid., 17.
6 Ibid., 18-20.
7 Ibid., 22.
8 Ibid., 25.
9 Ibid., 29.
10 Ibid., 98-104.
11 A. A. Allen, *Price of God's Miracle-Working Power* (Miracle Valley, AZ: A. A. Allen Revivals Inc., 1950).
12 L. Allen, *God's Man of Faith and Power*, 106-108.
13 Ibid., 167-169.
14 Ibid., 143-144.
15 Ibid., 155.
16 Ibid., 159.
17 Ibid., 161-162.
18 Ibid., 165.
19 Ibid., 173-175.
20 Harrell, *All Things Are Possible*, 68.
21 Ibid., 70.
22 Allen Spragget, *Kathryn Kuhlman: A Woman Who Believed in Miracles,* segment on Allen according to Knox County Criminal Court (New York: Signet Classics, published by the New American Library Inc., 1970), 32-33.
23 Harrell, *All Things Are Possible,* 70.
24 Ibid., 71.
25 Ibid., 70-71.
26 Personal interview with R. W. Schambach on March 22, 1996, El Paso, Texas.
27 Harrell, *All Things Are Possible,* 74.
28 Ibid., 72.
29 Ibid., 71.
30 Ibid., 74.
31 Personal interview with Helen McMaines on April 29, 1996.